Digital Governance and E-Government Principles Applied to Public Procurement

Rajesh Kumar Shakya
The World Bank, USA

A volume in the Advances in Electronic Government, Digital Divide, and Regional Development (AEGDDRD) Book Series

IGI GLOBAL
DISSEMINATOR OF KNOWLEDGE

www.igi-global.com

Published in the United States of America by
IGI Global
Information Science Reference (an imprint of IGI Global)
701 E. Chocolate Avenue
Hershey PA 17033
Tel: 717-533-8845
Fax: 717-533-8661
E-mail: cust@igi-global.com
Web site: http://www.igi-global.com

Library of Congress Cataloging-in-Publication Data

Names: Shakya, Rajesh Kumar, 1966- editor.
Title: Digital governance and E-government principles applied to public procurement / Rajesh Kumar Shakya, editor.
Description: Hershey, PA : Information Science Reference, 2017. | Includes bibliographical references.
Identifiers: LCCN 2016056013| ISBN 9781522522034 (hardcover) | ISBN 9781522522041 (ebook)
Subjects: LCSH: Government purchasing--Case studies. | Internet in public administration--Case studies.
Classification: LCC JF1525.P85 D54 2017 | DDC 352.5/30285--dc23 LC record available at https://lccn.loc.gov/2016056013

This book is published in the IGI Global book series Advances in Electronic Government, Digital Divide, and Regional Development (AEGDDRD) (ISSN: 2326-9103; eISSN: 2326-9111)

British Cataloguing in Publication Data
A Cataloguing in Publication record for this book is available from the British Library.

Advances in Electronic Government, Digital Divide, and Regional Development (AEGDDRD) Book Series

ISSN:2326-9103
EISSN:2326-9111

Mission

The successful use of digital technologies (including social media and mobile technologies) to provide public services and foster economic development has become an objective for governments around the world. The development towards electronic government (or e-government) not only affects the efficiency and effectiveness of public services, but also has the potential to transform the nature of government interactions with its citizens. Current research and practice on the adoption of electronic/digital government and the implementation in organizations around the world aims to emphasize the extensiveness of this growing field.

The Advances in Electronic Government, Digital Divide & Regional Development (AEGDDRD) book series aims to publish authored, edited and case books encompassing the current and innovative research and practice discussing all aspects of electronic government development, implementation and adoption as well the effective use of the emerging technologies (including social media and mobile technologies) for a more effective electronic governance (or e-governance).

Coverage

- Citizens Participation and Adoption of E-Government Provision
- Adoption of Innovation with Respect to E-Government
- ICT Infrastructure and Adoption for E-Government Provision
- Frameworks and Methodologies for E-Government Development
- E-Government in Developing Countries and Technology Adoption
- Public Information Management, Regional Planning, Rural Development
- Online Government, E-Government, M-Government
- E-Governance and Use of Technology for Effective Government
- Social Media, Web 2.0, and Mobile Technologies in E-Government
- Current Research and Emerging Trends in E-Government Development

IGI Global is currently accepting manuscripts for publication within this series. To submit a proposal for a volume in this series, please contact our Acquisition Editors at Acquisitions@igi-global.com or visit: http://www.igi-global.com/publish/.

The Advances in Electronic Government, Digital Divide, and Regional Development (AEGDDRD) Book Series (ISSN 2326-9103) is published by IGI Global, 701 E. Chocolate Avenue, Hershey, PA 17033-1240, USA, www.igi-global.com. This series is composed of titles available for purchase individually; each title is edited to be contextually exclusive from any other title within the series. For pricing and ordering information please visit http://www.igi-global.com/book-series/advances-electronic-government-digital-divide/37153. Postmaster: Send all address changes to above address.

Titles in this Series

For a list of additional titles in this series, please visit: www.igi-global.com

Handbook of Research on Sub-National Governance and Development
Eris Schoburgh (University of the West Indies, Jamaica) and Roberta Ryan (University of Technology Sydney, Australia)
Information Science Reference • copyright 2017 • 625pp • H/C (ISBN: 9781522516453) • US $285.00 (our price)

Agent-Based Modeling in Humanitarian Interventions Emerging Research and Opportunities
John McCaskill (University of Texas at Dallas, USA)
Information Science Reference • copyright 2017 • 99pp • H/C (ISBN: 9781522517825) • US $115.00 (our price)

Impacts of the Media on African Socio-Economic Development
Okorie Nelson (Covenant University, Nigeria) Babatunde Raphael Ojebuyi (University of Ibadan, Nigeria) and Abiodun Salawu (North-West University, South Africa)
Information Science Reference • copyright 2017 • 328pp • H/C (ISBN: 9781522518594) • US $175.00 (our price)

Population Growth and Rapid Urbanization in the Developing World
Umar G. Benna (Ahmadu Bello University, Nigeria) and Shaibu Bala Garba (Qatar University, Qatar)
Information Science Reference • copyright 2016 • 358pp • H/C (ISBN: 9781522501879) • US $205.00 (our price)

Political Discourse in Emergent, Fragile, and Failed Democracies
Daniel Ochieng Orwenjo (Technical University of Kenya, Kenya) Omondi Oketch (Technical University of Kenya, Kenya) and Asiru Hameed Tunde (Umaru Musa Yar'adua University, Nigeria)
Information Science Reference • copyright 2016 • 412pp • H/C (ISBN: 9781522500810) • US $185.00 (our price)

International Perspectives on Socio-Economic Development in the Era of Globalization
Saurabh Sen (Sunbeam College for Women, India) Anshuman Bhattacharya (Sunbeam College for Women, India) and Ruchi Sen (Sunbeam College for Women, India)
Business Science Reference • copyright 2016 • 288pp • H/C (ISBN: 9781466699083) • US $175.00 (our price)

IGI GLOBAL
DISSEMINATOR OF KNOWLEDGE

www.igi-global.com

701 East Chocolate Avenue, Hershey, PA 17033, USA
Tel: 717-533-8845 x100 • Fax: 717-533-8661
E-Mail: cust@igi-global.com • www.igi-global.com

Editorial Advisory Board

Table of Contents

Detailed Table of Contents

importance of Public Procurement for Innovation (PPI); and the intermediation of PPI. E-procurement, GPP, and PPI expand the aspects of enterprise resource planning systems, sustainability, and innovation, allowing the automation of internal business processes and providing the procurement-related platforms that support automation at a global level. The benefits of e-procurement, GPP, and PPI include reduced transaction time, increased productivity, improved standardization, enhanced sustainability, and simplified global procurement.

The use of Information and Communication Technologies (ICTs) plays a significant role in the economic, technological and social progression of a country. Corruption in government agencies and institutions is a serious problem in many countries in the world, especially in under-developed and developing countries. The use of ICT tools such as e-governance can help to reduce corruption. In this chapter, the authors discussed the application of e-government principles to mitigate corruption. Based on the available literature, this study identified some potential elements of e-government, which are currently practised around the world and how they are interrelated to fight against corruption. Finally, the authors present an evidence-based e-government anti-corruption framework.

While e-procurement provides efficiency and cost-savings, are governments that are utilizing these systems really getting what they want, particularly when procuring services? While e-procurement provides governments methods to communicate better with service providers and have access to more service providers, do the systems allow for collaboration? As there is a significant amount of research the issues related to procurement in the U.S., this chapter will use it as an example to demonstrate the need to collaborate and not just communicate. For years there has been discussion on the issues and reforms to the U.S. federal procurement process. One of the major issues is communications and collaboration. Goodrich (2015) provided in his Federal Times article "6 simple fixed for the federal procurement process." Five of the six areas involve communications and collaboration: poorly conceived documentation; contracting offices and program offices working as a team rather than independent; lengthy procurement decisions; government understands what they bought; and talk with industry. This chapter provides the background of the procurement process, current trends and recent approaches. It explores how the Alpha contracting method could be applied to Contracts by Negotiations / Full and Open procurements. Finally, it provides a Collaborative Government Model which takes a holistic and strategic approach to collaboration. There is a need to approach this collaboration in a strategic manner as it includes facets such as hierarchy, networking, and inter-personal interactions that are not linear in nature.

Digital transformation in the public sector is an inevitable requirement for governments due to the growing complexity and interconnections of information systems, and to the demands of citizens, who are becoming better informed and are increasingly looking to more agile and innovative services. However, despite the willingness of many governments and public institutions, the results do not always tally with the original objectives. In the case of public procurement in Portugal, it could be said that digital transformation experience had an unexpected success in the European context, through a business model that is still quite unique in Europe. This result is much owed to the strong political determination, the experience gained from pilot projects, and to the involvement of many stakeholders, who contributed, in a consistent and innovative way, to the definition of the system. The system is not perfect: there are many challenges that need to be addressed in the coming years. Yet, it has enabled the Portuguese public administration to significantly grow in the digital era, so that today the State has a database containing structure information about public procurement, which is a unique case in many countries.

In this chapter the author, who has served as one of the lead administrators and designers of Turkey's e-procurement platform (EKAP) discusses the development of the system since May 2009. Specific focus and discussion will be on three main choices on how to develop the system. Will it be mandatory or voluntary? Is it better to create a platform centrally or delegate responsibility to individual public/private parties? How will applications in the platform be introduced, step by step or all at once? The author argues that as a centralized and mandatory e-procurement platform and developed step by step, EKAP successfully transformed public procurement procedures in Turkey, thanks to right choices made regard to the development of the system.

The Georgian public procurement system has undergone significant Public Financial Management reforms over the last few years. The goal of creation, introduction and management of the Georgian Electronic Government Procurement (Ge-GP) system was delegated upon the State Procurement Agency, which succeeded in ensuring the development of the software for the Ge-GP system under the assistance of the National Agency of Public Registry. The Ge-GP system was created within less than one year. From the first of December, 2010 all the paper-based tenders were abolished and electronic procurement has become the single platform. Through the introduction of electronic procurement platform, the Georgian procurement system has become considerably more transparent and nondiscriminatory, encouraging free and fair competition and minimizing the risk of corruption. Experience of the Georgian e-Procurement System could be one of the motivating factors for the countries working towards public procurement reform.

ChileCompra (CC) is the procurement authority of Chile. Purchases are made independently by the public entities, but CC is responsible for market regulation and management of the electronic platform, where transactions are made. ChileCompra was launched on 2003, within a deep State modernization process which started by the end of the 90s. ChileCompra was born with the mission of generating a substantial change in public procurement, as the previous system was neither responding to market needs nor to the accountability which citizens demanded. The objective was the creation of a transparent, efficient, and – most of all - accessible system, which would create equal business opportunities to companies of all sizes, especially for micro and small ones. ChileCompra manages the public procurement market, facilitating the acquisition of goods and services for public authorities; with high levels of transparency and equal opportunities for every enterprise, especially the smallest

Preface

Public procurement is the government activity most vulnerable to waste, fraud and corruption due to its complexity, size of financial flows it generates and the close interaction between public and private sectors. To improve efficiency in use of public resources, Governments seek to strengthening the Public Financial Management. Governments therefore intend to adopt the electronic-Government Procurement (e-GP) or e-Procurement to provide a platform for increasing transparency in procurement procedures and practices; improving efficiency in the procurement processes, by minimizing the procurement cycle time, maximizing value for money, and fostering accountability; improving confidentiality, integrity and authenticity of transactions between the procurement entities and the suppliers; and facilitating proper monitoring, reporting and planning of public procurements. Procurement policy regulates the public sector's interactions with domestic and international markets in ways that directly impact national efficiency and competitiveness.

The governance of procurement is pivotal to public trust in Government and is a barometer for the quality of public administration, making it a priority target for strengthening in Government. Good governance is the most challenging issue in case of traditional procurement environment. Despite having sound procurement legislation in place, monitoring and evaluation in adherence to the principles of procurement as well as ethical and efficient performance of the public entities considering value for money and socio-economic development are mostly compromised. Widespread and effective enforcement of such legislations is hardly possible because of numerous human and bureaucratic factors entrenched traditionally. Efficacy of procurement tools and measures are easily compromised at the implementation level abusing furtively for personal and political gains nurturing the epidemic and pervasive corruptions. Only with the use of innovative approaches may facilitate curbing such undeniable challenges persistent in traditional procurement environment. Transforming the complete procurement processes and practices into electronic environment with adequate tools and measures could facilitate invigorating good governance in the public procurement sector.

Modern e-Procurement is made up of various functions that, as concepts, are largely stand-alone, but need to be integrated in order to serve procurement management of the Government. It should cover end-to-end processes and practices of public procurement, and should be compliant with the public procurement laws, regulations, practices and based on the lessons learned from the international practices. E-Procurement system implemented with clear understanding of the purpose of use help leverage the electronic platform for improving procurement process and practices. Mere use of incomplete functions and processes do not give desired benefits. Following definition provides a comprehensive understanding of the e-Government Procurement (e-GP) System:

An e-GP system is defined as the collaborative use of information and communications technologies by government agencies, bidding community, regulatory, oversight agencies, other supporting service providers, and civil society in conducting ethical procurement activities of the government procurement process cycle for the procurement of goods, works and service, and management of contracts ensuring good governance and value-for-money in public procurement, and contributing to the socioeconomic development of country. (Shakya, 2015, p. 141)

Traditional procurement environment is challenged and prone to numerous compromises with the legislative, procedural, operational and ethical behavioral requirements, which spans the whole life cycle, from the identification of the need to procurement, through supplier selection and contracting, to the delivery of the required goods or services and (where relevant) the underlying policy outcome through to the disposal of the asset(s) or service closure or re-competition exercise. In absence of effective enforcement of procurement acts and regulations, and consistent and mandatory procurement performance monitoring and evaluation, traditional procurement systems cannot be reliable and always remains prone to errors. In traditional procurement, accountability is diluted by the decretory options enjoyed by the authority of the buying organizations, and untraceable activity records of other individuals involved in the procurement process.

E-Procurement is now proving to be the ideal environment for the public procurement in many countries around the world, which facilitates to implement all public procurement governance principles very effectively and seamlessly along the procurement cycle despite e-procurement is still treated just as one of the tools for carrying out only few of the functions of the public procurement cycle. Hence the adaptation of the e-Procurement has become very slow, and benefits reported are questionable.

The topics discussed in the book include different aspects of e-Procurement system implementations, covering the unique compilation of e-GP policy guidance, research findings to practitioners oriented e-GP implementation case studies from around the world, which provides holistic body of knowledge on e-Government Procurement.

AN OVERVIEW OF CHAPTERS

The first chapter of the book is titled *Digital Governance and e-Government Principles: E-Procurement as Transformative* which introduces the capacity of digital governance to address key aspects of reform of traditional procurement, the growing complexity of government, and the governance challenges of many developing countries. The chapter reviews the problems of traditional procurement, the distinction between simple versus complex procurement, and new modalities, and notes that the prevailing procurement model has been built on a framework designed for simple and manual procurement. The chapter provides e-GP policy guidelines to the public policy makers, and also discusses on the practical lessons of using e-GP System. Additionally, the chapter discusses how e-Government principles applied in e-procurement can play a critical role in resolving some of the challenges in public procurement.

The second chapter explains the critical success factors and implementation of e-procurement systems; the barriers to e-procurement implementation; the perspectives on electronic public procurement; the Interpretive Structural Modeling (ISM), Structural Equation Modeling (SEM), and e-procurement; the prospect of Green Public Procurement (GPP); the importance of Public Procurement for Innovation (PPI); and the intermediation of PPI. E-procurement, GPP, and PPI expand the aspects of enterprise resource planning systems, sustainability, and innovation, allowing the automation of internal business processes and providing the procurement-related platforms that support automation at a global level.

Corruption in government agencies and institutions is a serious problem in many countries in the world, especially in under-developed and developing countries. The third chapter unveils the e-Government principles in anti-corruption framework for the use in the public procurement sector. The chapter shows how the use of Information and Communication Technologies (ICTs) can play a role in the economic, technological and social progression of a country. The chapter discusses the application of e-government principles to mitigate corruption. Finally, the authors present an evidence-based e-government anti-corruption framework.

The fourth chapter starts the presentation of research findings and country and region specific case studies in using e-GP system. The chapter analyzes the importance of communication and collaboration in case of using e-GP system through an example of United States federal procurement processes. The chapter also provides a Collaborative Government Model which takes a holistic and strategic approach to collaboration.

The fifth chapter provides a case study on the Digital transformation of the public procurement sector in Portugal. Despite the willingness of many governments and public institutions, the results do not always tally with the original objectives. In the case of public procurement in Portugal, it could be said that digital transformation experience had an unexpected success in the European context, through a business model that is still quite unique in Europe.

The sixth chapter discusses the development of the Turkish e-Procurement system, its approach to implementation, and the requirement of right policy choices for the success of introducing innovative systems.

The Georgian public procurement system has undergone significant Public Financial Management reforms over the last few years. Through the introduction of electronic procurement platform, the Georgian procurement system has become considerably more transparent and nondiscriminatory, encouraging free and fair competition and minimizing the risk of corruption. Experience of the Georgian e-Procurement System could be one of the motivating factors for the countries working towards public procurement reform. The seventh chapter is dedicated presenting the unique success story of the Georgian e-GP system (Ge-GP).

Chapter 8 focuses on the evolution of the Chilean public procurement system, lessons learned and challenges, and the conditions to make it a complete electronic procurement process. ChileCompra (CC) is the procurement authority of Chile. ChileCompra is currently a strong system, with high levels of transparency and efficiency. ChileCompra is now facing second generation challenges, like the strengthening of the public procurement role in the socio economic national development.

Chapter 9 explores the topic of electronic government procurement (e-GP) in Latin America and the Caribbean (LAC), the factors that affected the development of such systems, how they evolved differently across the region and the challenges going forward. The information included in this chapter will provide valuable insight on how e-GP implementation has been a key element in public procurement reform in LAC as well as important lessons from the region. The findings will be useful for stakeholders with an interest in public procurement modernization and reform including: policy makers, heads of procurement, academics, civil society and international development organizations.

Chapter 10 focuses the e-Procurement case of India and highlights that public procurement in any country acts as a barometer of public confidence in fairness and transparency of public institutions. A number of cases related to corruption in public procurement have been highlighted by media on regular basis. These incidents raise questions regarding robustness of the procurement framework in vogue in the country. The chapter covers the importance of public procurement, difference between public and corporate procurement, overview of procurement framework of India, and e-GP initiatives by the Government of India and status thereof.

Chapter 12 reviews the existing literature and reports on e-procurement benefits experience of a large Australian municipal council and shares the lessons learned from the experience of the council.

Chapter 13 analyzes the reform of public procurement systems in Russia and Ukraine in the context of electronization, as well as a comparative analysis of the effectiveness of such reforms. The chapter sets a goal to determine the prospects of expanding the scope of e-procurement based on the analysis of the implementation of the reform of public procurement systems effects in Russia and Ukraine.

The book as a whole discusses on the premise of achieving significant outcomes from the e-Procurement platform embracing it as the mainstream procurement platform applying e-government principles that enhances good governance through sustainable tools and measures of digital governance adequately implemented.

Rajesh Kumar Shakya
The World Bank, USA

REFERENCES

Shakya, R. K. (2015). e-Procurement for good governance in public procurement. Saarbrucken, Germany: Scholars' Press.

Acknowledgment

I thank my wife Dr. Dhandu Rani Shakya, my son Ayush Shakya and daughter Ayusha Shakya for the patience and support during the development of this book. Without their consistent support this would have been impossible.

I want to thank and acknowledge the work of each of the authors that contributed the book. I thank their dedication, their patience, and their ideas that led this book to be a pillar of knowledge in e-Government Procurement (e-GP).

I thank my Editorial Advisory Board, and especially Dr. Paul Schapper and Dr. Khi Thai, who reviewed the chapters and provided comments and valuable suggestions for enhancing the quality of the book.

Rajesh Kumar Shakya
The World Bank, USA

Chapter 1
Digital Governance and E-Government Principles:
E-Procurement as Transformative

Rajesh Kumar Shakya
The World Bank, USA

Paul Roland Schapper
Curtin University, Australia

ABSTRACT

This chapter focuses on the capacity of digital governance to address key aspects of reform of traditional procurement, the growing complexity of government, and the governance challenges of many developing countries. The chapter reviews the problems of traditional procurement, the distinction between simple versus complex procurement, and new modalities, and notes that the prevailing procurement model has been built on a framework designed for simple and manual procurement. Modernization efforts to address these issues have often been scoped around the robust governance institutions of advanced economies and are not good matches to the very different realities in many middle income and emerging economies. The chapter discusses how e-Government principles applied in e-procurement can play a critical role in resolving some of the challenges in public procurement.

DOI: 10.4018/978-1-5225-2203-4.ch001

INTRODUCTION

Public procurement comprises a substantial share of the national economy in almost all countries. In many markets, the public sector is by far the largest player.

Public procurement is a key link between the public financial system and social and economic outcomes, and as such is a major determinant of the quality of community services and the effectiveness of infrastructure investments. This function cuts across almost all areas of planning, program management, and budgeting. National planning and budget development, including responses to national crises and natural disasters as well as the provision of regular services, involve the prioritization and sometimes fast-tracking of new service programs, development projects and asset creation, which are all enacted by procurement.

Procurement policy often regulates the public sector's interactions with domestic and international markets in ways that directly impact national efficiency and competitiveness. Public procurement is also a common vehicle for business and industry policies, and most regional and bilateral trade agreements have significant procurement provisions aimed at granting reciprocal access to domestic government procurement markets.

The OECD (2002) estimated for OECD member countries as a whole, the ratio of total procurement to GDP is 19.96% and for non-member countries the ratio is 14.48%. The governance of public procurement also plays a key role in public trust in government and is a barometer for the quality of public administration, often making it a priority target for reform in many governments.

For these reasons, the strengthening governance in procurement has been described as the single most significant option for development in many countries. However, in many countries with poor governance, much of the strengthening of procurement implies fundamental changes in a variety of governance institutions involving a scope that would go well beyond procurement per se.

TRADITIONAL MANAGEMENT OF PROCUREMENT

The traditional management of public procurement had its origins in an era when government procurement focused primarily on basic goods and military equipment: For most of history, public procurement has been only a little more complicated than personal expenditure, and procurement personnel have been warehouse officials and accounts-payable staff, often unqualified in complex procurement. In those earlier times, public procurement was a relatively minor part of national economies.

Modern day reality is quite different. The OECD (2013) has recognized that "public procurement is the government activity most vulnerable to waste, fraud and corruption due to its complexity, the size of the financial flows it generates and the close interaction between the public and the private sectors". Traditional procurement barely distinguished between simple and high-risk complex procurement. In that environment, many opportunities for improved social and economic outcomes have been invisible because the relevant management and planning information has been inaccessible.

Poor governance in procurement invariably reduces development outcomes and has been shown as likely to reduce foreign direct investment. The International Monetary Fund (IMF) (1998) identified national consequences of poor governance in procurement in terms of:

- Over-spending on capital;
- Under spending on asset maintenance;
- Poor quality infrastructure, and
- Reduced government revenues.

That IMF review concluded that poor governance at the early planning level of procurement can result in infrastructure that reduces national growth - investment becomes a disinvestment. The poor quality and under-spending on maintenance also implies that what infrastructure exists has lower economic productivity.

As public procurement has become more complex and involved greater risks, inherent problems have become more evident including a lack of management information and market knowledge, inefficient procedures, high compliance costs for suppliers and government departments, simplistic and ineffective procurement methodologies, and a profound lack of transparency.

The Governance Dilemma

The proper governance of modern public procurement is concerned both with the value for money of procurement, and the means by which the outcome is reached. The means by which best practice procurement outcomes are achieved have two broad goals – those that help sustain the value for money objective and other goals of the government, and those that protect the management integrity surrounding the use of public funds.

There have been two divergent schools of thought in relation to the pursuit of governance strengthening and procurement reform. One advocates strong prescribed processes governed by rigid and detailed regulations and elimination of discretion. The other advocates greater provision for management flexibility and market knowledge, with a focus on performance and value for money. Exchanging prescriptive procurement regulations for professional standards and market expertise has much to recommend it especially for high-risk complex procurement such as for information technology contracts or major works.

A shift in the procurement regime from regulatory conformance to value for money performance requires an effective accountability framework and comprehensive procurement skills. Effective accountability generally implies at a minimum, high levels of transparency and reporting, clear lines of responsibility and authority, an effective compliance framework, and an audit function that is knowledgeable in procurement. Similarly, for the reform model, there are often implicit assumptions of an effective audit role, high levels of transparency, compliance enforcement, monitoring of conflicts of interest, understanding of value for money, an effective media oversight, understanding of basic procurement rules, understanding of law, etc.

These conditions are often not found even in developed countries with relatively robust governance, and are rare in developing country contexts where often the institutional and capacity conditions for effective governance are weak or simply do not exist. Where there are weak institutions, poor capacity and unreliable administration, the reform model generally recommends the elimination, as far as possible, of official flexibility, but in doing so relegates procurement to become a set of mechanical rules, which often seriously compromise value for money outcomes and greatly increase risks to the objectives of the procurement, while generally remaining readily corruptible from the same underlying factors.

The dilemma for developing countries (and some developed jurisdictions) is how to gain greater performance from procurement including reducing the governance risks and risks to the objectives of the procurement, without departing substantially from a compliance framework imposed because of weak institutions and capacity. For many developed country governments and for emerging economies where procurement governance is generally weak, procurement reform frequently seems dependent on what is often a remote goal of strengthening of governance in the government generally, as a pre-requisite to better value for money.

The challenge becomes more tangible if public procurement is considered in terms of 'portfolio' analysis, or more simply in terms of simple, low cost / high volume procurement versus complex, high cost / low volume procurement. Breaking down the procurement portfolio into its parts can reveal how performance for important parts of procurement can be strengthened without weakening existing regulations or controls regardless of their effectiveness or otherwise. The following sections show that there can be technological solutions for some of these issues for some types of procurement, such as the need for greater transparency, as well as the reduction in manual procedures and discretion, which can be delivered by online technology with a reduction in governance risk.

Digital Governance

The digital governance required today to ensure that public procurement is efficient and productive is central to the planning, monitoring and management of the modern State and its budget. These governance requirements are numerous and include 'spend' analyses of multiple public procurement entities, market trends, performances of many potential contractors and also procurement officials and supplier performances. These governance requirements cannot expect to be delivered within a paper environment. In reality, for some complex cases, the paper environment for procurement is unable to deliver almost any of these requirements. Indeed, the paper environment has often been characterized by:

- High process costs associated with testing the market;
- Poor and outdated market intelligence;
- Obsolete supplier profiles;
- Maverick spending (off contract);
- Inefficient payments processes;
- Obsolete audit information;
- Error-prone contract management tracking.

Each of these issues can be significantly diminished through e-Government applications. A range of other common procurement issues would also be partly or wholly addressed by e-procurement systems. Examples include:

- Problems in the quality of national bidding, and even larger bidders are often not well-prepared, being short on capacity and guidelines for preparing bids, a dominant reliance on newspaper notices and advertising and advertising that is often on non-business days, in obscure local newspapers that escape audit and monitoring, and reduce competition;
- A lack of national or provincial statistics on procurement other than what can be deduced from financial reports;
- Procurement planning that is often poor. Procurement plans are developed but not in standard formats;
- Blacklists maintained by individual entities in isolation;
- Limited or no standardization of major assets such as vehicles, so multiple inventories are maintained;
- Little trust of the public procurement system amongst many private sector entities who often trust the government less than their competitors. Payment of commissions is common;
- Bidding processes that are time consuming and expensive;

- Grievance redresses that are considered to favor agencies and are avoided by many businesses.

Paper-based procurement for many purchases involves a quoting system that limits competition and facilitates collusion. For more strategic procurement, the paper environment has often restricted information access and competition. Paper-based or manual information transactions are also vulnerable to common types of corruption, some of which can easily be eliminated by technology. In the modern complex government environment, traditional paper-based procurement procedures deliver neither good governance nor performance (Shakya, 2016).

E-PROCUREMENT AS TRANSFORMATIVE

Procurement technology or e-procurement represents an effective measure for enhancing transparency and documentation in public procurement and has the potential to transform many procurement procedures and practices without demanding the trauma and risk of abandoning familiar regulations in favor of what can seem to be an untested model usually against the advice of risk-averse procurement lawyers and more particularly the interests vested in the status quo.

Information technology can transform many aspects of procurement management, but the nature of this transformation varies between countries and also between procurement modalities. Depending on the context, aspects of the transformation may include the production of management information, administrative cultural change, competition, transparency, and corruption for routine procurement. Differentiation is also required between complex high-risk high cost procurement versus low-risk small value routine procurement. Potential savings from the implementation of e-procurement have been estimated to be in the range of 5-8% of the procurement value. Other financial benefits have been found both for suppliers and buyers.

However, cost reduction is a relatively minor aspect amongst the opportunities raised by the technology. E-procurement can also automate many procurement processes including supplier selection for some sorts of procurement, and opens the way for new efficient procurement modalities that can increase market access and competition and also can decentralize much procurement down to the point of service within the government (such as in schools). E-procurement has been shown to eliminate entirely some forms of corruption such as the demand for 'speed money' for some procedures.

E-procurement has the potential to strengthen governance through its capacity to enhance transparency and improve access to management and accountability information, while simultaneously reducing scope for procedural discretion, thereby resolving, for some contexts, the procurement dilemma discussed above. Many of the benefits of e-procurement are equally applicable to government and the business sector. In addition, the value of e-procurement for suppliers both in terms of efficiency (market access, ease of bidding, document transfers, transactions) and market information can promote the take-up of business technologies through the wider economy.

Reported Benefits from E-Procurement

E-Procurement can automate many procurement processes including supplier selection for some sorts of procurement that can increase market access and competition and also decentralise much procurement down to the point of service within the government (such as in schools). Benefits have been reported Aberdeen Group (2007) in terms of:

- Reduction in inventory value of up to 80%;
- Reduction in maverick buying – improved compliance of 30%
- Reduction in errors due to elimination of manual processes;
- Reduction in purchase-to-pay processes by 90%;
- Reduced procurement cycle time by up to 80%;
- Improved relations with suppliers who in turn have benefited from reduced transaction costs and improved efficiency;
- Improved analytical capacity and management control.

E-Procurement has, in some countries, eliminated at least one form of coercion – specifically the practice of physically preventing competitors from approaching and depositing a document in the bid box. Other examples include the following:

- The Austrian Federal Procurement Agency centralizes purchases for federal authorities through e-Procurement functionalities. EU (2010) reported savings of € 178 million against a procurement volume of € 830 million. Benefits significantly outweigh the annual maintenance costs of € 5 million, which are less than 3% of the savings.
- As from 1 February 2005, all contracting authorities in Denmark accept only electronic invoices. This reform affects approximately 15 million invoices a year, and applies to the entire public sector, from ministries to nursery schools. The use of e-Invoicing saves the public € 100 million every year, on top of savings in internal administrative processes.
- India - in the state of Andhra Pradesh where an e-Procurement system was launched in January 2003, tenders processed through the e-Procurement plat-

form in the pilot phase during 2003-04 claimed a reduction of 16% in the quotations (Bikshapathi, RamaRaju & Bhatnagar, 2006) in comparison to the previous year when the procurement was manual, and a reduction in tender cycle time from 130 days to 32 days.

- The Italian Emilia Romagna's agency Intercent ER offers e-Procurement services including e-Marketplace, e-Catalogues and e-Auctions and is the reference point for 539 administrations (90% of local agencies). In 2008 it processed transactions amounting to some €419 million, delivering efficiency benefits estimated at €67.5 million and time-savings of 45 man-years.
- The Korean Government has reported "significant cost savings, a 5-fold increase in productivity, and drastic reductions in corruption.
- The Government of Kazakhstan also reported significant savings from its partly developed system (Kazakhstan, 2011).
- In Norway, the Ehandel platform is helping authorities to achieve 20-40% reductions in the time taken to handle orders, receipt of goods and invoicing and delivering price savings in the region of 2-10%.
- A Portuguese study compared the best bids for public works contracted by 50 Portuguese public hospitals in 2009 (using paper based systems) and 2010 (using e-Procurement). It concluded that a cost reduction of 18% had been achieved in 2010, due to the increase in competition generated by e-Procurement.
- Scottish Executive (Government) improved contract pricing with an additional 1.5 percent discount on stationery due to automated payment using Visa procurement cards. Major reduction in administration costs, elimination of 45,000 invoices as a result of electronic consolidated invoicing, reduction in number of purchase-to-pay related processes from 45 to 4.
- In the UK, the Buying Solutions site reported in its 2008/09 annual report that it had facilitated sales of over £5 billion, delivering £732 million in savings. The UK also reported savings frequently exceeding 10% (and even up to 45%) through the use of e-auctions.
- The Office of Government Commerce (OGC) in the UK reported transactions savings of £41 per transaction for small value off-the-shelf purchasing systems, which freed up significant amounts of staff time, reduced order error rates and substantially reduced off-contract ordering ('maverick purchasing') (OGC, 2005).
- Philippine Government E-Procurement Service, the Government of the Philippine has reported savings from e-procurement as follows:
    - Various drugs / Medicines (53%)
    - Equipment for electrification projects (43%)
    - Printing of letterheads (42%)

    - IT equipment & supply / delivery of construction materials (33%)
    - Supplies / Material Services (25%)
    - Construction supplies, IT equipment (19%)
    - Electrical / mechanical supplies & equipment (17%)
    - Various office supplies / equipment (15%)
    - Office Supplies / Materials (15%)
- The Aberdeen Group (2008) reported that public sector enterprises have significantly improved their performance as a result of e-procurement initiatives with lower transaction costs, lower maverick spend, and lower transaction cycle times. Automating the order-payment cycle has led to reductions in manual processing of procedural error-prone tasks, allowing staff to focus on more productive activities. Some of the targeted benefits from a survey of e-procurement projects (2008) included a 47% reduction in transaction costs, a 63% improvement in process efficiency, 43% improvement in compliance, and 23% improvement in transparency.
- A World Bank survey (2007) of fourteen countries where e-procurement had been introduced, found that users of e-procurement were almost equally divided between those that considered the primary benefit of e-procurement was in terms of transparency, and those that considered efficiency as the primary outcome. Qualitative benefits reported from users included:
    - Reduced time for the procurement process;
    - Improved access to procurement opportunities via a single national portal;
    - Improved transparency;
    - Reduced errors in process and documentation for buyers;
    - More sophisticated market intelligence;
    - Increased market access.

The examples listed above were frequently the results of stronger management and coordination facilitated by technology, rather than from technology per se. For this reason, as for much of e-government generally, e-procurement is essentially a procurement reform program, rather than a technology or legal program, and is usually accompanied by changes in work practices and procurement methodologies to allow full use of the capabilities of the technology. The increase in competition from e-procurement is a source of substantial savings, through providing greater visibility and ease of access to the government market. Other value for money benefits arise from transactional efficiencies, improved management information and governance.

Transparency, Reporting and Assessment

The potential for e-Procurement to strengthen transparency (an essential component of accountability) has been reported in research for over ten years. Technology reduces the marginal cost of management and audit information from high to almost zero. E-Procurement also provides more significant and timely procurement information that creates the potential for regular analysis and reporting for many stakeholders. This information aspect cannot be expected to function effectively in the paper environment. Examples of applications of improved management information include:

- Spend analyses by department that provide the intelligence for strategic procurement development;
- Management of whole-of-government framework agreements that should require standardised reporting on a weekly or daily basis in an analytical format;
- 'Buy-domestic' industry development policies that require spend analyses to review programme effectiveness and compliance;
- Open-markets and cross-border trade policies and agreements that often require spend analyses, potential savings and levels of cross-border trade;
- Audit of procurement activities that require timely access to information from numerous widely dissipated small value transactions.
- Annual budgeting that requires analyses of the scheduled payment stream of major contracts, and the forward estimates of regular spend;
- Cross-agency complex analyses required to manage blacklisted suppliers;

The success of any management strategy for improving public expenditure depends largely on its ability to access, organize and analyze expenditure data. Access to accurate, timely and comprehensive spend data provides intelligence on spending patterns, inventory, performance and compliance. This information helps identify efficiency opportunities and market opportunities.

Interpreting the Benefits

Some benefits (such as transparency and improved access to management and audit information) are difficult to quantify, but this does not make them any less valid. Some savings can be realized in terms of hard cash, while others may improve efficiency and strengthen integrity but not be cashable.

The foregoing discussion identified the benefits of a well-conceived and implemented e-procurement strategy. Benefits have been described in qualitative and quantitative terms. With public procurement accounting for between 15%-20% of the national economy, this level of savings potential is substantial and the benefit / cost ratio should be overwhelming even without considering the qualitative benefits. It is likely that the qualitative benefits are even more important.

Caveats apply to all of these results, insofar as stakeholders themselves have reported most of them. However, in the light of the magnitude of public procurement, even the most conservative estimates of benefits dwarf the costs of implementing e-Procurement.

Many of these benefits from e-procurement only become available where there is a capacity to reform the practice of procurement. The reform drivers involving political backing, effective bureaucratic leadership, expertise, and procurement skills but these may not be understood or available within a government. Where the introduction of technology is not accompanied by the reform of work practices then the benefits may be small. Good technical systems can also be handicapped by the lack of strategic objectives, resulting in multiple systems between various departments and geographic areas and leading to a fragmentation of services, and a dissipation of the potential for leveraged buying and planning and analysis.

Finally, there have been cases where users on both sides of the market have raised objections to the introduction of information technology or e-procurement. The reasons for these have often included resistance to greater transparency and competition.

PROCUREMENT MODALITIES AND TECHNOLOGY

Technology opens the door to the efficient application of procurement methodologies such as e-auctions and e-framework agreements, and also enables the deployment of efficient e-purchase cards. The low cost access to management information in e-procurement enables the strengthening of control, oversight, efficiency and planning capabilities as well as competition.

Figure 1 shows, in terms of portfolio analysis, the ways that technology applications can impact on public procurement. The third quadrant (strategic contracting) typically accounts for 70-80% of public procurement by value, while the second quadrant (simple high value competitive contracting) accounts for 70-80% of the number of procurement transactions. The potential impact of technology is quite different in each of these areas.

For major acquisitions, such as large infrastructure, e-procurement advertises opportunities, and manages contract and planning information, and document flows. The advertising of these major projects on the Internet may improve competition, but this is likely to be a modest gain in many cases because these projects tend to be mostly relevant for larger companies, which are more likely to be effectively

Figure 1. E-procurement applications
Source: Schapper, Veiga Malta, & Gilbert (2009)

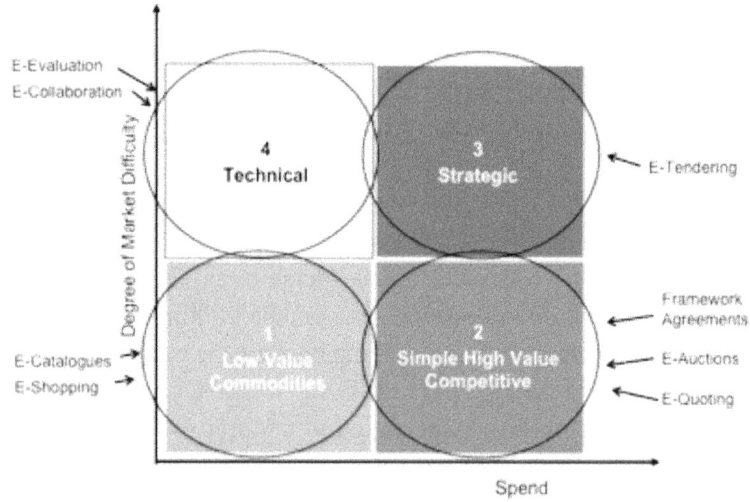

networked into this information anyway. The major gains from e-procurement for complex high risk contracting are contract and budget planning, contract management, transparency, and efficiency and integrity in document management (for example e-procurement abolishes the vulnerable physical bid box).

For the more common lower value procurement, the role of e-procurement is to manage competitive bidding amongst a significant range of suppliers, via framework agreements, quotations or reverse auctions. The objective of e-procurement in these cases is the promotion of competition, price reductions, and strengthening of transparency by the use of online processes and reducing or eliminating transactional discretion. E-procurement can also be applied to this level of procurement in a way that excludes the operator from the selection process and thereby can strengthen governance and reduce malpractice.

The opportunities for technology to streamline manual processes in procurement come through at many levels both for suppliers and buyers in the payment cycle, financial management integration, approvals, reporting, etc. The degree of manual processing in simple and complex procurement which can be streamlined with a well-designed and functional e-procurement system can be appreciated through an understanding of all of the elements that make up typical supply chain processing which includes search, requests for quotations, authorisations, financial reconciliations, audit and reporting.

Framework Agreements and Reverse Auctions

A major aspect of Figure 1 is the application of framework agreements. E-procurement greatly facilitates framework agreements by allowing larger numbers of suppliers to be managed and for online and mobile e-quoting systems for example. Framework agreements have many potential benefits and have been in place in some jurisdictions for many years, but are almost unheard of in other administrations. Framework agreements often operate more effectively when in the online environment, and indeed sometimes cannot operate in the paper context. Framework agreements are part of the modern procurement toolkit both in government and in the private sector, with potential benefits that include:

- Lower contract prices
- Reduced costs of process
- Efficient emergency operations
- Efficient use of scarce capacity
- Enhanced governance
- Enhanced budget planning

These instruments are applicable in a wide range of circumstances that include:

- Where there is frequent re-ordering based on similar specifications;
- The volume of supplies required cannot be precisely predicted;
- Unpredictable delivery dates;
- Independent buying units acquiring the same supplies;
- Small buying units lack the capacity to arrange and manage their contracts;
- Crisis planning (such as for natural disasters) cannot accommodate the time required for traditional processes;
- No single supplier is considered to have sufficient capacity;
- A choice of suppliers is considered desirable.

The use of framework agreements is focused primarily on low value simple goods, services and works. The efficiency savings from these instruments helps explain why some jurisdictions, such as in UK and Australia, undertake fifty percent or more of their transactions through framework agreements.

Another modality that requires online technology to be practical on any meaningful scale is that of reverse auctions. Reverse auctions can have many of the same benefits as framework agreements, and the boundary between framework agreements and reverse auctions can disappear in a well-designed procurement system. For example, framework agreements often allow for 'mini-competitions', that operate best when online, where suppliers that are part of the framework agreement then bid competitively for each procurement opportunity that arises over the life of the framework. This bidding can also be conducted via an auction (including Dutch action). It is generally not best practice for an auction to be conducted outside of a pre-existing framework agreement of one form or another because, for example, ineligible bidders subsequently disqualified or bidders who refused the conditions of contract would mean that the process would need to be repeated. Therefore, reverse auctions usually have a pre-qualification process that should be similar in scope to a framework agreement.

Reform Myths and Ambiguities

The potential roles of technology in procurement are often misunderstood. The interpretation of benefits and limitations depend on the assessor's standpoint. Different perceptions arise depending on, for example, whether the focus is for strong versus emerging economies, whether there are robust or weak governance environments, or whether the concern is with the large (generally works) contracts or on the smaller goods, works and services contracts. Also, the potential varies according to how the e-procurement system is centralized or decentralized and what is meant by centralization or decentralization. For each of these circumstances, the potential of e-procurement is different, so the question of benefits and impact of e-procurement can be ambiguous; the answer varies according to the context.

Sometimes there has been uncertainty as to whether procurement reform should precede the introduction of technology – whether e-procurement leads or lags reform. In practice, reform of procurement within the paper environment is difficult and confronts the dilemma discussed above between whether more or less regulation should be imposed. Some of these issues can be diminished or avoided by allowing e-procurement to lead reform through greater transparency and other benefits.

A further source of confusion has often been whether e-procurement can adequately be delivered by the financial management information system (FMIS). Financial packages often include components marketed as 'e-procurement'. However, these often have their origins in private industry supply lines and can be a poor fit for government procurement requirements without expensive customization and even more expensive upgrades when new versions of the FMIS appear. Here again the understanding also depends on the point of reference. The idea that the FMIS can deliver the e-procurement services is usually espoused by government officials and technocrats, whom procurement is about mere financial transactions: the government procures by paying a supplier, and this payment needs to be recorded against the appropriate budget line and reported as such, etc. However, while many have assessed this option, few governments have adopted the FMIS model: this model has little to do with public procurement and does almost nothing to address the challenges in modern procurement as is discussed previously.

There has sometimes been a presumption that all 'e' procurement is good. For example, it was once assumed that e-reverse auctions would revolutionize procurement but this has not happened and reverse auctions are used for only a small fraction of procurement transactions in most countries. It has also been assumed that PKI digital signatures would revolutionize authentication in procurement, but this has not happened: PKI is little used in online commerce, and its use has in several cases been withdrawn in favour of more business-friendly and more reliable methods.

Some technical specialists understand e-procurement as a file management system or that e-procurement refers to the interface between government buyers and suppliers, such as e-auctions, bidding, etc., thus ignoring the great benefits that arise from the workflow management and analytical functions of e-procurement. Similarly, e-procurement has sometimes been taken to represent a form of semi-automated buying or in terms of e-Bay, etc., which can be common in large private sector warehouses and assembly lines, but which is almost unheard of in government.

A lesson has been that e-procurement or e-procurement can refer to many different models, developments and functions, not all of which will be consistent with government policies or practices. Although e-procurement preferably reflects a unitary concept, in reality it often refers to a collection of tools and functions and collaboration among many stakeholders.

FUNCTIONALITY

The e-procurement technology architecture should provide public sector buyers, suppliers and the general public with secure access to an integrated range of procurement systems, tools and services, consisting of the following high-level components.

- **A Procurement Portal** Service which will provide informational and transactional services
- **A Supplier Register**, which will record basic details of suppliers interested in doing business with any part of the public sector;
- **A Buyer Register**, which will host the details of procurement entities participating in e-procurement and their designated procurement officers.
- **Information Services**, giving access to public sector procurement-related information such as news, publications and policies, as well as discussion forums;

- **An e-Bidding system**, which will facilitate the online advertising of bid invitations, and the secure transmission of electronic bid documents between buyers and bidders for public sector contracts;
- **Catalogue-based ordering system** to provide public sector buyers with facilities to order from online catalogues of goods available under contracts agreed with suppliers.
- **Quotations, Framework Agreements, E-Auctions;**
- **Direct purchasing and quoting system;**
- **E-Payments system**, which will facilitate online payments for the suppliers for the goods/services procured through the e-procurement system by the public procurement entities
- **Procurement Management Information System** inclusive of several key sub-systems
- **Procurement Planning and Inventory Management**
- **Regular and ad hoc reporting system** on procurement, such as performance data and trends;

As the primary access mechanism for the e-procurement services and systems will be via the Internet, users within the public sector will require access to Internet/ Government secure intranet to participate in e-procurement. However, except for e-auctions / reverse auctions, the Internet quality of service should not be especially demanding – most countries have sufficient infrastructure, even via mobile phone technology.

Procurement Management Information System

At the heart of the e-procurement system should be a Procurement Management Information System (PMIS) that is as essential to modern procurement as the Financial Management Information System (FMIS) is to modern financial management. The PMIS provides for contract management, tracking, planning, performance assessments, audit and reporting.

A standardised quality assured workflow process should be developed within the e-procurement system. The opportunity should be exploited to use the consolidation of the PMIS to also review current rules and management processes of the procuring entities to identify those that can be streamlined, modified or abolished for the electronic environment. The Procurement Management Information System will become the Procurement Management *and* Information System.

The PMIS must include workflow and authorisation trails, and all information transactions in any part of the procurement process including contract management, contract planning, and interactions between stakeholders.

The system should also have the following capacities:

- **Contract Variations**: To record and publish price variations to the awarded price per line item. A full audit trail of the contract and price variations is recorded
- **Contract Extension**: The system should manage the contract extension process. Many contracts are let for an initial period with the option to exercise extensions for further periods. The system should provide an early warning report of contracts that are due to complete their current term.
- **Contract Recall**: The system should manage the contract recall process. Many contracts are let for an initial period with the option to exercise extensions for further periods.

There should also be a capacity to facilitate aggregation obtaining better prices through returns to scale.

Further improvements in public procurement expenditure can be achieved by integrating Inventory Management systems with the PMIS. Capturing the key inventory data, removal of obsolete items data in the PMIS, laying down guidelines in procurement policy regarding minimum inventory levels for emergency situations, inventory management, disposal of obsolete items by way of sale through e-Auction etc can lead to substantial efficiency gains. So that for example, while inventory may be decentralised, this should not mean that its management should not be coordinated – there can be scope to identify stock surpluses in one part of government before reordering takes place in another part of the same government.

LEGAL AND REGULATORY FRAMEWORK

E-procurement has consequences for a range of business and public sector legislation although it is often possible to initiate some elements of e-procurement without legislative amendment and an e-procurement strategy should recognise this in its schedule of phased implementation. Legislation that allows for rules to be developed and changed without requiring major change to the legislation has some advantage in dealing with the evolving issues in procurement. Some specific legislation may have already been enacted in relation to electronic commerce including issues such as authentication, privacy and security of data.

The basic core legislative requirements for e-procurement and e-commerce generally are simply for there to be legal status provided for:

- Electronic documents
- Electronic signatures

In addition to procurement law requirements relating to e-documents and e-signatures, procurement regulations or rules need to be framed taking into account circumstances that would affect the e-procurement environment. These rules should also align the procurement process to take advantage of the strengths of the electronic environment rather than duplicating the process directly from the paper environment.

Procurement rules should include management practices and transactions in the electronic environment, and operating circumstances:

- Inconsistencies between electronic and hardcopy documentation from government agencies, and from the private sector;
- The malfunction of government facilities before closing time set for electronic bid lodgement;
- Electronic bid opening procedures;
- Electronic bid management security, encryptions standards for data;
- Electronic contract development for template and document consistency and economy;
- Online pre-tendered contracts;
- Online catalogues;
- Mobile technology options;
- IT Security
- Application Usage Policy (includes clause on limited liability)
- Disaster Recovery Planning
- Backup requirements
- Archival rules
- E-Payments/ Receipts rules
- Open Contracting policies

When quotations are requested in a traditional manual system, typically a minimum of 3-5 quotes are expected before the procuring authority can proceed with the procurement and select the supplier. Upon adoption of e-quoting, the best of the entire set of vendors offering the required product can be selected (100% sampling) without adding to procurement officer workload. The electronic mode allows for evaluating quotations from any number of suppliers without adding any cost or affecting the timelines of procurement.

Governments may consider whether they are to have a policy on e-procurement access through Internet cafes and mobile phones to increase access whee connectivity is weak. Access through Internet cafes conflicts with PKI authentication.

Policies or practices on bid submission closure times should be re-visited. Usually, bid closure time is during business hours and at times when Internet traffic is heavy. In countries where connectivity is poor this increases the risk of non-delivery. The policy can equally be set for midnight or any other hour when traffic is low. On the other hand this would mean that paper delivery of a bid would effectively close at a different time from e-delivery, but this may not be important depending on online bid box security.

Other rules and policies should also be reviewed. For example, all communications should be directed to be via the questions and answers facility. It should be noted that these policies are required regardless of the platform - whether the e-procurement system itself is built in-house, outsourced or whether it is contracted on a fee for service basis – the core issues are mostly not the technology platform but rather about management in the information environment

- Electronic records management;
- Consumer protection and privacy;
- Laws pertaining to legal evidence;
- Data protection and confidentiality;
- Intellectual property, copyright;
- Codes of practice.

However, these areas are generally not pre-requisites for the initial application of e-procurement.

Signatures and Authentication

As a general principle signature legislation should conform to international standards to ensure interoperability with similar legislation in other countries. Since the UNCITRAL Model Law on Electronic Commerce (1996), countries have been adopting laws on this issue. However, there are no universal international standards in this area, and such laws therefore have a limited scope as they are applied only to domestic transactions in each country, without any regulation on the wide range of cross-border transactions.

Within ASEAN and EU countries UNCITRAL model law on e-Commerce (1996) this issue is evident. These governments have adopted the 1996 Model Law and e-signatures are used but has been interpreted differently by different jurisdictions thereby curtailing its application for cross border procurement. Apart from government procurement there is little evidence that cross border trade has been inhibited, because private trading partners generally do not rely on these procedures.

There is a need to promote agreements among the countries that, taking into consideration their own national regulations, establish the basis for the mutual recognition of electronic signatures.

To address this situation, UNCITRAL elaborated the Convention on International Electronic Communications, which has been signed by 18 countries (2011) among which are China, Russian, Korea, Paraguay, Colombia, Honduras and Panama.

This Convention, adopted by the General Assembly of November 23, 2005, has the goal of promoting legal certainty and trading predictability when electronic communications are used in international contracts. It applies to the determination of the location of the parties involved in an electronic environment; the time and place the electronic communications are sent and received; the use of automated message systems to generate agreements; and the criteria applied to determine the functional equivalence between the electronic communications and the paper documents, including the "original" paper-based documents, as well as the methods for electronic authentication and handwritten signature.

The UNCITRAL Convention (2006) is now consistent with the technological neutrality principle, moving away from Public Key Infrastructure (PKI), and accepting any authentication method that allows on the one hand the determination of the identity of a person and on the other hand establishing the personal involvement of that person. It also admits agreements between parties, antecedents and the proportionality between means and purposes, including the further proof, thus admitting the scope for activities to be risk rated in determining the approach to authentication. Such methods are considered as the functional equivalence of electronic signatures with traditional laws required by goal of promoting legal certainty.

IMPLEMENTATION

Political and institutional leadership are the most important elements of an e-procurement reform strategy. There is a requirement for a central lead procurement agency (which may also be the entity responsible for the e-procurement system) to have the capacity and authority to drive the procurement reforms without which e-procurement will be of limited value. Such reforms include standard bidding documents, whole of government framework agreements, policies around the use of e-bidding and e-reverse auctions, whole-of-government policies for online catalogues and security.

Without adequate leadership, there is a high risk that developments will be fragmented and that systems will not be interoperable or will not have common core data capture that will enable proper performance assessments and financial integration.

Fragmentation will also exacerbate security risks and add to costs of development and maintenance. This lead institutional role will require the authority to:

- Mandate a government-wide framework for e-procurement, including preferably a single integrated system;
- Develop implement and monitor e-procurement operating and systems policies specified elsewhere in this volume;
- Minimize separate developments of various e-procurement systems that may lack interoperability or result in potentially expensive duplicate investments or developments;
- Minimize imposition of multiple system requirements, costs and confusion for suppliers;
- Ensure transparency and efficiency for all stakeholders.

Ideally there will be an independent procurement policy and oversight body, and a separate central procurement office with strategic operational roles of leading and maintaining the e-procurement system and arranging instruments such as whole-of-government framework agreements that will occupy the system. There also needs to be a capacity to arrange interdepartmental working groups / committees to develop various aspects such as BPR.

These institutional capacities may need to be supported by legislative changes before e-procurement can be made fully effective, and can affect the rollout schedule for e-procurement.

Issues in Implementation

- It is common in the South Asia region in particular, for fees to be attached to online registration and / or downloading of bidding documents. In the case of Andhra Pradesh, document download incurs no charge while bid submission incurs a fee, while Bangladesh imposes a supplier registration fee. In the case of Kazakhstan there is a policy for accelerating e-procurement rollout and so registration is free, as are all of the processes.
- In most cases, government retains the option of paper bids even while it is implementing e-procurement. This is intended to addresses the need for buyers and suppliers to adjust and where connectivity is unreliable. However, this transition period should be kept to a minimum as it also slows the rate of take-up of the systems and can defeat the purpose of promoting e-procurement.
- Some governments have had a preference for e-reverse auctions. In several cases, there have been major concerns about collusion in the e-auction bidding process, and in one case the government has required bidders to physi-

cally assemble in a common facility to participate in bidding so that they could be individually supervised. This is non-compliant with the MDB requirement that the system prevent bidders from being aware of each other's participation.

- A common problem is in relation to digital certificates. The issuance of digital certificates is a potential weakness in the PKI framework. There is a commercial relationship between the digital certificate provider and the government provider. The 2006 UNCITRAL Convention now recognises that PKI is not a standard, and there are now competing authentication technologies that are less costly and more easily understood by business users. These new Technologies including biometrics and tokens seek to overcome the disadvantages of PKI. Many countries are proceeding with e-procurement without mandating the use of certified digital signatures including Australia, Singapore, UK and USA. Some countries that had previously adopted PKI have since abandoned this. Significant work is also proceeding in relation to the application of biometrics online, for example in the MERCOSUR (IAC, 2011) framework in Latin America. For major contracts, digital signatures are not a substitute for traditional due diligence. It can also be noted that for e-procurement there is no requirement for the 'Public Key' from suppliers – a private key (e.g. a password) is just as good, and may have stronger authentication characteristics in the e-procurement environment.
- In the case of Russia, Belarus and Kazakhstan there is an agreement that the e-procurement system operate seamlessly between all members of the Custom Union, while there is a similar requirement for members within the EU. One approach is for the member states of these market entities to adopt a policy of mutual recognition, such that a government provider who has a digital certificate from one jurisdiction automatically has recognition in all member states, without need to re-register. This is not satisfactory to the MDBs because the concept behind an international competitive bidding procedure is that it be open to bidders from almost everywhere, rather than just within a closed trading bloc. An alternative solution is for reputable international commercial certification authorities also be recognised. New developments are underway, targeted at cross border trade.
- Some e-procurement developments do not have good quality disaster recovery / backup. This can be a major concern. Sometimes, Disaster Recovery sites back up only the data. If the system applications are destroyed it may take significant time to re-establish the service. A significant delay could be disastrous in the light of the scope of modern public procurement. The disaster recovery site should be able to recover data and the applications and re-establish the service within minutes. This may be achieved by operating

a remote disaster recovery site as a mirror site. The delay in response time between the primary and mirror site can be managed with appropriate replication technologies.

- In a few instances e-procurement has not proceeded in a coordinated fashion across a government but is fragmented between ministries or departments. A centralised coordinated approach is greatly superior in terms of cost, efficiency and interoperability. For example fragmentation multiplies security costs and weaknesses, and also requires suppliers to deal with multiple sites. A centralised unitary system does not imply the centralisation of procurement, as discussed in the following section.
- Finally, the risk management requirement for monitoring of the e-reverse auction system for market abuse such as collusion may be difficult to realise. The capacity and systems for review and assessment may exist, but the data is likely to be ambiguous.

Where third party service providers host the system, there may need to be audits undertaken of the provider. The scope for the government to undertake this, or to receive independent audit reports, must be part of the service agreement.

Centralisation vs. Decentralisation

An e-procurement strategy should preferably be a unitary system across all government entities and between different levels of government. This makes better use of the technology and particularly minimises duplicating security management, catalogue management, duplicate supplier registries, etc, and interoperability issues. It also simplifies a single log-on for suppliers and therefore greater supplier efficiencies and enhances the prospects of alternative procurement methodologies such as framework agreements.

Sometimes this is presumed to represent the centralisation of procurement but this is not the case. It represents a unified information infrastructure for procurement rather than centralisation of procurement itself. Individual entities and levels of government can remain fully responsible and in control of what they buy, how much they buy and when they buy it – procurement remains decentralised but is utilising a common infrastructure, just as it utilises other common national infrastructures for commerce such as the national currency, national laws, and national banking systems. Sometimes, provision is made for individual ministries and levels of government to be able to customise the system for their own management purposes without sacrificing the unitary aspects. Where multiple systems are unavoidable, as a minimum there should be a single sign-on and a common portal between these.

Capacity Building

E-procurement has implications for procurement training: a result of a good e-procurement strategy can be a streamlining in the overall training requirements for public procurement. Between 70%-80% of all procurement transactions are for low value standard or routine acquisitions of goods and services. E-procurement should enable procurement methods that largely automate the procedures for these transactions. The majority of procurement officials deal only with transactions at this level and their training and oversight should be simplified to engaging with user-friendly online systems that confine activity to within a robust risk management framework. Relatively few procurement officials should deal with the more strategic high value and complex procurement.

Capacity building is also often considered to be a major requirement for the online engagement of suppliers into e-procurement and in some cases it has been thought that a significant obstacle would be the lack of preparedness of suppliers. However this is almost invariably incorrect. In most cases, the experience has been that suppliers have adopted the technology with ease, even where there has been little pre-existing presence of online services.

Security

The e-procurement systems and management should be administered under an adequate governance framework to ensure security. This requires not only that the appropriate security tools (firewalls, encryption, time locks) are in place but also that the management around the system is secure. There are international IS risk audit standards and methodologies that apply, such as those published by the Information Systems Audit and Control Association (ISACA) that link with organization-wide risk management concepts and approaches, such as COSO ERM, ARMS and ISO 31000. A good country system will be compliant and regularly audited against such international standards. The requirement for active risk management and audit to international standards is often best assured by including this requirement as part of the e-procurement service provider agreement. Audit findings should be available to users or clients at least in summary form. The claim that system audit findings, at least in some reasonably meaningful level, must remain confidential because of security should not be accepted – clients including governments must be able to assess their risks and audit findings should be drafted to enable this. Where the systems are provided from an external source (for example a Cloud service) then issues arise such as transparency of controls – requirements in the service level agreement (SLA) are the key to managing risks of external providers and need to be consistent with international standards of risk management.

At the time of writing, there is no comprehensive and commonly accepted standard to address the technical risks in cloud environments. There does exist, however, a hierarchy of approaches such as checklists and scenario generation techniques that require the user to have only a minimum knowledge of information systems security. To have a well-defined scope for the checklist, cloud managers can follow the formats that are provided by British Standards or the US National Security Agency (NSA). The NSA suggests using 18 areas for information security assessment, which is more comprehensive than the British Standards. It is suggested to follow the NIST's guidelines for ranking threats, use NSA's 18 areas of information security assessment, and use checklists for vulnerability assessments that can lead an organization to estimate probabilities of the occurrence of incidents and quantify information security risks (ISACA, 2011, p. 6).

CONCLUSION

Good governance is the most challenging issue in case of traditional procurement environment. Despite having sound procurement legislation in place, monitoring and evaluation in adherence to the principles of procurement as well as ethical and efficient performance of the public entities considering value for money and socio-economic development are mostly compromised. Widespread and effective enforcement of such legislations is hardly possible because of numerous human and bureaucratic factors entrenched traditionally. Efficacy of procurement tools and measures are easily compromised at the implementation level abusing furtively for personal and political gains nurturing the epidemic and pervasive corruptions. Only with the use of innovative approaches may facilitate curbing such undeniable challenges persistent in traditional procurement environment. Transforming the complete procurement processes and practices into electronic environment with adequate tools and measures could facilitate invigorating good governance in the public procurement sector.

Implementation of e-procurement has been accepted as one of the most promising and feasible options for governments in delivering enhanced governance in the acquisition of goods, works, and services for the public sector. Again, since the time the governments started introducing e-Procurement to resolved problems in traditional procurement, it seems that the e-Procurement systems are being used just as one of the optional channels for procurement. Adaptation of the e-Procurement has become very slow, and benefits reported are questionable. One of the key factors of slow adaptation of e-Procurement environment lies in the perception that the countries implementing e-Procurement treat e-Procurement either as one of the procurement methods, just as one of the options, or treat it procurement platform parallel to the traditional procurement environment. The focus on leveraging the electronic procurement environment is diluted somewhere on the political agenda or just on a temporal propaganda instead of establishing e-Procurement as the mainstream platform for procurement.

REFERENCES

Aberdeen Group. (2007). *The Spend Analysis Benchmark Report.* Aberdeen Group. Retrieved from https://www.unspsc.org/Portals/3/Documents/Aberdeen_Spend_Analysis_Report.pdf

Aberdeen Group. (2008). *The e-Procurement benchmark report.* Aberdeen Group. Retrieved from http://onget.net/documents/Aberdeen_eproc_sept2008.pdf

APEC. (1999). *Non-Binding Principles on Government Procurement: Report by the Chair of the Government Procurement Experts Group.* Retrieved from http://mddb.apec.org/documents/2006/GPEG/GPEG2/06_gpeg2_005.pdf

Arrowsmith, S. (2002). The EC Procurement Directives, national procurement policies and better governance: The case for a new approach. *European Law Review, 27*(1), 3–24.

Arrowsmith, S. (2009). EC Regime on Public Procurement. In Thai, K. V. (Ed.), International Handbook of Public Procurement (pp. 251-289). CRC Press, Taylor and Francis Group.

Arrowsmith, S., Linarelli, J., & Wallace, D. (2000). *Regulating Public Procurement: National and International Perspectives.* Kluwer Law International.

Australian Government. (2001). Department of Finance, Financial Management and Accountability Act 1997 No. 154 of 1997 as amended.

Australian Government. (2008). Department of Finance, Commonwealth Procurement Guidelines. Financial Management Guidance No.1.

Bikshapathi, K., RamaRaju, P., & Bhatnagar, S. (2006). *E-Procurement in Government of Andhra Pradesh, India.* Retrieved from siteresources.worldbank.org/INTEGOVERNMENT/Resources/APeProcurement.doc

Brookings. (2009). *Effective and Transparent Governance of Public Expenditures in Latin America and the Caribbean - Revitalizing Reforms in Financial Management and Procurement.* Washington, DC: Brookings Institution - Transparency and Accountability Project.

EU. (2010). *EC Green Paper on expanding the use of e-Procurement in the EU*. European Commission. Retrieved from http://ec.europa.eu/internal_market/consultations/docs/2010/e-procurement/green-paper_en.pdf

IAC. (2011). *Ibero-American social electronic identification framework*. Approved by the XIII Ibero American Conference of Ministers of the Federal Administration and Reform of the State, Asunción, Paraguay.

ISACA. (2011). *Risk Perception and Trust in Cloud*. Retrieved from http://www.isaca.org/Journal/archives/2010/Volume-4/Pages/Risk-Perception-and-Trust-in-Cloud.aspx

Jones, D. S. (2002). Procurement Practices in the Singapore Civil Service: Balancing Control and Delegation. *Journal of Public Procurement*, *2*(1), 29–53.

Kaufmann, D., Kraay, A., & Mastruzzi, M. (2006). *Measuring Corruption: Myths and Realities*. Washington, DC: The World Bank.

Kazakhstan. (2011). *Kazakhstan Centre for E-Commerce website*. Retrieved from https://ecc.kz

Krüger, K. (2009). Ban-on-negotiations in tender procedures: Undermining the best value for money. In International Handbook of Public Procurement (pp. 631-658). CRC Press, Taylor and Francis Group.

New Zealand. (2006). *Mandatory Rules for Procurement by Government Department*. Retrieved from http://www.procurement.govt.nz/procurement/pdf-library/agencies/Mandatory%20Rules%20for%20Procurement%20by%20Departments.pdf/view

OECD. (2002). *Government Procurement: A synthesis report*. Retrieved from https://www.oecd.org/gov/budgeting/43506020.pdf

OECD. (2006). *Methodology for Assessment of National Procurement Systems*. Retrieved from http://www.oecd.org/dataoecd/1/36/37130136.pdf

OECD. (2008). *Fighting Cartels in Public Procurement*. Retrieved from http://www.oecd.org/dataoecd/45/63/41505296.pdf

OECD. (2013). *Public Governance Reviews Public Procurement Review of the State's Employee's Social Security and Social Services Institute in Mexico*. Retrieved from https://books.google.com/books?isbn=9264197303

OECD/DAC. (2003). *Mainstreaming the Procurement Function into the Public Expenditure Policy and Effectiveness Dialogue (OECD/DAC)*. World Bank Roundtable, Paris, France. Available at www.oecd.org

OGC. (2005). *e-Procurement in Action*. Office of Government Commerce. Retrieved from http://www.umic.pt/images/stories/publicacoes/embedded_object[1].pdf

Schapper, P. R., Veiga Malta, J., & Gilbert, D. (2009). An Analytical Framework for the Management and Reform of Public Procurement. In International Handbook of Public Procurement (pp. 87-103). CRC Press, Taylor and Francis Group.

Shakya, R. K. (2016). E-Procurement: Paradigm Shift From the Traditional Public Procurement. In *Procurement and Contract Management for the Curious: Why Study Procurement and Contract Management?* (pp. 1544–1880). Curious Academic Publishing. Retrieved Nov 11, 2016 from http://amzn.to/1T3kl4T

World Bank. (2001). *Colombia: Country Procurement Assessment Report*. Washington, DC: The World Bank.

World Bank. (2004). *Chile: Country Procurement Assessment Report*. Washington, DC: The World Bank.

World Bank England and Wales. Northern Ireland. (2006). *The Public Contracts Regulations, No 5*. Retrieved from http://www.oecd.org/unitedkingdom/39647169.pdf

Chapter 2
Mastering Electronic Procurement, Green Public Procurement, and Public Procurement for Innovation

Kijpokin Kasemsap
Suan Sunandha Rajabhat University, Thailand

ABSTRACT

This chapter explains the overview of Electronic Procurement (e-procurement); the critical success factors and implementation of e-procurement systems; the barriers to e-procurement implementation; the perspectives on electronic public procurement; the Interpretive Structural Modeling (ISM), Structural Equation Modeling (SEM), and e-procurement; the prospect of Green Public Procurement (GPP); the importance of Public Procurement for Innovation (PPI); and the intermediation of PPI. E-procurement, GPP, and PPI expand the aspects of enterprise resource planning systems, sustainability, and innovation, allowing the automation of internal business processes and providing the procurement-related platforms that support automation at a global level. The benefits of e-procurement, GPP, and PPI include reduced transaction time, increased productivity, improved standardization, enhanced sustainability, and simplified global procurement.

DOI: 10.4018/978-1-5225-2203-4.ch002

INTRODUCTION

The application of electronic procurement (e-procurement) ranges from the use of commonly available tools (e.g., web browsers and e-mails) to the use of dedicated e-procurement systems (e.g., interorganizational information systems) (Hassan, Tretiakov, Whiddett, & Adon, 2014). E-procurement is widely advocated as an effective tool to promote the participation of small and medium-sized enterprises (SMEs) as well as micro enterprises in the public procurement market (Albano, Russo, Castaldi, & Zampino, 2015). E-procurement enables organizations to reduce business costs, reduce paperwork, manage purchasing processes (Teo, Lin, & Lai, 2009), and access wider markets (Gunasekaran, McGaughey, Ngai, & Rai, 2009). Gunasekaran and Ngai (2008) indicated that the supply chain of a company cannot be successfully integrated without the adoption of e-procurement systems.

Procurement has a key role in sustainability as policies and practices need to extend beyond organizations' boundaries incorporating their whole supply chains (Meehan & Bryde, 2011). A green economy that incorporates a vision of environmental sustainability and equitable social development requires a fundamental rethinking of the existing economic models which center on growth (Otsuki, 2011). The high impact of green public procurement (GPP) on production activities positively affects the probability that companies invest (at both technological and organizational levels) in the innovative solutions (Testa, Iraldo, & Frey, 2011).

Public procurement for innovation (PPI) is widely acknowledged as an important demand-side innovation policy instrument which occurs when a public purchaser either seeks to trigger innovation by demanding products that do not yet exist, or by choosing products which have innovative characteristics (Georghiou, Edler, Uyarra, & Yeow, 2013). PPI is at the essence of many innovation policy initiatives across the Organization for Economic Cooperation and Development (OECD) and at the European Union (EU) level (OECD, 2011). To focus on PPI as an innovation policy tool is to support and stimulate the demand for and adoption of innovation for the sake of generating the economic benefit for suppliers and supply chains, on top of the social benefit generated by the public sector organizations (Edler & Yeow, 2016).

This chapter aims to bridge the gap in the literature on the thorough literature consolidation of e-procurement, GPP, and PPI. The extensive literature of e-procurement, GPP, and PPI provides a contribution to practitioners and researchers in order to maximize the impact of e-procurement, GPP, and PPI in both the public and private sectors.

BACKGROUND

Intensifying competition in today's business environment has highlighted the need to optimize the management of supply chains. Developments in the information and communication technology (ICT) are important tools to manage supply chains effectively (Toktaş-Palut, Baylav, Teoman, & Altunbey, 2014). Procurement (i.e., a vital part of supply chain management) has been significantly impacted by the new technologies (Bayazit, 2014). In recent years, an increasing trend has been observed in the adoption of e-procurement systems, which help in the integration of the procurement process throughout the supply chain (Toktaş-Palut et al., 2012). When the traditional procurement system is analyzed, it can be considered that the process is implemented by using phone, fax, and other communication channels, showing how the procurement system is developed over time (Hawking, Stein, Wyld, & Foster, 2004).

Many studies have reported on the effectiveness of the EU procurement directives, mostly in terms of the impact on the openness of public procurement and the impact on cross-border trade (Gelderman, Ghijsen, & Schoonen, 2010). The European Commission believes that the solution to integrating government procurement into the single market lies in e-procurement (Khorana, Ferguson-Boucher, & Kerr, 2015). The EU-compatible public procurement regime is being consolidated throughout the Central and Eastern Europe (CEE) region (Engelbrekt, 2011). Alongside the remarkable efforts executed by the European governments to promote the adoption of GPP, legislative interventions, and operational tools have been developed by the United States (Swanson, Weissman, Davis, Socolof, & Davis, 2005), Canada (Brammer & Walker, 2011), South Africa (Bolton, 2006), Asia (Ho, Dickinson, & Chan, 2010), Australia (Chang & Kristiansen, 2006), and Japan (Brammer & Walker, 2011).

A demand-based innovation policy can be defined as a set of public measures that aim at increasing the demand for innovation, at improving the conditions for the adoption of innovations and improving the articulation of demand in order to promote the creation and diffusion of innovation. The rationale for demand-based innovation policies is stimulated by the various market and system failures that affect the translation of needs into functioning markets for innovative products, the need for improvement of public services and the solution or mitigation of societal problems, and the strengthening of competitiveness through the creation of a lead market (Edler & Georghiou, 2007).

ASPECTS OF ELECTRONIC PROCUREMENT, GREEN PUBLIC PROCUREMENT, AND PUBLIC PROCUREMENT FOR INNOVATION

This section emphasizes the overview of e-procurement; the critical success factors and implementation of e-procurement systems; the barriers to e-procurement implementation; the perspectives on electronic public procurement; ISM, SEM, and e-procurement; the prospect of GPP; the importance of PPI; and the intermediation of PPI.

Overview of Electronic Procurement

The global environment has necessitated governments to adopt the systematic aspect of integrating suppliers, customers, and information linkages in an endeavor to create and sustain value for public services (Dorasamy, 2013). In recent years, government organizations are expressing the growing interest in the adoption of e-procurement systems in order to achieve many of the benefits that their counterparts in the private sector have reported (Rahim & Bantwal, 2012). E-procurement alters the activities of purchasing and transforms the purchasing process from a tactical into a strategic activity (Huang, Tran, Nguyen, & Nazir, 2016) reflected by the public administration (Pomazalová & Rejman, 2013; Shakya, 2015).

In the past decade, electronic mechanisms have started to overcome the conventional methods of procurement for both governments and enterprises because of the cost and time-saving effects of e-procurement (Genis-Gruber & Tas, 2013). In the public sector, governments must aim for the optimum supply of products and services from suppliers in terms of cost, quality, timeliness, risk management, and ethical practices (Dorasamy, 2013). In today's global economy, organizations are focusing on customer-oriented business models to use information technology (IT) not only for suppliers and customers, but also for effective communication and collaboration with public agencies (Rehan, 2013). IT has been applied to support the exchange of products, services, and information between organizations (Oliveira & Joia, 2013).

The term e-procurement refers to the integration of procurement process, which includes operations, such as negotiation, ordering, receipt, and post-purchase processes (Croom & Brandon-Jones, 2007). Morris et al. (2000) defined e-procurement as the procurement system that utilizes the Internet technologies and services to manage an organization's processes, ranging from requisition to payment. As a result of the increasing use of the Internet, a number of Internet-based e-procurement applications including e-sourcing, e-catalogs, e-marketplaces, and electronic contracts management systems have been developed (Bayazit, 2014).

E-procurement is the business-to-government (B2G) e-commerce venture that can benefit from the Internet (Reddick, 2007) and is a critical component of the government's supply chain initiatives toward providing an innovative solution in dealing with the inefficient public procurement that has received a lot of criticism and negative perception (Ambali, 2010). E-procurement is an important system that facilitates effective communications between buyers and suppliers while providing opportunities for making the system more flexible and efficient (Bayram & Vayvay, 2013).

For many organizations, e-procurement has become a necessity (Nagle, Finnegan, & Hayes, 2009) and has the potential to provide cost and time reductions while ordering products or services from suppliers (Andrade, Alturas, & Oliveira, 2012). E-procurement is not the recently discovered process as there are many attempts of using electronic systems for developing the automated procurement technology for organizations, such as electronic data interchange (EDI) and electronic workflow systems (Gunasekaran & Ngai, 2008). The increased use of the Internet offers greater opportunity for e-procurement, which can offer the viable electronic alternatives to the traditional paper-based processes (Eadie, Perera, & Heaney, 2013).

Regarding e-procurement, the most common tool utilized when partnering with the private sector is a contract (Bromberg, Saldivar, & Fudge, 2012). E-procurement is an organizational use of IT in establishing contracts and purchasing products or services (Robinson, Wale, & Dickson, 2010) and involves the use of the Internet and related technologies to perform purchasing activities over the Internet (Mital, Pani, & Ramesh, 2014). E-procurement systems emerge promoting a more integrated, efficient, and performance-based vision of procurement (Puschmann & Alt, 2005), facing a wider range of challenges coping with the strategic procurement issues and giving a central role to contract and its evaluation (Vincent-Jones, 2006).

There are many research studies about e-procurement practices. Davila et al. (2003) executed a research on the equilibrium point for the optimum e-procurement system that should be used by companies which have different attitudes toward technology. Panayiotou et al. (2004) worked on the case study about the Greek purchasing process and indicate the problems which may occur. Croom and Brandon-Jones (2007) evaluated the validity of the forecasts performed by earlier studies making predictions about the changes and improvements caused by e-procurement systems. Gunasekaran et al. (2009) explored the current state of e-procurement in SMEs located in the Southcoast of Massachusetts, United States. Wu et al. (2007) included two dimensions of the intensity of e-procurement use: coordination use (i.e., the use of e-procurement as a strategic tool to facilitate information exchange with suppliers, such as sharing product and inventory planning information with suppliers) and transactional use (i.e., the use of e-procurement to facilitate transactions, such as electronically placing the orders with suppliers).

The benefits of e-procurement are numerous in terms of enhancing transparency of transactions, saving time and lowering costs, increasing productivity, and standardizing and integrating processes (Filho & Mota, 2012). The solution of e-procurement include a redesign of the processes and use of suitable instruments in order to trim down the entire process of procurement (Comite, 2012). E-procurement solutions should be related to the purchasing strategies and the different steps of the purchasing process (Rehme, Kindstrom, & Brege, 2005). Using e-procurement solutions allows buyers to collaborate with suppliers throughout the purchasing process to cut the lead time, reduce the probability of stock out, and lower the bullwhip effect (Truong, 2016).

Through e-procurement, individual business activities can be completed much more quickly; they are not restricted by office hours and may not even need human intervention, thus increasing the capacity to complete transactions on a real-time basis. Because the virtual e-procurement portals are web-based, buyers can search suppliers worldwide, meaning a wider selection of products and services are available to the organization. With the e-procurement applications supporting various languages, currencies, international taxation, financing, and shipping regulations, it is simple for buyers and suppliers in different countries to communicate toward business growth and economic development.

Critical Success Factors and Implementation of Electronic Procurement Systems

E-procurement success factors include cost factors, time factors, process simplification factors, and the volume of e-transactions factors (Podlogar, 2007). The supply market characteristics and product characteristics can explain the emergence of various e-procurement systems (Pani, 2007). Economic theory suggests that the success of e-procurement depends on the number of bidders who participate in procurement auctions (Genis-Gruber & Tas, 2013). E-procurement benefits greatly depend on the operational and strategic organizational assimilation of e-procurement with different levels of success (Vaidya, 2007). E-procurement performance is measured as a combination of cost savings, order quality, and satisfaction of fulfillment as perceived by buyers (Vaidyanathan, Devaraj, & D'Arcy, 2012).

The implementation of e-procurement should be based on a gradual enrolled in the plan of development of electronic government (e-government) in the field of public administration (Martín & Peñalvo, 2013). E-government services must be redesigned to ensure that the benefits of ICT systems are completely realized (Kasemsap, 2016a). Organizations need to manage the portfolio of e-procurement systems to realize the full potential of the Internet (Agrahari, 2007). The concept of software agents is recognized as a method to automate the activities related to e-procurement process (Patra, 2007). The informed buyer environment promoted by e-procurement platforms (Bakos, 1997) may lead suppliers to a competitive price-taking equilibrium, improving buyers' benefits (Wang & Seidmann, 1995).

To help ensure that an e-procurement solution provides the intended return on investment, the applications, servers, and enterprise network infrastructure must effectively work together in terms of organizational culture, managerial skills, human resource management, and capabilities to manage interorganizational relationships and IT infrastructure (Imamoglu & Rehan, 2011). Significant investment in technology and human capital is required for the implementation of e-procurement systems (Steinfeld & Thai, 2013). If effectively implemented, e-procurement platforms may promote the full sourcing information to any procurer, increase competition between suppliers, and enhance better procurement performances (Costa & Tavares, 2014).

Because the e-procurement applications are internet based, they allow for both vertical and horizontal trading communities to be developed. This means buyers can consolidate buying power and it establishes the opportunities for new supply chains. E-procurement applications can be configured to suit the individual needs or both the buyer and the supplier, and can grow with the organization as needs be. It is important to select suppliers for both the current requirement as well as possible future need so that gaining an understanding of the technical infrastructure development plans of suppliers will help buyers select the potential partners and will make e-procurement implementation successful in both the public and private sectors.

Barriers to Electronic Procurement Implementation

Implementing an e-procurement system is a challenge for local government (Hashim, 2012). Many impediments to the adoption of e-procurement systems are expensive investment, fast obsolescence, risks involved in applying uncertain technology to core processes, problems integrating with existing systems, lack of common standards for e-commerce software development, and lack of suppliers accessible through e-procurement system (Teo et al., 2009). Sheng (2008) indicated that the major challenges in e-procurement implementation include business process integration, technological issues, value creation, and change management.

A lack of a qualified workforce, cultural barriers, and security problems significantly obstruct the development of e-procurement activities (Yamamoto & Karaman, 2007). Inadequate IT infrastructure of suppliers is found to be the most important barrier to the adoption of e-procurement systems (Toktaş-Palut et al., 2014). The challenges encountered during implementation of e-procurement include the lack of skilled personnel, multi-departmental implementation, inadequate IT infrastructure, challenges in the implementation of state-wide system, the need to regulate e-procurement market, and perspectives on federal state setup (Somasundaram, 2007).

Perspectives on Electronic Public Procurement

Electronic public procurement is the Internet-based interorganizational information system that is intended to facilitate government-to-business (G2B) or government-to-government (G2G) electronic communication, information exchange and transaction support through web access or value-added network (Vaidya, Campbell, Soar, & Gardner, 2012). Electronic public procurement provides a new method of communication between contracting authorities and economic operators, as well as being one of the most important areas in the development in the business-to-business (B2B) e-commerce (Martín & Peñalvo, 2013).

Electronic public procurement represents an important source of financing for regional development (Novosák, Hájek, & Machu, 2013) and is the primary issue which citizens are the most sensitive to in terms of how public money is spent (Demirbas, Eroglu, & Çetinkaya, 2013). Electronic public procurement have been adopted as a solution in order to respond to the sensitivity of citizens because of the benefits promised (Demirbas et al., 2013). Electronic public procurement of products and services is a strategic activity for governments for three major reasons: it has a relevant economic impact; it is relevant for potential improvements in governments' public services; and it affects both the competitiveness of nations and the welfare of citizens (Previtali, 2012).

The digitalization of electronic public procurement will sustain the desired transformative returns only if these efforts are accompanied by a reformative evolution of public procurement professionals (Roman, 2013). In many countries, approximately 20 to 25 percent of public funds has been estimated to have lost through the corruption in public procurement (Ishak & Said, 2015). Electronic public procurement is an important area warranting further attention in government reform, as electronic systems for procurement have the ability to help reduce corruption (Neupane, Soar, & Vaidya, 2015). Electronic public procurement solutions, in contrast to the electronic private procurement solutions, tend to be much more complex and advanced due to the fact that after a given procurement threshold value they must adhere to the legal and policy framework as this is defined by the European Commission (Christos, Ziouvelou, Yovanof, & Ramfos, 2011).

Interpretive Structural Modeling, Structural Equation Modeling, and Electronic Procurement

Interpretive structural modeling (ISM) is widely used to indicate the interactions among the elements of the specific systems, such as barriers and benefits of e-procurement (Toktaş-Palut et al., 2014). Talib et al. (2011) viewed ISM as an interpretive model, defining the relations among variables in complex systems by representing them in the hierarchical configuration. Gorvett and Liu (2006) evaluated the risks in the company by using ISM and explored the risk profile of the company. Singh and Kant (2008) utilized ISM in order to understand the relationships among the barriers to knowledge management. Chandramowli et al. (2011) performed a case study about the difficulties of developing landfill sites in order to realize the urban planning issues. Luthra et al. (2011) applied ISM to examine the relationships among the barriers to green supply chain management for the Indian automotive industry.

Structural equation modeling (SEM) can be used for multivariate data as it is appropriate for illustrating the relationships between exogenous and endogenous latent variables in one model (Aibinu & Al-Lawati, 2010). SEM is the widely used tool for psychology, sociology, and econometrics (Golob, 2003). There are many studies of e-procurement systems using SEM. Madeja and Schoder (2003) analyzed the impacts of e-procurement adoption process on electronic business (e-business) success. Ho et al. (2004) explored the direct impacts of e-procurement on supply chain orientation from the buyer–seller perspectives.

Lee and Quaddus (2006) conducted an e-procurement study in Singapore about the impacts of buyer–supplier relationship on the decision of e-purchasing adoption. Vaidyanathan and Devaraj (2008) studied the impacts of the quality of the information flow process and the quality of logistics fulfillment on the satisfaction of e-procurement performance. Konradt et al. (2012) explored the effects of organizational and technical perspectives on usability and commercial transactions in B2B e-commerce. In addition, Devaraj et al. (2012) examined the effects of mixing flexibilities and purchase volumes on e-procurement performance by using SEM.

Prospect of Green Public Procurement

Green public procurement (GPP) is one of the most important sustainability issues in global supply chain. To date, many researches in the field of public procurement are mostly focused on the issues, such as the development of green procurement implementation tools within public policy (Walker & Brammer, 2009), potential versus real benefits of green procurement (Hall & Purchase, 2006), the obstacles that can negatively affect GPP practices (Zhu, Geng, & Sarkis, 2013), and the utilization of environmental procurement criteria (Nissinen, Parikka-Alholaa, & Ritab, 2009). The strategic decision by the top management in implementing e-procurement technologies is mainly concentrated on managing the supply of external resources and preferred to focus on the implementation of green supply chain activities to increase the environmental performance with e-procurement technologies (Kamarulzaman & Eglese, 2015).

Thomson and Jackson (2007) indicated that GPP in the United Kingdom is encouraged through legislation, providing information and dismantling knowledge-related barriers. In Norway, many environmental criteria regarding GPP are developed by the National Environmental Panel (Fet, Michelsen, & de Boer, 2011). Green specifications for a wide range of the commonly procured products have been developed in Hong Kong (Ho et al., 2010). Zhu et al. (2013) showed the crucial role of GPP knowledge in strengthening GPP drivers, such as procurement regulations. GPP initiatives can be used to facilitate the inclusion of green waste compost in contract specifications and enable public bodies to close the recycling loop (Dawson & Probert, 2007) and to stimulate innovation (Günther & Scheibe, 2006).

The importance of the presence of GPP documents in promoting GPP practices has been highlighted by many studies (Meehan & Bryde, 2011). Enhancing the influence of GPP documents can be the important perspective toward improving in the adoption of GPP practices (Testa, Annunziata, Iraldo, & Frey, 2016). Opportunities for incorporating environmental aspects into contract clauses are important in order to ensure that the environmental criteria of the tender documents are fulfilled by the purchased products and services during the contract period (Palmujoki, Parikka-Alhola, & Ekroos, 2010).

Many GPP initiatives have cost implications for local government, which may clash with other priorities (Preuss, 2007). Public authorities have encountered several obstacles in adopting GPP practices (Testa, Iraldo, Frey, & Daddi, 2012). Among the main obstacles are the lack of organizational resources for political support and of information on the environmental impact of the products, the difficulties in finding suppliers, the lack of effective procurement guidelines from higher-order authorities, and of cooperation between authorities (Walker & Brammer, 2009).

Importance of Public Procurement for Innovation

Public procurement for innovation (PPI) is the significant demand-side innovation policy instrument (Edler & Georghiou, 2007) which occurs when a public organization places an order for the fulfillment of certain functions within a reasonable period of time through a new product (Edquist & Zabala-Iturriagagoitia, 2012). This product may be a product or a service or a combination of the two, which may be called a system (Georghiou et al., 2013). The innovation-related activity occurs when a public purchaser either attempts to stimulate innovation by demanding products that do not yet exist, or by selecting products with innovative features (Georghiou et al., 2013).

Edquist and Zabala-Iturriagagoitia (2012) proposed a taxonomy of PPI involving two dimensions. The first dimension focuses on the end user of the resulting product and includes two different categories (i.e., direct PPI and catalytic PPI). Direct PPI occurs when the procuring organization is the end user of the purchased product, while catalytic PPI is when the procuring agency functions as the coordinator for different end users (Caloghirou, Protogerou, & Panagiotopoulos, 2016).

The second dimension refers to the character of the resulting innovation and consists of three categories (i.e., pre-commercial procurement, adaptive PPI, and developmental PPI). Pre-commercial procurement refers to the procurement of research and development (R&D)-based solutions and not to the development of an actual product. Pre-commercial procurement is a matter of R&D funding geared toward very specific goals. Adaptive PPI occurs when the procured product is new only to the country of procurement and involves incremental innovation. Developmental PPI implies that the new-to-the-world products are created as a result of the procurement process regarding radical innovation (Edquist & Zabala-Iturriagagoitia, 2012).

The important challenges for PPI are about evaluating the market and its opportunities, both in terms of what is already offered and in terms of what the market can deliver if asked for by the public buyer; being able to understand the individual's requirement and the functional improvements through innovation; establishing incentive structures that reflect the risk–reward distribution, to ensure that those organizational units that deliver the risk also share the reputational benefits related to innovation (Edler & Yeow, 2016); and being able to implement the innovation and change organizational procedures, routines, and capacities needed to do so.

Intermediation of Public Procurement for Innovation

The perspective on PPI has identified which factors concerning the process and capabilities of the buying organization are the approaches to buying and adopting innovation in the public sector (Rolfstam, 2013). To establish those enabling factors significantly provides the challenges for buying organizations and creates the possibilities for the intermediation to support the PPI (Edler & Yeow, 2016). Intermediation of PPI provides a link between at least two entities which need to connect in order to generate innovation, but which do not do so sufficiently without having a linking device or linking support (Klerkx & Leeuwis, 2009).

Intermediation of PPI can be the direct approach, bringing actors together and supporting their interaction, or the indirect approach, supporting actors to better understand others, their preferences, and interests as well as the objects of the transfer, such as knowledge, technological artifacts, and products (Edler & Yeow, 2016). Intermediation of PPI serves a large variety of roles, and has been analyzed in various streams of literature. Intermediation is recognized at a systems level, whereas intermediaries are not so many brokers between distinct parties, but instruments to support systemic functions in the innovation systems (Hekkert, Suurs, Negro, Kuhlmann, & Smits, 2007) or the directed change of socio-technical systems (van Lente, Hekkert, Smits, & van Waveren, 2003).

FUTURE RESEARCH DIRECTIONS

The classification of the extensive literature in the domains of e-procurement, GPP, and PPI will provide the potential opportunities for future research. E-procurement, GPP, and PPI make it easier to purchase products and services from the preferred vendors on the sustainable and innovative perspectives. Strategic outsourcing means asking the third-party vendor to work for company on a contractual basis (Kasemsap, 2016b). Cloud computing is a new style of computing in which virtualized resources are provided as the services over the Internet (Kasemsap, 2015a). In cloud-based supply chain, logistics process is handled using cloud computing services in which shipping schedule, shipping notice, receiving notice, and payment information are stored and shared through cloud computing applications (Kasemsap, 2015b). An examination of linkages among e-procurement, GPP, PPI, strategic outsourcing, and cloud computing in global supply chain would seem to be viable for future research efforts.

CONCLUSION

This chapter highlighted the overview of e-procurement; the critical success factors and implementation of e-procurement systems; the barriers to e-procurement implementation; the perspectives on electronic public procurement; ISM, SEM, and e-procurement; the prospect of GPP; the importance of PPI; and the intermediation of PPI. E-procurement, GPP, and PPI expand the aspects of enterprise resource planning systems, sustainability, and innovation, allowing the automation of internal business processes and providing the procurement-related platforms that support automation at a global level. E-procurement, GPP, and PPI allow procurement professionals across the globe to effectively communicate information, organizing the global procurement process and reducing time and costs without compromising on standards and quality.

The benefits of e-procurement, GPP, and PPI include reduced transaction time, increased productivity, improved standardization, enhanced sustainability, and simplified global procurement. The fulfillment of e-procurement, GPP, and PPI is necessary for public sector organizations that seek to serve suppliers and customers, increase public performance, strengthen competitiveness, and achieve continuous success in the public sector. Therefore, it is essential for public sector organizations to enhance the utilization of e-procurement, GPP, and PPI toward satisfying customer requirement. Applying e-procurement, GPP, and PPI has the potential to improve organizational performance and reach strategic goals in both the public and private sectors.

REFERENCES

Agrahari, A. (2007). Analyzing e-procurement adoption efforts: Case study of an Indian steel manufacturer. In A. Pani & A. Agrahari (Eds.), *E-procurement in emerging economies: Theory and cases* (pp. 197–231). Hershey, PA: Idea Group Publishing. doi:10.4018/978-1-59904-153-7.ch008

Aibinu, A. A., & Al-Lawati, A. M. (2010). Using PLS-SEM technique to model construction organizations' willingness to participate in e-bidding. *Automation in Construction*, *19*(6), 714–724. doi:10.1016/j.autcon.2010.02.016

Al-Hakim, L., Abdullah, N. A., & Ng, E. (2012). The effect of inter-organization trust and dependency on e-procurement adoption: A case of Malaysian manufacturers. *Journal of Electronic Commerce in Organizations*, *10*(2), 40–60. doi:10.4018/jeco.2012040103

Albano, G. L., Russo, F. A., Castaldi, G., & Zampino, R. (2015). Evaluating small businesses' performance in public e-procurement: Evidence from the Italian government's e-marketplace. *Journal of Small Business Management*, *53*(Suppl. 1), 229–250. doi:10.1111/jsbm.12190

Ambali, A. R. (2010). Determinants of e-government satisfaction: The case study of e-procurement. In H. Rahman (Ed.), *Handbook of research on e-government readiness for information and service exchange: Utilizing progressive information communication technologies* (pp. 465–479). Hershey, PA: IGI Global. doi:10.4018/978-1-60566-671-6.ch023

Andrade, P., Alturas, B., & Oliveira, T. (2012). Electronic procurement: The supplier perspective. In J. Varajão, M. Cruz-Cunha, & A. Trigo (Eds.), *Organizational integration of enterprise systems and resources: Advancements and applications* (pp. 213–232). Hershey, PA: IGI Global. doi:10.4018/978-1-4666-1764-3.ch012

Arnold, U., & Schnabel, M. (2008). Economic effects of electronic reverse auctions: A procurement process perspective. In D. Parente (Ed.), *Best practices for online procurement auctions* (pp. 57–76). Hershey, PA: IGI Global. doi:10.4018/978-1-59904-636-5.ch005

Bakos, J. Y. (1997). Reducing buyer search costs: Implications for electronic marketplaces. *Management Science*, *43*(12), 1676–1692. doi:10.1287/mnsc.43.12.1676

Bayazit, O. (2014). Investigating adoption of e-procurement systems: An empirical study. *International Journal of Information Systems and Supply Chain Management*, *7*(2), 47–66. doi:10.4018/ijisscm.2014040103

Bayram, S., & Vayvay, Ö. (2013). E-procurement system and adoption for SMEs. In *Supply chain management: Concepts, methodologies, tools, and applications* (pp. 950–966). Hershey, PA: IGI Global. doi:10.4018/978-1-4666-2625-6.ch055

Bircan, T., & Çeviker-Gürakar, E. (2015). Business networks and public procurement in Turkey. In V. Benson & S. Morgan (Eds.), *Implications of social media use in personal and professional settings* (pp. 249–267). Hershey, PA: IGI Global. doi:10.4018/978-1-4666-7401-1.ch013

Bobar, V., Mandic, K., & Suknovic, M. (2015). Bidder selection in public procurement using a fuzzy decision support system. *International Journal of Decision Support System Technology*, *7*(1), 31–49. doi:10.4018/ijdsst.2015010103

Bolton, P. (2006). Government procurement as a policy tool in South Africa. *Journal of Public Procurement*, *6*(3), 193–217.

Brammer, S., & Walker, H. (2011). Sustainable procurement in the public sector: An international comparative study. *International Journal of Operations & Production Management*, *31*(4), 452–476. doi:10.1108/01443571111119551

Bromberg, D., Saldivar, K., & Fudge, M. (2012). E-procurement: Understanding implementation. In A. Manoharan & M. Holzer (Eds.), *E-governance and civic engagement: Factors and determinants of e-democracy* (pp. 72–92). Hershey, PA: IGI Global. doi:10.4018/978-1-61350-083-5.ch004

Caldwell, N., & Howard, M. (2011). *Procuring complex performance: Studies of innovation in product-service management*. New York, NY: Routledge.

Caloghirou, Y., Protogerou, A., & Panagiotopoulos, P. (2016). Public procurement for innovation: A novel eGovernment services scheme in Greek local authorities. *Technological Forecasting and Social Change*, *103*, 1–10. doi:10.1016/j.techfore.2015.10.016

Chandramowli, S., Transue, M., & Felder, F. A. (2011). Analysis of barriers to development in landfill communities using interpretive structural modeling. *Habitat International*, *35*(2), 246–253. doi:10.1016/j.habitatint.2010.09.005

Chang, H. S., & Kristiansen, P. (2006). Selling Australia as “clean and green”. *The Australian Journal of Agricultural and Resource Economics*, *50*(1), 103–113. doi:10.1111/j.1467-8489.2006.00330.x

Christos, G., Ziouvelou, X., Yovanof, G., & Ramfos, A. (2011). An open source e-procurement application framework for B2B and G2B. In M. Cruz-Cunha & J. Varajão (Eds.), *Innovations in SMEs and conducting e-business: Technologies, trends and solutions* (pp. 76–97). Hershey, PA: IGI Global. doi:10.4018/978-1-60960-765-4.ch005

Comite, U. (2012). Innovative processes and managerial effectiveness of e-procurement in healthcare. In A. Manoharan & M. Holzer (Eds.), *Active citizen participation in e-government: A global perspective* (pp. 206–229). Hershey, PA: IGI Global. doi:10.4018/978-1-4666-0116-1.ch011

Costa, A. A., & Tavares, L. V. (2014). Social e-business as support for construction e-procurement: E-procurement network dynamics. *Automation in Construction*, *43*, 180–186. doi:10.1016/j.autcon.2014.03.019

Croom, S., & Brandon-Jones, A. (2007). Impact of e-procurement: Experiences from implementation in the UK public sector. *Journal of Purchasing and Supply Management*, *13*(4), 294–303. doi:10.1016/j.pursup.2007.09.015

Davila, A., Gupta, M., & Palmer, R. (2003). Moving procurement systems to the Internet: The adoption and use of e-procurement technology models. *European Management Journal*, *21*(1), 11–23. doi:10.1016/S0263-2373(02)00155-X

Dawson, G. F., & Probert, E. J. (2007). A sustainable product needing a sustainable procurement commitment: The case of green waste in Wales. *Sustainable Development*, *15*(2), 69–82. doi:10.1002/sd.307

Deasy, M., White, G. R. T., Parfitt, S., & Ringwald, K. (2014). Asymmetric procurement in the public sector. *Strategic Change*, *23*(1/2), 21–29. doi:10.1002/jsc.1957

Demirbas, T., Eroglu, E., & Çetinkaya, Ö. (2013). The benefits and barriers of electronic public procurement system: A case study on public hospitals in Turkey. In P. Ordóñez de Pablos, J. Lovelle, J. Gayo, & R. Tennyson (Eds.), *E-procurement management for successful electronic government systems* (pp. 131–146). Hershey, PA: IGI Global. doi:10.4018/978-1-4666-2119-0.ch008

Devaraj, S., Vaidyanathan, G., & Mishra, A. N. (2012). Effect of purchase volume flexibility and purchase mix flexibility on e-procurement performance: An analysis of two perspectives. *Journal of Operations Management*, *30*(7/8), 509–520. doi:10.1016/j.jom.2012.08.001

Dorasamy, N. (2013). Conditions determining the success of public e-procurement. In N. Pomazalová (Ed.), *Public sector transformation processes and Internet public procurement: Decision support systems* (pp. 185–209). Hershey, PA: IGI Global. doi:10.4018/978-1-4666-2665-2.ch009

Eadie, R., Perera, S., & Heaney, G. (2013). Electronic procurement in the construction industry. In N. Pomazalová (Ed.), *Public sector transformation processes and Internet public procurement: Decision support systems* (pp. 118–161). Hershey, PA: IGI Global. doi:10.4018/978-1-4666-2665-2.ch007

Edler, J., & Georghiou, L. (2007). Public procurement and innovation: Resurrecting the demand side. *Research Policy*, *36*(7), 949–963. doi:10.1016/j.respol.2007.03.003

Edler, J., & Yeow, J. (2016). Connecting demand and supply: The role of intermediation in public procurement of innovation. *Research Policy*, *45*(2), 414–426. doi:10.1016/j.respol.2015.10.010

Edquist, C., & Zabala-Iturriagagoitia, J. M. (2012). Public procurement for innovation as mission-oriented innovation policy. *Research Policy*, *41*(10), 1757–1769. doi:10.1016/j.respol.2012.04.022

Engelbrekt, K. (2011). EU enlargement and the emboldening of institutional integrity in Central and Eastern Europe: The “tough test” of public procurement. *European Law Journal*, *17*(2), 230–251. doi:10.1111/j.1468-0386.2010.00546.x

Federici, T. (2009). Introducing e-procurement in a local healthcare agency. In A. Scupola (Ed.), *Cases on managing e-services* (pp. 218–237). Hershey, PA: IGI Global. doi:10.4018/978-1-60566-064-6.ch015

Fet, A., Michelsen, O., & de Boer, L. (2011). Green public procurement in practice: The case of Norway. *Society and Economy*, *33*(1), 183–198. doi:10.1556/SocEc.33.2011.1.13

Filho, J. R., & Mota, F. P. (2012). Public e-procurement implementation: Insights from the structuration theory. In K. Vaidya (Ed.), *Inter-organizational information systems and business management: Theories for researchers* (pp. 222–233). Hershey, PA: IGI Global. doi:10.4018/978-1-60960-768-5.ch014

Gelderman, K., Ghijsen, P., & Schoonen, J. (2010). Explaining non-compliance with European Union procurement directives: A multidisciplinary perspective. *JCMS: Journal of Common Market Studies*, *48*(2), 243–264.

Genis-Gruber, A., & Tas, B. K. (2013). Does national culture affect e-procurement implementations?: Analysis of differences through a unified model. In M. Khosrow-Pour (Ed.), *E-commerce for organizational development and competitive advantage* (pp. 171–190). Hershey, PA: IGI Global. doi:10.4018/978-1-4666-3622-4.ch009

Georghiou, L., Edler, J., Uyarra, E., & Yeow, J. (2013). Policy instruments for public procurement of innovation: Choice, design and assessment. *Technological Forecasting and Social Change*, *86*, 1–12. doi:10.1016/j.techfore.2013.09.018

Golob, T. F. (2003). Structural equation modeling for travel behavior research. *Transportation Research Part B: Methodological*, *37*(1), 1–25. doi:10.1016/S0191-2615(01)00046-7

Gorvett, R., & Liu, N. (2006). *Interpretive structural modeling of interactive risks*. Paper presented at the 2006 Enterprise Risk Management Symposium, Chicago, IL.

Gunasekaran, A., McGaughey, R. E., Ngai, E. W. T., & Rai, B. K. (2009). E-procurement adoption in the Southcoast SMEs. *International Journal of Production Economics*, *122*(1), 161–175. doi:10.1016/j.ijpe.2009.05.013

Gunasekaran, A., & Ngai, E. W. T. (2008). Adoption of e-procurement in Hong Kong: An empirical research. *International Journal of Production Economics*, *113*(1), 159–175. doi:10.1016/j.ijpe.2007.04.012

Günther, E., & Scheibe, L. (2006). The hurdle analysis. A self-evaluation tool for municipalities to identify, analyse and overcome hurdles to green procurement. *Corporate Social Responsibility and Environmental Management*, *13*(2), 61–77. doi:10.1002/csr.92

Hall, M., & Purchase, D. (2006). Building or bodging? Attitudes to sustainability in UK public sector housing construction development. *Sustainable Development*, *14*(3), 205–218. doi:10.1002/sd.265

Hashim, R. (2012). Issues in electronic procurement project implementation in local government. In J. Wang (Ed.), *Project management techniques and innovations in information technology* (pp. 285–296). Hershey, PA: IGI Global. doi:10.4018/978-1-4666-0930-3.ch017

Hashim, R., & Mazuki, M. A. (2013). Electronic procurement (e-procurement) implementation in municipalities: Lessons learned. In P. Ordóñez de Pablos, J. Lovelle, J. Gayo, & R. Tennyson (Eds.), *E-procurement management for successful electronic government systems* (pp. 220–238). Hershey, PA: IGI Global. doi:10.4018/978-1-4666-2119-0.ch014

Hassan, H., Tretiakov, A., Whiddett, D., & Adon, I. (2014). Extent of e-procurement use in SMEs: A descriptive study. *Procedia: Social and Behavioral Sciences, 164*, 264–270. doi:10.1016/j.sbspro.2014.11.076

Hawking, P., Stein, A., Wyld, D. C., & Foster, S. (2004). E-procurement: Is the ugly duckling actually a swan down under? *Asia Pacific Journal of Marketing and Logistics, 16*(1), 3–26. doi:10.1108/13555850410765140

Hekkert, M., Suurs, R. A. A., Negro, S. O., Kuhlmann, S., & Smits, R. (2007). Functions of innovation systems: A new approach for analysing technological change. *Technological Forecasting and Social Change, 74*(4), 413–432. doi:10.1016/j.techfore.2006.03.002

Ho, C. F., Wu, W. H., & Tai, Y. M. (2004). *An e-procurement impact model based on supply chain orientation: An empirical investigation*. Paper presented at the 4th Workshop on Knowledge Economy and Electronic Commerce, Kaohsiung, Taiwan.

Ho, L. W. P., Dickinson, N. M., & Chan, G. Y. S. (2010). Green procurement in the Asian public sector and the Hong Kong private sector. *Natural Resources Forum, 34*(1), 24–38. doi:10.1111/j.1477-8947.2010.01274.x

Huang, D. C., Tran, Q. D., Nguyen, T. Q., & Nazir, S. (2016). Initial adoption vs. institutionalization of e-procurement in construction firms: The role of government in developing countries. In *Web design and development: Concepts, methodologies, tools, and applications* (pp. 1417–1437). Hershey, PA: IGI Global. doi:10.4018/978-1-4666-8619-9.ch064

Imamoglu, M. Y., & Rehan, M. (2011). Evaluation of Turkish public e-procurement systems: An analysis of critical success factors. In D. Piaggesi, K. Sund, & W. Castelnovo (Eds.), *Global strategy and practice of e-governance: Examples from around the world* (pp. 144–156). Hershey, PA: IGI Global. doi:10.4018/978-1-60960-489-9.ch009

Ishak, M. W., & Said, J. (2015). Assessing the role of anti-corruption initiatives in reducing lobbyist involvement in e-procurement: A case study of Mardi. *Procedia Economics and Finance, 31*, 485–494. doi:10.1016/S2212-5671(15)01182-X

Kamarulzaman, N. H., & Eglese, R. W. (2015). Managing purchasing with different e-procurement solutions. In E. Sabri (Ed.), *Optimization of supply chain management in contemporary organizations* (pp. 246–279). Hershey, PA: IGI Global.

Kasemsap, K. (2015a). The role of cloud computing adoption in global business. In V. Chang, R. Walters, & G. Wills (Eds.), *Delivery and adoption of cloud computing services in contemporary organizations* (pp. 26–55). Hershey, PA: IGI Global. doi:10.4018/978-1-4666-8210-8.ch002

Kasemsap, K. (2015b). The role of cloud computing in global supply chain. In N. Rao (Ed.), *Enterprise management strategies in the era of cloud computing* (pp. 192–219). Hershey, PA: IGI Global. doi:10.4018/978-1-4666-8339-6.ch009

Kasemsap, K. (2016a). The roles of business process modeling and business process reengineering in e-government. In J. Martins & A. Molnar (Eds.), *Handbook of research on innovations in information retrieval, analysis, and management* (pp. 401–430). Hershey, PA: IGI Global. doi:10.4018/978-1-4666-8833-9.ch015

Kasemsap, K. (2016b). The role of strategic outsourcing in global business. In G. Alor-Hernández, C. Sánchez-Ramírez, & J. García-Alcaraz (Eds.), *Handbook of research on managerial strategies for achieving optimal performance in industrial processes* (pp. 325–357). Hershey, PA: IGI Global. doi:10.4018/978-1-5225-0130-5.ch016

Kassim, E. S., & Hussin, H. (2013). A success model for the Malaysian government e-procurement system: The buyer perspective. *International Journal of Electronic Government Research*, *9*(1), 1–18. doi:10.4018/jegr.2013010101

Khorana, S., Ferguson-Boucher, K., & Kerr, W. A. (2015). Governance issues in the EU's e-procurement framework. *JCMS: Journal of Common Market Studies*, *53*(2), 292–310.

Klerkx, L., & Leeuwis, C. (2009). Establishment and embedding of innovation brokers at different innovation system levels: Insights from the Dutch agricultural sector. *Technological Forecasting and Social Change*, *76*(6), 849–860. doi:10.1016/j.techfore.2008.10.001

Konradt, U., Lückel, L., & Ellwart, T. (2012). The role of usability in business-to-business e-commerce systems: Predictors and its impact on user's strain and commercial transactions. *Advances in Human-Computer Interaction*, *2012*, 1–11. doi:10.1155/2012/948693

Kotwani, A. (2013). Transparency and accountability in public procurement of essential medicines in developing countries. In *Supply chain management: Concepts, methodologies, tools, and applications* (pp. 1437–1452). Hershey, PA: IGI Global. doi:10.4018/978-1-4666-2625-6.ch085

Krysiak, M. K., Tucker, C., Spitzer, D., & Holland, K. (2008). E-procurement: State government learns from the private sector. In A. Anttiroiko (Ed.), *Electronic government: Concepts, methodologies, tools, and applications* (pp. 1566–1583). Hershey, PA: IGI Global. doi:10.4018/978-1-59904-947-2.ch118

Lee, J. Y. (2007). The government e-procurement system in Korea. In A. Anttiroiko & M. Malkia (Eds.), *Encyclopedia of digital government* (pp. 896–900). Hershey, PA: IGI Global. doi:10.4018/978-1-59140-789-8.ch134

Lee, W., & Quaddus, M. (2006). *Buyer–supplier relationship in the adoption of e-purchasing in the small and medium printing industries in Singapore: An empirical test using structural equation modelling*. Paper presented at the 10th Pacific Asia Conference on Information Systems (PACIS 2006), Kuala Lumpur, Malaysia.

Leistner, C. N. (2013). Measuring the impact of tools on the leanness of e-procurement processes. In D. Graham, I. Manikas, & D. Folinas (Eds.), *E-logistics and e-supply chain management: Applications for evolving business* (pp. 44–88). Hershey, PA: IGI Global. doi:10.4018/978-1-4666-3914-0.ch004

Lin, A., & Chen, S. (2013). Structuring information systems-in-use: Studying the replication of an e-procurement system through a practice lens. *Journal of Global Information Management, 21*(1), 1–18. doi:10.4018/jgim.2013010101

Luthra, S., Kumar, V., Kumar, S., & Haleem, A. (2011). Barriers to implement green supply chain management in automobile industry using interpretive structural modeling technique: An Indian perspective. *Journal of Industrial Engineering and Management, 4*(2), 231–257. doi:10.3926/jiem.2011.v4n2.p231-257

Madeja, N., & Schoder, D. (2003). *The adoption of e-procurement and its impact on corporate success in electronic business*. Paper presented at the 3rd International Conference on Electronic Business (ICEB 2003), Singapore.

Manthou, V., Bialas, C., & Stefanou, C. J. (2016). Benefits and barriers of e-sourcing and e-purchasing in the healthcare sector: A case study. In P. Papajorgji, F. Pinet, A. Guimarães, & J. Papathanasiou (Eds.), *Automated enterprise systems for maximizing business performance* (pp. 71–87). Hershey, PA: IGI Global. doi:10.4018/978-1-4666-8841-4.ch005

Marín, J. L., Rodríguez, M., Marín, Á., Calmeau, R., Alvarez, J. M., & Labra, J. E. (2013). Euroalert.net: Aggregating public procurement data to deliver commercial services to SMEs. In P. Ordóñez de Pablos, J. Lovelle, J. Gayo, & R. Tennyson (Eds.), *E-procurement management for successful electronic government systems* (pp. 114–130). Hershey, PA: IGI Global. doi:10.4018/978-1-4666-2119-0.ch007

Martín, S. B., & Peñalvo, F. J. (2013). Electronic government systems for e-procurement procedure in the EU. In P. Ordóñez de Pablos, J. Lovelle, J. Gayo, & R. Tennyson (Eds.), *E-procurement management for successful electronic government Systems* (pp. 29–51). Hershey, PA: IGI Global. doi:10.4018/978-1-4666-2119-0.ch003

Meehan, J., & Bryde, D. (2011). Sustainable procurement practice. *Business Strategy and the Environment*, *20*(2), 94–106. doi:10.1002/bse.678

Mital, M., Pani, A., & Ramesh, R. (2014). Determinants of choice of semantic web based software as a service: An integrative framework in the context of e-procurement and ERP. *Computers in Industry*, *65*(5), 821–827. doi:10.1016/j.compind.2014.03.002

Morris, A., Stahl, A., & Herbert, R. (2000). *E-procurement: Streamlining processes to maximize effectiveness*. Houston, TX: Luminant Worldwide Corporation.

Nagle, T., Finnegan, P., & Hayes, J. (2009). From tough negotiation to complex integration: Implications of adversarial and collaborative relationships on electronic procurement systems. *Information Resources Management Journal*, *22*(4), 64–84. doi:10.4018/irmj.2009061904

Nath, R., & Angeles, R. (2005). Relationships between supply characteristics and buyer-supplier coupling in e-procurement: An empirical analysis. *International Journal of E-Business Research*, *1*(2), 40–55. doi:10.4018/jebr.2005040103

Neupane, A., Soar, J., & Vaidya, K. (2015). Anti-corruption capabilities of public e-procurement technologies: Principal-agent theory. In *Business law and ethics: Concepts, methodologies, tools, and applications* (pp. 355–373). Hershey, PA: IGI Global.

Nissinen, A., Parikka-Alholaa, K., & Ritab, H. (2009). Environmental criteria in the public purchases above the EU threshold values by three Nordic countries: 2003 and 2005. *Ecological Economics*, *68*(6), 1838–1849. doi:10.1016/j.ecolecon.2008.12.005

Novosák, J., Hájek, O., & Machu, J. (2013). Public procurement in the Czech Republic: Focused on regional development and e-procurement. In N. Pomazalová (Ed.), *Public sector transformation processes and Internet public procurement: Decision support systems* (pp. 210–226). Hershey, PA: IGI Global. doi:10.4018/978-1-4666-2665-2.ch010

OECD. (2011). *Demand-side innovation policies*. Paris, France: Organization for Economic Cooperation and Development.

Oliveira, A. F., & Joia, L. A. (2013). E-procurement associated with MRO: The case of Caixa Econômica Federal. In P. Ordóñez de Pablos, J. Lovelle, J. Gayo, & R. Tennyson (Eds.), *E-procurement management for successful electronic government systems* (pp. 52–72). Hershey, PA: IGI Global. doi:10.4018/978-1-4666-2119-0.ch004

OMahoney, J., Heusinkveld, S., & Wright, C. (2013). Commodifying the commodifiers: The impact of procurement on management knowledge. *Journal of Management Studies*, *50*(2), 204–235. doi:10.1111/joms.12008

Otsuki, K. (2011). Sustainable partnerships for a green economy: A case study of public procurement for home-grown school feeding. *Natural Resources Forum*, *35*(3), 213–222. doi:10.1111/j.1477-8947.2011.01392.x

Palmujoki, A., Parikka-Alhola, K., & Ekroos, A. (2010). Green public procurement: Analysis on the use of environmental criteria in contracts. *Review of European Community & International Environmental Law*, *19*(2), 250–262. doi:10.1111/j.1467-9388.2010.00681.x

Panayiotou, N. A., Gayialis, S. P., & Tatsiopoulos, I. P. (2004). An e-procurement system for governmental purchasing. *International Journal of Production Economics*, *90*(1), 79–102. doi:10.1016/S0925-5273(03)00103-8

Pani, A. K. (2007). Perspectives from IOIS, EDI, and channel management: Research issues in e-procurement. In A. Pani & A. Agrahari (Eds.), *E-procurement in emerging economies: Theory and cases* (pp. 1–20). Hershey, PA: Idea Group Publishing. doi:10.4018/978-1-59904-153-7.ch001

Patra, M. R. (2007). A service-oriented agent-based model for electronic procurement. In A. Pani & A. Agrahari (Eds.), *E-procurement in emerging economies: Theory and cases* (pp. 233–264). Hershey, PA: Idea Group Publishing. doi:10.4018/978-1-59904-153-7.ch009

Peck, F., & Cabras, I. (2011). The impact of local authority procurement on local economies: The case of Cumbria, North West England. *Public Policy and Administration*, *26*(3), 307–331. doi:10.1177/0952076709356859

Podlogar, M. (2007). E-procurement success factors: Challenges and opportunities for a small developing country. In A. Pani & A. Agrahari (Eds.), *E-procurement in emerging economies: Theory and cases* (pp. 42–75). Hershey, PA: Idea Group Publishing. doi:10.4018/978-1-59904-153-7.ch003

Pomazalová, N., & Rejman, S. (2013). The rationale behind implementation of new electronic tools for electronic public procurement. In N. Pomazalová (Ed.), *Public sector transformation processes and Internet public procurement: Decision support systems* (pp. 85–117). Hershey, PA: IGI Global. doi:10.4018/978-1-4666-2665-2.ch006

Preuss, L. (2007). Buying into our future: Sustainability initiatives in local government procurement. *Business Strategy and the Environment, 16*(5), 354–365. doi:10.1002/bse.578

Preuss, L., & Walker, H. (2011). Psychological barriers in the road to sustainable development: Evidence from public sector procurement. *Public Administration, 89*(2), 493–521. doi:10.1111/j.1467-9299.2010.01893.x

Previtali, P. (2012). European public e-procurement: The Italian experience. In A. Manoharan & M. Holzer (Eds.), *Active citizen participation in e-government: A global perspective* (pp. 230–249). Hershey, PA: IGI Global. doi:10.4018/978-1-4666-0116-1.ch012

Puschmann, T., & Alt, R. (2005). Successful use of e-procurement in supply chains. *Supply Chain Management: An International Journal, 10*(2), 122–133. doi:10.1108/13598540510589197

Rabaey, M. (2013). A complex adaptive system thinking approach of government e-procurement in a cloud computing environment. In P. Ordóñez de Pablos, J. Lovelle, J. Gayo, & R. Tennyson (Eds.), *E-procurement management for successful electronic government systems* (pp. 193–219). Hershey, PA: IGI Global. doi:10.4018/978-1-4666-2119-0.ch013

Rahim, M. M., & Bantwal, A. P. (2012). Perceived benefits from a local government public procurement initiative: A diffusion of innovation perspective. In K. Vaidya (Ed.), *Inter-organizational information systems and business management: Theories for researchers* (pp. 251–271). Hershey, PA: IGI Global. doi:10.4018/978-1-60960-768-5.ch016

Reddick, C. G. (2007). Government e-procurement through the Internet. In A. Anttiroiko & M. Malkia (Eds.), *Encyclopedia of digital government* (pp. 901–905). Hershey, PA: IGI Global. doi:10.4018/978-1-59140-789-8.ch135

Reddy, K., & Rampersad, R. (2013). Black economic empowerment, ICT, and preferential public procurement in South Africa. In N. Pomazalová (Ed.), *Public sector transformation processes and Internet public procurement: Decision support systems* (pp. 254–275). Hershey, PA: IGI Global. doi:10.4018/978-1-4666-2665-2.ch012

Rehan, M. (2013). An analysis of public e-procurement system: An overview of Turkish system. *International Journal of Technology Diffusion, 4*(4), 66–81. doi:10.4018/ijtd.2013100104

Rehme, J., Kindstrom, D., & Brege, S. (2005). Know your why's how's: Towards a contingency model for industrial e-procurement. In N. Shin (Ed.), *Strategies for generating e-business returns on investment* (pp. 125–142). Hershey, PA: Idea Group Publishing. doi:10.4018/978-1-59140-417-0.ch006

Resca, A., & Federici, T. (2013). Implementing e-procurement in public healthcare: The knowledge management issue. In *Supply chain management: Concepts, methodologies, tools, and applications* (pp. 984–1001). Hershey, PA: IGI Global. doi:10.4018/978-1-4666-2625-6.ch057

Robinson, P., Wale, D., & Dickson, G. (2010). *Events management.* Cambridge, MA: CABI Publishing. doi:10.1079/9781845936822.0000

Rolfstam, M. (2013). *Public procurement and innovation: The role of institutions.* Cheltenham, UK: Edward Elgar Publishing. doi:10.4337/9780857930521

Roman, A. V. (2013). The "mental revolution" of the public procurement specialist: Achieving transformative impacts within the context of e-procurement. In N. Pomazalová (Ed.), *Public sector transformation processes and Internet public procurement: Decision support systems* (pp. 1–16). Hershey, PA: IGI Global. doi:10.4018/978-1-4666-2665-2.ch001

Shakya, R. K. (2015). *Good governance in public procurement: An evaluation of the role of e-procurement system* (3714138, Capella University). ProQuest Dissertations and Theses, 225.

Sheng, M. L. (2008). Global integrated supply chain implementation: The challenges of e-procurement. In F. Tan (Ed.), *Global information technologies: Concepts, methodologies, tools, and applications* (pp. 3243–3249). Hershey, PA: IGI Global. doi:10.4018/978-1-59904-939-7.ch229

Singh, M. D., & Kant, R. (2008). Knowledge management barriers: An interpretive structural modeling approach. *International Journal of Management Science and Engineering Management, 3*(2), 141–150.

Somasundaram, R. (2007). Challenges in implementation of e-procurement in the Indian government. In A. Pani & A. Agrahari (Eds.), *E-procurement in emerging economies: Theory and cases* (pp. 76–100). Hershey, PA: Idea Group Publishing. doi:10.4018/978-1-59904-153-7.ch004

Steinfeld, J. M., & Thai, K. V. (2013). Technology advancement and e-procurement in the US. In N. Pomazalová (Ed.), *Public sector transformation processes and Internet public procurement: Decision support systems* (pp. 68–84). Hershey, PA: IGI Global. doi:10.4018/978-1-4666-2665-2.ch005

Swanson, M., Weissman, A., Davis, G., Socolof, M., & Davis, K. (2005). Developing priorities for greener state government purchasing: A California case study. *Journal of Cleaner Production, 13*(7), 669–677. doi:10.1016/j.jclepro.2003.12.011

Talib, F., Rahman, Z., & Qureshi, M. N. (2011). An interpretive structural modelling approach for modelling the practices of total quality management in service sector. *International Journal of Modelling in Operations Management, 1*(3), 223–250. doi:10.1504/IJMOM.2011.039528

Tarantini, M., Loprieno, A. D., & Porta, P. L. (2011). A life cycle approach to green public procurement of building materials and elements: A case study on windows. *Energy, 36*(5), 2473–2482. doi:10.1016/j.energy.2011.01.039

Teo, T. S. H., Lin, S., & Lai, K. (2009). Adopters and non-adopters of e-procurement in Singapore: An empirical study. *Omega: International Journal of Management Science, 37*(5), 972–987. doi:10.1016/j.omega.2008.11.001

Testa, F., Annunziata, E., Iraldo, F., & Frey, M. (2016). Drawbacks and opportunities of green public procurement: An effective tool for sustainable production. *Journal of Cleaner Production, 112*, 1893–1900. doi:10.1016/j.jclepro.2014.09.092

Testa, F., Iraldo, F., & Frey, M. (2011). The effect of environmental regulation on firms' competitive performance: The case of the building & construction sector in some EU regions. *Journal of Environmental Management, 92*(9), 2136–2144. doi:10.1016/j.jenvman.2011.03.039 PMID:21524840

Testa, F., Iraldo, F., Frey, M., & Daddi, T. (2012). What factors influence the uptake of GPP (green public procurement) practices? New evidence from an Italian survey. *Ecological Economics, 82*, 88–96. doi:10.1016/j.ecolecon.2012.07.011

Thomson, J., & Jackson, T. (2007). Sustainable procurement in practice: Lessons from local government. *Journal of Environmental Planning and Management, 50*(3), 421–444. doi:10.1080/09640560701261695

Timmermans, B., & Zabala-Iturriagagoitia, J. M. (2013). Coordinated unbundling: A way to stimulate entrepreneurship through public procurement for innovation. *Science & Public Policy, 40*(5), 674–685. doi:10.1093/scipol/sct023

Toktaş-Palut, P., Baylav, E., Teoman, S., & Altunbey, M. (2014). The impact of barriers and benefits of e-procurement on its adoption decision: An empirical analysis. *International Journal of Production Economics*, *158*, 77–90. doi:10.1016/j.ijpe.2014.07.017

Truong, D. (2016). The relationship between B2B e-procurement solutions and the purchasing portfolio: An empirical study. *International Journal of Knowledge-Based Organizations*, *6*(2), 55–69. doi:10.4018/IJKBO.2016040104

Vaidya, K. (2007). Organizational assimilation of e-procurement: An institutional perspective and the research model. In A. Pani & A. Agrahari (Eds.), *E-procurement in emerging economies: Theory and cases* (pp. 21–40). Hershey, PA: Idea Group Publishing. doi:10.4018/978-1-59904-153-7.ch002

Vaidya, K., Campbell, J., Soar, J., & Gardner, S. (2012). Assimilation of inter-organizational information systems: Insight from change resistance theory in public electronic procurement. In K. Vaidya (Ed.), *Inter-organizational information systems and business management: Theories for researchers* (pp. 18–32). Hershey, PA: IGI Global. doi:10.4018/978-1-60960-768-5.ch002

Vaidyanathan, G., & Devaraj, S. (2008). The role of quality in e-procurement performance: An empirical analysis. *Journal of Operations Management*, *26*(3), 407–425. doi:10.1016/j.jom.2007.08.004

Vaidyanathan, G., Devaraj, S., & D'Arcy, J. (2012). Does security impact e-procurement performance? Testing a model of direct and moderated effects. *Decision Sciences*, *43*(3), 437–458. doi:10.1111/j.1540-5915.2012.00354.x

van Duinkerken, W., Batenburg, R., & Versendaal, J. (2008). The added value of e-procurement for buyer-supplier interaction. In N. Kock (Ed.), *Encyclopedia of e-collaboration* (pp. 14–20). Hershey, PA: IGI Global. doi:10.4018/978-1-59904-000-4.ch003

van Lente, H., Hekkert, M., Smits, R., & van Waveren, B. (2003). Roles of systemic intermediaries in transition processes. *International Journal of Innovation Management*, *7*(3), 1–33. doi:10.1142/S1363919603000817

Vincent-Jones, P. (2006). *The new public contracting: Regulation, responsiveness, relationality*. Oxford, UK: Oxford University Press. doi:10.1093/acprof:oso/9780199291274.001.0001

Walker, H., & Brammer, S. (2009). Sustainable procurement in the United Kingdom public sector. *Supply Chain Management: An International Journal*, *14*(2), 128–137. doi:10.1108/13598540910941993

Wang, E. T. G., & Seidmann, A. (1995). Electronic data interchange: Competitive externalities and strategic implementation policies. *Management Science*, *41*(3), 401–418. doi:10.1287/mnsc.41.3.401

Wu, F., Zsidisin, G. A., & Ross, A. D. (2007). Antecedents and outcomes of e-procurement adoption: An integrative model. *IEEE Transactions on Engineering Management*, *54*(3), 576–587. doi:10.1109/TEM.2007.900786

Yamamoto, G. T., & Karaman, F. (2007). Barriers to e-procurement adoption: The Turkish case. In A. Pani & A. Agrahari (Eds.), *E-procurement in emerging economies: Theory and cases* (pp. 101–125). Hershey, PA: Idea Group Publishing. doi:10.4018/978-1-59904-153-7.ch005

Yu, S., Mishra, A. N., Gopal, A., Slaughter, S., & Mukhopadhyay, T. (2015). E-procurement infusion and operational process impacts in MRO procurement: Complementary or substitutive effects? *Production and Operations Management*, *24*(7), 1054–1070. doi:10.1111/poms.12362

Zhu, Q., Geng, Y., & Sarkis, J. (2013). Motivating green public procurement in China: An individual level perspective. *Journal of Environmental Management*, *126*, 85–95. doi:10.1016/j.jenvman.2013.04.009 PMID:23666074

KEY TERMS AND DEFINITIONS

Electronic Government: The use of information technology to improve the activities of public sector organizations.

Government: The act or process of governing, especially the control and administration of public policy in a political unit.

Information Technology: A broad term that includes the development, installing and use of anything to do with computing and telecommunications.

Innovation: The process of translating an idea or invention into a product or service that creates value.

Policy: The set of basic principles and associated guidelines, formulated and enforced by the governing body of an organization, to direct and limit its actions in pursuit of long-term goals.

Procurement: The act of buying products and services.

Public Sector: The part of the economy that is controlled or funded by the government.

Supplier: The individual that provides products or services.

Chapter 3
Application of E-Government Principles in Anti-Corruption Framework

Arjun Neupane
University of Southern Queensland, Australia

Jeffrey Soar
University of Southern Queensland, Australia

Kishor Vaidya
University of Southern Queensland, Australia & University of Canberra, Australia

Sunil Aryal
Federation University, Australia

ABSTRACT

The use of Information and Communication Technologies (ICTs) plays a significant role in the economic, technological and social progression of a country. Corruption in government agencies and institutions is a serious problem in many countries in the world, especially in under-developed and developing countries. The use of ICT tools such as e-governance can help to reduce corruption. In this chapter, the authors discussed the application of e-government principles to mitigate corruption. Based on the available literature, this study identified some potential elements of e-government, which are currently practised around the world and how they are interrelated to fight against corruption. Finally, the authors present an evidence-based e-government anti-corruption framework.

DOI: 10.4018/978-1-5225-2203-4.ch003

INTRODUCTION AND BACKGROUND

Corruption in government agencies and institutions is a serious problem in many countries in the world, especially in under-developed and developing countries. It is a barrier that hinders the country's economic, technological and social progression (Neupane, Soar, Vaidya, & Aryal, 2014). In under-developed and developing countries, trillions of dollars is spent on goods and services for the public welfare but can be misused because of an inappropriate and non-transparent government work and services. Reports of World Bank, United Nations (UN), Transparency International, Organisation for Economic Co-operation and Development (OECD), Asian Development Bank (ADB) and other government agencies suggest that corruption in public services is at alarming levels particularly in developing countries (Olken & Pande, 2011). Much literature has proposed that Information and communication Technology (ICT) tools such as e-government can be useful to combat corruption and increase transparency and accountability in government work and services (Aladwani, 2016; Shakya, 2012, S. Kim, Kim, & Lee, 2009). E-government uses ICTs or internet based inter-organizational information systems to improve government processes and services in a transparent and accountable way. There are various applications of ICT tools in practice around the globe that successfully connect government with citizens, and businesses.

The main purpose of this Chapter is to contribute to the existing literature about the application and use e-government application to promote public work efficiency, quality, effectiveness, transparency, accountability in government work and services to mitigate the risk of corruption. Most importantly, this chapter discusses the principles of e-government, and their applications to reduce corruption. In addition, we develop an anti-corruption framework that can help mitigate corruption in public sectors. We discuss and analyse prior research cases to support the anti-corruption framework.

The chapter is structured as follows. Firstly, it discusses e-government principles. Secondly, it presents the evidence of applications of e-government to reduce corruption. Next, we discuss the anti-corruption framework with different potential factors to reduce the misuse of public office for private gain. The discussion of the findings, conclusions and recommendation for future research is presented in the final sections.

E-GOVERNMENT PRINCIPLES

Governments across the globe have been improving service delivery in innovative and effective ways to their citizens, businesses, and governments. Many countries have already adopted e-government with the aim of improving service delivery. The main key principles of implementing those projects is to replace the traditional paper based systems to modernised internet based inter-organisational information systems to achieve maximum cost saving, fast and reliable quality service to the citizens, businesses, and governments. The underlying principle is to improve the day to day government work and services by reducing the transaction time and cost, better quality management of work and services, to improve the relationship between different government departments, to enhance transparency and accountability and reducing the risk of corruption (Bhatnagar & Singh, 2010; Mohammad, Almarabeh, & Ali, 2009). E-government is a key enabler of connected government and technology plays a potential role of integration of public information and services. In recent years, many scholars have identified different successful e-government principles, including digital transformation, strong management support and funding of the project (Ke & Wei, 2004), a number of challenges, capacity building (Dwivedi, Weerakkody, & Janssen, 2012; Gil-García & Pardo, 2005), and the for high level of sponsorship for the project.

E-government is a long-term project of the government for transforming all government activities through the internet based integrated information systems. E-government added new concepts as an anti-corruption tool and improve transparency and accountability (Bertot, Jaeger, & Grimes, 2010), watchdog of government work and services by civil society (Linders & Wilson, 2011). Strong management support is required to implement e-government. Government in developing countries still requires a commitment to reform the public administration and digitize the delivery of work and services.

Every two years the United Nations (UN) publishes e-government survey results by the Department of Economic and Social Affairs. The UN e-government survey 2014 e-government development index, which is shown in Figure 1 and indicates the level of transparency and abuse of corruption. The Republic of Korea is in the top rank with 0.94 followed by Australia 0.91, Singapore 0.90, France 0.89, Netherlands 0.889, Japan 0.887, United States of America 0.87, United Kingdom of Great Britain and Northern Ireland 0.86, New Zealand 0.86 and Finland 0.84 respectively. Nepal (0.23), Afghanistan (0.19), and Myanmar (0.18) are at the bottom of e-government index indicating high levels of corruption in government. Similarly, Somalia is the country with the lowest e-government index (0.013).

Based on the UN e-government survey results, developing countries still have a number of challenges to implement e-government and they are slow in making plans to adopt this technology. Strong leadership is required to face the challenges to implement e-government. Furuholt and Wahid (2008) identified three key important challenges for adoption e-government including management, infrastructure, and human factors. Political leadership is consider to be one of the key success factors

Figure 1. E-government development index of top 10 countries
Source: UN E-government Survey 2014

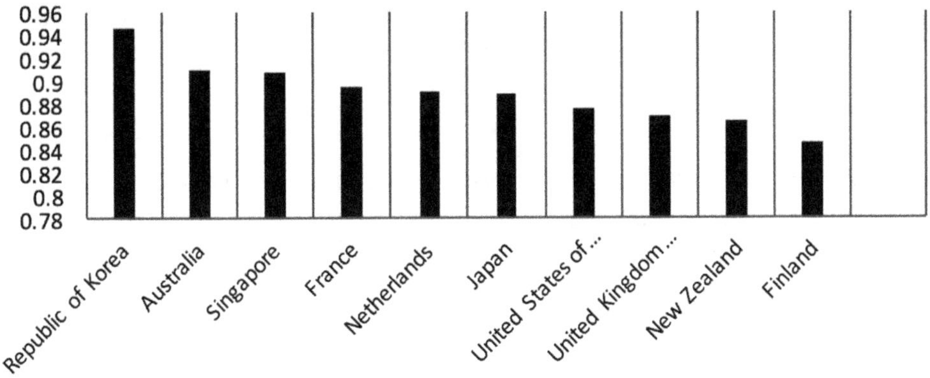

to run e-government for the enhancement of the government accountability and transparency (Ahn & Bretschneider, 2011; Furuholt & Wahid, 2008; Kifle & Low Kim Cheng, 2009; Luk, 2009). There are other potential barriers to implement the e-government in developing countries including poor ICT infrastructure, finance, skilled personnel, poor data systems and lack of compatibility, cultural issues, and bureaucracy (Gichoya, 2005). Further, research on ICT and e-government adoption in the context of Bangladesh conducted by Imran and Gregor (2010),authors developed a process model for e-government adoption and interrelationship with eleven major barriers for example lack of knowledge, lack of planning and strategy, existing bureaucratic processes, lack of experts and professionals, political will and leadership, infrastructure, socio-economic conditions, law and rules and others.

E-GOVERNMENT APPLICATION TO REDUCING CORRUPTION

Potential applications of e-government are in public services, government administration, democratic processes, connection with citizens, and private sector (Rahman & Ramos, 2013). Weerakkody, Irani, Lee, Osman, and Hindi (2015) did comprehensive review of the literature on e-government research and showed the summary of thirty six research work of e-government benefits including cost reduction, better service, combating identity fraud, increasing accountability, great access information, reducing corruption and many more. Some of the studies are concerned about the application of e-government to fight against corruption. Elbahnasawy (2014) used large panel dataset for the empirical investigation of the impact of e-government and internet adoption for the battle of the corruption and results found that e-government is a powerful ICT tool in reducing corruption. Kim et al. (2009) research evaluates the anti-corruption system called OPEN (Online Procedures Enhancement for Civil application) is used in the Seoul Metropolitan Government, an evaluation concluded that OPEN systems found four strategies to fight corruption including accesses to information and empowerment, prevention, enforcement, and capacity building. Table 1 summarise key studies since 2010 of e-government as an anti-corruption systems with different case study.

Table 1. Literature summary of e-government to reduce corruption

E-government / ICTs	Descriptions and study context	Corruption variables	Authors
E-government / e-governance	The study examines the role of e-governance systems in Bangladesh for the modernization of public administration as well to control corruption and poverty reduction.	Human Intervention, Usefulness, Transparency and accountability	(Bhuiyan, 2011)
E-government	The study examine the case study reports (e-government) local government in Seoul, South Korea-Gangnam-gu.	Transparency and accountability	(Ahn & Bretschneider, 2011)
ICTs, Social Media and Collaborative e-government	The study used the literature review, content and web site analysis to examine the interrelationship between ICTs, social media and collaborative e-government to facilitate transparency.	Transparency, Collaboration, Monitoring	(Ae Chun et al., 2012)
E-government	The study links e-government and administrative corruption on the perception of Jordanians citizens.	People's perceptions	(Abu–Shanab, Harb, & Al–Zoubi, 2013)
E-government	The study investigates the relationship between transparency and e-government based on two measures the corruption perceptions index (CPI) and the Open budget index (OBI).	Transparency	(Abu-Shanab, 2013)
E-government	The study examines the relationship among e-government maturity, corruption, economic prosperity and environmental degradation based on available archival data and authors found e-government indirectly impacts on corruption.	Awareness raising	(Krishnan, Teo, & Lim, 2013)
E-government	The study analysed more than 200 countries data and found that e-government can be an effective tool to reduce corruption.	Transparency, Openness, Accountability, Human interventions	(C.-K. Kim, 2014)
ICTs- Electronic Monitoring Systems (EMS)	The research is examining and exploring the effectiveness of ICTs – Electronic Monitoring Systems (EMS) in China to reduce corruption, and the authors found that EMS has a positive effect to reduce corruption.	Monitoring, User satisfaction	(Xinli, 2015)
ICTs	The study used a secondary data from 97 countries for the investigation of the relationship between ICT penetration among businesses, government and citizens in the country and countries level of corruption.	Deterrent, Automation	(Shrivastava & Bhattacherjee, 2015)
ICTs and e-government	The study discusses the role of ICTs as a means of tackling corruption in Nigeria. The Study reviews the literature on ICTs help for access to information and transparency, sharing information, monitor to public spending and demand accountability, and tackle corruption.	Transparency, Accountability, Monitor	(Adamu, Shatimah, & Aliyu, 2016)

Table 1 suggests that e-government is one of the essential tools to reduce corruption. E-government application such as e-procurement or online procurement is one of the important ICT tools already implemented by many public and private organisations for the automation of procurement processes. The main aims of implementing e-procurement system are increasing transparency and accountability, reducing the transaction costs, increasing trust between government and its partners, improve efficiency and quality, and reducing human intervention in government bidding systems (Neupane, 2014; Kishor Vaidya, Sajeev, & Gao, 2005). The e-procurement has also justified the role of e-procurement to reduce corruption in government procurement (Neupane, Soar, Vaidya, & Yong, 2012, 2014), the potential anti-corruption factors of e-procurement (Neupane, Soar, & Vaidya, 2014).

For example, Azmi and Rahman (2015) study demonstrated case of Malaysia using e-procurement to mitigate public procurement fraud. Azmi and Rahman (2015, p. 150) research finding confirmed that 'e-procurement can dispute political and economic forces in government purchasing processes, manage demands and interference when rewarding government contracts, and be used efficiently at the nexus of government and businesses'. Likewise, Lupu and Lazar (2015) research confirm that greater use of e-government to reduce corruption in some European Union (EU) and non-EU states. Lupu and Lazar (2015, p. 370) research model suggest that '1% in the index of e-government can result in a decrease in corruption by 6.7% for EU countries and 6.3 for non-EU member'. Another project e-government and its ability to reduce corruption case of Estonia by Karv (2015) and study concluded that e-government to desertion of middle-man in government work and services and also enhanced more transparency and accountability. Furthermore, we can take a good case country example of how the e-government projects help to increase transparency in government procurement process: South Korea (Government-Procurement System (GePS), Singapore (One-stop e-procurement portal GeBIZ, eCitizen portal), Andhra Pradesh India (E-government project), Brazil e-procurement project (COMPRASNET), E-government Australia and so on.

In the current market, there are different internet based information systems such as e-procurement, e-informing, e-sourcing, e-tendering, e-reverse auctioning, e-ordering, e-intelligence, e-contract management, web based Enterprise Resource Planning, e-government, e-participation, e-governance and many more (Neupane, Soar, Vaidya, & Aryal, 2014). Table 2 demonstrates the most common types of e-procurement and e-government systems and their explanations.

Every system plays a significant role to automate existing systems into web based digital systems and it has specific work and functionality. The main motive to implement this system is to improve public sector operation and service delivery, including interacting with government business partners, and citizenship empowerments through real time access to information. E-government is one of the best government

Table 2. Types of e-procurement and e-government system

E-procurement and e-government system	Description	Authors(S) & Year
e-Contract Management	The use of information technology for improving the efficiency and effectiveness of contracting processes of companies.	(Angelov & Grefen, 2008; Yang & Zhang, 2009)
e-Democracy	E-democracy refers to the use of ICT to communicate between government and citizens for the purpose of information sharing, voting and polling, or discussion. It supports the democratic decision making processes.	(Macintosh, 2004; Saxena, 2005)
e-Governance	Electronic governance involves the use of ICTs to transact the business of government including level of government services 24/7, greater information accessibility, and reduce service cost. It emphasises the application of ICTs in governance systems and processes The main aim is to reform the theory and practice of legitimate decision making and policy formulation to meet the demand of the civil society.	(Asgarkhani, 2005; Saxena, 2005)
e-Government	E-government (also known as an e-gov, internet government, digital government, on-line government, or connected government) describes the digital interaction between government institutions and public. The main application of e-government is to empower citizens and businesses to transact government business online, it can enhance economic development of the country, thereby allowing greater public access and faster information responses, lower costs, provide more up-to-date and complete information, reduced corruption and many other benefits.	(Asgarkhani, 2005; Mistry & Jalal, 2012; Ojha, Palvia, & Gupta, 2008)
e-Informing	Gathering and distributing purchasing information both from and to internal and external parties using Internet technology.	(Boer, Harink, & Heijboer, 2001; De Boer, Harink, & Heijboer, 2002; Essig & Arnold, 2001)
e-Intelligence	Management information system with spend analysis tools	(Eakin, 2003; Harink, 2003)
Electronic social media	Electronic social media uses the internet technology for interaction among users. Social media includes blogs, wikis, social networking sites (e.g. Facebook), micro-blogging services (e.g. Twitter), multimedia sharing services (e.g. Flicker, YouTube) Crowdsourcing, Circumvention, online communities etc.	(Arpit, 2012)
e-Markets	E-markets are meeting venues for component suppliers and purchasers, who use exchange mechanism to electronically support the procurement process.	(Block & Neumann, 2008; Fuks, Kawa, & Wieczerzycki, 2009)

continued on following page

Table 2. Continued

E-procurement and e-government system	Description	Authors(S) & Year
e-MRO and Web based Enterprise resource planning (ERP)	The process of creating and approving purchasing requisitions, placing purchase orders and receiving the goods or services ordered via a software system based on Internet technology, e-MRO deals with indirect items (MRO,), web-based ERP deals with product-related items.	(Bruno, Esposito, Mastroianni, & Vellutino, 2005; De Boer et al., 2002; Fink, 2006; Gunasekaran, McGaughey, Ngai, & Rai, 2009)
e-Ordering	The use of Internet to facilitate operational purchasing process, including ordering (requisitioning), order approval, order receipt and payment process.	(Harink, 2003; Reunis, Santema, & Harink, 2006)
e-Participation	E-participation is one of the applications of electronic government that serves to encourage two-way communication between government and citizens, educate citizens about the rationale and complexity of policy making, legitimise government decisions, and provide the opportunities of mutual learning.	(Phang & Kankanhalli, 2008)
e-Reverse Auctioning	Internet based reverse auction technology which focuses on the price of the goods and services auctioned.	(Carter et al., 2004; Teich, Wallenius, & Wallenius, 1999)
e-Services	Electronic services refer to utilising ICT in different areas such as service provider, service receiver, and channels of service delivery. Public agencies (Government) are the service provider that provides a service to the citizens as well as business (service receiver) and the Internet is the main channel of service delivery. The main application is to provide a better customer services and assist different opportunities including e-filling, email, e-forms and the like.	(Beynon-Davies, 2005)
e-Sourcing	Process of identifying new suppliers for specific categories of purchasing requirements using Internet technology.	(De Boer et al., 2002; Fuks et al., 2009; Knudsen, 2003)
E-Submission	It is the process of online submission of electronic document like tender document that is specially designed to facilitate the bidders' submissions of their bids through e-submission.	(Neupane, Soar, & Vaidya, 2012; Salin & Abidin, 2011)
e-Tendering	The process of sending requests for information and prices to suppliers and receiving the response using Internet technology.	(Betts et al., 2010; De Boer et al., 2002)
Public e-procurement	Public e-procurement is defined as the use of ICT such as internet or web-based system by government institutions in their procurement activities. It integrates and automates the procurement processes in order to improve transparency and accountability in government procurement.	(Croom & Brandon-Jones, 2005; Davila, Gupta, & Palmer, 2003; Joongi, 2006; Leipold, Klemow, Holloway, & Vaidya, 2004; Mahmood, 2010; K. Vaidya, 2007)

(Neupane, 2014; Neupane, Soar, Vaidya, & Aryal, 2014)

Table 3. Summary of e-government to reduce corruption

Anti-corruption factors	Description	Logic to achieve benefits	Main target	E-government
Automation	Replacing manual activities by systems	Reduces opportunities for corruption as it removes human agents	Petty bribes in government operation	Any ICT tools and technology
Transparency	Operations/activities are visible to anyone	Removes opportunities for discretion	Small and large scale corruption	Government web portal where all information is published
Accountable	Making people in authorities responsible for their actions	Discourage corruption as people in authorities will be careful before making any decisions	Large scale corruption (public procurement)	Systems which keep track of actions by each individual
Detection in operations	Monitoring and evaluating daily and aggregated actions	Finding suspicious actions	Petty bribery and large scale corruption	Audit and control functions in systems such as e-procurement
Preventive detection	Monitoring individual (social media) to detect preparations for corruption	People in authorities interact with the other party before taking any action in the case of corruption	Large scale corruption and public procurement	Social media and social network analysis
Awareness raising	Make public aware of government rules and regulations	If people are aware, they are better able to resist arbitrary treatment	Petty bribery	Websites and any other ICT tools
Reporting	Mobilising communities and public to report instances of corruption	It is easy to take corrective actions if wrong-doing is reported on time and discourage authorities to involve in corruption	Small and large scale corruption	Website, Social media, electronic anonymous complaint box
Deterrence	Publishing income and assets of any public employee	Discourage corruption as any imbalance in income and property can be easily identified	Small and large scale corruption	Website, social media
Promoting ethical attitudes	Engaging the public through trainings and discussions to promote anti-corruption attitudes	Awareness and education motivates public to observe and report instances of corruption	Public awareness	Social media, websites, videos

Figure 2. The proposed research anti-corruption framework

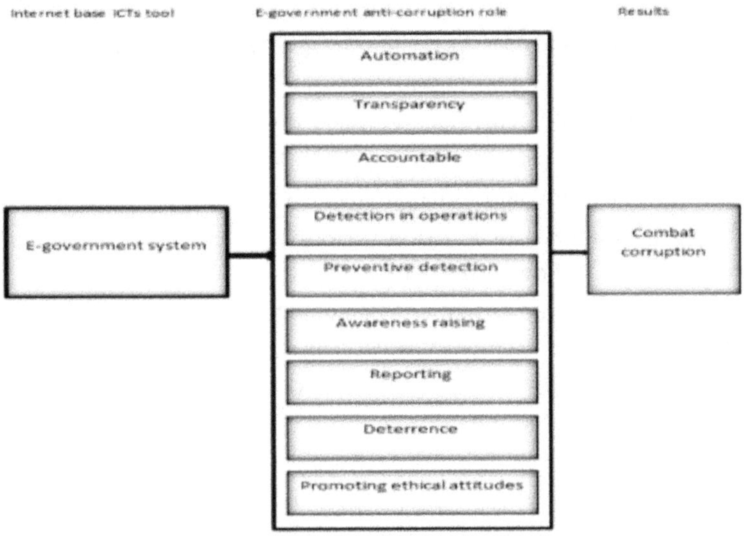

system to promote more public participation in the government programme and it also changes the way of interactions between people with government (Lee & Huang, 2014). E-government uses the web 2.0 tools that create an interactive environment for more open sharing information to the citizens (Uthayasankar, 2014).

There are different factors of an e-government application to reduce corruption. Table 3 summarises e-government or other ICTs tool anti-corruption factors with description adapted from (Grönlund, 2010, p. 15).

Table 3 presents various ICT tools or any-corruption factors that can be used to combat corruption in government work and services. Automation is one of the key elements to automate the existing government processes and also to reduce corruption in public institutions (Neupane, Soar, Vaidya, et al., 2012). In Afghanistan, the automation in customs procedures helps to reduce face-to-face contact and the negotiation in Customs- business relationship and increased both transparency and national consistency (McLinden & Durrani, 2013) . Through a government web-portal public can view and search government spending and contracts. In addition, watchdog group can also download government data and analyse them for better monitoring government work. E-government services can improve awareness of government law and regulations. Figure 2 depicts the proposed research framework and clearly presents the potential application of e-government or other web based ICT enabled technology anti-corruption factors helps to combat corruption.

DISCUSSION AND IMPLICATION FOR FUTURE RESEARCH

In this chapter, we reviewed the prior literature on e-government and related other ICT enabled technology, e-government principles, and application of e-government to reduce corruption. The main contribution of this research work is to demonstrate governments around the world, academic scholars, international agencies, and International Non-Governmental Organisation (INGO). E-government has potential benefits not only automate the existing systems to digitize the work and services, but also reduces corruption in the public sector. The main motivation for implementing e-government to more public engagement in government services, to make more transparent and accountable government work and services, maintain good relationship with other agencies and public-servant, higher productivity in terms of reducing the operating costs, and more efficient in public administrative procedures.

This research work is significant for academic scholar, government institutions, international agencies, including the World Bank, Asian Development Bank, African Development Bank, Transparency International, the United Nations and Other government's donor organisation they are investing huge amounts of money every year to implement e-government or other types of ICTs system for the transformation of public service. In an academic sense, this work is very useful and offered an anti-corruption framework based on the discussion of available literature on e-government and other benefits of internet based ICT system in public service. This framework is offered to assist in policy development in developing countries that have still some barriers to adoption of e-government to deliver the anticipated impacts on the economy, and technological and social development. Consequently, this research concept demonstrates that e-government systems is a central value added application for the government to provide better quality and service to the citizens, business and other agencies. The future research work will need to work on cross-sectional country data analysis, large-scale survey research. Another method called Design Science Research (DSR) methodology can also use that focuses on the development of anti-corruption artefacts in order to solve public corruption problems. This study recommends that governments explore the opportunities offered by e-government systems.

CONCLUSION

This chapter presented the potential anti-corruption elements of e-government or internet based inter-organisational information systems in a public organisation. This chapter, discussed e-government principles to minimise the operation costs, real time quality service to the citizens, business, and governments, and enhance transparency and accountability, improve day-to-day government activities, and reduce the risk of miss use of public service. Most importantly, this chapter explored the application of e-government application to fight corruption. The study summarises the literature of e-government as an anti-corruption systems. This chapter discussed the importance of anti-corruption factors, including automation, transparency, accountability, detection in operations, preventive detection, awareness raising, reporting, deterrence, and promoting ethical attitudes and proposed an anti-corruption framework based research. This research work demonstrated that e-government having a central instrument to assist the government and its agencies in the efficient of public resources and ultimately positive and significant effect on reducing corruption in the public sector, which may help for better economic, and social development of all the countries.

REFERENCES

Abu-Shanab, E. A. (2013). *The Relationship between Transparency and E-Government: An Empirical Support.* Paper presented at the Electronic Government and Electronic Participation, Joint Proceedings of Ongoing Research of IFIP EGOV and IFIP ePart 2013EGOV/ePart Ongoing Research, Koblenz, Germany.

Abu–Shanab, E. A., Harb, Y. A., & Al–Zoubi, S. Y. (2013). E–government as an anti–corruption tool: Citizens perceptions. *International Journal of Electronic Governance*, *6*(3), 232–248. doi:10.1504/IJEG.2013.058410

Adamu, H., Shatimah, A., & Aliyu, M. (2016). Role of Information and Communication Technology as a Means of Tackling Corruption in Nigeria. *International Journal of Innovative Research and Creative Technology*, *1*(5), 478–480.

Ae Chun, S., Luna-Reyes, L. F., Sandoval-Almazán, R., Carlo Bertot, J., Jaeger, P. T., & Grimes, J. M. (2012). Promoting transparency and accountability through ICTs, social media, and collaborative e-government. *Transforming Government: People,Process and Policy*, *6*(1), 78–91.

Ahn, M. J., & Bretschneider, S. (2011). Politics of E-Government: E-Government and the Political Control of Bureaucracy. *Public Administration Review*, *71*(3), 414–424. doi:10.1111/j.1540-6210.2011.02225.x

Aladwani, A. M. (2016). Corruption as a source of e-Government projects failure in developing countries: A theoretical exposition. *International Journal of Information Management*, *36*(1), 105–112. doi:10.1016/j.ijinfomgt.2015.10.005

Angelov, S., & Grefen, P. (2008). An e-contracting reference architecture. *Journal of Systems and Software*, *81*(11), 1816–1844. doi:10.1016/j.jss.2008.02.023

Arpit, B. (2012). E-Government and Social Media as Openness and Anti-Corruption Strategy. *Research Journal of Management Sciences*, *1*(1), 48–52.

Asgarkhani, M. (2005). Digital government and its effectiveness in public management reform: A local government perspective. *Public Management Review*, *7*(3), 465–487. doi:10.1080/14719030500181227

Azmi, K. S. A., & Rahman, A. A. L. A. (2015). E-Procurement: A Tool to Mitigate Public Procurement Fraud in Malaysia? *The Electronic Journal of E-Government*, *13*(2), 150-160.

Bertot, J. C., Jaeger, P. T., & Grimes, J. M. (2010). Using ICTs to create a culture of transparency: E-government and social media as openness and anti-corruption tools for societies. *Government Information Quarterly*, *27*(3), 264–271. doi:10.1016/j.giq.2010.03.001

Betts, M., Black, P., Christensen, S. A., Dawson, E., Du, R., Duncan, W., & Nieto, G. et al. (2010). Towards secure and legal e-tendering. *Journal of Information Technology in Construction*, *11*, 89–102.

Beynon-Davies, P. (2005). Constructing electronic government: The case of the UK inland revenue. *International Journal of Information Management*, *25*(1), 3–20. doi:10.1016/j.ijinfomgt.2004.08.002

Bhatnagar, S. C., & Singh, N. (2010). Assessing the Impact of E-government: A Study of Projects in India. *Information Technologies & International Development*, *6*(2), 109–127.

Bhuiyan, S. H. (2011). Modernizing Bangladesh public administration through e-governance: Benefits and challenges. *Government Information Quarterly*, *28*(1), 54–65. doi:10.1016/j.giq.2010.04.006

Block, C., & Neumann, D. (2008). A decision support system for choosing market mechanisms in e-procurement. *Negotiation, Auctions, and Market Engineering*, *2*, 44–57. doi:10.1007/978-3-540-77554-6_3

Boer, L., Harink, J., & Heijboer, G. (2001). *A model for assessing the impact of electronic procurement forms*. In *10th International Annual IPSERA Conference*, Jönköping, Sweden.

Bruno, G., Esposito, E., Mastroianni, M., & Vellutino, D. (2005). Analysis of public e-procurement web site accessibility. *Journal of Public Procurement*, *5*(3), 344.

Carter, C. R., Kaufmann, L., Beall, S., Carter, P. L., Hendrick, T. E., & Petersen, K. J. (2004). Reverse auctionsgrounded theory from the buyer and supplier perspective. *Transportation Research Part E, Logistics and Transportation Review*, *40*(3), 229–254. doi:10.1016/j.tre.2003.08.004

Croom, S. R., & Brandon-Jones, A. (2005). Key issues in e-procurement: Procurement implementation and operation in the public sector. *Journal of Public Procurement*, *5*(3), 367–387.

Davila, A., Gupta, M., & Palmer, R. (2003). Moving Procurement Systems to the Internet: The Adoption and Use of E-Procurement Technology Models. *European Management Journal*, *21*(1), 11–23. doi:10.1016/S0263-2373(02)00155-X

De Boer, L., Harink, J., & Heijboer, G. (2002). A conceptual model for assessing the impact of electronic procurement. *European Journal of Purchasing & Supply Management*, *8*(1), 25–33. doi:10.1016/S0969-7012(01)00015-6

Dwivedi, Y. K., Weerakkody, V., & Janssen, M. (2012). Moving towards maturity: Challenges to successful e-government implementation and diffusion. *ACM SIGMIS Database*, *42*(4), 11–22. doi:10.1145/2096140.2096142

Eakin, D. (2003). Measuring e-procurement benefits. Summit: Canada's Magazine on Public Sector Purchasing.

Elbahnasawy, N. G. (2014). E-government, internet adoption, and corruption: An empirical investigation. *World Development*, *57*, 114–126. doi:10.1016/j.worlddev.2013.12.005

Essig, M., & Arnold, U. (2001). Electronic procurement in supply chain management: An information economics based analysis of electronic markets. *Journal of Supply Chain Management*, *37*(4), 43–49. doi:10.1111/j.1745-493X.2001.tb00112.x

Fink, D. (2006). Value decomposition of e-commerce performance. *Benchmarking: An International Journal*, *13*(1/2), 81–92. doi:10.1108/14635770610644592

Fuks, K., Kawa, A., & Wieczerzycki, W. (2009). *Improved e-sourcing strategy with multi-agent swarms.* Paper presented at the Computational Intelligence for Modelling Control and Automation International Conference, Vienna, Austria.

Furuholt, B., & Wahid, F. (2008). *E-government Challenges and the Role of Political Leadership in Indonesia: the Case of Sragen.* Paper presented at the Hawaii International Conference on System Sciences. doi:10.1109/HICSS.2008.134

Gichoya, D. (2005). Factors affecting the successful implementation of ICT projects in government. *The Electronic Journal of E-Government, 3*(4), 175-184.

Gil-García, J. R., & Pardo, T. A. (2005). E-government success factors: Mapping practical tools to theoretical foundations. *Government Information Quarterly, 22*(2), 187–216. doi:10.1016/j.giq.2005.02.001

Grönlund, Å. (2010). Using ICT to combat corruption - tools, methods and results. In C. Strand (Ed.), *Increasing transparency and fighting corruption through ICT-empowering people and communities* (pp. 7–27). SPIDER - The Swedish Program for ICT in Developing Regions.

Gunasekaran, A., McGaughey, R. E., Ngai, E. W. T., & Rai, B. K. (2009). E-Procurement adoption in the Southcoast SMEs. *International Journal of Production Economics, 122*(1), 161–175. doi:10.1016/j.ijpe.2009.05.013

Harink, J. H. A. (2003). *Internet technology to purchase* (PhD Thesis). University of Twente, Netherland.

Imran, A., & Gregor, S. (2010). Uncovering the Hidden issues in e-Government adoption in a least Developed Country: The Case of Bangladesh. *Journal of Global Information Management, 18*(2), 30–56. doi:10.4018/jgim.2010040102

Joongi, K. (2006). *National Integrity Systems:Transparency International Country Study Report: Republic of Korea.* Transparency International Secretariat Alt Moabit 96, 10559. Retrieved from http://www.transparency.org

Karv, J. (2015). *E-Government and its ability to reduce corruption-The case of Estonia* (Master Thesis). Lund University, Lund, Sweden.

Ke, W., & Wei, K. K. (2004). Successful e-government in Singapore. *Communications of the ACM, 47*(6), 95–99. doi:10.1145/990680.990687

Kifle, H., & Low Kim Cheng, P. (2009). E-government Implementation and Leadership: The Brunei Case Study. *Electronic. Journal of E-Government, 7*(3), 271–282.

Kim, C.-K. (2014). Anti-corruption initiatives and e-government: A cross-national study. *Public Organization Review, 14*(3), 385–396. doi:10.1007/s11115-013-0223-1

Kim, S., Kim, H. J., & Lee, H. (2009). An institutional analysis of an e-government system for anti-corruption: The case of OPEN. *Government Information Quarterly, 26*(1), 42–50. doi:10.1016/j.giq.2008.09.002

Knudsen, D. (2003). Aligning corporate strategy, procurement strategy and e-procurement tools. *International Journal of Physical Distribution & Logistics Management, 33*(8), 720–734. doi:10.1108/09600030310502894

Krishnan, S., Teo, T. S., & Lim, V. K. (2013). Examining the relationships among e-government maturity, corruption, economic prosperity and environmental degradation: A cross-country analysis. *Information & Management, 50*(8), 638–649. doi:10.1016/j.im.2013.07.003

Lee, C., & Huang, T.-y. (2014). *E-government Use and Citizen Empowerment: Examining the effects of online information on political efficacy*. Academic Press.

Leipold, K., Klemow, J., Holloway, F., & Vaidya, K. (2004). The World Bank e-procurement for the selection of consultants: Challenges and lessons learned. *Journal of Public Procurement, 4*, 319–339.

Linders, D., & Wilson, S. C. (2011). What is open government?: one year after the directive.*Proceedings of the 12th Annual International Digital Government Research Conference: Digital Government Innovation in Challenging Times.* doi:10.1145/2037556.2037599

Luk, S. C. Y. (2009). The impact of leadership and stakeholders on the success/failure of e-government service: Using the case study of e-stamping service in Hong Kong. *Government Information Quarterly, 26*(4), 594–604. doi:10.1016/j.giq.2009.02.009

Lupu, D., & Lazăr, C. G. (2015). Influence of e-government on the Level of Corruption in some EU and Non-EU States. *Procedia Economics and Finance, 20*, 365–371. doi:10.1016/S2212-5671(15)00085-4

Macintosh, A. (2004). Characterizing e-participation in policy-making.*Proceedings of the 37th Annual Hawaii International Conference on.*

Mahmood, S. A. I. (2010). Public procurement and corruption in Bangladesh confronting the challenges and opportunities. *Journal of Public Administration and Policy Research, 2*(6), 103-111.

McLinden, G., & Durrani, A. Z. (2013). Corruption in Customs. *World Customs Journal, 7*(2), 3–10.

Mistry, J. J., & Jalal, A. (2012). An empirical analysis of the relationship between e-government and corruption. *The International Journal of Digital Accounting Research, 12*(18), 145-176.

Mohammad, H., Almarabeh, T., & Ali, A. A. (2009). E-government in Jordan. *European Journal of Scientific Research, 35*(2), 188–197.

Neupane, A. (2014). *The potential of public e-procurement technology to reduce corruption in public procurement* (PhD Thesis). University of Southern Queensland, Toowoomba, Australia.

Neupane, A., Soar, J., & Vaidya, K. (2012). Evaluating the anti-corruption capabilities of public e-procurement in a developing country. *The Electronic Journal on Information System in Developing Countries*, *55*(2), 1–17.

Neupane, A., Soar, J., & Vaidya, K. (2014). Anti-Corruption Capabilities of Public E-Procurement Technologies: Principal-Agent Theory. In K. J. Bwalya (Ed.), *Technology Development and Platform Enhancements for Successfull Global E-government Design.* IGI Global. doi:10.4018/978-1-4666-4900-2.ch010

Neupane, A., Soar, J., Vaidya, K., & Aryal, S. (2014). The potential for ICT tools to promote public participation in fighting corruption. In C. M. Akrivopoulou & N. Garipidis (Eds.), Human Rights and the Impact of ICT in the Public Sphere. Hershey, PA: Information Science Reference, IGI Global. doi:10.4018/978-1-4666-6248-3.ch010

Neupane, A., Soar, J., Vaidya, K., & Yong, J. (2012). Role of public e-procurement technology to reduce corruption in government procurement. *Proceedings of the 5th International Public Procurement Conference (IPPC5).*

Neupane, A., Soar, J., Vaidya, K., & Yong, J. (2014). Willingness to adopt e-procurement to reduce corruption: Results of the PLS Path modeling. *Transforming Government: People,Process and Policy*, *8*(4), 500–520.

Ojha, A., Palvia, S., & Gupta, M. (2008). A model for impact of e-government on corruption: Exploring theoretical foundations. In J. Bhattacharya (Ed.), *Critical thinking in e-governance* (pp. 160–170). New Delhi: Gift Publishing.

Olken, B. A., & Pande, R. (2011). Corruption in developing countries. *Annual Review of Economics. Annual Reviews*, *4*(1), 479–509.

Phang, C. W., & Kankanhalli, A. (2008). A framework of ICT exploitation for e-participation initiatives. *Communications of the ACM*, *51*(12), 128–132. doi:10.1145/1409360.1409385

Rahman, H., & Ramos, I. (2013). Technology Development and Platform Enhancements for Successful Global E-Government Design. In K. J. Bwalys (Ed.), Stages of E-Government Maturity Models: Emergence of E-Governance at the Grass Roots (p. 228). Academic Press.

Reunis, M. R. B., Santema, S. C., & Harink, J. H. A. (2006). Increasing e-ordering adoption: A case study. *Journal of Purchasing and Supply Management*, *12*(6), 322–331. doi:10.1016/j.pursup.2007.01.006

Salin, A. S. A. P., & Abidin, Z. Z. (2011). *Information and communication technologies and local governance trend: A case study of a smart city in Malaysia*. Paper presented at the 2010 International Conference on Business and Economics Research, Kuala Lumpur, Malaysia.

Saxena, K. (2005). Towards excellence in e-governance. *International Journal of Public Sector Management*, *18*(6), 498–513. doi:10.1108/09513550510616733

Shakya, R. K. (2012). *Procurement governance framework: Success to e-government procurement (E-GP) system implementation*. Retrieved from http://woppaa.org/wp-content/uploads/2012/09/PAPER-II.16-PROCUREMENT-GOVERNANCE-FRAMEWORK.pdf

Shrivastava, U., & Bhattacherjee, A. (2015). ICT as a corruption deterrent: a research note.*Proceedings of the Seventh International Conference on Information and Communication Technologies and Development*. doi:10.1145/2737856.2737864

Teich, J., Wallenius, H., & Wallenius, J. (1999). Multiple-issue auction and market algorithms for the world wide web. *Decision Support Systems*, *26*(1), 49–66. doi:10.1016/S0167-9236(99)00016-0

Uthayasankar, S. (2014). *Exploring the application of web 2.0 technologies in the context of e-government* (PhD thesis). Brunel University.

Vaidya, K. (2007). *Electronic Procurement in the Australian Public Sector: The Organizational Assimilation Process and Its Impact on Public Procurement Performance*. University of New England.

Vaidya, K., Sajeev, A., & Gao, J. (2005). E-procurement assimilation: an assessment of e-business capabilities and supplier readiness in the Australian public sector.*Proceedings of the 7th international conference on Electronic commerce*. doi:10.1145/1089551.1089630

Weerakkody, V., Irani, Z., Lee, H., Osman, I., & Hindi, N. (2015). E-government implementation: A birds eye view of issues relating to costs, opportunities, benefits and risks. *Information Systems Frontiers*, *17*(4), 889–915. doi:10.1007/s10796-013-9472-3

Xinli, H. (2015). Effectiveness of information technology in reducing corruption in China: A validation of the DeLone and McLean information systems success model. *The Electronic Library*, *33*(1), 52–64. doi:10.1108/EL-11-2012-0148

Yang, J., & Zhang, R. Y. (2009). *The research and analysis of e-procurement for iron and steel enterprises*. Paper presented at the International Conference on Information Management, Innovation Management and Industrial Engineering, Xian, China.

KEY TERMS AND DEFINITIONS

Automation: Automation is one of the key elements to avoid human intervention in government work and services which can be achieved from the implementation of e-government that automate the existing system into digitize system.

Corruption: According to World Bank and Transparency International "corruption is the misuse of the public office for private gain. Corruption is one of the chronic diseases of many governments around the world and ICTs is one of the best option to eliminate.

E-Government: The use of ICTs or other internet based inter-organisational information systems to automate the government systems with goal of increase transparency, accountability, cost reduction, more citizen engagement, enhance more quality work and services. Ultimately, it also helps to reduce corruption.

Ethical Attitudes: E-government helps to more public engagement, online discussion, and awareness of government law and regulations.

Preventive Detection: E-government helps to provide batter monitoring networks and individuals.

Reporting: E-government provides the platform for the public to easily access real time information at a single click. The citizens can analyse the government report and easily take a corrective action if the government is doing wrong. The public can easily report through e-government complaint box.

Transparency: The use of information and communication technologies (ICTs) or internet based any organisational systems to promote more transparency and accountability in government work and services.

Chapter 4
Managing Collaboration in E-Procurement

Robert J. Wright
Capella University, USA

Jacqueline M. Shiner
Norwich University, USA

ABSTRACT

While e-procurement provides efficiency and cost-savings, are governments that are utilizing these systems really getting what they want, particularly when procuring services? While e-procurement provides governments methods to communicate better with service providers and have access to more service providers, do the systems allow for collaboration? As there is a significant amount of research the issues related to procurement in the U.S., this chapter will use it as an example to demonstrate the need to collaborate and not just communicate. For years there has been discussion on the issues and reforms to the U.S. federal procurement process. One of the major issues is communications and collaboration. Goodrich provided in his Federal Times article "6 simple fixed for the federal procurement process." Five of the six areas involve communications and collaboration: poorly conceived documentation; contracting offices and program offices working as a team rather than independent; lengthy procurement decisions; government understands what they bought; and talk with industry. This chapter provides the background of the procurement process, current trends and recent approaches. It explores how the Alpha contracting method could be applied to Contracts by Negotiations / Full and Open procurements. Finally, it provides a Collaborative Government Model which takes a holistic and strategic approach to collaboration. There is a need to approach this collaboration in a strategic manner as it includes facets such as hierarchy, networking, and inter-personal interactions that are not linear in nature.

DOI: 10.4018/978-1-5225-2203-4.ch004

INTRODUCTION

Regardless of which country you are in, a significant amount of the governments' budgets are procurement-based for goods and services. As a large cost-driver, realizing efficiency and cost-savings has become a priority and as a result, federal and local governments all over the world are moving to E-procurement systems. (Cabras, 2010, p. 1134). Cabras (2010) states that "E-procurement is seen as a powerful means of achieving efficiency and 'has an indirect effect on cash savings by providing the access to good deals." (p. 1134). Takach (2008) describes E-procurement as "the process by which governments save costs and increase ease of use by uploading paper-based forms onto a website, so the public can download them." (p. 16). Most systems also include the ability for the supplier to create an account to track opportunities. (Takach, 2008, p.16). The result is "easier and cheaper bidding" as there are more participants responding to the bid requests creating greater competition. (Takach, 2008, p.16).

Purchasing of commodities is straight-forward as the government is able to clearly define their requirements. Services are not as easy to procure as governments may not be able to clearly define what it is that they require. Simply communicating the requirement out to suppliers may not be enough. Merriam-Webster (n.d.). defines communicate as "to give information about (something) to someone" or "to get someone to understand your thoughts or feelings." Which is what the E-procurement system is doing successfully with the purchasing of goods. The definition for collaborate is "to work with another person or group in order to achieve or so something" (Merriam-Webster, n.d.). Unfortunately, most E-procurement systems are one-way systems where information is communicated from the government to the supplier and supplier back to government. When procuring services, governments need to collaborate more than communicate. There are some systems that have "social media" type systems arrangements where there is more "real-time" collaboration but collaboration also has its own "issues." what is the implication here.

Today's public managers engage in collaborations in order to address complex problems and/or to carry out the mission of their organization in a more effective manner. This imperative compels such public officials to venture beyond their traditional hierarchical operating arrangement and work with other, like-minded individuals as it concerns a particular governmental service domain (Frederickson, 1999; Agranoff, 2004; Goldsmith & Eggers, 2004; Meeks et al, 2006; Campbell, 2012; Shakya, 2015). Importantly, these other individuals are not under each other's control as they work together in a shared-power environment with the aim of mitigating a problem or delivering a complex service.

But what transpires when these individuals engage in a collaboration? Do we find that the hierarchical structure drives the nature of the collaborative operating environment or does the network that binds the "like-minded" participants provide the core direction in terms of eventual actions and outcomes? In turn, insights in terms of these important queries can be explored as it relates to the complex operating environment associated with the government procurement function. Implicitly, the manner in which collaboration emerges within the E-procurement function calls for a consideration upon those facets inherent in a more strategic, holistic management framework in which complexity is the norm.

For years there has been discussion on the issues and reforms to the federal procurement process. In 2003, Congress passed the Service Acquisition Reform Act which created the Acquisition Advisory Panel which was tasked in reviewing the laws, regulations and government-wide policies on and to make recommendations to the Administrator of the Office of Federal Procurement Policy ("OFPP") (Report of the Acquisition Advisory Panel to the Office of Federal Procurement Policy and the United States Congress, 2007, p. ix.). This report was originally to be submitted at the end of 2003 but was extended until the end of 2006 (Report of the Acquisition Advisory Panel to the Office of Federal Procurement Policy and the United States Congress, 2007, p. ix.). As Goodrich (2015) states that because of this report, "…much has been done to address the 'mechanics of procurement,' but little has been done to address the human aspect of procurement, either on the government or the contractor sides."

Goodrich (2015) identifies six areas that needs to be "fixed." Five of the six areas involve people interactions. The first is "improve requirements" which Goodrich (2015) identifies as the "biggest challenge" in procurement. The government tends to be prescriptive in their procurement requests but provide "poorly conceived documentation" (Goodrich, 2015). Industry are the experts and should be determining how to perform the work based on government requirements and not following prescriptive methods from the government who are not experts (Goodrich, 2015). The second area is that the government needs to demand that the contracting offices work with program offices rather than be an independent organization (Goodrich, 2015). Contracts and programs needs to work as a team. Third is that the procurement decisions are taking too long and the government needs to just "make decisions" (Goodrich, 2015). Fourth is that government needs to understand what they bought (Goodrich, 2015). This goes back to the requirements definition. When the government does develop clear definitions, the contractor will their best to produce what they think the government is asking to procure. Goodrich (2015) states that "we have seen many situations where the government is asking for more, or for something different from what I actually bought." Last is that the government needs to talk with industry and create an environment where the government can get good market data and understood solutions and alternatives (Goodrich, 2015). This paper explores one of the main issues in procurement which is communications and collaboration.

While these issues are U.S. specific, they can also be applied internationally and has been experienced by one of the chapter's author who is a practitioner.

Purpose and Scope

Regardless of which country you are in, procurement procedures tend to be highly regulated. For example, the EU has specific rules for advertising procurement needs, invitations to tender and the awarding of contracts (Cabras, 2010, p. 1135). In the experience of the Author, these procedures tend to be similar regardless of the country. As there is significant documentation available on the U.S. federal government procurement methods, the purpose and overarching concern, then, of this chapter proposal is to review the current U.S. federal government procurement system for one of its weaknesses which is collaboration and provide a holistic model to approach this issue (Literature reference here). Like the E.U., the U.S. has a substantial and complex set of rules governing the federal government's purchasing process called the Federal Acquisition Regulations (FAR) (The U.S. Small Business Administration, SBA.gov, n.d.). The U.S. Federal Government does not use the term "procurement" but uses instead the term "acquisition." The Federal Acquisition Regulations defines the period of acquisition as starting with the requirements definition through final contract deliverable (2.1 C.F.R. § 2.101 [b][2], 2016). To improve understanding of the Government requirements, the Federal Acquisition Regulations encourages exchanging information, not only early in the process but throughout the life of the procurement, with all interested parties which includes "...potential offerors, end users, Government acquisition and supporting personnel, and others involved in the conduct or outcome of the acquisition" (15.2 C.F.R. § 15.201 [a] [b], 2016). Collaborating with this diverse group of interested parties, where capacity and trust are relevant to the success of the procurement, can be considered a compound implementation and face critical challenges.

The scope of this chapter will include an overview of the Contract by Negotiations / Full and Open procurement basics which uses communications as well as Alpha contracting which uses collaboration during the procurement cycle. The authors will explore how the Alpha contracting / sole source procurement method (collaboration) could be applied to Contracts by Negotiations / Full and Open procurements (communications) even with the restrictive procurement procedures where there are multiple potential offerors using collaborative technology. In addition, the authors will present a Collaborative Government Model which takes a holistic and strategic approach to collaboration (See Figure 1). Using this new model and technology may improve the success of the current weakness in collaboration in the area of the E-Procurement system.

Figure 1. Collaborative government model

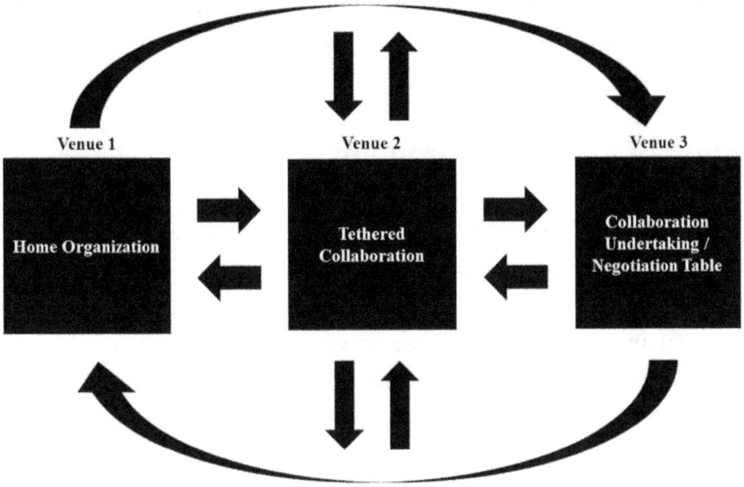

Trends and Recent Approaches

To address the collaboration weakness, the federal government is moving to "Agile Procurement" which is based on the Agile Methodology of program management. What is Agile? It is an alternative to traditional project management and helps teams respond to unpredictability through incremental, iterative work cadences (The Agile Movement, n.d.). The federal government is applying the Agile methodology to procurement. At the National Contract Management Association Government Contract Management Symposium held in December 2015, this was the main focus of the event. Members from different departments including Department of Defense and General Services Administration were on panels and were presenters on the move to using Agile program management methodology in procurement. In one of the presentations, the Agile Values were presented and first on the list of most important items was "individuals and interactions" versus important but not the focus of "processes and tools" (Brantley, 2015). And third on the list of four was most important "customer collaboration" versus important but not the focus of "contract negotiation" (Brantley, 2015). In addition, the presentation states that the focus of Agile procurement is on information and collaboration (Brantley, 2015). This is attributed to the "information revolution" and "knowledge workers" (Brantley, 2015). The program management style "emphasized the importance of customer – project team collaboration" (Brantley, 2015). While it may increase communications and collaboration, there are a diverse group of people that are engaged throughout the procurement process. It includes but is not limited to: contracting; fiscal; legal;

technical personnel; combatant commander or chief of mission, as appropriate; as well as industry counterparts to all. Perhaps a way to improve communications is to employ methods used in the federal government method called Alpha / sole source procurement.

Application of Alpha Procurement

Alpha / sole source procurement process "…involves many activities performed jointly by the Government and contractor teams" (Alpha Contracting, n.d.). This nearly mirrors the definition of collaboration provided earlier. There are many advantages to using Alpha /sole source procurement one of which is improvement of communications which decreases the number of Request for Proposals (RFP) iterations during the proposal phase as well as reduces the number of revisions and rework due to poorly written requirements that lead to misunderstandings, errors, and mistakes during the implementation phase (Alpha Contracting, n.d.). It streamlines and expedites the procurement process and eliminates any unnecessary processes and reviews (Alpha Contracting, n.d.). This process could be modified and used in the Full and Open Procurements with the use of collaboration technology where information is shared and distributed to all simultaneously. As this process requires collaboration it is important to understand the potential difficulties that may be encountered and how to address them.

Explore New Management Approach via Collaboration Model

As discussed above, throughout the procurement process, collaboration is required and involves a diverse group of organizations including public and private entities. There is a need then to approach this collaboration in a strategic manner as it includes facets such as hierarchy, networking, and inter-personal interactions that are not linear in nature. In turn, this service mosaic suggests an approach in which the collaboration, from a strategic management approach, can be aligned with venues of actions by today's public manager. Intrinsic in such a multi-dimensional operating condition assumes varying perspectives, changing time dimension (for action), varied communication streams, and multi-behavioral actions by public manager as driven by particular venue engagement area. Figure 1, the Shiner-Wright Collaborative Government Model, provides a holistic collaboration model to approach this diverse group.

- **Venue 1:** Home organization. Each participant in the procurement collaboration, whether public or private, receives tasks and performance expectations as driven by superior-subordinate relationship as framed by hierarchical operating and rule arrangement. In addition, a return on investment is maintained and articulated from top-down. These "forces" may contradict each other as public and private organizations tend to have disparate motivation factors and define return on investment differently.

- **Venue 2:** *Tethered* operating condition (Wright, 2009). Currently in the Full and Open procurement method, we see that the Public Administrator attempts to mediate the demands of the home organization while addressing the needs of the other participants of the collaboration during the ongoing solution development process. Importantly, we need to consider that as the Public Administrator becomes more entrenched in the activities of the collaboration, he/she will eventually find him/herself *tethered* to the home organization as the various (conflicting/differing) dispositions of the collective are addressed as program (collaboration-driven) action are realized in a mutually satisfactory fashion (Wright, 2009). In turn, the Public Administrator must be mindful of those actions which may place him/her in a condition of job peril as efforts to reconcile the demands and needs of the home organization with those inherent within the emerging collaboration while *tethered* between the two entities and their corresponding operating venues (Wright, 2009).
- **Venue 3:** Collaboration Arena. Again, each participant must work in the collaborative arena as driven by his/her positive inter-personal skills, yet mindful of the demands/challenges inherent in terms of functioning a negotiator with limited organizational resources to expend while balancing the need to realize a take-away from the collaboration that meets or exceeds the return on investment as articulated by his/her supervisor and Overhead Executive (leadership) of the home organization.

This strategic approach from above has been identified as a need as based upon literature as driven by complex problems encountered by today's public agency who must grapple and consider facets of today's complex collaborative undertakings that are accordingly engender (Frederickson, 1999; Agranoff, 2004; Goldsmith & Eggers, 2004; Meeks et al, 2006; Campbell, 2012; Shakya, 2015). This condition and/or assumption applies to today's federal E-Procurement system.

Procurement Basics / Overview

The federal government will procure supplies and services from for-profit organizations and non-profit organizations. Traditionally a Request for Proposal (RFP) or Request for Quote (RFQ) will be used for procurements with for-profit organizations. Request for Proposals (RFPs) are negotiated and are more complex while Request for Quotes (RFQs) are not negotiated as they are "simplified acquisitions" and are under a certain threshold dollar amount established in the Federal Acquisition Regulations (FAR). For non-profit organizations, the government normally uses Request for Acquisition (RFA) or Annual Program Statement (APS) for grants or cooperative agreements. The difference between working with for-profit organizations versus non-profit organizations is that the government exercises a higher level of control over the for-profit organization in obtaining results. For non-profit organizations, the government may use a grant which does not include a substantial involvement from the government as the recipient of the funds will be doing what is inherently their work. The government can also use a cooperative agreement which is similar to for-profit procurements where the government will have more control over the results but not as much as the for-profit organizations. In the for-profit procurements, the government may spell out in great detail how to perform the requirements while the government will provide the non-profit with just their objectives for the program. For-profit organizations do have a procurement method that is similar to the non-profit method and this is known as performance-based contracting method. The government can combine procurement methods. There are procurements where the government will include both a for-profit type procurement and a non-profit type procurement, i.e. a Request for Proposal (RFP) may have a grant component or a Request for Acquisition (RFA) may have a Request for Proposal (RFP) or Request for Quote (RFQ) component.

The largest type of procurement in the U.S. federal government is known as "Contract by Negotiation" specifically "Full and Open" which "…means that all responsible sources are permitted to compete" (2.1 C.F.R. § 2.101 [b][2], 2016). As discussed earlier, over the years there have been issues with the process costing the federal government, contractors as well as tax payers in re-work or major revisions to programs as requirements during the proposal phase are not clearly defined making it difficult for bidders to provide proposals that meet the government requirements. The federal government is purchasing more services than product and as such the procurement process is not as straight-forward as it has been historically (O'Connell, 2012). O'Connell (2012) provided the statement from Roger, president of the Coalition for Government Procurement in 2012, that in the 90's "…maybe 60 to 70 percent of maybe even a little bit higher, were product-based acquisition. Waldron said that as of June 2012 procurement of services makes up 55 to 65 percent of total acquisitions (O'Connell, 2012). Services procurement Request for Proposals (RFP) involves the government to write requirements for what it is they want to purchase. The government has to understand what their requirements are and how to ask for them in a way that the contractor can deliver.

Regardless of the type, these procurements are typically requested, managed and awarded via an electronic system. This does not mean that there is little or no human interaction. The procurement process begins when someone within the government identifies a need. The requiring organization will put together an acquisition team that consists of "all those who will be responsible for significant aspects of the acquisition, such as contracting, fiscal, legal, and technical personnel" (7.1 C.F.R. § 7.104 [a], 2016). This team is not limited to just those in the same department. As the Federal Acquisition Regulation (FAR) states, if the requested goods or services is in a designated area or supporting a diplomatic or consular mission, the combatant commander or chief of missions should also be included (7.1 C.F.R. § 7.104 [a], 2016). In some instances, the requirement may be needed for two or more departments within an agency and can even be more than one agency engaged. All of these government people should be involved with the development of the acquisition. In addition, the government may also reach out to industry for their inputs on the requirements using one or many methods which include: industry to small business conference; public hearings; market research; one-on-one meetings; pre-solicitation notices; draft requests; Request for Information (RFI); pre-solicitation or preproposal conferences; and site visits (15.2 C.F.R. § 15.201 [c], 2016). Based on inputs from all of these sources, a written acquisition plan is developed and needs to have concurrence from the acquisition team. Upon completion of this plan, the planner is responsible for coordinating with the contracting officer as well as the cognizant small business specialist with the procurement strategy and acquires their approval (7.1 C.F.R. § 7.104 [b] [c], 2016). The request is posted to the appropriate system for the for-profit organizations or non-profit organizations to respond. Upon receipt of the proposals, another team of technical and contracts staff will review the responses based on the criteria developed with the acquisition plan and decide who will be awarded the work. As the Contracting Officer issuing the Request for Proposal (RFP) must incorporate all the different stakeholders' interests which may be conflicting, one can understand why there are issues with the federal procurement process.

Scope of Federal / Enabling Legislation

As stated earlier, the Federal Acquisition Regulations (FAR) encourages procurement teams to reach out to industry for their inputs on the requirements, to collaborate with industry. During the pre-proposal period, that is before the Request for Proposal (RFP) is published, the government should reach out to industry for input to identify and resolve concerns regarding the acquisition strategy, including proposed contract type, terms and conditions, and acquisition planning schedules; the feasibility of the requirement, including performance requirements, statements of work, and data requirements; the suitability of the proposal instructions and evaluation criteria, including the approach for assessing past performance information; the availability of reference documents; and any other industry concerns or questions (Federal Acquisition Regulation 15.2 C.F.R. § 15.201 [c], 2016).

Methods recommended by the Federal Acquisition Regulations (FAR) includes: industry to small business conference; public hearings; market research; one-on-one meetings; pre-solicitation notices; draft requests; Request for Information (RFI); pre-solicitation or preproposal conferences; and site visits (15.2 C.F.R. § 15.201 [c], 2016).

Throughout the procurement proposal life cycle, general information and future requirements may be disclosed at any time (Federal Acquisition Regulation 15.2 C.F.R. § 15.201 [f], 2016). However, after the Request for Proposal (RFP) has been released, the contracting officer becomes the only point of contact for industry and only the contracting officer may exchange information with the potential bidders (Federal Acquisition Regulation 15.2 C.F.R. § 15.201 [f], 2016). Should the contracting officer disclose to one or more potential offerors information necessary to respond to the Request for Proposal (RFP), the contracting officer must disclose the information to the public as soon as practicable (Federal Acquisition Regulation 15.2 C.F.R. § 15.201 [f], 2016). This rule is to ensure that no one potential offeror has an unfair advantage over the other offerors (Federal Acquisition Regulation 15.2 C.F.R. § 15.201 [f], 2016). The only time that the information is not shared with all is when the information may reveal the offerors confidential business strategy which is protected under the Federal Acquisition Regulation 3.104 or Subpart 24.2 (Federal Acquisition Regulation 15.2 C.F.R. § 15.201 [f], 2016). While the regulations do not prohibit or restrict communication between the government and industry, the regulations states that it must be one individual, the contracting officer. And yet, with the fear of protest and the desire to ensure that all information is shared equally with all potential bidders, the majority of contracting officers take a strict interpretation of the law and limit their communications with the potential bidders.

The traditional proposal process is as follows. The contracting officer releases the Request for Proposal (RFP) by either one of the electronic systems such as fedbizops.com or e-mail. Upon receipt of the Request for Proposal (RFP), industry reviews the documentation and develops questions they may have on the requirements. There will be a specific date in the Request for Proposal (RFP) for industry to submit questions to the contracting officer. No questions will be accepted by the government after this date. After receipt of the questions, the government reviews all of the submitted questions and answers them. There is a hard submittal date for industry to submit their proposal, as such, while they wait for responses to questions they must continue with their proposal process and make assumptions. The government typically does not provide the date for when they will provide the answers to the questions. There are no communications between the contracting officer and industry during this period. The answers to the questions should be provided with sufficient time for industry to adjust their proposals, however, as the contracting officer needs to ensure that the answers are approved from all of the contributing stakeholders, many times the answers are not provided until just a few days before the bidders must submit their proposals. In these cases, industry may ask for a submittal deadline extension which may or may not be granted. Upon receipt of the answers, there is not another opportunity for bidders to ask clarification questions should the answers be incomplete, conflicting with another requirement, or unclear. As such, the bidders need to interpret what the responses mean and make assumptions in their respective proposals. If during this process, there was more communication or collaboration between the government and industry, the proposal process may not take as long as it does now and the government would potentially get proposals that best meet their requirements. Using collaboration technology tools and the methods used in alpha / sole source procurement where there is true "collaboration" between the government and industry could improve this issue.

Key Concerns

For years, there has been discussion on the issues and reforms to the federal procurement process. In 2003, Congress passed the Service Acquisition Reform Act which created the Acquisition Advisory Panel which was tasked in reviewing the laws, regulations and government-wide policies on and to make recommendations to the Administrator of the Office of Federal Procurement Policy ("OFPP") (Report of the Acquisition Advisory Panel to the Office of Federal Procurement Policy and the United States Congress, 2007, p. ix.). Due to the complexity of federal government procurement, this report was originally to be submitted at the end of 2003 but was extended until the end of 2006 (Report of the Acquisition Advisory Panel to the Office of Federal Procurement Policy and the United States Congress, 2007, p. ix.). The report includes multiple "key themes." The first is that the government needs to ensure effective and appropriate use of commercial practices which includes the need to enhance competition with better requirements definition (Report of the Acquisition Advisory Panel to the Office of Federal Procurement Policy and the United States Congress, 2007, p. 7). Next, the report encourages the government to open competition as commercial organizations do, not to limit the competition but to send to all available potential competitors (Report of the Acquisition Advisory Panel to the Office of Federal Procurement Policy and the United States Congress, 2007, pp. 8-10). Third, the report recommends that the government should adopt more commercial practices such as the use of fixed priced contracts and again mentions using well-defined requirements (Report of the Acquisition Advisory Panel to the Office of Federal Procurement Policy and the United States Congress, 2007, p. 11). According to the report, the government needs to enhance accountability and transparency as procurement is accomplished through the use of interagency contracts (Report of the Acquisition Advisory Panel to the Office of Federal Procurement Policy and the United States Congress, 2007, p. 13). The report also recommends that the government improve small business participation (Report of the Acquisition Advisory Panel to the Office of Federal Procurement Policy and the United States Congress, 2007, p. 22). While some of the issues are straight-forward and can easily be addressed, there is a theme with the majority of the issues and it involves the complexity of government procurement and the underlying problem of collaborating with a wide range of stakeholders. As Goodrich (2015) states this report has caused the government "...to address the 'mechanics of procurement,' but little has been done to address the human aspect of procurement, either on the government or the contractor sides."

Goodrich (2015) identifies six areas that need to be "fixed." Five of the six areas involve people interactions or collaboration. The first is "improve requirements" which Goodrich (2015) identifies as the "biggest challenge" in procurement. The government tends to be prescriptive in their procurement requests but provide "poorly conceived documentation" (Goodrich, 2015). As discussed earlier, the government engages a wide range of people in developing of the requirements for their proposals. This complex collaboration inherently causes issues and makes it difficult to develop clear and concise prescriptive methods on how to perform the work. Rather than have the government spend the time and effort in prescribing how to perform the work, the government should provide what outcome and requirements they expect and allow the industry, who are the experts, to determine how to perform the work based on government requirements (Goodrich, 2015). The second area is that the government needs to demand that the contracting offices work with program offices rather than be an independent organization (Goodrich, 2015). Contracts and programs needs to work as a team. Again, this is a collaboration issue. Often times the programs team develops the requirements without the engagement of the contracts department. When the contracts department reviews the documentation, they tend to make adjustments they see fit and these changes could inherently change the technical requirements. Industry, who is developing a response to the proposal requirements, will follow what is provided in the Request for Proposal (RFP) and if the contracting officer changed a technical requirement, the government may end up with products or services that they do not want. Third is that the procurement decisions are taking too long and the government needs to just "make decisions" (Goodrich, 2015). With all the different people involved in the procurement process, the issues with collaboration and getting all parties to agree is causing the government to take too long to make decisions. Fourth is that government needs to understand what they bought (Goodrich, 2015). Again, this is the issue with collaboration and goes back to the requirements definition. When the government does develop clear definitions, the contractor will do their best to produce what they think the government is asking to procure. Goodrich (2015) states that "we have seen many situations where the government is asking for more, or for something different from what I actually bought." Last, is that the government needs to talk with industry and create an environment where the government can get good market data and understood solutions and alternatives (Goodrich, 2015). While the government already has many entities engaged in the procurement process, to leave industry out of the develop requirements phase adds to the poor requirements definition as they may be asking for something that is not available in the market and/or too expensive to develop.

Procurement collaboration within a for-profit organization can be complicated. According to the Project Management Body of Knowledge [PMBOK] (2013) for-profit organization stakeholders includes: the sponsor, the one who is paying for the program; customer and users; sellers; business partners; organizational groups; functional managers; and other stakeholders such as procurement, financial institutions, and government regulators (A Guide to the Project Management Body of Knowledge., 2013, pp. 32 – 33). In the implementation of public policy, you have all of these, including the sellers in which the work may be outsourced to and can also include inter-agencies, for-profit organizations or non-profit organizations plus you have Congress, executive branch, other governments, other Agencies, pressure groups, political parties, judiciary branch, communications media and individual citizens (Anderson, 2015, p. 247). This is where the politics can cause friction. Power may be shared amongst several or many of these organizations and conflict over value may cause problems (Cline, 2000, p. 552). In the procurement process, as discussed earlier, all of these stakeholders must be engaged and approve the procurement plan. This tends to cause the requirements to be lacking leading to bidders proposing solutions that do not need the government's needs. Cline (2000) offers the solution which is that the individual or agency should build institutions or mechanisms that create a cooperative environment (p. 552). But how does the individual and/or agency do that? The procurement / program has the same requirement that it is the program manager's job to manage the stakeholders' expectations and ensure that the team interacts with the stakeholders in a professional and cooperative manner (A Guide to the Project Management Body of Knowledge., 2013, p. 32). The individual and/or agency could use the Project Management Body of Knowledge [PMBOK] (2013) systematic method of analyzing the stakeholders using quantitative and qualitative methods to identify their relationship to the program as well as communication / influencing methods (A Guide to the Project Management Body of Knowledge., 2013, p. 395). This method would be advantageous to the individual and/or agency to ensure that they have captured all of the stakeholders and understand how to engage them in the implementation of the policy. But it may not resolve the conflict inherent in collaboration.

Again, using the federal procurement problem as an example, Sarantis, Charalabidis, and Askounis (2010) state that stakeholder management is a significant issue and that it must be addressed. (p. 18). As noted earlier, government procurements are unsuccessful because of absence of vision or strategy and poor program management. This may be in part due to lack of stakeholder management. Successful program management, according to Sarantis, Charalabidis, and Askounis (2010) requires bringing in the disparate organizations, cultures and people together to create a harmonious and workable solution (p. 17). The knowledge management system should include stakeholder information which includes the expected role of the stakeholder so that the program can ensure each participant's commitment to the program (Sarantis, Charalabidis, and Askounis, 2010, p. 18). The process provided by the Project Management Body of Knowledge [PMBOK] (2013) would be an ideal method to collect this data.

With the potential of many stakeholders, it is obvious that communication is key to a successful implementation. Cline (2000) states that communications need to have clarity and consistency in form and content (p. 560). Clear and concise communications can lead to a better designed program (Cline, 2000, p. 560). The program should use communications to build trust, increase cooperation, and increase the "right" kind of involvement from the stakeholders (Cline, 2000, p. 560). The Project Management Body of Knowledge [PMBOK] (2013) provides a method to develop a communication management plan where you will take into account: who needs what information and when, where the information should be stored, the format of the information should be stored, how the information will be retrieved and whether time zones, language barriers and cross-cultural considerations needs to be taken into account (A Guide to the Project Management Body of Knowledge., 2013, p. 290). The government is just starting to address this issue of collaboration between the government and industry by implementing Agile procurement. With collaboration technological solutions available today such as wikis, blogs, forums, RSS feeds, opinion polls, community chats and social networking which allows for "for robust real time collaboration at a distance that in many situations can be as effective as traditional face-to-face forms of collaboration" why does the government continue to use the traditional method described above where the communication which is not real time and is limited? (Wahl & Kitchel, 2016, p. 28). While the use of these tools may facilitate real time collaboration, we still encounter the inherent issue that comes with collaborating with so many different stakeholders.

Lessons Learned

On February 4, 2011, Daniel Gordon, then Administrator for Federal Procurement Policy issued a memorandum entitled "'Myth-Busting': Addressing Misconceptions to Improve Communication with Industry during the Acquisition Process" that was issued to chief acquisition officers; senior procurement executives; and chief information officers (Office of Federal Procurement Policy, 2011). The memorandum states:

Some agency officials may be reluctant to engage in these exchanges out of fear of protests or fear of binding the agency in an unauthorized manner; others may be unaware of effective strategies that can help the acquisition workforce and industry make the best use of their time and resources (Office of Federal Procurement Policy, 2011, p. 1).

The memorandum points out that the issue is not just with the government side but with industry as well. It states that some in the industry may be concerned that talking with the government may create a conflict of interest and preclude them from competition on the procurement (Office of Federal Procurement Policy, 2011, p. 1). The memorandum recommends that the procuring agency develops a vendor communication plan which discusses how the agency will "reduce unnecessary barriers, publicize communication opportunities, and prioritize engagement opportunities for high-risk, complex programs or those that fail to attract new vendors during re-competitions" (Office of Federal Procurement Policy, 2011, pp. 2-3). The memorandum provides ten myths or misconceptions about vendor communications and provides the fact including the law or regulation and guidance (Office of Federal Procurement Policy, 2011, pp. 5-11).

Directions / Trends

While this memorandum was written in 2011, limited communications between the government and industry during the proposal phase continues to date. At the National Contract Management Association (NCMA) World Congress 2016 that will take place in July 2016 there will be two sessions dedicated to this topic. The first is titled "Mythbusting—Communication with Industry" with the panelists: Jeffrey Claar, Senior Procurement Analyst, ACC-Orlando; Joseph Giunta, Executive Director/Principal Assistant Responsible for Contracting, Army Contracting Command (ACC) – Orlando; and Lesley Sullivan, Policy Branch Chief, ACC-Orlando. The session description is "Learn how to encourage and enhance communication between government and industry. Hear a variety of methods to actively engage industry early in the communication process in order to benefit from industry's knowledge of available products and technology" (National Contract Management Association (NCMA) World Congress 2016 Breakout Sessions, 2016). The second session is titled "Can We Talk? A Frank and Open Dialogue Between Government and Industry" lead by Millisa Gary, Procurement Ombudsman, General Services Administration with panelists: David Drabkin, Principal, Drabkin and Associates, LLC; Mike Pullen, Director, Strategic Operations, CGI Federal; and Jacqueline Shiner, OSA Proposals LLC. The session description is

Communication is key to successful partnerships and acquisition outcomes. Yet government and industry have not mastered the art of meaningful communication. What does industry need from government to navigate the federal marketplace? How can government leverage partnerships that foster innovation and drive value to government wide customers? Let's examine this lack of communication and the barriers preventing a healthy and productive dialogue between government and industry (National Contract Management Association (NCMA) World Congress 2016 Breakout Sessions, 2016).

While the government continues to address this issue, the problem continues to exist. The solution may not be issuing a memorandum or holding sessions, it requires understanding the fundamental issues with communications with so many parties and how to address these issues. With the advancement of collaboration technologies like wikis, blogs, forums, RSS feeds, opinion polls, community chats and social networking, the government could use methods used in the Alpha / sole source procurement method.

ALPHA / SOLE SOURCE PROCUREMENT

Scope and Definition

"Alpha" procurement or "sole source procurement" is when the federal government sole sources to a specific company.

Quander and Woppert (2010) describes alpha contracting as a collaborative effort to streamline the procurement process from beginning to end. (p. 2). Alpha contracting is also known as Integrated Product Team (IPT) and is a teaming approach "developed to involve a concerted effort among the government's contracting representatives, technical representatives, and contractor personnel" (Quander and Woppert, 2010, p. 2).

Why isn't Alpha contracting always used? There are strict requirements for a project to be sole sourced. The Federal Acquisition Regulations (FAR) refers to this as "Other than Full and Open Competition" (6.3 C.F.R. § 6.300, 2016). This process is limited to procurements that meet one or more of the following criteria: there is only one supplier of the goods or services required by the agency; there is an unusual and compelling urgency for the goods or services; to mobilize industry for engineering, development, research capability expert services; an international agreement; the goods or services are authorized or required by a statute; the goods or services are required for national security; or it is in the public interest (Federal Acquisition Regulation 6.3 C.F.R. § 6.302, 2016). To use alpha contracting, a justification must be created and the contracting officer must certify to the accuracy and completeness of the justification as such this type of procurement is not frequently used (Federal Acquisition Regulation 6.3 C.F.R. § 6.302, 2016).

Alpha contracting goals are to enhance communications reduce costs and procurement time, and improve the acquisition process without sacrificing contract objectives and requirements (Quander & Woppert, 2010, p. 2). These goals are very similar to the Agile Program Management methodology in which the federal government is planning on using for the Full and Open procurement as discussed earlier. Unlike the Full and Open procurement methodology described above, Alpha contracting is not restricted in the communications as there is only one offeror. The procurement process, starting with the development of the Request for Proposal (RFP) engages the offeror with the government to ensure that the requirements are written satisfactory to both parties. The process continues the same as described for the full and open process but unlike that process, questions may be asked at any time and there is an open dialog between the offeror and government. Agile procurement could take a similar approach to the procurement process that Alpha contracting does. As the government has not yet implemented the Agile procurement method, we have used than Alpha procurement method which has a proven successful track record and available documentation as the model for improvement of collaboration. Again, the use of collaboration technology allows the government more "flexibility" in communications with industry. This however, does not resolve the inherent issues with collaboration as we have discussed earlier in the Collaboration model section.

Implementation of a Collaboration Model

As stated earlier, with the advancement of collaboration technology, government could use technical solutions available today that provide robust real time collaboration and work with industry as they do in the Alpha contracting procurement process. While this may not resolve all of the collaboration issues, it would remove a portion of the issues. To use the words from Goodrich (2015) this would at least address the "mechanics of procurement." This still does not resolve the human aspect of procurement, either on the government or the contractor sides (Goodrich, 2015).

SHINER-WRIGHT COLLABORATION MODEL

- **Venue 1-Home Organization:** The Alpha procurement approach is characterized as a collaborative undertaking as driven by its Integrated Product Team (IPT) framework (Quander &Woppert, 2010, p. 2). However, we find that each participant in the procurement collaboration, whether public or private, receives tasks and performance expectations as driven by superior-subordinate relationship as framed by hierarchical operating and rule arrangements of their home organization. Thus, insofar the premise of Alpha procurement is to improve the federal procurement requirements per procurement, participants must grapple with the various demands of their overhead executives while they attempt to anticipate the challenges inherent in terms of developing and maintaining a collaborative undertaking from both the immediate and long-term vantage.

  Attention will turn to notions such as aligning the demands of their home organization with the reality of engaging in a collaborative undertaking in which resources may be scarce and individual dispositions may not emerge as necessarily cooperative in nature. This concern emerges as key when the initial planning actions revolve around the justification for a sole source procurement approach. Respective organizational imperatives can involve, for instance, challenges relating to "how" a return on investment will be captured from their involvement in the IPT. Pressures can manifest in diverse fashions as each participant defines their involvement in a dynamic development effort that involves multiple perspectives of command and control.
- **Venue 2-Tethered Collaboration (Wright, 2009):** Within this venue the Public Manager and Industry member must communicate the emerging needs and expectations of the collaboration to the upper management of the home organization. The core needs associated with Alpha contracting involves areas concerning how contracting and program offices partner as well as to the degree to which the federal procurement officials consult industry for solution development purposes per eligible procurement. This iterative solution development effort calls for the Public Manager and Industry member to engage program (collaboration-driven) action while he/she is tethered to the home organization (Wright, 2009). This duality compels today's Public Manager and Industry member to be mindful of those actions which may place him/her in a decision making posture that can transpire into conditions of (job) peril (Wright, 2009).

  The nature of this peril needs to be mitigated by the Public Manager and Industry member while fostering harmony within the collaboration as based upon workable solutions associated with the particular procurement (Sarantis,

Charalabidis, and Askounis, 2010, pp. 17-18). The knowledge management system centers, moreover, around the expected role of the stakeholder so that the program can ensure each participant's commitment to the program (Sarantis, Charalabidis, and Askounis, 2010, p. 18). The participants of Alpha contracting have the advantage in that communications can be engaged as there is only one offeror; this condition can help to inculcate a robust knowledge management system. This robust system is closely related to a justification for the eligible procurement a based upon the capacity of the contracting officer to certify the accuracy and completeness of the justification as such this type of procurement is not frequently used (Federal Acquisition Regulation 6.3 C.F.R. § 6.302, 2016).

- **Venue 3-Collaboration Undertaking:** Each participant must work in the collaborative arena as enabled by his/her positive inter-personal skills. Such individuals must be mindful of the challenges inherent in terms of functioning as a productive negotiator within the confines of the collaborative undertaking. The aim, then, of the Alpha procurement approach can be construed as rendering timely decisions per procurement as based upon improved knowledge of what is procured through effective consults with the associated, involved industry. Accordingly, clear and concise communications can lead to a better designed procurement program scope (Cline, 2000, p. 560). An appropriate program scope, as driven by the Alpha procurement requirements, should build trust, increase cooperation, and increase the "right" kind of involvement from the stakeholders from an information management vantage (Cline 2000, p. 560).

  In turn, the Alpha procurement scope starts with the development of the Request for Proposal (RFP) so as to actively engage industry with the government in order to ensure that the requirements are written in accordance with the needs of both parties. These activities are undertaking to realize the Alpha contracting goals. These goals aim to enhance communications, reduce costs and procurement time, and improve the acquisition process without sacrificing contract objectives and requirements (Quander & Woppert, 2010, p. 2).

DISCUSSION

While Alpha / sole source contracting has been successful and in most instances meets the goals to enhance communications, reduces costs and procurement time, and improves the acquisition process without sacrificing contract objectives and requirements, using this method for full and open procurement will not "fix" all the issues of communications in these collaborative teams. With full and open, there will not be just one bidder but could be as few as three and as many 30. As we add each additional member of the IPT, the collaboration issues as defined in our model compounds. In order to work with all the IPT members, the goal of reducing cost and procurement time is in jeopardy. The government used a method very similar to what we have discussed here for the General Services Administration procurement "One Acquisition Solution for Integrated Services (OASIS)." General Services Administration used nearly all the options available to include: public hearings; market research; one-on-one meetings; pre-solicitation notices; draft requests; Request for Information (RFI); pre-solicitation and preproposal conferences as well used a government developed collaboration tool (Interact) where questions and answers were posted. The draft Request for Proposal (RFP) was released to industry for comment in March 2013, the Request for Proposal in August 2013 and awarded in May 2014. There were 74 large businesses and 123 small business firms awarded contracts. Some in the industry may feel that this procurement time was long and costly. Others may feel that the process was inclusive and satisfactory. Was the length of time for the procurement due to the volume of bidders or did the collaboration "issue" also play a role?

CONCLUSION AND RECOMMENDATIONS

Collaboration transpires through a variety of communication channels while mediating complex, ever-changing operating ecologies that are driven by a diverse set of personalities. These ecologies can be influenced by: 1) one's home organization; 2) the transitional space in which the participants of the collaboration must reconcile the often unrelenting oversight of their home organization while attempting to develop key (formal/informal), partnering arrangements within the emerging collaboration; and 3) the "area" in which the collaboration is developed, planned, and codified. The participants who ultimately are organizationally tasked with the responsibility to accrue benefits from a collaborative undertaken must quickly become experts managing developmental activities in these three venues.

These venues can be construed as a framework for collaboration that is not necessarily linear in nature, nor is it driven entirely by the traditional hierarchical reporting arrangements, yet reflects a dependence upon linear activity as well as recognition of the needs that are vital to one's home organization as manifested in the traditional superior-subordinate reporting structure. So, then, how does this multi-dimensional system of collaboration imply for the conduct of today's Public Administration?

Simply put, if those public, private, and/or non-profit organizations who partake in a collaborative undertaking do not recognize that a set of formal as well as infor-

Figure 2. Collaboration cycle

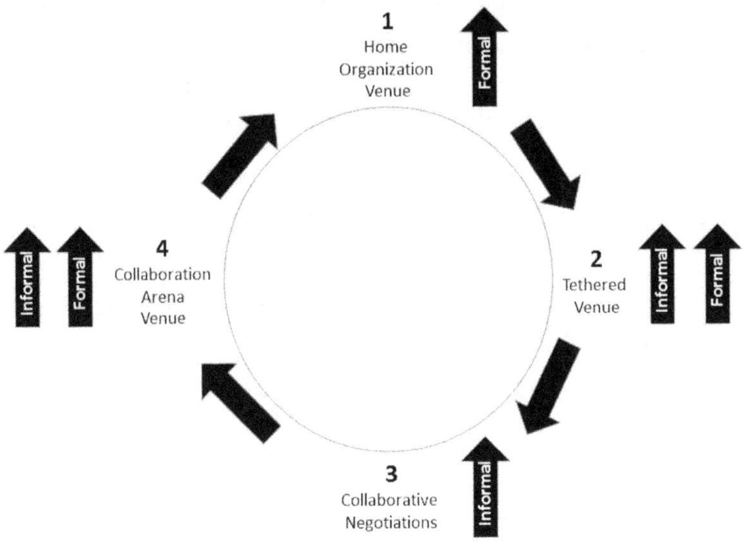

mal actions need to occur in a methodical, purposive manner, then the outcomes of this shared-power realm will not meet the real or perceived expectations of its participants as rooted in the needs of their respective home organization. The nature of this overall charge is reflected in a Collaboration Cycle (see Figure 2).

In terms of this cycle, we can find that the collective actions that emerge intrinsic to the three Collaboration Venues are mediated by informal as well formal interactions. Such actions enable the collaborative entities to solve problems and attain momentum in order to implement a business vision that can become fickle in relations to its operating ecology. In this sense, we see that these operating imperatives are consistent in terms of those collaborative activities undertaken in relation to Alpha Procurement as manifested in the actions of its IPT.

Alpha Procurement highlights the import of the activities intrinsic to the three venues of the Shiner-Wright Model as driven by the Collaboration Cycle. In this sense, the government can "fix" the modes and frequency of communications with industry but that does not necessarily resolve the issues encountered during the procurement process as discussed earlier. Government and industry needs to be cognizant of the collaboration issues as identified in this chapter and develop a total solution.

When we move to an E-procurement system, we lose some of the human interaction. This condition requires industry and government to remain aware of the complexities engendered by the nature of the collaboration linked to the various E-procurement systems that are either emerging or existing both on the domestic as well as international fronts. E-procurement must then be approached, from a public management vantage that takes into account the multi-dimensional nature of today's collaboration that operates along multiple planes of interactions as manifested in both hierarchical and non-hierarchical functional arrangements. In essence, the nature of this operating ecology can be considered from the tethering framework as prescribed by the Shiner / Wright Collaboration Model.

REFERENCES

A Guide to the Project Management Body of Knowledge. (2013). Newton Square, PA: Program Management Institute.

Acquisition Systems. (n.d.). Retrieved from: https://www.acquisition.gov/?q=Acquisition_Systems

Agranoff, R. (2003). *Leveraging Networks: A Guide for Public Managers Working Across Organizations*. Bloomington, IN: Indiana University, School of Public and Environmental Affairs.

Agranoff, R. (2004). Another look at bargaining and negotiating in intergovernmental management. Journal of Public Administration: Research and Theory, 14(4), 495–512. doi:10.1093/jopart/muh033 doi:10.1093/jopart/muh033

Al-Hakim, L., Abdullah, N. A. H. N., & Ng, E. A. H. N. (2012). The Effect of Inter-Organization Trust and Dependency on E-Procurement Adoption: A Case of Malaysian Manufacturers. Journal of Electronic Commerce in Organizations, 10(2), 40–60. doi:10.4018/jeco.2012040103 doi:10.4018/jeco.2012040103

Anderson, J. E. (2015). Public Policymaking. Stamford, CT: Cengage Learning.

Brantley, W. (2015, December). Agile Project Management for Improved Contract Development and Execution. In *Government Contract Management Symposium*. Symposium conducted at the meeting of National Contract Management Association, Washington, D.C.

Cabras, I. (2010). Use of E-procurement in Local Authorities Purchasing and Its Effects on Local Economies: Evidence from Cumbria, UK. European Planning Studies, 18(7), 1133–1151. doi:10.1080/09654311003744209 doi:10.1080/09654311003744209

Campbell, D. (2012). Public managers in integrated services collaboratives: What works is workarounds. Public Administration Review, 72(5), 721–730. doi:10.1111/j.1540-6210.2012.02545.x doi:10.1111/j.1540-6210.2012.02545.x

Cline, K. D. (2000). Defining the implementation problem: Organizational management versus cooperation. Journal of Public Administration: Research and Theory, 10(3), 551–571. doi:10.1093/oxfordjournals.jpart.a024281 doi:10.1093/oxfordjournals.jpart.a024281

Collaborate. (n.d.). In *Merriam-Webster Dictionary*. Retrieved September 04, 2016, from http://www.merriam-webster.com/dictionary/collaborate

Communicate. (n.d.). In *Merriam-Webster Dictionary*. Retrieved September 04, 2016, from http://www.merriam-webster.com/dictionary/communicate

Contracting, A. (n.d.). *Defense Acquisition University (DAU) Acquisition Community Connection*. Retrieved from: https://acc.dau.mil/CommunityBrowser.aspx?id=24962

Dillard, M., Jr. (2014, November). Applying Agile Methodology to Acquisition and Contracting Support. In *Government Contract Management Symposium*. Symposium conducted at the meeting of National Contract Management Association, Washington, DC.

Federal Acquisition Regulation. 2.1 C.F.R. § 2.101 (b)(2) (2016). Retrieved from: https://www.acquisition.gov/?q=browsefar

Federal Acquisition Regulation. 6.3 C.F.R. § 6.300. (2016). Retrieved from: https://www.acquisition.gov/?q=browsefar

Federal Acquisition Regulation. 7.1 C.F.R. § 7.104 [a]. (2016). Retrieved from: https://www.acquisition.gov/?q=browsefar

Federal Acquisition Regulation. 15.2 C.F.R. § 15.201. (2016). Retrieved from: https://www.acquisition.gov/?q=browsefar

Federal Acquisition Regulations (FAR), The U.S. Small Business Administration, SBA. gov. (n.d.). Retrieved from: https://www.sba.gov/content/federal-acquisition-regulations-far

Frederickson, H. (1999). The repositioning of American public administration. *PS Political Science & Politics*, *32*(4), 701–711. doi:10.1017/S1049096500056547

Golden, W., Hughes, M., & Scott, M. (2003). Implementing E-Government in Ireland: A Roadmap for Success. *Journal of Electronic Commerce in Organizations*, *1*(4), 17–33. doi:10.4018/jeco.2003100102

Goldsmith, S., & Eggers, W. (2004). *Governing by network*. Washington, DC: Brookings Institution Press.

Goodrich, S. (2015, February). 6 simple fixed for the federal procurement process. Federal Times. Retrieved from: http://www.federaltimes.com/story/government/acquisition/blog/2015/02/20/procurement-fix-legislation-rule/23754523/

Meek, J., Schildt, K., & Witt, M. (2006). *Local government administration in a metropolitan context*. University of LaVerne.

National Contract Management Association (NCMA) World Congress 2016 Break-out Sessions. (2016, July). Retrieved from: http://www.ncmahq.org/wc16/speakers/sessions

O'Connell, M. (2012, June). Services Acquisition Reform Act (2003). Federal News Radio. Retrieved from: http://federalnewsradio.com/acquisition/2012/06/services-acquisition-reform-act-2003/

Office of Federal Procurement Policy. (2011, February 2). "Myth-Busting": Addressing Misconceptions to Improve Communication with Industry during the Acquisition Process. Memorandum for Chief Acquisition Officers; Senior Procurement Executives; Chief Information Officers. Washington, DC: Daniel I. Gordon, Administrator for Federal Procurement Policy, Author.

Quander, A. Y., & Woppert, J. N. (2010, September). Analysis of Alpha Contracting from Three Perspectives: Government Contracting, the Government Program Office, and Industry. Retrieved from Defense Acquisition University (DAU) Acquisition Community Connection: https://acc.dau.mil/CommunityBrowser.aspx?id=417098

Report of the Acquisition Advisory Panel to the Office of Federal Procurement Policy and the United States Congress. (2007, January). Retrieved from: http://www.ndia.org/Advocacy/AcquisitionReformInitiative/Documents/4-24102_GSA.pdf

Sarantis, D., Charalabidis, Y., & Askounis, D. (2010). A goal-driven management approach based on knowledge exploitation for e-government programs. International Journal of Electronic Government Research, 6(3), 14–30. doi:10.4018/jegr.2010070102

Chapter 5
Digital Transformation in the Public Sector: Electronic Procurement in Portugal

Isabel da Rosa
Universidade de Lisboa, Portugal

João de Almeida
Independent Researcher, Portugal

ABSTRACT

Digital transformation in the public sector is an inevitable requirement for governments due to the growing complexity and interconnections of information systems, and to the demands of citizens, who are becoming better informed and are increasingly looking to more agile and innovative services. However, despite the willingness of many governments and public institutions, the results do not always tally with the original objectives. In the case of public procurement in Portugal, it could be said that digital transformation experience had an unexpected success in the European context, through a business model that is still quite unique in Europe. This result is much owed to the strong political determination, the experience gained from pilot projects, and to the involvement of many stakeholders, who contributed, in a consistent and innovative way, to the definition of the system. The system is not perfect: there are many challenges that need to be addressed in the coming years. Yet, it has enabled the Portuguese public administration to significantly grow in the digital era, so that today the State has a database containing structure information about public procurement, which is a unique case in many countries.

DOI: 10.4018/978-1-5225-2203-4.ch005

INTRODUCTION

Digital transformation (DT) – the use of technology to radically improve performance or reach of enterprises – is becoming a hot topic for companies across the globe (MIT Center for Digital Business and Capgemini Consulting, 2013).

The era of digital transformation is here to stay. It is happening in our lives in ways we have not even begun to grasp, but it is there. One need only think about the proliferation of social networks, and in particular on how they influence relationships, impact on electoral results, etc. But, if this is a very obvious example, many others are not so obvious, albeit equally relevant.

While the public sector is no exception to this avalanche of transformations the world has witnessed, it is not always agile enough to successfully drive this transformation process. Moreover, the confidence of citizens in the public administration ability to reinvent and modernize itself today seems more lost than ever, as the result of the austerity measures and economic instability that has already dealt a cruel hand on some countries and had its repercussions on many others, through globalization and the interdependencies that have been established.

According to a survey conducted by Accenture, European citizens across five countries were asked how confident they felt about their governments' ability to deliver services that will meet the needs and expectations of citizens in the future. More than 62% said they were not confident. To stay connected to their constituents, public leaders both at Member State and European levels need to usher in a new accountability framework (Masson, 2014).

In the specific case of public procurement, according to an OECD recommendation, public procurement is a crucial pillar of strategic governance and services delivery for governments. Because of the sheer volume of spending it represents, well governed public procurement can and must play a major role in fostering public sector efficiency and establishing citizens' trust. Well-designed public procurement systems also contribute to achieving pressing policy goals such as environmental protection, innovation, job creation and the development of small and medium enterprises (OECD, 2015).

If digital reform is added to an effective reform of public procurement, which today one cannot forgo, then there would be an opportunity for transforming public service. Portugal was, in this field, a surprising and unexpected case study. In fact, without making it explicitly known, the Portuguese government made the bold decision of making e-procurement compulsory on 1 November 2009 through a solution based on Cloud service resources.

The purpose of this article, which as part of studies on digital transformation seeks to explain the reasons why the Portuguese model is so effective, is to understand that decision and put it into context.

With this in mind, the article is divided into the following sections: introduction, background on digital transformation, description of the Portuguese case in respect of the legal reform and the implemented electronic system, analysis of the case in the context of digital transformation, lessons learned and current challenges, and, finally, the conclusions.

BACKGROUND

According to the declaration on the digital transformation of European industry and enterprises stemming from the conference on the digital transformation of European industry and enterprises, held in Brussels in February this year, digital technologies are currently driving the 'fourth industrial revolution' (Conference on Digital Transformation, 2016).

Empowered by digital investments, disruptive business models and improved production processes, European companies are generating international market opportunities with new products and services. In today's globalized world, the transition to a digital economy is essential for Europe's competitive edge and to deliver much needed economic growth and jobs. This is what drove the analysis of electronic public procurement in this current turmoil.

To this end, and although the topic of digital transformation has exponentially increased in many fields over the last two years, in particular in consultancy and in the academy, this work has focused on the analysis carried out by George Westerman and co-authors in his recent work on the leading role of digital transformation.

The rationale behind this choice is that this analysis is essentially based on the activity of companies worldwide and, on the other hand, because this is a quite diversified business sector. This study explains that successful transformation is a clear, two-fold framework: where to invest in digital capabilities, and how to lead the transformation.

The authors' attention was most captured by the component of how to lead the transformation because in the case of Public Procurement the decision about "what" – to implement electronic public procurement – was a political decision. So, how to implement Electronic Public Procurement is where the challenge lies and is related to the field of leadership. Leadership capabilities are essential to achieving true digital transformation; they turn digital investment into digital advantage.

The four key elements of leadership (Westerman, Bonnet, & Mcaffe, 2014) are:

- **Creating a Digital Vision:** Digital transformation starts when you create a transformative vision of how the organization will be different in the digital world;
- **Engagement of Employees:** Engaging employers means getting everyone moving towards the same direction;
- **Creating Governance System:** Establish the right model digital governance model is critical, since it acts as the rudder to steer digital initiatives in the right direction;
- **Creating IT/Business Synergies:** Building strong relationships between IT and business people and the right digital skills will help to build and continually reap the benefits from a well-designed digital platform.

E-Procurement Concept - e-Procurement refers to the use of Internet-based (integrated) information and communication technologies (ICTs) to carry out individual or all stages of the procurement process, including search, sourcing, negotiation, ordering, receipt, and post-purchase review. While there are various forms of e-Procurement that concentrate on one or many stages of the procurement process, such as e-Tendering, e-Marketplace, e-Auction/Reverse Auction, and e-Catalogue/Purchasing, e-Procurement can be viewed more broadly as an end-to-end solution that integrates and streamlines many procurement processes throughout the organization (Vaidya, Sajeev, & Callender, 2006)

THE 2008 THREE PILLARS PUBLIC PROCUREMENT REFORM

Strongly motivated by the need to conform the Portuguese public procurement system to the EU law, especially Directives 2004/17/EC and 2004/18/EC, the 2008 reform was based on three essential pillars: a new public contracts code as the primary public procurement law, an institutional framework based on the National Public Procurement System and a fully-fledged e-procurement system.

Public Contracts Code

EU regulations on Public Procurement aim to promote transparency, fairness and a competitive public procurement across the EU's single market, fostering business opportunities and generating economic growth and job creation.

In the case of the 2004 EU directives package (Directives 2004/18/EC and 2004/17/EC) that regulated the procurement procedures for major contracts (Bovis, 2006) until 2014, they addressed the creation of an internal market for public procurement and were based on the Treaty provisions related to the single market.

The aim of these directives was not to provide a general framework for implementing other objectives, such as ensuring best value for taxpayers' money, preventing corruption, or ensuring transparency and accountability (Arrowsmith, 2005), which, as in other aspects of procurement policy, should still be considered a matter to be dealt with at Member State level. This explains why so many Member States have set their own regulations and requirements applicable to contracts the value of which is below the Directives' thresholds.

Approved by Decree-law 18/2008, the Portuguese Public Contracts Code (PCC) primarily aimed at transposing the above mentioned EU 2004 procurement directives into the national legal system.

Public procurement contracts, including supplies, services, works, and works and services concessions are regulated by the PCC and all entities classified as contracting authorities by the EU directives fall within the scope of and must comply with it. These include the central government, the regional and local authorities and the bodies governed by public law (regardless of their public or private nature).

However, the PCC went further than the minimum mandatory scope of the required transposition by promoting a major shift in the Portuguese public procurement system, as the legislator made use of its relative freedom to regulate contracts below the Directives' thresholds and opted to set out, in many ways, a similar framework for contracts above and below the Directives thresholds (Almeida & Fautino, 2009) and set an innovative and bold public procurement model to foster non-discrimination, competition, transparency and accountability in public procurement contracting (Tavares, A gestão das aquisições públicas: guia de aplicação do Código dos Contratos Públicos, 2009).

Drawing on the external pressure of the EU to transpose the 2004 Directives, it should be emphasized that the Code eventually became the decisive instrument of change towards a new paradigm based on e-procurement in 2008. In tandem with the supplementary legislation described in Table X below, the Code added a new DNA to the Portuguese public procurement system – the use of electronics in the contract preparation phase (until the award of the contract) and the disclosure of procedures and opening of the procurement market to society, guaranteed through the combination of electronic means of data transfer and of e-procurement platforms (transactional system component) with the availability of a single public contracts portal, the BASE Portal.

No other innovation brought in by the 2008 Code can be considered more striking than the transformation into a fully-fledged e-procurement system. While it had been promised for the entire UE since the "Manchester Declaration" (ministerial declaration approved unanimously on 24 November 2005, Manchester, under the auspices of the United Kingdom EU Presidency) with the assumed target of "By 2010 at least 50% of public procurement above the EU public procurement threshold will be carried out electronically", Portugal had already achieved 91% of this target in 2010 (IMPIC, I.P., 2011).

Reality has shown the appropriateness of the legislator. The new legislation has introduced an unparalleled level of transparency, at a time when most Portuguese people believed that contract formation procedures, even open tenders, were "rigged" and did not satisfy the principle of equal treatment or, at best, the system did not promote competition and prevented or made it hard for new players to enter the system, especially SMEs. While it is true that electronics on its own does not necessarily open doors to an ideal world, there is however a recognition that it removed from contract formation procedures most discriminatory practices and, when supported by a portal such as BASE, it served most of the interests of stakeholders involved in public procurement, either those on the demand and supply side, or the inspection bodies and society in general (the right of scrutiny over the management of taxpayers' money).

The most striking aspects of this reform are that its adoption is mandatory, even though "electronics" and "paper" were allowed to coexist during a transitional period, and the legal enforcement by which contracts are void if formed through non-electronic media.

Even if from a technological viewpoint this profound change posed no major, let alone insurmountable difficulties to any EU Member State, the fact is that only the mandatory nature of its adoption now prescribed in the 2014 Directives was to bring about change and, from the limit dates set at EU-wide level, the following causes were said to have slowed down the process:

- A relative distrust of public powers and economic operators on the degree of openness and increased facilitated access to domestic/national markets by international market players (protectionist tensions), for example, in that e-Procurement enables some context costs associated to the physical location of companies and of target markets of their products and services be close to irrelevant (once language difficulties are sorted out, e-procurement makes it financially feasible, perhaps even interesting, for a Finnish architecture office to bid in a public works tender launched by a municipality in the Portuguese hinterland, or, conversely, for a Portuguese software company to bid in a public tender for the selection of a system to monitor the marine environment around Helsinki. There is no need for teams to travel to the sites, and there are no communication costs involved, for e.g., costs for shipping documents and mock-ups);
- Poor promotion of the e-Procurement system as regards aspects other than contract awarding (up to the e-tendering phase) that deal with the integrated management of public organizations (the interfacing with public finance

management and other areas, applications and tools used in the management of public organizations, ERPs, CRMs, etc., with the aim of increasing their efficiency);
- The classical resistance to change, perhaps more noticeable in some sectors of public administration rather than in private economy, which is much more exposed to more demanding global levels of competition and faces the key challenge of innovation as an "approach" to survival.

Against this background, one of the questions most often heard among stakeholders in the early years of the reform was: "What about Portugal? Is the decision to take the lead the right one?

While it is true that the national public market provided (even) easier access to economic agents from other EU countries, nonetheless the pioneering role of Portugal in this area:

- increased transparency, providing more and better methods of preventing corruption;
- afforded more competition between economies of scale (better prices and savings);
- prepared the Portuguese companies, in particular the SMEs, to access electronic public procurement markets, which, in adopting the new 2014 Directives, will become the rule in the Single Market, and
- enabled the formation of a cluster of service providers linked to e-procurement, from e-platform operators to public procurement consultants (as "e-public procurement" is turning into "public procurement").

By introducing, in 2008, electronics as the new (mandatory) paradigm in the public contracts formation in Portugal (See Table 2), the Code and its supplementary legislation impacted tremendously on the public procurement lifecycle and helped change workflows, processes and working methodologies of both contracting authorities and economic operators. To some extent the Code brought Portugal to a leading position and prepared the country well in advance for what the EU came to set as targets for the use of electronics in 2014, through Directive 2014/24.

National System of Public Procurement

The National Public Procurement System (NPPS) was established in 2007 while the preparatory work on the new Public Contracts Code was already being finalized. Its main aim was the optimization of purchases of categories of goods and services likely to be centralized, led by the National Agency for Public Procurement (ANCP),

Table 1. 2008 reform legislative package

	LEGAL ACT	SUBJECT MATTER
A	Decree-Law 37/2007 (DRE, 2007)	Defines the National System of Public Purchases (NSPP) and creates the National Agency for Public Procurement (NAPP) as the entity responsible for the system's management
	Regulation 330/2009 (DRE, 2009)	Regulates the functioning of the National System of Public Procurement
B	Decree-Law 18/2008 (DRE, 2008)	PUBLIC CONTRACTS CODE (PCC) – new primary public procurement law
C	Decree-Law 143-A/2008 (DRE, 2008)	Electronic Platforms and data communication forms
	Order 701-A/2008 (DRE, 2008)	Approves the key standard forms related to contract notices and contract award notices that are published in the "*Diário da República Eletrónico*" (e- Official Journal)
	Order 701-B/2008	Setup of an Advisory Committee in charge of monitoring the application of the Public Contracts Code
	Order 701- D/2008	Defines the model of statistical data to be reported by contracting authorities
	Order 701- E/2008	Defines the model of the data reports to be completed and provided by contracting authorities in/through the Public Procurement Portal www.base.gov.pt
	Order 701- F/2008	Regulates the setup, operation and management of the Public Procurement Portal (www.base.gov.pt)
	Order 701-G/2008	Sets out the requirements and conditions of use of electronic platforms by the contracting authorities and regulates their terms of operation
	Order 701- H/2008	Approves the mandatory content of the execution project of public works and the procedures and standards to be adopted
	Order 701- I/2008	Establishes the "Observatory of Public Works", and approves its operational rules
	Order 701-J /2008	Defines the model of statistical data to be reported by contracting authorities

A – Setup of central purchasing system and body **B** – Code of Public Contracts (transposing the EU 2004 Directives into the national legal system) **C** – Specific e-Procurement and implementing provisions

the nature and policy instruments of which are those typical of a Central Purchasing Body (CPB), in addition to some policy-making and coordination powers besides those relating to centralized purchases. The NPPS, led by the ANCP until 2012 and based on a network of Ministerial Purchasing Units, comprised the affiliated entities (direct administration services and public institutions) and voluntary entities,

Table 2. Key deadlines set forth by Directive 2014/247EU

Key deadlines set forth by the Directive 2014/24/EU	
E-Noticing, including all procurement documents,	18 April 2016
Full e-procurement including e-Tendering for Central Purchasing Bodies	18 April 2017
Full e-procurement including e-Tendering for other public contracting authorities	18 October 2018

who joined the system through accession agreements for purchasing purposes under framework agreements provided by the CPB (Municipalities and Municipality-Owned Companies, Regional Authorities, State Owned Companies).

More recently, through Decree-Law 117-A/2012, of 14 June, the ANCP merged with other two entities (GERAP, set up to deal with some shared services in the field of human resources and public finance management, and the IT Centre for Public Administration, which had been until then a unit within the Ministry of Finance) into a new body of public law, the Agency for Shared Services in the Public Administration (eSPap).

So, the institutional framework has significantly evolved within the last 10 years (2007-2016) as the key competences and responsibilities of the public procurement system have been assigned to seven different public bodies throughout this period. Figure 2 below shows the evolution of actors and distribution of key functions:

- **National Public Procurement System (NPPS)**
    - **ESPAP**: Former ANCP (Ministry of Finance) – Manages the National System of Public Procurement and acts as a generalist central purchasing body
    - **UMC**: Ministerial Purchasing Units (one per Ministry)
    - **SPMS**: Central purchasing body for the Health Sector
- **National Information System and Regulation**
    - **IMPIC (Ministry of Planning and Infrastructures)**: Public Contracts Portal (BASE) and Electronic Platforms Regulation
    - **GNS (National Security Office)**: Accreditation of Security Auditors
- **Private Electronic Platforms Operators**
    - 6 licensed to operate in the Market (May, 2016)
- **National Auditing Authorities**
    - Court of Auditors
    - Inspectorate-General of Finance, Ministerial Inspectorates (Sectoral)
    - Competition Authority

The key entities who contribute to the strategy and policy making, implementation, monitoring and control of public procurement in Portugal can be grouped under the following four functions as shown below in Figure 1:

The Portuguese institutional framework does not comprise an independent Review Body as in other countries. In case the request for review is rejected by the Contracting Authority (CA), the Economic Operator (EO) has to make use of the judicial system through the Administrative Courts.

Figure 1. 2016 KEY public entities in public procurement governance

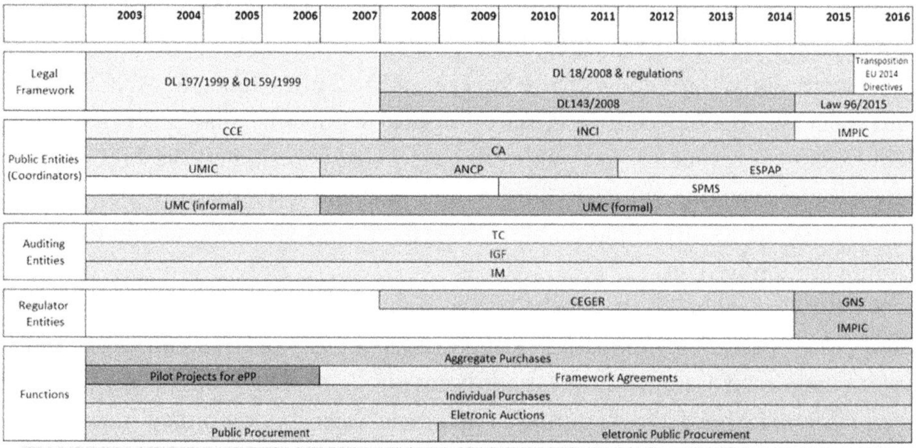

The Star of the Reform: e-Procurement System

It must nevertheless be noted that the most remarkable aspect – and incidentally more lasting – of the 2008 reform was precisely the setup of a fully-fledged e-procurement system which proved to be the "star of the reform" and the reason why it was referred to as the "Portuguese case" at international level. In fact, from a substantive viewpoint of the legal reform, in addition to some creative solutions (for example, the swapping of the sequential order of eligibility and awarding, the harbinger of the EU solution adopted by Directive 2014/24/EC), most of the legislator's solutions were circumscribed by the European directives. Where the legislator surprised the most was precisely in respect of e-procurement – due to the change in strategy, anchored within a short transitional period during which paper and electronics coexisted, followed by the imposition of electronics in the formation process of almost all public contracts.

It comes as no surprise that the more skeptical prophesized the deadlock of the public administration, claiming that it was not prepared for such a revolution, and alerting to the possibility of the breakdown in the supplies of essential utilities to schools, security forces, prisons, etc. None of those catastrophist scenarios have materialized.

Although the great turning point in the public procurement national system occurred in 2008, with the adoption of the new PCC, the fact is that the profound changes that became visible in that year had been in the pipeline since 2002.

The Roadmap

In fact, it all started with the setup of the Knowledge Society Agency (UMIC) by Resolution of the Council of Ministers No. 135/2002, of 20 November, and the assignment to this new body of the task to devise and propose a strategy for development of information society and electronic government in Portugal, as well as an implementation plan covering the period from 2003 to 2006.

In June 2003, the Council of Ministers approved, among a set of strategic documents aiming at stimulating the changeover towards an information society, the National Plan of Electronic Procurement, the first roadmap towards the adoption of a fully-fledged e-procurement system in Portugal. Until 2007, this national plan encompassed the implementation of 8 (eight) pilot projects completed in 8 (eight) ministries through the use of the 4 (four) B2B platforms (Business to Business) that existed in the private market at the time. It should be stressed that the scope of the pilot projects was limited to internal preparatory tasks, e.g. the collection and aggregation of needs for joint procurement or conduction of e-auctions as an allowed method under the negotiated procedure at the time.

By showcasing the potential benefits of a broader e-procurement system, the implementation of these pilots has been critical to induce a structural change both at the level of procedures and working methodologies and, more importantly, the attitudes towards public procurement management which was calling for a new mind-set to be adopted by the key stakeholders.

The positive impact of pilot projects went well beyond the sole "electronic perspective" of matters and solutions - where the conduct of e-auctions deserves to be highlighted - and has significantly contributed to initiate a broader transformation. It was, indeed, within the pilot projects that a number of contracting authorities experienced, for the first time ever, a different collaborative atmosphere enabling them to share and aggregate needs, to setup the first specialized units within ministries and other contracting authorities in charge of managing the procurement and setting the minimum standards for the public consumption of some pre-selected cross-cutting categories of goods and services.

Key Features of the System

In clear contrast with a much less ambitious attitude adopted by the majority of Member States, and following a transitional period of one year, the electronic procurement became mandatory in Portugal as of 1 November 2009.

The PCC made, itself, a bold and comprehensive commitment to electronic procurement (Tavares, 2010) and translated into the legal provisions a solid, determined and ambitious political decision about a new public procurement system highly anchored in the use of electronic communications as a means to make it more transparent and efficient.

The rule is, in fact, that all public procurement procedures in Portugal must be performed electronically, from the publication of the contract notice to the publication of the contract award notice and the contract itself: all tender documents must be produced, published, notified and stored electronically; all economic operators must submit their applications, tenders, documents, requests for clarification, claims, etc., electronically; all communications between these two parties must be done electronically. Additionally, for all procedures encompassing the publication of notices, the contract formation phase must run on a certified electronic platform, i.e., the contracting authority documents must be published, notified and stored on an electronic platform; all economic operators must submit their applications, tenders, documents, requests for clarification, claims, etc., through an electronic platform.

The implementation of this model required the availability of electronic platforms and the Portuguese legislator opted to rely on a market of electronic platform operators (instead of a model based on a single public platform). Decree-Law 143-A/2008, of 25 July, and Ordinance 701-G/2008, of 29 July, were adopted with the aim of regulating the activities of platform operators, and the key features and functionalities these platforms should be ready to offer in order to be granted the licence to operate.

The Law 96/2015, of 17 August 2015, (DRE, 2015) repealed DL 143-A/2008 and introduced the legal definition of electronic platform as "a technological infrastructure that consists of a number of computer applications, resources and services required for the operation of electronic procedures relating to national public procurement, and through which these procedures are carried out" (Article 2(e)).

The National Security Office (NSO) is the organisation under the Presidency of the Council of Ministers responsible for certifying electronic platforms in terms of electronic security. In May 2016, six certified electronic platforms were allowed to operate in Portugal.

The second pillar of the Portuguese e-public procurement model is the public contracts portal: portal BASE. This portal is a centralised database that contains extensive information about all public contracts and is automatically fed by the DRE - electronic official journal (www.dre.pt), the electronic platforms and by contracting authorities, depending on the type of procedure and the phase within the procurement cycle.

The Business Model

Simultaneous with the decision on mandatory electronic public procurement, Portugal also opted for a decentralised approach to e-procurement platforms, in contrast

Figure 2. The Portuguese e-public procurement framework

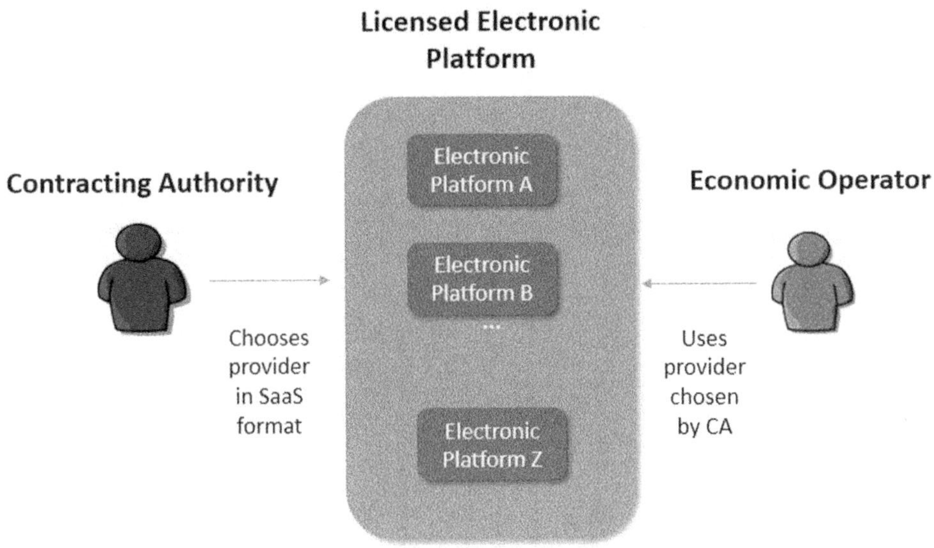

to several countries across Europe where e-procurement implementation models relied on the mandatory use of a single national platform (Assar & Boughzala, 2008) (European Commission, 2009). The CAs may select the most suitable platform from a set of electronic platforms licensed by a Supervisory Board offering general and differentiated services, whose list is available on the public contracts portal (IMPIC, IP, 2016) and EOs must be registered and use the various platforms at the same time (see Figure 3). In the decentralised approach, the e-procurement platform market is regulated and each member must comply with strict security and safety requirements (Betts, et al., 2006) (Polemi & Papastergiou, 2006). As expected, the existence of several platforms increased competition and stimulated the development of more capable solutions, integrating business processes, promoting green procurement, boosting collaboration and enhancing electronic supply chain management (Arantes, Aguiar Costa, & Valadares, 2013).

As explained further ahead in this paper, this very option may have been among the critical success factors that allowed the public procurement system to overcome the difficulties raised by a slight high political rotation with concrete impacts at the level of the Public Administration and several strategic changes within a slightly short period of time if we consider the structural kind of reforms at stake. Notwithstanding, as in any other alternative, its practical deployment has shown positive and negative aspects that are recognised at both national and international levels.

On the positive side, it is important to stress that the model:

Figure 3. SaaS business model

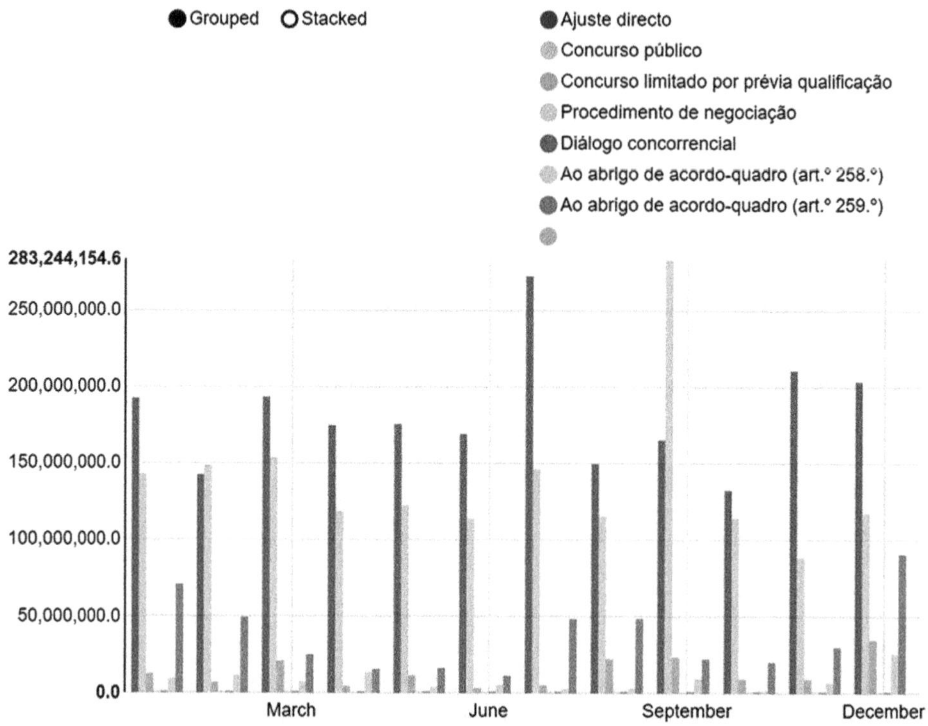

For a more accurate representation of this figure, please see the electronic version.

- Allows a very fast "Time to Market";
- Promotes a competitive market among private electronic platform operators;
- Fosters innovation as a result of such competition and as a result of a more demanding public client;
- Requires a low initial investment and entry cost for public entities;
- The accreditation process regarding the security requirements of the platform and the operational conditions of the provider exempts Contracting Authorities from worrying about this complex task they are not prepared for and have no resources to undertake by themselves.

On the negative side, the following coud be highlighted as weaknesses of the model:

- Each economic operator must use multiple e-platforms;
- Lack of interoperability among e-Platforms;

- Difficulty to prevent some risks of anti-competitive behavior and conduct (both relating to the scope of services to be rendered and prices) from platform operators which was calling for a better regulatory framework. The Law 96/2015, of 17 August 2015 has responded to this challenge and today a proper enforcement scheme is in place.

New Levels of Transparency and Accountability

In its unique view of the electronic model of the information system, the Public Contracts Code provides for the establishment of a Web Portal to register contracts awarded under its legal framework.

One of the main reasons that supported the creation of this type of solution was the fact that direct awards - a fairly frequent type of public procurement procedure where suppliers can participate by invitation - were considered a black box within public expenditure. To avoid that, it became mandatory to disclose these contracts through a Web-based solution. Besides promoting transparency in the conduct of these procedures, which in the past were only known to the participating entities, the legislator wanted also to ensure its effective enforcement by determining that if this type of procedures were not disclosed on the Portal, the corresponding contract would not be paid. This enforcement mechanism significantly contributed to contracting authorities being more careful when complying with the regulations and, as a consequence of a much higher degree of compliance, the accuracy and completeness of information has increased significantly.

It should be noted that this type of information on the internal operations of the Public Administration had never come under the public eye in such a direct manner before. Such a transparency brought into direct awards induced a "silent revolution" in the behavioral culture of people and organizations and prompted a quite exacerbated scrutiny of the data published on the Portal in the early days of its existence.

Also of utmost importance was the need to provide a single information repository regarding all public procurement procedures enabling policy makers and market operators, from both demand and supply sides, to have a 360º view over the system. This aspect was quite visionary at that time, and not all stakeholders understood the implications of this measure, which was the establishment of a centralized repository of the life cycle of public contracts, in addition to the decentralized model of transactions processed through private platforms.

For the first time ever, it became possible to trace public contracts from the pre-award phase up to the post-award phase within an integrated information system.

The Public Contracts Portal: A Contracts Register

The public contracts Portal, called and known as "BASE", is a complex information system that automatically collects data, via the Internet, from various sources and from the electronic forms completed by contracting authorities in the reserved area. The system comprises a database the purpose of which is to centralize in a single repository the information from the entire Portuguese public administration. Accessed at www.base.gov.pt, it has a reserved access area for contracting authorities who, using the same link, can access their data either introduced directly by them or fed into the system by the electronic platforms. Its public component comprises also a specific subsystem for procedures related to works and public works, called the Public Works Observatory. The data entered in the Portal since August 2008 are an extremely valuable asset, enabling the Portuguese public administration to analyze information in many different ways, to profile public expenditure and its evolution across different macroeconomic scenarios and already significant time series, to carry out forecasts and analyses and, last but not least, to monitor compliance with the PCC in quantitative terms. By the end of May 2016, there were around 645 000 contracts registered in the system. Since August 2013, the uploading of the image of the document itself became mandatory.

Several stakeholders play a relevant role in interacting with the system's architecture, especially as regards the forwarding of information concerning the transactions related to the contract formation phase. Once electronic public procurements in the contract formation phase became mandatory, since 1 November 2009, electronic platforms have had to be used for all public procedures. Although electronic platforms are not mandatory in the case of direct awards, electronic means do have to be used. Transactions made on these e-platforms must be automatically forwarded to the BASE Portal through an interoperability system, for which a feasible technological solution had to be found, consisting of a number of *Web services* for the safe transmission of reported data.

One of the relevant stakeholders is the Portuguese printing house and mint (INCM - Imprensa Nacional Casa da Moeda), as it is responsible for the authentication system and the automatic transmission of notices concerning public procurement procedures. Cooperation with that entity is, therefore, particularly relevant. Firstly, because system developments in the user authentication component were no longer necessary, thus reducing efforts and implementing a good practice by reusing existing solutions. Secondly, not only because of the visibility of notices on a portal dedicated to public procurement, but also because integration with INCM has a very strong impact on the database: the integration of public notices automatically generates the procedures. As to the contracting authorities, they are responsible for ensuring the registration and execution of contracts using the forms available in the BASE

Figure 4. Key processes run through the e-platforms, official journal and BASE Portal

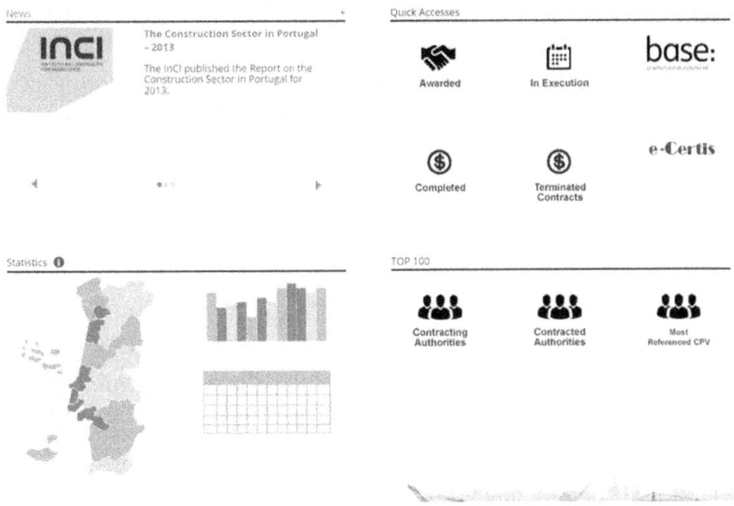

reserved area. However, plans are in the pipeline to ensure the automatic transmission of this information in the future by developing *Web services* connected to the internal systems of each entity.

The BASE Portal keeps extensive information about most public procurement procedures and contracts, some of which is public and available online in real time, and some is stored and analyzed for reporting and policy purposes.

The model is a very simple one and is shortly described as follows:

For procedures conducted upon invitation, indicated by red arrows on Figure 4, all documents including the invitation to tender, contract specifications/requirements and respective tenders have to be transacted through electronic channels. While the use of electronic platforms is not mandatory for procedures by invitation, indicated by yellow arrows on Figure 4, still many contracting authorities are opting for electronic platform services to manage them. In any case, regardless of the means of communication effectively used, the publication of the contract information on the BASE Portal by the contracting authority is always mandatory in order to ensure completeness of information. This information includes, among others, details about the contacting authority, the economic operator, as well as the subject matter and the value of the contract. An important aspect of the publication of this information relating to contracts originated by a direct award (red arrows) is that, according to the PCC, the contract is null and void if the information is not published on the BASE Portal.

For procedures open to the competition (yellow arrows), some additional information is to be sent to the Base Portal. As defined in the legal framework, all notices are published in the electronic official journal DRE (www.dre.pt) by registered contracting authorities. The DRE sends a copy of the notice to the BASE Portal, by automatic means, and immediately registers the procedure into the database. From this moment onwards, contracting authorities (using the same login credentials as for accessing the DRE) can manage the procedure and contract related information in BASE Portal. Economic operators can both access notices on the DRE, or on the BASE Portal. In the last case some structured criteria are available for search. As mentioned before, it is mandatory that all published procedures are conducted through/within a certified electronic platform. The electronic platform automatically feeds the BASE Portal, through a *web services* infrastructure, with information about the procedures and contracts of the client contracting authority. The technical and functional documentation for the *web services* is public available on BASE as recommended in the legal regulation (IMPIC, IP, 2016).

In the public interface, it is possible to find a statistic area, in which some graphics and global amounts can be calculated in real time, organized by type of procedure, type of contract and by year.

Figure 5 shows an example of a graphic related to global amount per type of procedure distributed along 2015.

It is possible to find in the media many references to data published on the BASE Portal as well as on other tools such as the DADOS.GOV Portal, which contains the open format files published on the public area of the BASE Portal.

Figure 5. Sample statistical graphic generated by BASE Portal in the public interface

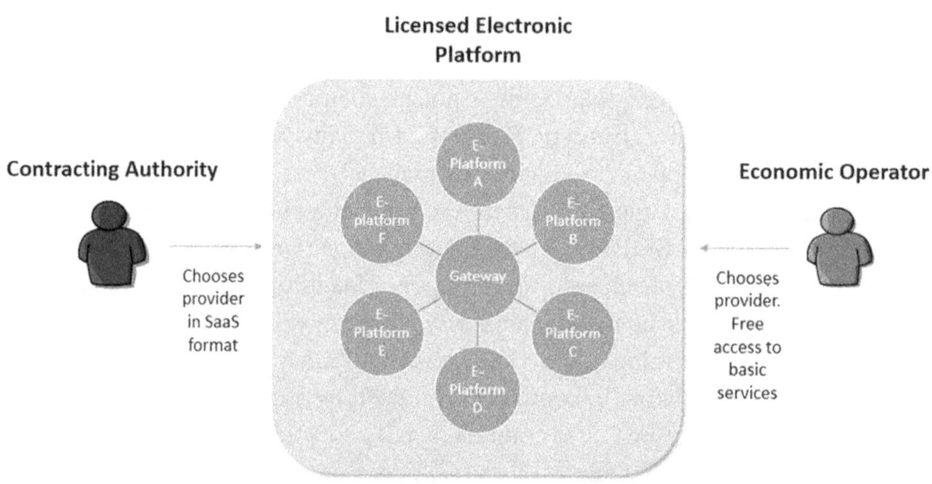

A Special View on Public Works: The Observatory - OOP.INCI.PT

Contracts related to public works have always have always been the subject of special attention from various governments. The Public Contracts Code introduced significant changes in this area and provides for the creation of a Public Works Observatory (PWO) - Ordinance 701-I/2008, of 29 July - with the aim of monitoring the most relevant aspects of the execution of public works contracts.

The PWO is a special information filter within the BASE database that ensures the access and visualization of a set of data, as well as the analysis and dissemination of the corresponding statistical data related to public works contracts. The PWO is a relevant working tool for all entities that develop studies and need various statistical data on the public works market.

It comprises an information search system allowing a quick access to data related to the contract formation phase, including the invited tenderers (where appropriate), the applicants (where appropriate), the tenderers and the contractors. Moreover, during the contract execution phase the current status of each contract and the causes for deviation from its agreed deliverables, deadlines and cost can be traced throughout. All this information builds on the data entered in the BASE Portal by the contracting authorities, either during the contract formation phase, with the transmission of the Contracting Report (an embedded xml form), or during the contract execution phase, through the transmission of the Annual Summary Report (where appropriate) and the Works Completion Report.

The PWO is a valuable instrument for analyzing the public works sector, providing important quantitative inputs to policy-making in this extremely important field of public procurement.

CASE ANALYSIS

As described above, the entire reform of the public procurement system in Portugal took place over several years and assumed a new shape in 2008 as a result of the legal reform that led to the publication of the Public Contracts Code, an integrated legal instrument applicable to the procurement of goods, services, public works and concessions. Although this legal instrument came into force in mid-2008, part of its scope, i.e., e-procurement, was only enforced almost a year later, in November 2009.

An important issue had a significant effect throughout the entire process: phased implementation, on a step-by-step basis.

The prior period that led the government to adopt the measures of the Code, which we know today, was essential to decision-making. For that reason, the study

Figure 6. Public works observatory main page

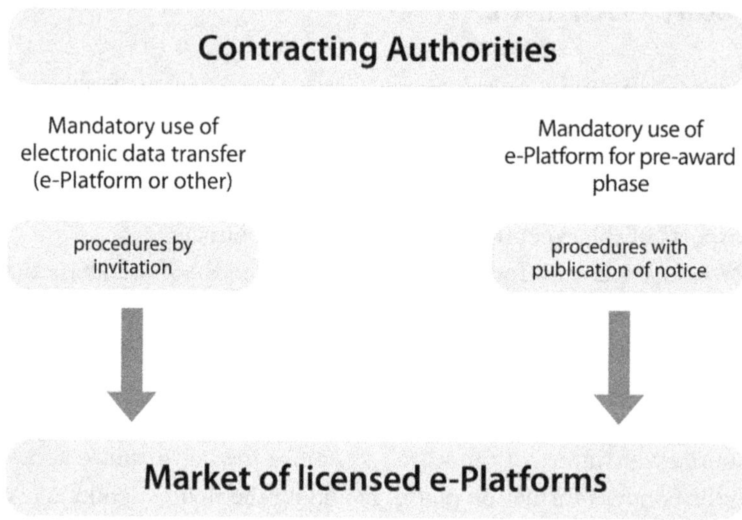

has taken the key success factors of digital transformation – creating a digital vision, engagement of employees, creating a governance system, and creating IT/business synergies – and analyzed the conditions associated with these factors in the Portuguese case that led to the measures that are still in force in Portugal.

As regards creating a digital vision – this vision, defined in 2004, marks the beginning of the system's reform through 4 pilot projects in 8 ministries. At the time, the solution to use tried and tested B2B tools available in the market and to not develop any central solution for the State seemed bold and very risky. The only way to assess whether this vision was feasible or not was to test it in the field. The vision, however, had been delineated and its potential had to be evaluated. These were Cloud service-based solutions for State services with everything that this entails in many aspects, and which are still the topic of lively debates in many areas. This vision was delineated by the UMIC mission unit with good political coverage at the time.

As regards the engagement of employees – this was decisive for the success of the pilot projects and underlined the government's decision to make electronic procurement compulsory. A large number of people from dozens of public institutions participated voluntarily in several specific working groups: legal analysis, product standardization, aggregated purchases, technical definition of specifications for IT solutions, etc. The heads of services and units were involved and these groups engaged multidisciplinary teams organized throughout a network covering the whole public administration, working intensely for 3 years. While the effect of the involvement of people was felt in different ways, they all agreed that this was a period of thorough team work in which people worked towards the same goal.

As regards the creation of a governance system – the establishment of a new unit (UMIC) and, most importantly, its statute of task-force strongly impacted on how the reform strategy unfolded. First, because it was assigned to a new institution, thus overcoming possible conflicts in previously existing institutions that were dealing with the same matters before and could feel targeted by the changes. Secondly, the fact that the political coverage of this mission unit was quite far-reaching helped to spread the message that this was a high priority issue in the government's agenda. Lastly, because it enabled the strategy to be centrally managed at top level in the government structure, with operationalization being carried out by the institutions under the coordination of UMIC.

As regards creating IT/business strategies – the pilot projects were decisive for the government's decision to make e-procurement compulsory and, above all, for choosing a model based on private providers, a solution hitherto highly innovative in the public sector in this area.

Moreover, besides supporting the implemented model, it also enabled the design of what later became the architecture of the Portuguese electronic system. This experience clarified two major issues:

- The providers must be technically and functionally in line with the legal framework;
- The State needs a solution to safeguard what is most important: data.

The certification of electronic platforms by a public entity solved the first of these issues, while the second issue was resolved through a system implemented to gather the information on public contracts: the Public Contracts Portal.

It is right and proper to say that the digital transformation in public e-procurement was much influenced by the government's strong emphasis on modernizing its processes and services provided to citizens.

LESSONS LEARNED AND CHALLENGES AHEAD

What Made the 2008 Reform a Success

The positive results of the 2008 reform would not have been achieved had the legal, institutional and technological issues not been properly adjusted. The entire strategy behind the reform took into consideration the need to establish and nurture an alliance between the Government and other stakeholders in the public procurement system – an alliance which often had to overcome "counter-reform" tensions which, albeit outnumbered, nevertheless fueled a near-state of anxiety during the originally planned transitional period (Jul 2008 – Jul 2009) and especially during its extended period (Jul 2009 – Nov 2009). The following positively contributed to the situation:

- The political determination to tread the path outlined in the roadmap, with the legal requirement to mandatorily adopt electronic media once the transitional period ended and to report sanctions if "procurement on paper" happened to be used, i.e., resulting in a null contract and possible disciplinary penalties imposed to the heads of the contracting authority);
- The testimonials of organizations that had already fully migrated to the new paradigm (nobody was really experiencing any disruption or catastrophe as anticipated by those more skeptical about the change – on the contrary, the feeling of a "breath of fresh air" in public procurement and the opportunity for public procurers (demand side) to participate in a transformational process and to reposition their badly recognized profession came into play and acted as the "new ally" in the reform. Showcasing has proved to be the last and decisive selling argument to bring more and more entities and professionals to the new system;
- The response of e-platform operators, who, besides their obvious interest in being part of the change led by public stakeholders, offered technically reliable solutions and allocated adequate resources to the "problem-solving front" that is to be expected within such a vast and fast transformation.

Seven years of a mandatory electronic public procurement system have proved that a cloud-based architecture, based on software as a service model, can successfully meet the business needs.

Security accreditation of operators proved to be a key point in the whole process because without this fundamental requirement it would be very difficult for Contracting Authorities to define these criteria in the procurement procedure.

The knowledge required for this purpose is vast and complex and, in Portugal, as in many other countries, knowledge of ICT varies greatly from one public entity to another, being scarce in most organisms, especially the smaller-sized ones.

What's Next for Portugal?

However, soon the Portuguese government realized that technical accreditation was not sufficient as the existing rules do not allow the imposition of sanctions in the event of infringement by the electronic platform operators, so it became crucial to update the legal framework to regulate this market.

Law 96/2015 not only sought to resolve this issue, but also resolved the issue, widely discussed in Europe, of the interoperability between e-Plaforms. The overall

Figure 7. Interoperability model

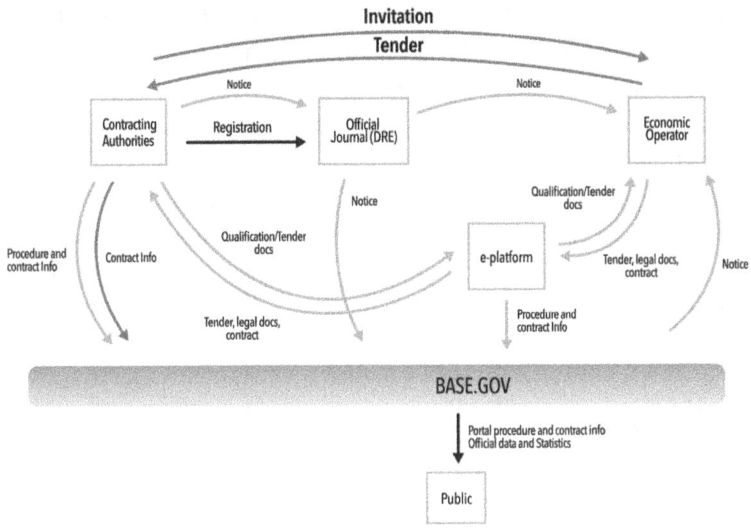

purpose here is to grant the economic operators the possibility of choosing the e-Platform they will use in a given procedure or transaction. To some extent, it aims at extending the principle of free choice, which today benefits only the contracting entities, to economic operators (supply side/suppliers).

This component of the legal framework will be further detailed by means of an Order to be published as soon as the ongoing architectural design phase is completed. If Portugal addresses this issue, it will have taken another giant step as leader in the development of public procurement solutions, because this will be a crucial point in the implementation of the European single market. However, it is also obvious that the maturity of this market is still relatively small for sufficient comfort to the solutions that currently foresee.

There is a tendency to increase measures, at European level, towards standardization to further consolidate an interoperability architecture, such as the creation CEN's Project Committee 'Electronic Public Procurement' (CEN/TC 440) which will proceed with the development of technical specifications that are intended to support electronic public procurement processes and their accompanying information flows. The deliverables being drafted in this Project Committee will provide business interoperability specifications and vocabulary in relation to e-Procurement, e-Notification, e-Tendering, e-Ordering and e-Fulfilment (CEN - CENELEC, 2016). Indeed, more than technology, interoperability is subject to the standardization of services and activities, which is still in its very early stages. In addition, the creation of a database with information from public contracts proved to be a fundamental part of the system. This piece of the puzzle allows the government to hold on to the information that would otherwise be kept only in private solutions, and hold a set of data analysis tools which can be applied according to the objectives.

It turns out that while there is still much to do in respect of reliability and data integrity, Portugal has reached in this field a fairly high level of development, hardly compared with other countries.

In this area, it has been proved that the system will benefit very much from automation mechanisms for data transfer under development. This is also a huge challenge for the Portuguese public administration because it implies more internal interoperability and the enforcement of the only-once principle.

CONCLUSION

The implementation of e-procurement in Portugal was, without any doubt, unusual within the European Union.

To some extent, it can be said that this was perhaps due to the following reasons:

- First, because it was the first country to adopt compulsory e-procurement for the pre-award phase;
- Because the model was based on solutions in Cloud Services, when few dared to do so at the time;
- Because it set forth in Europe a level of transparency in public contracts unheard of before;
- Because it introduced the certification of e-platforms;
- Because the architecture of the electronic system is based on an interoperability network between private and public systems;

And, finally, because despite the various unusual circumstances, what came out of it was a true and profound digital transformation.

There have already been repercussions from the learning acquired from the implemented model. In 2015, the e-procurement system was reformed and e-platforms became a regulated activity supervised by the State, in addition to the technical accreditation process already implemented.

This diploma makes room for an interoperability solution to cater for the principle of free choice of platform for Awarding Entities, and also for Economic Operators. Its future implementation could represent a major leap forward in interoperability across borders.

Finally, this profound revolution process began and was prepared with the establishment of UMIC in 2003 and with the implementation of pilot processes in 8 Ministries of the Portuguese Public Administration.

The rationale behind the implemented model has its roots in this history of unparalleled strong leadership and vision.

In the light of digital transformation, it can be said that:

- It was essential to define a clear vision of the model to be implemented, and to carry out tests;
- The engagement of people as a team was the driving force behind the strong sense of unity;
- Having a mission unit with clear capacities and power to coordinate the pilot projects led to this governance structure being accepted and coordinated by all stakeholders;

and

- The experience of pilot projects enabled the system's architecture to be designed as it is today, by integrating several private and public elements in harmony.

To briefly summarize it, leadership in this case, as in many others, was without a doubt a differentiating and decisive factor in the achieved results.

REFERENCES

Almeida, J., & Fautino, P. (2009). Implementing national measures on public procurement under the EC Directives: the portuguese experience.*International Public Procurement Conference.*

Arantes, A., Aguiar Costa, A., & Valadares, L. (2013). The Evaluation Of Mandatory E-Public Procurement In Portugal: Perceptions And Results Of The National Survey (2010-2012).*1st European Conference on e-Public Procurement* (pp. 63-74). Barcelona, Spain: ebook.

Arrowsmith, S. (2005). *The Law of Public and Utilities Procurement.* Sweet & Maxwell.

Assar, S., & Boughzala, L. (2008). Empirical evaluation of e-procurement platforms in France. *International Journal of Value Chan Management*, 30-42.

Betts, M., Black, P., Christensen, S., Dawson, E., Du, R., Duncan, W., . . . Gonzalez, J. (2006). Towards secure and legal e-tendering. ITcon, 89-102.

Bovis, C. (2006). *EC Public Procurement: Case Law and Regulation*. Oxford, UK: Oxford university Press.

CEN - CENELEC. (2016, June). *Work Programme 2016 - European standardization and related activities*. Retrieved from CEN-CENELEC Management Centre: http://www.cencenelec.eu/news/publications/publications/cen-cenelec-wp2016_en.pdf

Conference on Digital Transformation. (2016, February 16). *Declaration on the digital transformation*. Retrieved from Digital Transformation 2016: http://www.digitaltransformation2016.eu/docs/declaration.pdf

DRE. (2007, February 19). *Diário da República, 1ª série*. Retrieved from Diário da Repúblic Eletrónico - DRE: https://dre.pt/application/file/517923

DRE. (2008a). *Diário da República, 1ª série*. Obtido de Diário da República Eletrónico - DRE: https://dre.pt/application/file/248099

DRE. (2008b). *Diário da República, 1ª série*. Obtido de Diário da República Eletrónico - DRE: https://dre.pt/application/file/239497

DRE. (2008c). *Diário da República, 1ª série*. Obtido de Diário da República Eletrónico - DRE: https://dre.pt/application/file/575266

DRE. (2009, July 30). *Diário da República, 2ª série*. Retrieved from Diário da República Eletrónico - DRE: https://dre.pt/application/file/757133

DRE. (2015). *Diário da República, 1ª série*. Obtido de Diário da República Eletrónico - DRE: https://dre.pt/application/file/70017225

European Commission. (2009). Smarter, faster, better eGovernment, 8th Benchmark Measurement. Brussels, Belgium: European Commission.

IMPIC, I.P. (2011). *Contratação Pública em Portugal – Relatório Síntese 2010*. Lisboa: IMPIC, IP.

IMPIC. IP. (2016a). *Condições Tecnicas de Interligação*. Obtido de Portal BASE: http://www.base.gov.pt/mediaRep/inci/files/base_docs/Req_Interligacao_PE_BASE_20160407.pdf

IMPIC. IP. (2016b, June 18). *Plataformas certificadas*. Retrieved from Portal BASE: http://www.base.gov.pt/Base/pt/PlataformasEletronicas/PlataformaEletronicasLicenciadas

Masson, B. (2014). *Digital disruption ushering in a new era of public services in Europe: a call to action.* Obtido de The Lisbon Council: http://www.lisboncouncil.net/publication/publication/117-delivering-public-service-for-the-future.html

MIT Center for Digital Business and Capgemini Consulting. (2013). *Digital transformation: A roadap for billion dollar organisations.* Retrieved from http://digitalcommunity.mit.edu/docs/DOC-1084

OECD. (2015, February 18). *OECD Recommendation of the Council on Public Procurement.* Retrieved from Decisions, Recommendations and other Instruments of the Organisation for Economic Co-Operation and Development: http://acts.oecd.org/Instruments/ShowInstrumentView.aspx?InstrumentID=320&InstrumentPID=348&Lang=en

Polemi, D., & Papastergiou, S. (2006). *A secure e-ordering web service.* Academic Press.

Tavares, L. (2009). *A gestão das aquisições públicas: guia de aplicação do Código dos Contratos Públicos.* Observatório de Prospectiva da Engenharia e da Tecnologia.

Tavares, L. (2010). *White paper: Public e-Tendering in the European Union: Trust in eVolution.* EVA - European Vortal Academy.

Vaidya, K., Sajeev, A. S., & Callender, G. (2006). Critical factors that influence e-procurement. Journal of Public Procurement, 6.

Westerman, G., Bonnet, D., & Mcaffe, A. (2014). *Leading digital.* Boston: Harvard Business Review Press.

Chapter 6 EKAP: Turkey's Centralized E-Procurement System

Umit Alsaç
Independent Public Procurement Consultant, Turkey

ABSTRACT

In this chapter the author, who has served as one of the lead administrators and designers of Turkey's e-procurement platform (EKAP) discusses the development of the system since May 2009. Specific focus and discussion will be on three main choices on how to develop the system. Will it be mandatory or voluntary? Is it better to create a platform centrally or delegate responsibility to individual public/private parties? How will applications in the platform be introduced, step by step or all at once? The author argues that as a centralized and mandatory e-procurement platform and developed step by step, EKAP successfully transformed public procurement procedures in Turkey, thanks to right choices made regard to the development of the system.

INTRODUCTION

The term "e-procurement" has probably been the trendiest word in the public procurement profession in recent years. Since the beginning of this millennium, along with development of several e-procurement systems such as KONEPS of the Republic of Korea, e-procurement was increasingly quoted as a panacea to well-known ills of public procurement procedures including corruption, fraud, collision, lack

DOI: 10.4018/978-1-5225-2203-4.ch006

of transparency and public oversight. However, what is understood from this term is not unique. Kohli (2012) defines e-procurement as "conducting on the internet the equivalent of the manual tendering process, with the ostensible objective of enhancing transparency and efficiency of public procurement". European Commission (2010) defines it as 'the use of electronic communications and transaction processing by government institutions and other public sector organisations when buying supplies and services or tendering public works.' Gardenal (2010) defines it as "a specific set of instruments, technologies and organizational solutions supporting public procurement processes, particularly considering the possibility to manage tendering procedures and auctions online (e-tendering, e-auctioning)". For the purpose of this chapter the term public e-procurement will be used to define "partial or complete conduct of public procurement procedures on an internet based platform specifically established for public procurement purposes".

Along with many other countries trying to establish a public e-procurement system, Turkey also looked for an e-procurement system to achieve the objectives written in the fifth article of the public procurement law no 4734 (PPL). These objectives are transparency, equal treatment, trust, confidentiality and timely and appropriate meeting of public needs. The institutional framework for e-procurement in Turkey includes, the Turkish Public Procurement Authority (PPA), an independent regulatory and supervisory public organization charged with oversight of public procurement in Turkey, contracting entities, suppliers and other government institutions in charge of various e-government applications to supplement the e-procurement system with information used in public procurement procedures such as tax identification numbers for suppliers who are legal persons and addresses of suppliers. PPA was established in 2002 after the enactment of the PPL same year. PPL was officially entered into force by the beginning of 2003 as one of the main reform laws enacted after the devastating economic crises of 2001 along with assistance from the World Bank, International Monetary Fund and the European Commission.

PPA's work on e-procurement dates back to 2004 when a working group was established to review best practices around the world in order to create an ideal e-procurement model for Turkey. This working group, whose one of the members was the author of this chapter, built a reference e-procurement model after these reviews and consultations with other stakeholders including contracting authorities and unions of suppliers. This model featured an establishment of a single centralized electronic public procurement platform that has to be used (in other words mandatory) by related parties including both contracting authorities and suppliers, established and improved step-by-step (PPA, 2007). In this chapter, the primary focus will be the decisions of PPA and perhaps the Turkish government on whether to establish a single centralized platform or multiple decentralized platforms, make its use mandatory or voluntary and open the platform with end-to-end features covering all procedures or open it with some applications and improve it over time. The author will argue that decisions to establish the e-procurement platform as a single centralized one, make its use mandatory for users and develop it step by step were ideal decisions for the Turkish e-procurement system and helped a smooth transition from paper based procurement to e-procurement though there are still missing blocks for reaching to end-to-end e-procurement which needs particular attention from now on.

BACKGROUND

The decision for governments to transform procurement procedures through e-procurement requires careful considerations. All the stakeholders, including contracting entities and their procurement personnel, suppliers and their personnel in charge of preparation, submission and follow-up of bids, auditors at various government entities who are charged with review of public procurement procedures, are very much used to paper based procedures. As a feature of human character, change and transformation is not easy. So there are various options that need to be considered before embarking on e-procurement transformation. The first decision to be made is how to develop an e-procurement system? Should the government establish a system all at once (end-to-end) to cover all procurement procedures from definition of the need to signing of a contract and all contract management issues such as payment, performance bonds and contract performance? Or, should the system be opened with various applications to cover selected steps of procurement procedures and be developed over time, in other words step-by-step? The second decision is on the institutional set-up of the system. Should the e-procurement system include single centralized platform? Or, should the government allow public or private parties to establish individual e-procurement platforms while regulating and accrediting the platforms? The third decision is on the mandate of the use of system? Should its use be mandatory for contracting authorities and/or suppliers or voluntary? Many national, regional or local governments around the world made these three decisions with impacts on the success and fate of e-procurement systems.

End-to-End vs. Step-by-Step System Development

A typical procurement procedure can be summarized as in Figure 1 below:

An end-to-end e-procurement system covers either all the steps mentioned in Figure 1 or at least the first two phases which ends with signing of the contract. An e-procurement system which is developed step-by-step typically includes applica-

Figure 1. Procurement procedure
(Karagoz, 2014)

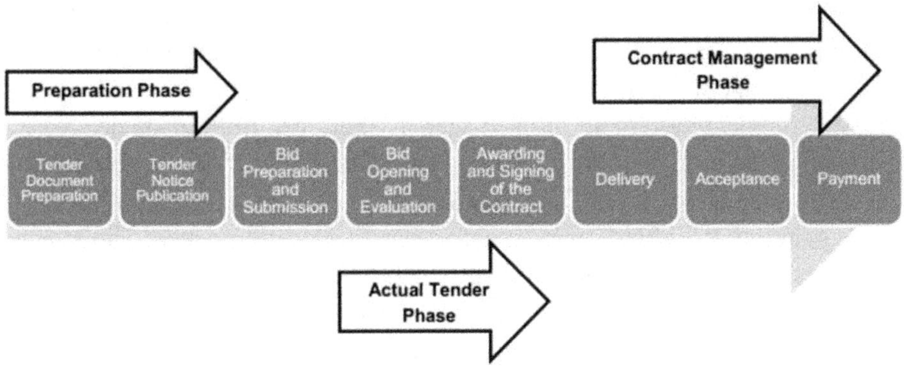

tions covering some of the steps in the procurement procedure while others are not included or are being developed.

The development of a system step-by-step has various advantages. First, it allows a smooth transition from paper based procurement procedures to electronic procedures. This way, resistance to change from stakeholders is somehow softened. Second, the cost of system development is dispersed throughout the time so initial investment requirement is reduced. Third, since the way procurement procedures are conducted changes by e-procurement, mistakes that can be made by users in the system are reduced. For example, if a contracting entity user makes a mistake in the time of notification of contract awards electronically, it can result in disputes. If applications in the system are introduced step-by-step, users get used to the system and the likelihood of making mistakes in its application becomes lower. Fourth, feedbacks can be gathered from stakeholders and those feedbacks can be used both to correct any mistakes made in applications finished so far and how to better develop new applications and make them more user friendly. In their road map to e-procurement, multilateral development banks (2004) including the World Bank, Asian Development Bank and Inter-American Development Bank recommend to start from less complex procedures. Similarly, United Nations E-Procurement Expert Group (2011) posits that in hybrid approaches combining on-line and off-line applications would be better for developing and less developed countries. They emphasize the difficulty of evolution to an end-to-end solution due to the nature and capacity of various stakeholders. The e-procurement platforms of the Philippines (PhilGEPS), Korea (KONEPS), Armenia, Russia and finally Turkey's EKAP are examples of e-procurement platforms developed step-by-step (UN, 2011; Niewadomska & Weiner, 2013).

Developing an end-to-end e-procurement system before it is officially used by contracting authorities and/or suppliers is not easy as mentioned above. However, if accomplished it brings about expected good outcomes of e-procurement sooner. First, an end-to-end system eliminates any paper based procedures so it doesn't carry on red tape to the new system. Second, it allows users to see advantages of the e-procurement system all at once such as shortened time spans needed from definition of the need to awarding of the contract and elimination of procedural errors such as rejection of a bid due to absence of a needed certificate if the system prevents submission of bids unless needed certificates are attached. Third, since it requires higher amounts of initial investments, it decreases the likelihood of any barriers to further development of the system inherent in the step-by-step approach, especially due to resistance to change from stakeholders. In other words, if huge sums of money are invested, it is more difficult to waste it especially if it is financed by public resources. If an end-to-end e-procurement system is built and opened for use, it has to be supported by intensive training sessions for users of the system from all stakeholders. Also, an end-to-end system needs good IT infrastructure for both contracting authorities and suppliers. If there are any parties who lacks technical requirements such as internet connectivity, in the absence of paper based alternatives, they will be unable to procure their needs. Portugal is a good example of a country that has end-to-end private e-procurement platforms used by contracting authorities since late 2009. Georgia also has a public e-procurement platform that is built as an end-to-end e-procurement system (called Ge-GP) and used since late 2010 (EBRD, 2015). Albania's e-procurement system (EPS) was again built as an end-to-end system and used since 2009 (Kashta, 2012).

Single Centralized Platform vs. Multiple Platforms

The institutional set up of the e-procurement system is another decision to be made before embarking on e-procurement project. This decision is, however, more related to how public procurement is regulated and administered in a country. Countries that have centrally regulated public procurement systems with a framework law or laws covering all or most type of public entities including central, regional and local governments, state economic enterprises are more likely to have single centralized e-procurement platforms. Georgia's Ge-GP, South Korea's KONEPS, Albania's EPS and Turkey's EKAP systems are examples of single centralized e-procurement platforms (EBRD 2015, UN 2011). On the other hand, countries that don't have comprehensive public procurement laws covering all types of public entities are more likely to have multiple e-procurement platforms. For example, PwC (2013) identified more than 300 e-procurement platforms operating in the EU. In the UK and Germany e-procurement infrastructures are strongly decentralized parallel to decentralized public procurement regulation (Racca & Albano, 2013). In Portugal, private e-procurement platforms compete with the national government's e-procurement platform (SNCP) for tenders of local governments and state economic enterprises for whom the use of SNCP is voluntary (EBRD, 2015). In Indonesia, local governments are entitled to build and operate their own e-procurement systems (ADB, 2013).

Single centralized platforms have many advantages. First, suppliers don't have to register, learn about and follow so many different platforms in order to see tender opportunities. Also, they don't have to pay fees in order to get registered in multiple platforms. This, in turn also decreases bid prices since suppliers reflect such costs in their pricing strategies. Second, in a single platform all procurement related information (tender notices, documents, contract award information etc.) can be found on a single web site which makes the oversight of public procurement easier (Syquia, 2007). Third, a single centralized platform can be better to promote competition because of its convenience and ease of use for suppliers. Fourth, a single platform is better suited to link with other e-government applications since interoperability issues are overcome more easily when dealing with just one platform. Fifth, establishing a single centralized platform is less costly. Last, a single centralized platform guarantees more standardized procurement procedures for both contracting authorities and suppliers (ADB, 2013; EBRD, 2015).

The advantages of single centralized platforms are disadvantages of multiple platforms due to their absence. In addition, since establishment of each e-procurement platform entails considerable set up costs, if the government decides to switch to a single centralized a-procurement platform model afterwards, a huge amount of resources will be wasted. However, there are considerable advantages of multiple platforms that can be thought of if a suitable framework exists. First, in a public e-procurement system with multiple platforms, all or most of the platforms are privately built and managed. This is the case in Portugal, Ukraine and the UK. Involvement of private sector in building and operating of e-procurement platform decreases the initial set up costs for governments. Though, a single centralized platform can also be privately built under a public private partnership model and reap cost benefits of this approach. Second, competition among different platforms encourages them to build more effective and user friendly systems. Third, in a country where procurement laws and regulations are decentralized and tailored to specific needs of different groups of contracting authorities (local governments, state economic enterprises etc.), multiple platforms are better suited to adapt the system to specific needs of contracting authorities. For example a single centralized platform may not incorporate some applications to a system (such as e-catalogues) if there is not much demand for them, whereas some platforms in a multiple platform system may add them in order to attract new customers to their platform.

Mandatory vs. Voluntary Use

How the system will be used, on a mandatory basis or voluntary basis is another decision to be made both before the platform/platforms are initiated and afterwards. Here, one fact should be clarified further. Mandatory/voluntary use for one type of users (contracting authorities) or both users (both contracting authorities and suppliers) and mandatory/voluntary use for different applications available in the platform throughout the procurement procedure (tender document preparation, tender notice publication, bid submission etc.) are two sides of this discussion. Different countries opt for different strategies in this regard. Some countries make the use e-procurement platform(s) mandatory for both users and for all tender phases available in the system. Typically, it is made mandatory through laws and with certain deadlines. Portugal and Georgia are typical examples of countries that have made the use of e-procurement platform(s) mandatory. Portugal made the use of those accredited multiple e-procurement platforms since November 2009 for purchases above the value of €5.000 after enactment of a series of laws and regulations in 2007-2008. Georgia made the use of Ge-GP mandatory for all procurement procedures since December 2010 after enactment of a new law same year (EBRD, 2015). New European Public Procurement Directives (2014/EC/24 for classical procurement and 2014/EC/25 for utilities procurement) accepted in April 2014, stipulate that electronic submission of bids will be mandatory for procurement of central purchasing bodies in March 2017 and for all contracting entities in September 2018. Some other countries, who have more or less developed e-procurement systems, don't make its use mandatory for contracting authorities. Ireland, Germany, the UK and the Netherlands can be counted as examples of those countries (Racca & Albano, 2013)

Making the use of e-procurement system mandatory has some clear advantages. It makes the transformation process from paper based procedures to e-procurement fast. It eliminates the potential of redundancy as regards this transformation among users of both contracting authorities and suppliers most of whom would probably be resisting the change. However mandatory use does not guarantee success, especially, when a sufficient infrastructure does not exist. For example, in the Philippines when PhilGEPS was first introduced in 2003, initial implementation and adaptation level was slow due to insufficiency of resources. Only about 25% of contracting authorities did have sufficient internet connectivity (Syquia, 2007). On the other hand, voluntary use lacks the advantages of mandatory use, namely fast adaptation and overcoming resistance to change. However, it has positive aspects as well. It eliminates any bottlenecks in procurement of public needs due to problems inherent in newly established e-procurement systems. For example, if some contracting authorities have problems with internet connectivity, as it was the case in the Philippines in early 2000s, they can opt for paper based procedures in order to procure their needs. It is also associated with prudent transformation from paper to e-procurement. If only those contracting authorities and suppliers who are technically ready use the system, their enthusiasm may increase the success of the system and eliminate any resistance to transformation which may be detrimental for e-procurement reform especially in early stages. Volunteer users are more prone to collaborate with e-procurement system developers and administrators and they can report any problems within the system (such as misinterpretation of a rule written in the law) and contribute to optimal solutions. However, voluntary use of the system should not curb competition in procurement. Even if a contracting authority is ready for the use of the system, if their suppliers are not ready for its use, it may decrease the number of bids on average and increase bid prices.

TURKEY'S E-PROCUREMENT SYSTEM: EKAP

Before going over the three decisions on how to develop an e-procurement system in Turkey, it is better to give some background information about the Turkish public procurement system. In Turkey, public procurement is regulated primarily by PPL No. 4734 which has been enacted in 2002 and enforced since the beginning of 2003. This law regulates procurement of goods, services, consultancy services and construction by contracting authorities. Contract execution phase is regulated by another law, the Public Procurement Contracts Law No. 4735. It typically covers all publicly financed procurements of central governments, local governments, state/municipal economic enterprises and social security institutions. Though, there are various exemptions from the PPL. Primarily these exemptions are commercial procurements (used for production of commercial goods and services) of state/municipal economic enterprises, procurements for national defense and intelligence and procurement of pharmaceuticals directly from pharmacies by patients under social security. Three procurement procedures prescribed in the PPL are open, restricted and negotiated procedures. There is also direct procurement which doesn't entail tenders and composed of simpler methods, generally used for single source procurement and procurements that have lower values (below 18.000 USD) (PPA, 2012).

As briefly mentioned in the introduction, PPA is the main regulatory and supervisory body in charge of public procurement in Turkey. Main duties of PPA are regulating procurements under the scope of the PPL, settlement of disputes between contracting authorities and suppliers during tender procedures within the scope of PPL, management of EKAP and training of contracting authorities and suppliers about the PPL and secondary regulations (PPA, 2012). Public procurement market in Turkey has a considerable size. According to statistics of PPA (2016), total size of public procurement market was 148 billion TL in 2015 (about 51 billion USD) which is about 7% of the GDP (PPA, 2016). Of this amount 128 billion TL (about 43.8 billion USD) is procured through normal procurement procedures within the scope of PPL, 12 billion TL (about 4.1 billion USD) is procured through exemptions and 8 billion TL is procured under direct procurement (about 3.1 billion USD).

EKAP: General Information

EKAP is the Turkish abbreviation for Electronic Public Procurement Platform. The term EKAP entered into the PPL in November 2008 when the PPL was amended to legalize the use of electronic means in public procurement procedures within the scope of the PPL. The fourth article of the PPL defines EKAP as *"the electronic environment, managed by the Authority, in which the contracting authorities and other stakeholders can conduct the proceedings related with the procurement process via internet"*. The additional article No:1 which is named also as EKAP stipulates that:

...stages related to procurement process, such as the tender notice, preparation and submission of the tender document, submission of the documents concerning participation and qualification, preparation, submission, and evaluation of the tenders, finalization and approval of the procurement, notification of the final tender decision, and signing of the contract as well as all sorts of notifications may be realized partly or wholly over the EKAP established by the PPA. The principles and procedures concerning the establishment and operation of the Electronic Public Procurement Platform as well as the use of electronic means during the procurement process shall be determined by the PPA (PPA, 2012).

After the amendment of the PPL in November 2008, the PPA conducted a service tender to outsource the software development services. The technical work of the e-procurement project started in May 2009 after signing of the service contract. Another tender was also conducted in the last quarter of November 2009 to procure hardware such as servers, memory discs needed for the system. Even though EKAP was not officially opened yet, an interface of EKAP was developed by February 2010 to register contracting authorities and suppliers. This process was supported by a call center, again established by the PPA, to assist registration of these stakeholders. After a very busy period of software development, hardware installation, application testing and stakeholder training period, EKAP was officially opened in September 2010 (Alsac, 2013). In Figure 2, a screenshot of EKAP web page is illustrated:

The layout of EKAP system is depicted in Figure 3 below:

As the Figure 3 above illustrates, EKAP system has 4 main components. The first component is the EKAP Contracting Authority module. This module has numerous applications developed for and used by contracting authorities including

EKAP

Figure 2. EKAP opening page

Figure 3. EKAP layout

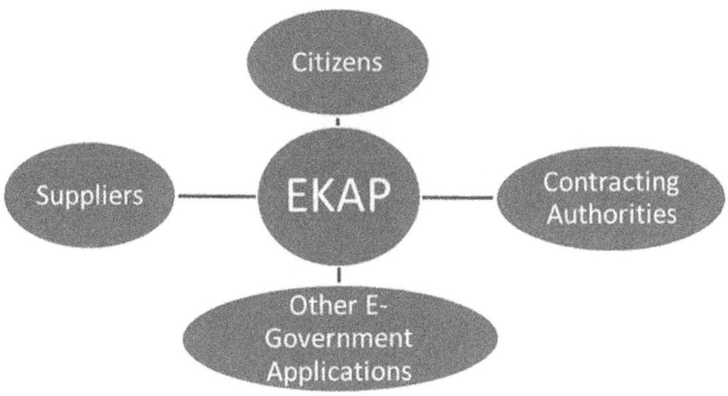

tender notice and tender document preparation, tender evaluation records, contract award notice preparation, e-bid opening and evaluation, submission of notifications, black list confirmation and various contract management applications such as records of payments and preparation of business experience certificates for contractors who have successfully finished their work. The second module is the Suppliers Module. This module has applications specifically developed for themselves such as downloading of tender documents using e-signatures, submission of e-bids, search for tender notices within areas of their interest and receipt of notifications from contracting authorities about the status of their proposals. These two components are only open to users of contracting authorities and suppliers and can be used after a login based on a user ID and a password. The third component is integration with other e-government systems used to gather information about contracting authorities and suppliers. This approach aims to retrieve information directly from its source and eliminate any duplications and disputes about such information which determines qualification of suppliers. The list of EKAP's integration with other e-government systems is as follows (EBRD, 2015):

- Ministry of Finance/Revenue Administration (information about the tax debts due, identity of legal persons, balance sheet and income statements),
- Social Security Institution (information about social security premium debts due),
- Ministry of Health- The Pharmaceuticals and Medical Devices Data Bank (information about sellers of medical devices and goods sold by them including quality certificates and authorizations given to sell those goods by producers),
- General Directorate of Population and Citizenship (information about identity of real persons),
- General Directorate of Public Accounting (information about identity of contracting authorities).

The fourth component is EKAP Citizens module, in other words EKAP's main page which contains procurement related information open for public in order to ensure public oversight and transparency in public procurement. Some of the applications available in this module are tender search, downloading of tender documents, inquiries about decisions taken by the PPA about disputes and downloading of public procurement bulletins which include tender notices and contract award notices.

Various numbers about EKAP are summarized in Table 1 (PPA, 2016). The numbers written in Table 1 illustrates the level of maturity EKAP system has achieved so far.

EKAP: Step-by-Step Development

EKAP system is not an end-to-end e-procurement system. Its development continues since September 2010 when it officially started to operate. PPA undertook the approach of step-by-step and cautious system development in order to alleviate any objections and resistance to electronic procedures and reduce potential mistakes in procurement procedures that can arise due to incompetence of individual users which may strengthen the position of stakeholders who are against transformation to

Table 1. EKAP by numbers (as of 31.12.2015)

Total number of registered contracting authorities	30.065
Total number of registered suppliers	101.343
Total number of individual users	479.995
Total number of tenders registered since Sep.2010	1.061.612
Total number of tenders where e-bids were submitted since June 2013	137
Total number of notifications sent from contracting authorities to suppliers via EKAP since January 2015	977.500
Total number of business certificates issued for contractors who have successfully completed their contracts	109.073

e-procurement. When EKAP was first opened in September 2010 it mainly provided following electronic applications for contracting authorities:

- Preparation of a needs report in order to define what is being procured and classify the needs according to the Common Procurement Vocabulary used in the European Union.
- Tender registration.
- Tender document preparation according to more than 30 specification and contract templates separated according to type of procurement (goods, services, consultancy and construction) and type of procedure (open, restricted and negotiated). This application was probably the most important one at that stage. Because, this application was based on a wizard that directs users of contracting authorities, who are in charge of tender document preparation, in accordance with law and regulations. For example, if a certain type of document has to be requested from bidders due to the size (estimated value)/nature of procurement (goods, services, works) (e.g. bank statements, experience certificates), this wizard mandatorily places this requirement into the tender document. This way, the potential of mistakes in tender document preparation was reduced substantially.
- Tender notice preparation and publication.
- Record of tender document sales (according to the PPL potential bidders have to either buy the tender document from the contracting authority or download it from EKAP using their e-signatures), record of paper bids submitted and evaluations(valid, economically most advantageous, rejected etc.) of bids by the tender commission.
- Record of tender commission members so that only those who are entitled can conduct work on EKAP for a particular tender.

- Black list confirmations (according to the PPL those in the black list of the PPA cannot be awarded a contract)
- Collection of monthly procurement data about procurements made via direct procurement clause of the PPL.
- Contract award notice preparation and publication.

The functionalities provided for suppliers were even more modest at this stage. Suppliers who are registered in EKAP were just entitled for tender notice search mechanisms and selection of sectors of their operation and receipt of tender notices in those selected sectors via their e-mails. Therefore, when EKAP was initially opened, it didn't allow for electronic bid submission, opening and evaluation.

After EKAP started to operate it was developed continuously. Thousands of minor bugs (such as removal of a rule that is not compatible with regulations or addition of a forward/back button needed on a specific page) were fixed and many new applications were added to the system to ease its use, to transfer more paper based procedures to electronic ones and incorporate any legal/regulatory rule changes into applications in EKAP. Table 2 below gives the list of major novelties added to EKAP since its opening (PPA, 2016).

As the Table 2 illustrates, there has been a continuous and step by step development trend in EKAP. The step-by-step development approach was a deliberate strategy of the PPA. This approach brought about many advantages and somehow was necessary due to resource limitations and resources. The advantages and necessities were as follows:

- This approach did not suddenly end paper based procedures. So, procurement personnel of both contracting authorities and suppliers adapted to EKAP system easily. This fact decreased tendency of user caused mistakes in procurement procedures and potential resistance to change.
- This approach was also needed due to resource limitations. The initial project team of the PPA who developed and opened EKAP consisted of 1 project manager, 3 public procurement experts and just 17 technical staff 15 of whom was personnel of the contractor mainly composed of software and hardware engineers. With just 21 staff, it was not technically possible to analyze all paper based procedures and transform them to electronic ones. Later in July 2011, the number of contractor's technical staff increased to 60, and this increase made development and testing of novel applications much easier.
- Another resource limitation was hardware. All transactions conducted on EKAP and documents uploaded (such as technical specifications) have to be recorded and backed up both for archiving purposes and as a cushion against events such as system shutdowns, cyber-attacks and fires in hardware rooms.

Table 2. Novel applications added to EKAP since September 2010

Time of Addition	Name of Application	Brief Explanation
December 2010	Tender Document Downloading via e-signatures	This application gives suppliers who are registered in EKAP the opportunity to download tender documents via their e-signatures if all tender documents are uploaded to EKAP by the contracting authority. This way, suppliers are relieved from the tender document purchasing requirement for bid submission.
December 2010	Integration with the Social Security Institution and the Revenue Administration	According to the PPL, suppliers who have tax and social security debts due con not be awarded a contract. This application gives contracting authorities the opportunity to inquire these debts from related e-government systems.
January 2012	Tender Diary	Suppliers who are registered in EKAP, can record tenders of their interest on their diaries in EKAP. This application informs suppliers about due dates of bid submission and any changes made to tender documents by contracting authorities.
March 2012	Mobile EKAP	Those who have EKAP on their mobile phones can use various applications of EKAP such as tender search.
May 2012	New Contract Award Notices	All contract award notices were renewed in order to give more concrete and varied information about contracts awarded, including trade name of the contractor, contract price vs. estimated value, total number of bids submitted.
May 2012	Integration with the Ministry of Health's (MoH) Pharmaceuticals and Medical Devices Data Bank (PMDDB)	According to regulations of the MoH, all pharmaceuticals and medical devices to be sold to public hospitals have to be registered in the PMDDB. This application gives contracting authorities functionality to make such inquiries directly from the PMDDB.
June 2012	Business Experience Certificate Preparation and Inquiry Module	Business experience certificates are required as a qualification document in most tenders conducted according to the PPL. They are given to successful contractors who have successfully fulfilled their contracts. Those engineers/ architects who control/manage construction works are also entitled for business experience certificates. This application gives contracting authorities opportunity to prepare these certificates according to 21 templates prescribed by regulations. This way, possible mistakes during preparation of these certificates are avoided. If these certificates are used by suppliers in a specific tender, the tender commission can inquire the validity of this certificate on EKAP and ensure that a fake certificate is not used.
September 2012	Tender Document Downloading via mobile e-signatures.	With this application, suppliers registered in EKAP can download tender documents via their mobile e-signatures in mobile EKAP application.

continued on following page

Table 2. Continued

Time of Addition	Name of Application	Brief Explanation
January 2013	Contract Management	With this application, contracting authorities started to report information about any additional works/deducted works to/from a specific contract, any price differences paid to the contractor due to inflation, payments to contractors, cancellation of contracts and causes of cancellation (e.g. bankruptcy of a contractor) to the PPA on EKAP. These figures are used in semi-annually statistical reports to give accurate figures about the size of public procurement market in Turkey.
June 2013	E-bid preparation/submission and e-tender evaluation at call-off stages of framework agreements.	According to the PPL, framework agreements can be used by contracting authorities for commonly procured goods and services. After a framework agreement is signed with at least three suppliers, mini competitions are conducted at call-off stages to make actual procurement. This application, transfers this procedure totally to EKAP and paper procedures are eliminated. Generally used in pharmaceutical and medical devices sectors.
December 2014	Electronic Notifications	All notifications from contracting authorities to suppliers are conducted on EKAP. This application finishes the use of paper based notifications and saves considerable amount of time compared to snail mails used in paper procedures.
January 2016	Direct Procurement Records	Contracting authorities started to record each procurement made using the direct procurement clause of the PPL. This is an alternative to monthly gross direct procurement data collection which was available on EKAP since its opening.

The system needs to have terabytes of cyber space for these purposes and so many servers, disks and cyber-attack prevention applications/devices. This in turn requires big initial hardware investments. If EKAP was opened as an end-to-end e-procurement system, the available hardware stock could not cope with enormous increase in data and recording of procurement could continue only for a few months. When another substantial hardware investment was made in the second half of 2014, the system was running up to its maximum potential. Disks were nearly full. So, the step-by-step approach also gave time for additional investments that has to be made for an extensive e-procurement system.

- The step-by-step approach also gave PPA the opportunity to receive feedbacks from users of EKAP to correct any errors inherent in the system, enhance current applications, design and develop new applications. The call center of EKAP was essential in this regard, since many bugs were fixed after they were delivered by EKAP users via the call center and project staff was being informed about which new applications would be more essential for EKAP users.

EKAP: A Single-Centralized E-Procurement Platform

EKAP is the only national public e-procurement platform in Turkey. Its status as a single centralized e-procurement platform stems from both the administrative structure of Turkey and public procurement system briefly described at the beginning of this section. Turkey's constitution foresees a strong control and oversight of central government over local governments. (Turkish Prime Ministry, 2016) No states exist in Turkey. Local governments are generally composed of municipalities. Even though mayors and members of municipal assemblies are elected, they are strictly controlled by the Ministry of Interior. Municipalities receive substantial financial assistance from central government because their primary source of income, real estate taxes, are not sufficient to meet their costs. This philosophy is reflected in the PPL since all types of governments and public entities including state/municipal economic enterprises are in the scope of the PPL. When the PPL was amended to legalize its development, EKAP was considered as a single-centralized public e-procurement platform which has to be administered and developed by the PPA. In the same manner, the PPA's status as a single national regulatory and supervisory authority in charge of public procurement, similarly led to the birth of a single-centralized e-procurement platform.

What did Turkey and the PPA achieve with a single centralized public e-procurement platform? Pretty much the same as other successful single centralized e-procurement platforms such as Korea's KONEPS:

- EKAP as a single centralized platform endured standardization in e-procurement procedures. PPL and public procurement regulations enforced by the PPA have hundreds of rules that administer public procurement regulations. A single centralized platform meant that those rules are applied uniformly in e-procurement procedures. If multiple platforms existed in Turkey, then some rules and regulations could be interpreted and transferred to electronic environment differently which could be harmful both for contracting authorities and suppliers and lead to disputes among stakeholders including managements of these portals.
- EKAP's status as an e-procurement platform administered by the PPA also ensured that rules and regulations were accurately transferred to the electronic environment since PPA is the regulator and EKAP was designed with and tested by contribution of public procurement experts, including author of this chapter, who have many years of expertise in regulation and review of public procurement procedures within the scope of the PPL.

- EKAP, as a single centralized platform prevented the need to retrieve public procurement related data from multiple platforms in order to construct public procurement statistics, as was the case in Portugal and Indonesia.
- EKAP has become the single source of public procurement related information including tender notices, tender documents and contract award notices. So, there has not been any need for suppliers to deal with hassle of registering in multiple platforms to follow tender opportunities. This fact combined with free registration opportunity for suppliers increased competition considerably. According to PPA's statistics, in tenders where tender documents were downloaded by suppliers on EKAP using e-signatures, a novelty of EKAP, the average number of bids submitted was 5,1. On the other hand, in tenders where tender documents could not be downloaded by suppliers on EKAP using e-signatures, thus had to be procured from the contracting authority, the average number of bids submitted was 2,6 in year 2012 (Alsac, 2013). The reason why tender documents cannot be downloaded using e-signatures on EKAP is because the size of the tender document exceeds the permitted amount which was 40 MB at that time but increased to 100 MB in 2015.
- EKAP as a single source of public procurement related information also made public oversight much easier since every citizen can see tender notices, tender documents, any disputes between contracting entities and suppliers that has been delivered to the PPA and contract award notices without any need to register and pay any fees. Especially, the application named "Tender at a Glance" gives such public data on a single sheet for each tender.
- EKAP's status as a single centralized platform administered by the PPA, a public organization, made it easier to integrate and link with other e-government applications, since public organizations are generally reluctant to share information with private sector organizations.

EKAP: A Mandatory E-Procurement Platform

EKAP's use has been mandatory for contracting authorities since its opening in September 2010. However, registration in EKAP was not mandatory for suppliers who have Turkish origin until January 2015. There are particular reasons why its use was mandatory for contracting authorities from its opening. First, public procurement rules and regulations are mostly focused on procedures that are conducted by contracting authorities. The roles of suppliers are mainly preparation and submission of bids and if there are any disputes, delivering of any complaints to the PPA for settlement. All other procedures are responsibilities of contracting authorities from preparation of tender documents to evaluation of bids and awarding of contracts. Second, most of the disputes brought to the PPA for settlement were due to mistakes (such as omission of a required qualification certificate in the tender document) made by contracting authorities in procurement procedures. Development and use of electronic applications intended for contracting authorities' use would decrease most disputes due to this fact. Third, one of the most beneficial aspects of transformation to e-procurement is collection of more reliable and in-depth procurement statistics. These statistics are collected by input from contracting authorities. If registration in and use of EKAP was not mandatory for contracting authorities, those statistics could not be collected as desired. Fourth, nearly half of PPA's income is fees collected from contracting authorities for tender notices published in the Public Procurement Bulletin (PPB) (PPA, 2016). Tender notices are prepared and submitted to the PPA via EKAP and published in the PPB available on EKAP. Collection of fees is controlled by an application that has integration with three commercial banks in which PPA has accounts. If tender notice fees are not deposited in PPA's accounts, then contracting authorities cannot submit their notices to the PPA for publication. Mandatory use of EKAP by contracting authorities ensures smooth flow of PPA's primary income.

Even though, EKAP's use has been mandatory for contracting authorities since opening of EKAP, use of not all applications were mandatory. For example, even though business experience certificate preparation and inquiry module became available on EKAP since January 2012, its use was not mandatory until September 2014. Similarly, e-bid preparation/submission and e-bid evaluation at call-off stages of framework agreements became available on EKAP in June 2013, but its use is still not mandatory. Also, use of contract management applications has not been mandatory for contracting authorities since June 2014, even though it was available on EKAP by January 2013. This is partly because PPA regulations didn't keep pace with EKAP's development of new application and partly because PPA and administrators of EKAP, including the author of this chapter, wanted to see how these novel applications work and receive feedback from users before making their use mandatory.

PPA statistics collected from EKAP show the effect of making its use mandatory. Figure 4 below show the trend in the number of contracting authorities registered in EKAP:

Figure 4 shows that the total number of contracting entities registered in EKAP has kept increasing since March 31, 2011 (6 months after EKAP's opening), but always have been considerably high because its use was mandatory. Another reason, why EKAP has such a high number of contracting authorities is decentralized structure of procurement in Turkey. Even departments in ministries and municipalities have their own budget and are entitled to register in EKAP as a separate contracting authority. So many contracting authorities have already been registered in EKAP since its opening, though some of them got registered afterwards because

Figure 4. The number of contracting authorities registered in EKAP

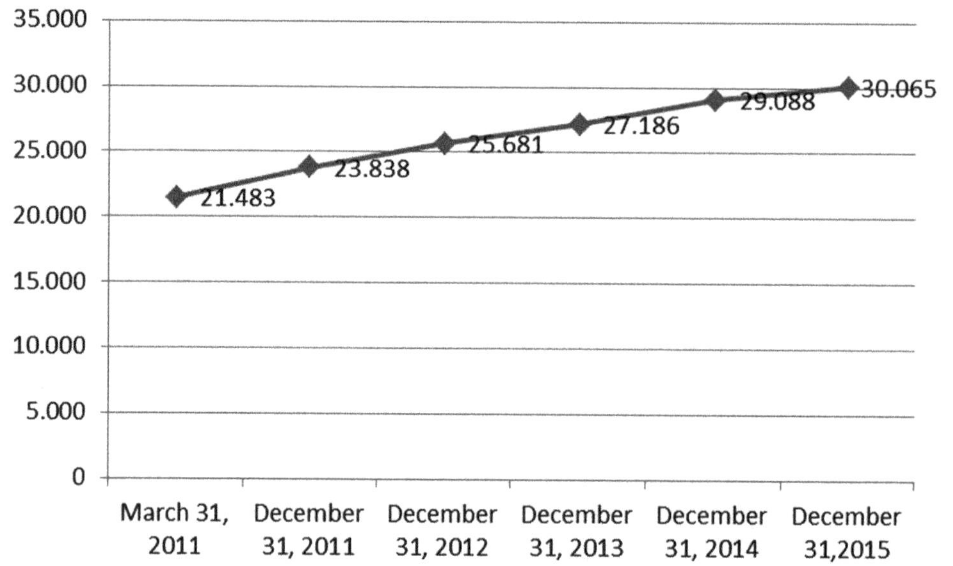

they were established after EKAP's opening or they have not used their own budgets for procurements before they registered in EKAP.

As mentioned above, registration in EKAP was not mandatory for suppliers who are of Turkish origin until the beginning of 2015. Until that time, suppliers were encouraged to register in EKAP by various advantages such as downloading of tender documents using e-signatures and e-bid preparation and submission at call-off stages of framework agreements. Figure 5 below shows the same registration trend for suppliers using PPA statistics collected from EKAP:

The Figure 5 illustrates that the number of suppliers registered in EKAP continuously increased between early 2011 and 2015-year end. However, the steepest increase happened after December 31, 2014 when EKAP registration became mandatory for suppliers of Turkish origin. The trend of increase became apparent even from 2013 year end to 2014 year end because the PPA announced in mid-2014 that EKAP registration would be mandatory for suppliers of Turkish origin by the beginning of year 2015. So, this statistics show that even with strong incentives, such as tender document downloading with e-signatures, suppliers were not allured to EKAP registration before it became mandatory. Another similar statistics is about the number of business experience certificates prepared in EKAP. As mentioned before, the use of business experience certificate preparation and inquiry application was not mandatory until September 2014 even though it became available on EKAP since January 2012. The Figure 6 below shows the number of business experience certificates prepared since this application became available on EKAP:

EKAP

Figure 5. The number of suppliers registered in EKAP

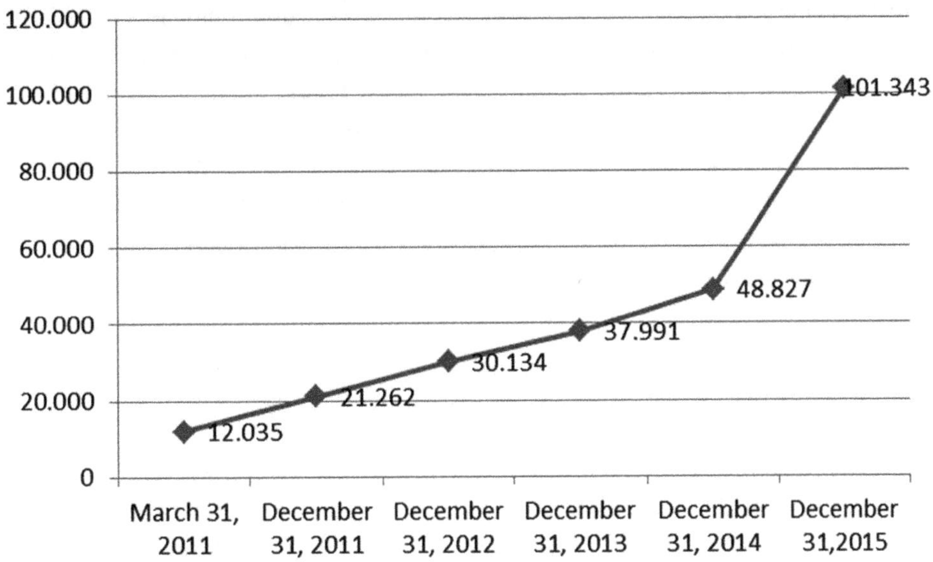

Figure 6. The number of business experience certificates prepared on EKAP

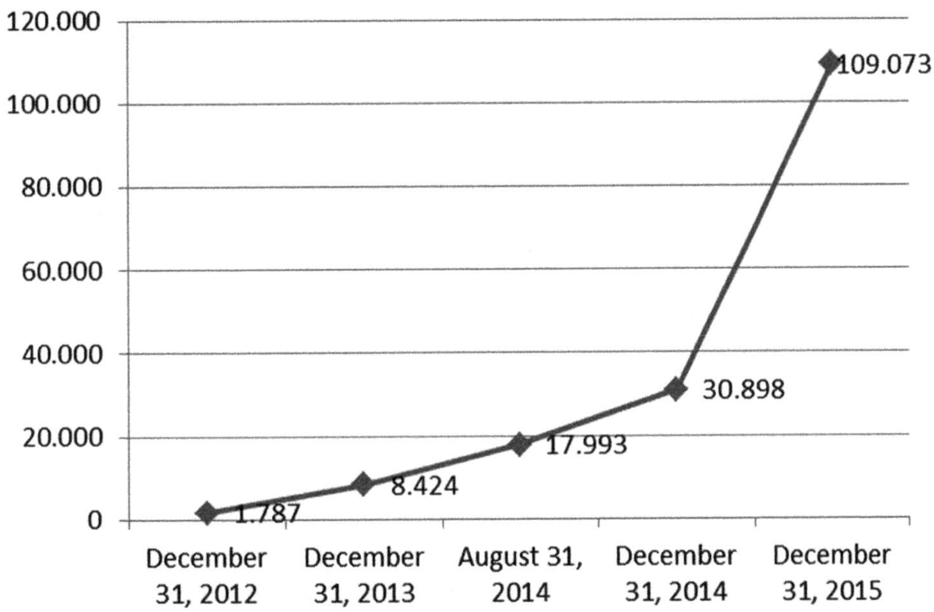

The Figure 6 illustrates that the increase in the number of business experience certificates was modest until September 2014, when the use of business experience certificate preparation application became mandatory. The number of certificates prepared on EKAP substantially increased after the regulation made its use mandatory. This statistics again show that, even with strong incentives to use electronic applications in procurement procedures and contract management, (in this case opportunity to prepare certificates with minimum errors and validate them on EKAP by electronic inquiries during tender evaluation stage) its use doesn't really take-off until regulation makes it mandatory.

CONCLUSION

After nearly 6 years since its opening, EKAP has fundamentally transformed public procurement procedures within the scope of PPL in Turkey. All tender documents are prepared on EKAP for tenders within the scope of the PPL, evaluation of bids are partially electronic (most qualification certificates are still submitted paper based) but fully recorded on EKAP, a comprehensive set of tender related information can be monitored which is essential for transparency and public oversight, a comprehensive set of tools are provided for contract management purposes and collection of statistics about execution of contracts and paperless (fully electronic) tenders have already started on EKAP at call-off stages of framework agreements. By electronic notifications from contracting authorities to suppliers of Turkish origin on EKAP, time intervals required for procurement procedures condensed, since notifications based on snail paper mails require much more time. Both contracting authorities and suppliers registered on EKAP have been happy with this information. A survey conducted by the PPA (2012), less than 2 years after EKAP was opened, showed that nearly 90% of contracting authority users said mistakes in procurement procedures were reduced after EKAP and nearly 95% of these users said EKAP eased procurement procedures for them. In the same survey, more than 90% of supplier users registered in EKAP said they were satisfied with EKAP and nearly 95% of these users said EKAP's tender document downloading by e-signatures and advanced tender search mechanism were best applications provided by EKAP for them. So, even within a short period of time after its opening, EKAP was very favorably esteemed by main stakeholders. According to a study conducted by (Niwadomska & Weiner, 2013), Turkey was ranked 5th in terms of e-procurement adaptation among 26 countries in which EBRD operates. Both these surveys and independent assessment by the EBRD show that EKAP has been a successful e-procurement system. Another indication of success is the interest of many other countries on EKAP including Kyrgyzstan,

Kosovo, Greece, Oman, Bahrain and Poland who have sent delegations to review EKAP for knowledge sharing from 2012 to 2015.

As this chapter illustrated with so many facts and figures, deliberate decisions by the PPA as to how to build an e-procurement system has determined EKAP's success. A step-by-step development strategy ensured smooth transformation from paper based procurement to e-procurement. It alleviated potential resistance to change and incorporated feedback of stakeholders for better system development. Also, modest initial investments and resources were sufficient to execute this strategy. Building a single and centralized e-procurement system was the best way for Turkey since the PPL and the PPA were based on centralized regulation and standardization in e-procurement and effective procurement data collection could be best achieved by a single centralized e-procurement platform. Making the use of EKAP mandatory for contracting authorities from the very beginning ensured that e-procurement applications were used to a great extent at the very beginning and expected outcomes such as reductions of mistakes in tender document preparation could be achieved sooner. Awaiting of mandatory EKAP registration for suppliers for more than 4 years after its opening reduced the use of EKAP's novel applications by suppliers and demonstrated that mandatory use would be better in Turkey. This fact also lengthened reaping of benefits such as improved competition, as the number of bids submitted substantially increases when tender documents are downloaded on EKAP by registered suppliers using e-signatures. These decisions were supported by comprehensive training for procurement personnel of both the contracting authorities and suppliers. PPA engaged in intensive information and training sessions for these two stakeholders both before the system was launched and afterwards until most users of the system got used to EKAP's applications and its legal framework. PPA embraced a different approach as a supplement to formal training sessions. This approach was called self-training for EKAP users via videos and manuals. Video guides were prepared and made available on EKAP in order to show how to use EKAP applications such as registration of tenders, preparation of tender documents and submission of e-bids. After major applications were added to EKAP, such as business experience certificate preparation and inquiry module, PPA posted manuals on EKAP to train EKAP users and show how these applications are used. Both formal training sessions and self-training tools decreased likelihood of user mistakes on EKAP and helped alleviate resistance to change.

Looking forward, EKAP needs some fundamental electronic applications in order to be a more sophisticated and en-to-end procurement system. E-bid preparation, submission and evaluation are still not available on EKAP, except call-off stages of framework agreements. This application should be developed further to make e-bid preparation, submission and evaluation possible for other type of tenders as well. The biggest obstacle for this application is the need for paper based qualification documents in tenders, when qualification documents cannot be electronically retrieved on EKAP from other e-government applications. In order to overcome this bottleneck, when inquiry on EKAP is not possible on EKAP, suppliers should be entitled to submit declarations at the bidding phase, and the only successful bidder should be required to submit paper based documents before signing of the contract. Even though direct procurements are recorded on EKAP, they are not advertised to inform potential suppliers for procurement opportunities. Procurement notices for direct procurements should be prepared and published on EKAP. Further, registered EKAP suppliers should submit quotations for direct procurements on EKAP using their signatures. This application is quite easier to adapt since there are not any paper based qualification documents required for direct procurements. By achieving these novelties, EKAP will be a more end-to-end e-procurement system and satisfaction of both contracting authorities and suppliers will increase.

REFERENCES

Alsac, U. (2013). The Developments of E-procurement in Turkey. In L. V. Tavares (Ed.), *E-Public Procurement in Europe: Public Management, Technologies and Processes of Change* (pp. 48–55). Lisbon: OPET Publishing.

Asian Development Bank. (2013). *E-Government Procurement Handbook*. Retrieved April 27, 2016, from http://www.adb.org/sites/default/files/institutional-document/34064/files/e-government-procurement-handbook.pdf

European Bank for Reconstruction and Development-EBRD. (2015). *Guide to Electronic Procurement Reform*. Retrieved April 25, 2016 from http://www.ebrd.com/what-we-do/sectors/legal-reform/public-procurement.html

European Commission. (2010). *Green Paper on Expanding the Use of e-Procurement in the EU Brussels*. European Commission.

Gardenal, F. (2010). Public E-procurement-Define, Measure and Optimize Organizational Benefits. *Proceedings of the* 4th *International Public Procurement Conference*. Retrieved April 24, 2016, from http://www.ippa.org/IPPC4/Proceedings/05e-Procurement/Paper5-1.pdf

Karagoz, H. (2014). Procurement Procedures at Unions of Public Hospitals. *Journal of Health Efficiency*, *2*, 26–31.

Kashta, R. (2012), E-procurement System in Albania, Impact and Lessons Learned. *Proceedings of the 5th International Public Procurement Conference*. Retrieved April 25, 2016, from http://www.ippa.org/IPPC5/Proceedings/Part2/PAPER2-5.pdf

Kohli, J. (2012). Red Flags in E-procurement/E-tendering for Public Procurement and Some Remedial Measures. *Proceedings of the 5th International Public Procurement Conference*. Retrieved April 24, 2016, from http://www.ippa.org/IPPC5/Proceedings/Part2/PAPER2-6.pdf

Multilateral Development Banks. (2004). *Electronic Government Procurement Roadmap*. Retrieved April 24, 2016, from http://idbdocs.iadb.org/wsdocs/getdocument.aspx?docnum=645469

Niewadomska, E., & Weiner, S. (2013). Measuring Success in Public Procurement Reform. *Law in Transition Online*, *2*, 6–21.

PricewaterhouseCoopers. (2013). *E-procurement Golden Book of Good Practice*. Retrieved April 27, 2016, from http://ec.europa.eu/archives/dgs/internal_market/studies/docs/e-procurement-golden-book-of-good-practice_en.pdf

Racca, G., & Albano, G. L. (2013). Collaborative Public Procurement and Supply Chain. In D. Martinez-Alfonso (Ed.), *The SAGE Handbook of Strategic Supply Management* (pp. 179–213). London: SAGE Publications Ltd. doi:10.4135/9781446269886.n8

Syquia, J. L. C. (2007). *Reforming Public Procurement in Emerging Market Countries. A USAID's sponsored view on procurement reform*. USAID. Retrieved April 27, 2016, from http://kdid.org/sites/kdid/files/resource/files/Reforming%20Public%20Procurement%20in%20Emerging%20Market%20Countries.pdf

Turkish Prime Ministry. (2016). *The Constitution of Turkey. Ankara, Turkey*. Turkish Prime Ministry. Retrieved April 27, 2016, from http://www.mevzuat.gov.tr/MevzuatMetin/1.5.2709.doc

Turkish Public Procurement Authority. (2006). *Annual Performance Report for the Year 2006*. Ankara, Turkey: Turkish Public Procurement Authority.

Turkish Public Procurement Authority. (2012a). *Public Procurement Law*. Ankara, Turkey: Turkish Public Procurement Authority. Retrieved April 27, 2016, from http://www2.ihale.gov.tr/english/4734_English.pdf

Turkish Public Procurement Authority. (2012b). *EKAP Survey for User Satisfaction*. Ankara, Turkey: Turkish Public Procurement Authority. Retrieved April 27, 2016, from http://www2.ihale.gov.tr/duyurular2012/20120404_EKAP_Kullanim_Anketi.pdf

Turkish Public Procurement Authority. (2016a). *2015 Report for Public Procurement Statistics*. Ankara, Turkey: Turkish Public Procurement Authority. Retrieved April 27, 2016, from http://dosyalar.kik.gov.tr/genel/Raporlar/2015_yil_sonu_kamu_alimlari_raporu_v2.pdf

Turkish Public Procurement Authority. (2016b). *Annual Performance Report for the Year 2015*. Ankara, Turkey: Turkish Public Procurement Authority. Retrieved April 27, 2016, from http://www2.ihale.gov.tr/duyurular2012/2015_Faaliyet_Raporu.pdf

United Nations. (2011). *Expert Group Meeting Report: E-Procurement: Towards Transparency and Efficiency in Public Service Delivery*. New York, NY: United Nations.

Chapter 7
Public Procurement Reform in Georgia:
The Way from Paper-Based Procurement to an E-Procurement System

Ana Chania
State Procurement Agency, Georgia

Kakha Demetrashvili
State Procurement Agency, Georgia

ABSTRACT

The Georgian public procurement system has undergone significant Public Financial Management reforms over the last few years. The goal of creation, introduction and management of the Georgian Electronic Government Procurement (Ge-GP) system was delegated upon the State Procurement Agency, which succeeded in ensuring the development of the software for the Ge-GP system under the assistance of the National Agency of Public Registry. The Ge-GP system was created within less than one year. From the first of December, 2010 all the paper-based tenders were abolished and electronic procurement has become the single platform. Through the introduction of electronic procurement platform, the Georgian procurement system has become considerably more transparent and nondiscriminatory, encouraging free and fair competition and minimizing the risk of corruption. Experience of the Georgian e-Procurement System could be one of the motivating factors for the countries working towards public procurement reform.

DOI: 10.4018/978-1-5225-2203-4.ch007

INTRODUCTION

The Georgian public procurement system has undergone significant Public Financial Management reforms over the last years. The Georgian Electronic Government Procurement (Ge-GP) system was launched in December 2010. Until then, the public procurement system was still believed to be the legacy of old times. There had been the cases of discriminatory treatment due to the absence of sufficient transparency; the cases of corruption were not exceptional. Due to the various reasons there had been the cases of favoritism and other unsound practices, the society had a distrust towards procurement system, access to tender-related data was very limited, the costs of participation in tenders was inevitably high, i.e. the amount of Georgian Lari GEL 200. All the tendering procedures were conducted on the basis of paper documents and all together led to lack of transparency, restricted competition, and high risk of corruption. Approximately 20 million paper documents were accumulated in State Procurement Agency (SPA) and it was almost impossible to collect and analyze data contained therein.

Another main problem was bureaucracy. Participation in paper-based tenders was associated with the collection of numerous documents, multiple visits of suppliers to procuring entities and other administrative bodies. It was mandatory to submit many such documents, which created additional administrative barriers. Except for the winners these documents were practically useless and meant the sheer waste of time and material resources for the other bidders. The problem of geographical inequality should also necessarily be mentioned. The regional companies were in unfavorable position as compared with Tbilisi-based (capital city of Georgia) companies, insofar as most of the procuring entities were located in the capital and regional companies had to visit Tbilisi at least four times to participate in a tender with no guarantees for winning it. According to the World Bank Report for 2008 the state procurement system of Georgia was rated as "high risk environment" with regard to corruption. Based on the foregoing and due to other reasons state procurement system of those time was regarded as inappropriate and inadequate for the reformer country.

The reform aimed to achieve five simple goals:

- **Transparency:** It was necessary to ensure the transparency of the expenditure of state resources for the society to have access to information whether for what and in what amount the state budget assignments were expended.
- **Non-Discrimination:** It was necessary to introduce such procedures, which would have placed all the players on the equal play grounds when participating in tender proceedings and would have excluded the possibility of discriminatory treatment. This was a rather complicated challenge, as there were

several factors, e.g. the geographical factor, giving preference to certain companies, which were located relatively closer to procuring entities.

- **Fair Selection:** In certain cases, the suppliers were unfairly disqualified for various reasons through giving them low grades, what was further supported by quite subjective and non-transparent evaluation system.
- **Simplified Procedures:** Participation in paper-based tenders was associated with rather complicated procedures, waste of time and material resources, what made many companies reluctant with the participation in tenders. It was necessary to simplify the procedures and remove the administrative barriers.
- **Getting Rid of the Papers:** The paper documents submitted to the agency were inefficient and non-reliable source of information and, at the same time, the procession of these documents and obtaining the necessary information was a rather complicated and time-consuming process. It was also difficult to issue the paper-based data as public information (difficulty in searching, processing, copying, etc.)

DEVELOPMENT OF E-PROCUREMENT

Georgia considered several models of the electronic system for the state procurement: the first one was the off-the-shelf e-Procurement product, rather expensive foreign model, which meant the gradual introduction of e-tenders. The other model considered was the in-the-house creation and introduction of the system within the shortest period practicable and at minimal cost, which system would have been fitted to dynamically reforming liberal business climate of Georgia. The preference was given to the second option. As a result, in less than one year it became possible to fully get rid of "paper-based tenders" and hold the state tenders only through the electronic system.

The goal of creation, introduction and management of the Ge-GP system was delegated upon the State Procurement Agency, which succeeded in ensuring the development of the software for the Ge-GP system under the assistance of the National Agency of Public Registry. The introduced innovations resulted in the creation of Ge-GP system, currently considered as one of the most transparent, fair and efficient electronic procurement systems in the world. According to the assessments of both the direct users of the system and various local and international organizations, the system is regarded as a commendable system as of to date. The transparent electronic procurement system made state tenders largely available for everyone and considerably simplified the procurement procedures. The Ge-GP system transparency and flexibility guarantee the systemic prevention of corruption, that minimizes the risks of unlawful practices. As a result, the level of competition has significantly increased in state tenders that provided for the disbursement of taxpayer resources in exceptionally transparent and fair environment. The established Ge-GP system, being the extensive database of information about the procurement market and performance of tender participants, enabled us to visualize and evaluate our achievements on the one part, and on the other to analyze the existing data for the identification of measures for further improvement of the system.

The current analysis, along with regular review of international experience, shows that irrespective of current achievements there are still much work to be done for the perfection of the Ge-GP. It can even be said that the reform of the state procurement system implies a continuous process. The major challenge of this field is rising awareness and professionalism of bidders and procuring entities; certain efforts are necessary for functional expansion of the system; one of the continuous processes is the analysis and monitoring of the performance of the parties involved in procurement proceedings.

Webpage of the SPA, i.e. www.procurement.gov.ge, is the official state procurement portal links the procuring entities and suppliers. At the same time, the system allows for any interested person to obtain the necessary information about any tender, specifics of state procurement market and field regulatory legislation through SPA webpage. The registered procuring entities publish tender announcements and documents in the Ge-GP through simple procedures, what makes it easy for the suppliers to find information about the needs of the state sector. Using multifunctional search fields both registered suppliers and interested persons with a guest status are able to find a tender announced with regard to procurement object they are interested in, to download the tender documentation free of charge, get registered in the Ge-GP and participate in the tender of their interest. Any user, registered in the Ge-GP, is also able to create its own profile, mark the procurement object of interest and receive an electronic notification (internal messages) upon the announcement of a tender with regard to marked procurement object. e-Procurement system is interconnected with other Georgian eGovernance subsystems: Company Registry, eGuaranties System (GREG), eTreasury, eBudget and intends to extend to electronic revenue system of the Ministry of Finance of Georgia.

PUBLIC PROCUREMENT LAW AS A FRAMEWORK

The first post-Soviet Law on Public Procurement (PPL) was adopted in July 1999, which was based on the UNCITRAL Model Law on Procurement of goods, Services and construction. This law was the first legal instrument that governed public procurement in Georgia. In 2006 significant amendments were made in the first Georgian PPL, abandoning UNCITRAL Standards, which was later in 2008 assessed by World Bank as "high risk environment" that needed substantial improvements and reforms (WB, 2008).

The Government of Georgia embarked on a public procurement reform in 2009, and promulgated a new PPL in 2010. The main purpose of the law was to ensure the efficient spending of state resources through a competitive process that was transparent and increased public confidence in the electronic system. Former paper-based tenders were challenged by a high risk of corruption, restricted competition, high compliance costs and lack of transparency. The target was to fully re-engineer the procurement business process.

The law is structured as framework legislation with substantial parts of the procurement process put into secondary legislation. The law regulates the process from planning of procurement till the conclusion of contract.

The purpose of the law is to:

- Ensure rational expenditure of financial resources designated for state procurement;
- Develop healthy competition in the areas of production of goods, supply of services and construction works necessary for the state needs;
- Ensure fair and non-discriminatory approach towards participants of the procurement in the course of implementation of the state procurement;
- Ensure publicity of the state procurement;
- Establish uniform system of state procurement and to promote public confidence towards such system.

The scope of the law covers purchases of goods, supply of services and construction works, made by contracting authorities which use funds from the state budget, Autonomous Republics' budgets and local budgets, funds of public bodies and grants or loans guaranteed by the state.

TYPES OF PROCUREMENT IN GE-GP

The Unified Electronic System is a core electronic platform, which is based on the reverse auction principle.

Ge-GP has delivered better transparency and increased accessibility to procurement information during all stages of the procurement process. All calls for competition (for the award of contracts whose annual estimated value is higher than GEL 5,000) are being published on a single eProcurement platform to which access is free for any interested person. The general public, including economic operators, can access public documents, such as procurement rules and regulations, tender notices and tender documents, tender award results and initiate an online complaint. All Data are collected in database, which is integrated with Business Intelligence (BI) System, providing more than 70 real time reports. All system modules are open and available for all registered users, as well as for those who are using Facebook accounts for the system login, so that creates more transparency for all interested parties. It is noteworthy that filing a complaint is free of charge.

Artificial subdivision of the contracts, with the intention to avoid the monetary limits, is not allowed. For this purpose, a special definition of homogenous objects of procurement is provided. In practice and in accordance with subordinate legislation, the Common Procurement Vocabulary (CPV) codes are used for determination of the homogenous objects of procurement. Where the first three digits of the CPV code are identical, it is considered that all the procurement objects with the same digits are homogenous.

There are different methods for awarding contracts:

- *Simplified electronic tender* is used for purchases of homogeneous objects with value between GEL 5,000 and GEL 200,000. In case of a simplified electronic tender the timeframe for the familiarization with the tender notice and tender documentation shall be at least one day from the instance of posting of the tender notice and tender documentation in the System. Within two days from the expiration of this term a bidder can submit a bid through the System and modify the price of the submitted bid based on the principle of reduction and considering the bid reduction step via electronic reverse auction. This method is carried out fully through the Unified Electronic System.
- *Electronic tender* is used for purchases of homogeneous objects with value equal or above GEL 200,000. In case of an electronic tender the timeframe for the familiarization with the tender notice and tender documentation must be at least fifteen days from the instance of posting the tender notice and tender documentation in the System. Within five days from the expiration of this term a bidder can submit a bid through the System and modify the submitted bid price based on the principle of reduction and considering the bid reduction step via electronic reverse auction. This method is also carried out fully through the Unified Electronic System (see Figure 1).
- *Design contest* is an alternative to public procurement procedure, which enables a procuring entity to procure design or/and cost calculation services, amongst them designing, planning, architectural and engineering plans or designs (see Figure 2).

Figure 1. Phases of conducting electronic /simplified electronic tenders in Ge-GP

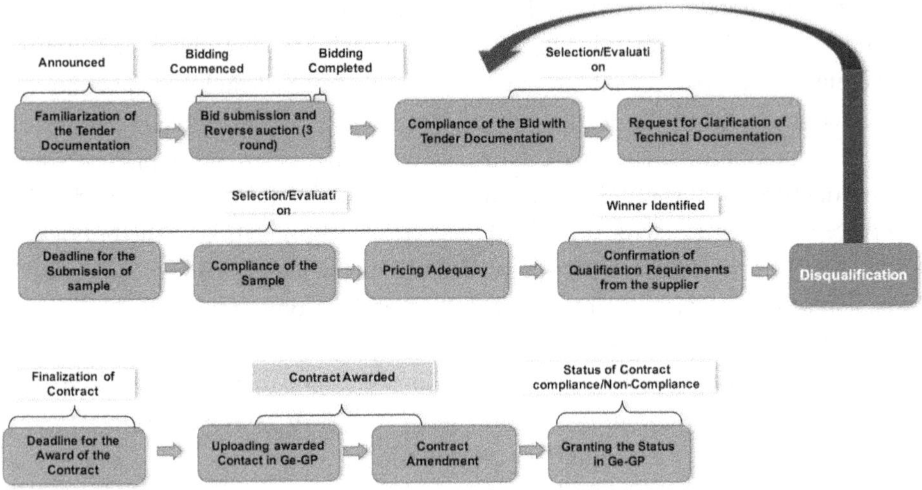

Figure 2. Phrases of conducting design contest in Ge-GP

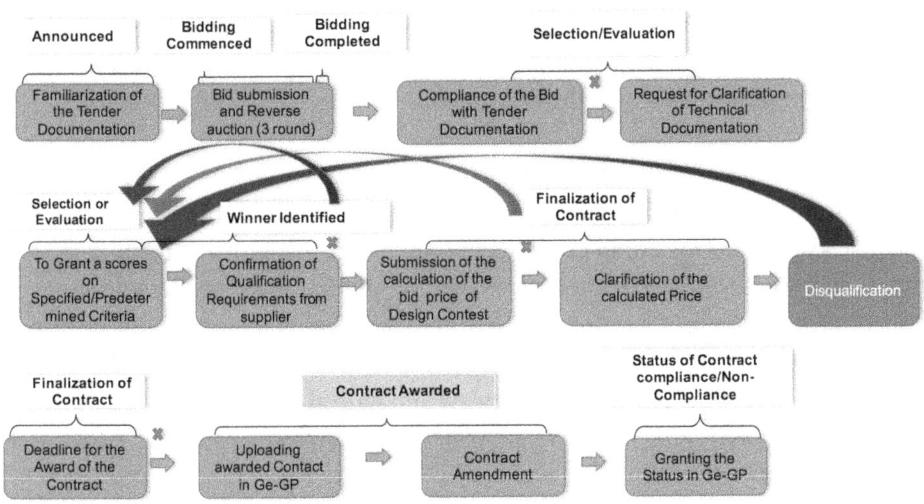

Until July 2015, the design contests were held according to the so-called "hard-copy" mechanism, meaning the submission of bids to procuring entities in envelopes. The absence of specific rules of conducting design contests and standardized methods of bidder evaluation provided for differentiated approaches on the part of procuring entities, feeling of ambiguity in suppliers and, quite often, for reasonable grounds to believe, that evaluation was "biased". As of to date the elaborated rules and the new electronic module developed on the basis thereof ensure not only the uniformity of standards but also the electronic publication of invitations for bids and documents. It is worth mentioning that the relevant documents are archived in the electronic system enabling any interested person to monitor the conducted design contests. The SPA developed and introduced uniform, universal algorithm for the evaluation of bidders, according to which the best quality/price bidder is easily identified using pre-determined quality criteria by a procuring entity, best bid price and priority factor of specific criteria. The application of the bid ranging automated system significantly simplified the management of the evaluation of bids, submitted by participants, by procuring entities on the one hand and on the other - eliminated the feeling of ambiguity in suppliers. SPA developed more than one practical guidelines to raise awareness of the users about the aforementioned innovations. Those guidelines are published on SPA official web-page under the heading "Guidelines for design Contest Module".

It should be mentioned, that like tenders, the design contest procedures are also subject to appealing to the Dispute Resolution Board, enabling any interested person to protect its rights.

- *Consolidated tenders* are unified and centralized state procurement procedure conducted by the SPA that involves the purchase of homogeneous procuring objects for different procuring entities.

Since 2012, for efficient allocation of budgetary resources, the respective Governmental Commission, under the intensive participation of SPA, has been conducting tenders with regard to certain procurement objects in a centralized manner through the so-called consolidated tenders. This way the state attains considerable economy on a procurement objects announced in a consolidated manner, what ensures more efficient and targeted budgetary expenditures.

From 2012 the consolidated tenders were announced within the unified electronic system for different types of fuels, personal and portable computers, A4 printing paper, tires and cellular network services (See Figure 3).

As of to date the Office for Consolidated Tenders is intensively engaged in analytical researches to identify the objects of the procurement which would have been reasonable in a consolidated manner in the context of efficient expenditure of budgetary resource. It should as well be mentioned with regard to the foregoing, that with a view to planning the consolidated tenders, their further monitoring, analysis and keeping relevant statistics, the new computer system CONSYS for the management of consolidated tenders was launched, which is located at the following address: https://ctd.spa.ge.

Figure 3. Phases of conducting consolidated tenders in Ge-GP

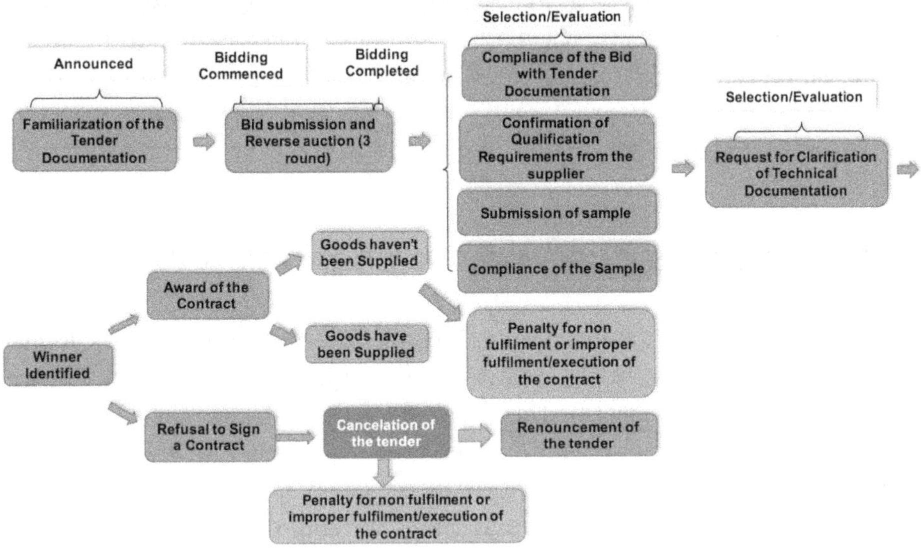

Registration within the system is mandatory for every procuring entity for each of them to present any information, requested by Governmental Tender Commission and SPA with regard to consolidated tenders, through the Consolidated Tenders Management System.

To make the use of the new system easier for procuring entities the User-Manual of Consolidated Tender Management System was developed, providing detailed directions and operational procedures.

The introduction of the Consolidated Tender Management System further enhanced not only correct and timely planning of consolidated tenders, but also keeping statistics and analysis, what is a priority for SPA and what has greatly promoted the updating of the data of procuring entities and evaluation of the adequacy of their demands.

- *Simplified procurement (direct contracting)* is used for purchases of homogeneous objects of value below GEL 5,000, purchases by diplomatic mission threshold is GEL 50,000, and in case of the Ministry of Interior, Ministry of Defense and State Protection Special Service of value below GEL 20,000. The use of this procedure is also permitted in certain circumstances provided in the law such as urgent necessity, exclusive rights etc. This method does not go through the Unified Electronic System; however, uploading of contracts in Contracts Management Reports (CMR) module is mandatory. A contracting authority may decide to perform simplified procurement electronically and use simplified electronic tender for purchases below GEL 5,000. Contracting authorities need to obtain a prior approval from the SPA to be able to use simplified procurement in four specific circumstances (in case of exclusive rights; urgent necessity; necessity to prevent the deterioration of the quality of an object and/or to ensure further operation thereof; necessity to implement an event of state and public importance without hindrance within the restricted timeframes).

WORLD BANK PROCUREMENT INTEGRATION IN GE-GP

In 2012, the World Bank conducted an assessment of the Georgian e-procurement system in order to explore the possibility of using the system for World Bank-financed projects. The assessment identified improvements and modifications required to make the e-procurement system meet the World Bank's requirements for the procurement of civil works and goods.

SPA undertook these modifications and, after almost two years of extensive internal work and close cooperation with the government and the private sector, the World Bank started using Georgia's e-procurement system in 2014 for the procurement of civil works with an estimated contract price below US $10 million, as well as for the procurement of goods below an estimated contract price of US $1 million.

In this context, there have been some major modifications of the e-procurement system:

1. E-Reverse Auction is not applicable;
2. Estimated contract price is disclosed. However, bidders can price their bids below or above such estimations;
3. Bids are disclosed in the system only if bidders agree. It should be noted that no single case has been reported where bidders refused to disclose their bids.

To support the sustainability of these changes, the World Bank has also conducted a number of training sessions and workshops for a wide-range of participants on these subject areas.

BUILT IN MODULES IN E-PROCUREMENT

Electronic Plan (e-Plan)

E-Plan module is the module, which contributes to more transparency and financial planning in public procurement. All contracting authorities are obliged to upload their annual procurement plans into the system via e-Plan module. This system is beneficial for business suppliers, since they can plan and maintain business activities in advance of publishing official public procurement notices. No public contracts can be concluded if the respective procurement was not planned and properly reflected in e-Plan. According to the authorities, this restriction could help to prevent possible law infringements.

Contracts Management Report (CMR)

Contracting authorities are not conducting direct purchases via the Unified Electronic System, they are obliged to upload simplified procurement (direct) contracts, any changes to contracts, their fulfilment and actual payments, and related documents of simplified procurement in the Contract Management Reports (CMR) module. Any interested person, even with guest user status which has authorization in Facebook, can find any kind of simplified procurement (direct) contracts in CMR Module.

SMP Module (Simplified Procurement Module)

SMP module (Simplified Procurement Module) is the module that obliges contracting authorities to obtain a prior approval from the SPA to be able to use simplified procurement in specific circumstances, i.e. in case of exclusive rights; urgent necessity; necessity to prevent the deterioration of the quality of an object and/or to ensure further operation thereof; necessity to implement an event of state and public importance without hindrance within the restricted timeframes.

Procuring entities are required to publicly justify their decisions on awarding public procurement contracts through simplified procurement procedure before making procurement and then confirm them with SPA through filing an application with the newly integrated into the unified electronic system SMP module for agreement of simplified procurements.

It should be mentioned, that based on the principle of transparency in public procurement procedures, the applications filled by procuring entities with SPA for obtaining a consent for the conduct of simplified procurement, became available for any interested person. Furthermore, the interested persons are able to provide their opinion regarding the applications of procuring entities, using 'Comments' function of the module, before SPA decision is made. After submission of application by a procuring entity the SPA makes a decision not earlier than two and not later than three business days on granting or non-granting consent. SMP module boosts transparency and compliance with the law of public procurement even for the exceptional cases to maintain maximal control of public spending.

Dispute Resolution Board (DRB) Module

For the improvement of public confidence in public procurement and ensuring the fair competition the Dispute Resolution Board (DRB) was set up within the agency on 10th of December, 2010. The DRB consists of six members. It is chaired by the Chairman of the SPA who also appoints two members of the DRB from among the SPA employees. Three other members represent the civil society. Representatives of NGOs are selected by a broad group of NGOs to serve as members of the Board under the principle of rotation for a one-year term.

Complaints on the procurement system may be addressed directly to the contracting authority, the DRB, or a court. As a General rule, any registered user has the right to submit a complaint against any decision of the contracting authority. A complaint is filled through the Unified Electronic System and is free of charge. Complaint is visible on-line and is linked to the tender. A complainant should indicate the legal basis of the complaint and submit it according to the template, which is generated automatically. In addition to the substance of the complaint, the complainant can upload through the Unified Electronic System other materials and evidence in support of the complaint.

It should be noted that the number of complaints has considerably increased over years (Figure 4).

This almost certainly suggests an increase in the confidence by economic operators in the SPA management and the remedies system to deal with legitimate complaints. Additionally, it should as well be mentioned, that a "Dispute review calendar" is published on the official webpage of the SPA, where any interested

Figure 4. Trend of complaints lodgment

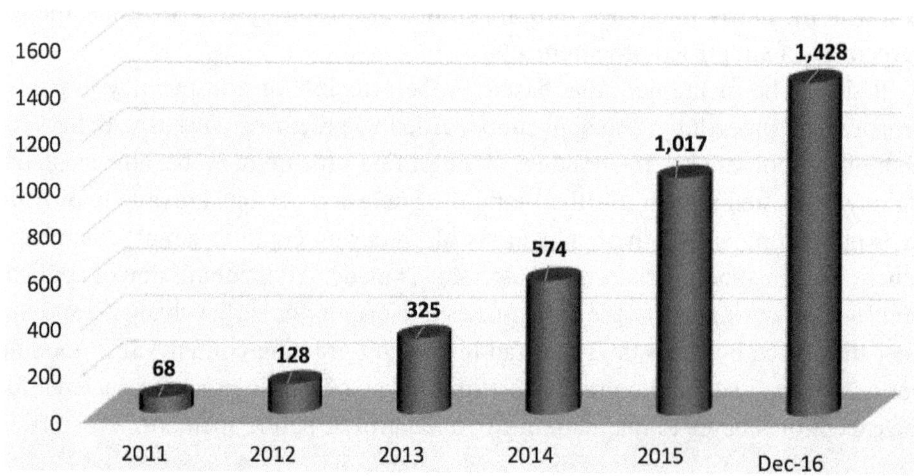

person can view the parties involved in the trial, as well as the date of trial. This calendar further enhances transparency and awareness of the interested parties.

Black and White Lists

The Agency also ensures the maintenance of the "Black" and "White lists". Black Listed suppliers are those, which are prohibited from the participation in public procurement procedures for a period of one year, because of their "unfair" action during the procurement procedure. Respectively, the Black List is integrated into the Ge-GP system, which automatically blocks blacklisted companies from the participation in a tender. The data concerning blacklisted suppliers is accessible on the official webpage of the agency www.procurement.gov.ge.

Apart from the Black List the SPA is also maintaining the list of qualified suppliers, which is called "White List". The suppliers from the white list are entitled to even more simplified procedures while participating in state procurement. It should as well be mentioned, that a brand-new rule regarding the new criteria for entry into the White List was enacted in 2015. This rule will, presumably, promote the registration of SMEs in this Register, what will further ensure non-discriminatory, equal treatment and will encourage bona fide suppliers irrespective of the size of their businesses.

Monitoring of Public Procurement Procedures

One of the key duties and tasks of SPA is the monitoring of tenders and design contests announced within the unified electronic system, public procurement contracts uploaded in CMR and ePLAN modules, and annual public procurement plans. Current capacities of the Monitoring Department are mostly consumed in the exercise of ex-post verifying legal compliance by the contracting authorities. Each step of the monitoring procedure is described and regulated in detail and, in general, a room for discretion by contracting authorities is reduced to the minimum.

Besides, SPA elaborated risk-based system according to various risk factors and criteria, which is built in the Ge-GP system and allows Monitoring Department to receive automated notifications/alerts. Through this system, numerous tenders are filtered according to higher risks and then are subject to comprehensive monitoring.

It should be also mentioned, that within the framework of the National Counter-corruption Strategy of Georgia and 2015-2016 Action Plan for the Implementation of the National Counter-corruption Strategy of Georgia, the SPA has undertaken to intensively participate in the provision for transparency and reduction of corruption risks in the field of public finances and public procurement.

With regard to the foregoing, the methodology for the disclosure of artificial splitting of public procurements was approved in December 2015, which promotes the disclosure of the cases of artificial splitting and violation of monetary thresholds in the course of procurement and ensures efficient and targeted operation of the respective personnel of SPA.

In addition to the above-mentioned actions, special workgroup was set up for conducting research on potential risks in the field of public procurement and improving efficiency of combating corruption. The main field of activity of this group is the focused analyses of the current situation in the field of public procurement, development of relevant proposals and recommendations for the removal of corruption risks, and reasons causing them.

CAPACITY BUILDING

In 2014, Training Centre was created in SPA to retrain the procurement specialists of procuring and supplier entities. The training course is led by highly qualified experts of state procurement field, who are selected according to their knowledge, qualification and experience. The training course is fully funded by SPA. Agency has also developed special unique software for the Training Centre in order to accomplish following tasks: online registration of trainees, pre and post-testing and statistical analysis. This software allows for impartial assessment of the knowledge of the trainees both before and after the training courses. Thousands of specialists employed in state agencies, local self-government and business-sector were trained. The system of training established by the SPA in its initial phase has shown significant achievements. However, the need for continuous building capacity of all stakeholders in the Georgian procurement system will need to be addressed in the forthcoming period. The role of the Training Centre of the SPA will therefore play a significant role.

E-PROCUREMENT AT A GLANCE

By the end of May 2016, total number of 32,055 users were registered in the Georgian Electronic Government Procurement, out of which 4,463 were procuring entities and 27,592 suppliers (Figure 5).

Registration in Ge-GP is free of charge. Any interested person with a guest-status are able to find any information concerning to e-tenders or simplified procurements (Direct Purchases). From 2010, more than one Million open contracts are

Figure 5. Users in Ge-GP

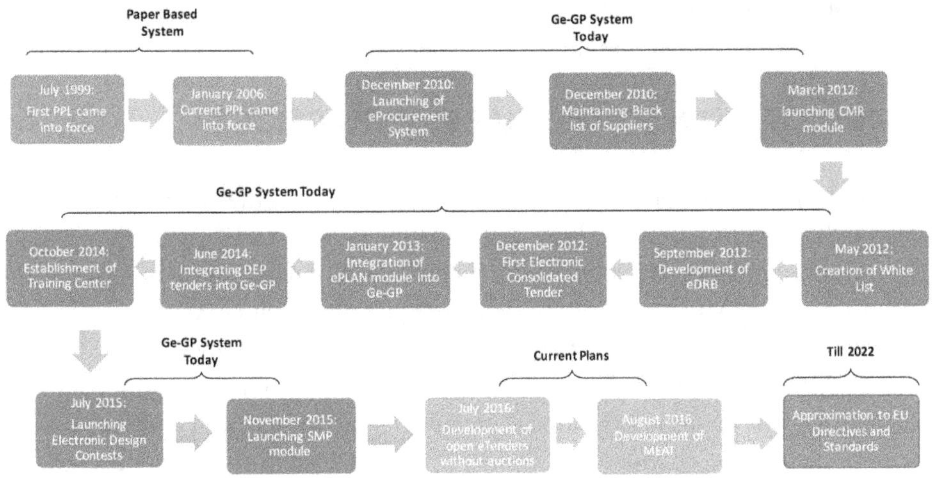

Figure 6. e-Tenders announced through Ge-GP

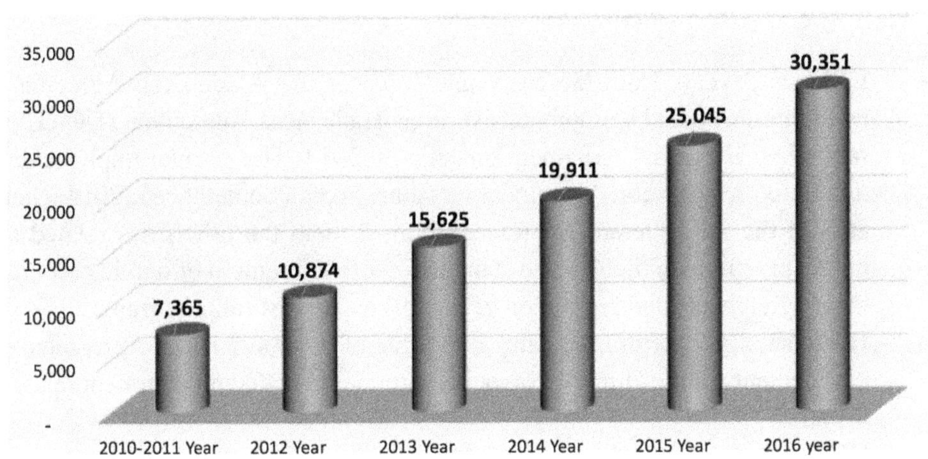

uploaded in Ge-GP. From 2010, more than 171,000 e-tenders (Figure 6) were announced through Ge-GP.

Due to large volume of annual public spending (more than 3,200,546,439 GEL in 2015), public procurement represents important factor in local economy. Between the years 2010-2016, savings (difference between estimated value and contract price) generated through GE-GP is more then 1,3 Billion GEL. In 2011, average number of bidders was 1.73, in 2012 - 1.75, in 2013 2.01, in 2014 average number of bidders in tenders reached - 2.02. It should as well be mentioned that the Ge-GP system is bilingual and the data contained therein is accessible for any user in the Georgian and English languages.

APPROXIMATION TO THE EU BEST PRACTICES

One of the major challenges remains to be the working on the commitments under Deep and Comprehensive Free Trade Area Agreement with the EU, which provides for gradual approximation of public procurement legislation and institutional framework with EU *acquis*. Article 145 of the Association Agreement (AA) obliges Georgia to develop the roadmap and implement it within timelines set by AA.

The Action Plan covers 8-year period (from the date of entry into force of the basic provisions of the Association Agreement, 01.09.2014) and is divided into 5 phases. Each phase provides for legislative and normative changes in accordance with the EU Directives, thus ensuring the approximation with the EU public procurement system.

In the course of legislative approximation and implementation process Georgia will undergo the following phases:

- **I Phase**: 3 years from the entry into force of the Association Agreement including Deep and Comprehensive Free Trade Area Agreement (DCFTA), ratified by Georgian Parliament on July 18, 2014. The gradual implementation of the Association Agreement was launched on September 1, 2014 when 80% of the AA entered into force, amongst them the provisions related to public procurement field, basic standards for the execution of public procurement agreements and regulation of the respective institutional frame;
- **II Phase**: 5 years from the entry into force of the Association Agreement – key elements of the Directive on public procurement and procurement related disputes;
- **III Phase**: 6 years from the entry into force of the Association Agreement – key elements of the Directive on sectors (water, energy, transport and postal sectors) and dispute settlement in sectors;
- **IV Phase**: 7 years from the entry into force of the Association Agreement – other (mandatory and optional) elements of the Directive on public procurement and procurement related disputes;
- **V Phase**: 8 years from the entry into force of the Association Agreement – other (mandatory and optional) elements of the Directive on sectors and dispute settlement in sectors,

Figure 7. Major reform phases

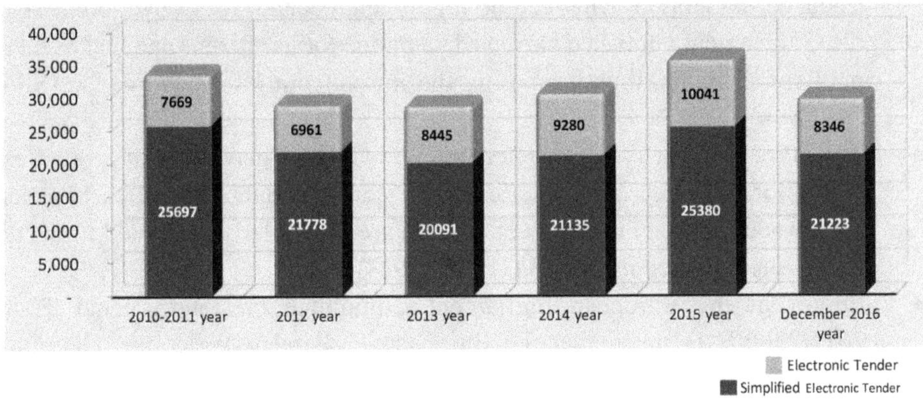

Based on the foregoing, it is apparent that the planned reform is far more comprehensive than only the approximation with the provisions of EU public procurement directives. Apart from the harmonization of legislation, Georgia has to ensure the adequate introduction and implementation of the new procedures and rules, which are based on transparency and non-discrimination principles. Major reforms will be implemented within the 8-year period of approximation with the EU *acquis*, the unified electronic system of public procurement will be further improved (see Figure 7). The aforementioned changes will promote free trade with the EU countries and increase competition on Georgian public procurement market.

EVALUATION OF GE-GP

Achievements of Georgian e-Procurement system have been explicitly acknowledged by different international organizations:

- The Georgian e-Procurement system was awarded the second place among 471 candidates from 71 countries in the United Nations' Public Service Annual Survey, Category: Preventing and Combating Corruption in the Public Service as the most prestigious international recognition in terms of public services around the world (SPA, 2011).
- EBRD Assessment of Public Procurement Law and Practice stated that the key components of Public Procurement policy are introduced in South-European countries, however only Georgia has high Compliance rating, as Georgia has best complied with and implemented the efficient procurement instruments recommended by the international best practice (EBRD, 2011).

- The electronic, transparent system of State Procurement was successfully introduced in Georgia, what can be highly appreciated. It is very good, when the Government published various data online for its citizens and makes them publicly available, thus promoting the introduction of e-governance (SPA, 2011).
- The eProcurement system implemented in Georgia may serve as a good example for Asia and other Pacific countries. The countries, which have not yet introduced the eProcurement system, are particularly interested in the reforms implemented in Georgia (PMC, 2014).
- Report of the European Parliament Committee on International Trade 2011/2306(INI) stated that the European Parliament Welcomes Georgia's new procurement system, Georgia should also serve as an example for the EU Member States in this area (SPA, 2011).
- Transparency International (TI) - In 2012 Georgia moved from 68th to 51st place in Corruption Perception Index, what was greatly promoted by the Georgian eProcurement system (TI, 2012).
- OECD - Georgia was highly appraised amongst the Eastern Partnership Countries in the field of state procurement (SPA, 2012).
- UNPAN - The UN recognized the Georgian eProcurement system as one of the best worldwide (SPA, 2012).
- According to EBRD 2012 Regional Public Procurement Legislation Self-Assessment Georgia is on the 1-st place amongst EBRD Regional 26 countries (EBRD, 2013).
- Transparency International (TI) – Georgia stated that Georgia's procurement system is state of the art and one of the most transparent and efficient systems in the world (TI, 2013).

REFERENCES

EBRD. (2011). *Public Procurement Assessment Review of laws and practice in the EBRD region*. EBRD.

EBRD. (2013). *Turning best practice into policy: public procurement reform agenda.* EBRD.

PMC, R. C. (2014). *Analysis of the State Procurement System of Georgia.* USAID Georgia.

SPA. (2011). *Annual Report*. Tbilisi: State Procurement Agency.

SPA. (2012). *Annual Report*. Tbilisi: State Procurement Agency.

TI. (2012). *Transparency International: Georgia 51st in 2012 Corruption Perceptions Index*. TI.

TI. (2013, June 14). Retrieved from http://www.transparency.ge/en/node/3117

WB. (2008). World Bank.

Chapter 8
Challenges in Chilean E-Procurement System:
A Critical Review

Guillermo Burr Ortuzar
ChileCompra, Chile

Claudio Loyola Castro
ChileCompra, Chile

Elena Mora Sevillano
ChileCompra, Chile

Catalina Uribe
ChileCompra, Chile

ABSTRACT

ChileCompra (CC) is the procurement authority of Chile. Purchases are made independently by the public entities, but CC is responsible for market regulation and management of the electronic platform, where transactions are made. ChileCompra was launched on 2003, within a deep State modernization process which started by the end of the 90s. ChileCompra was born with the mission of generating a substantial change in public procurement, as the previous system was neither responding to market needs nor to the accountability which citizens demanded. The objective was the creation of a transparent, efficient, and – most of all - accessible system, which would create equal business opportunities to companies of all sizes, especially for micro and small ones. ChileCompra manages the public procurement market, facilitating the acquisition of goods and services for public authorities; with high levels of transparency and equal opportunities for every enterprise, especially the smallest ones. Through the electronic platform www.mercadopublico.cl – which is the biggest electronic marketplace in the country – public organizations are connected to suppliers within a transparent and efficient system based on a solid regulatory framework whose governing principles are universality, accessibility,

DOI: 10.4018/978-1-5225-2203-4.ch008

and non-discrimination. ChileCompra is currently a strong system, with high levels of transparency and efficiency. As other public procurement national systems, ChileCompra is now facing second generation challenges, like the strengthening of the public procurement role in the socio economic national development. This chapter focuses on the evolution of the Chilean public procurement system, lessons learned and challenges, and the conditions to make it a complete electronic procurement process.

INTRODUCTION

The significant market share attained by Medium and Small Enterprises (MSE) within the Chilean government procurement system is the result of permanent actions of the Directorate of Government Procurement and Contracting (ChileCompra) aimed at reducing barriers to entry and market failures to which smaller providers seem to be especially sensitive. The fact that the measures are of a general nature and application has led some observers to believe that there are not specific measures for MSE in the Chilean government procurement system. Thirteen (86%) broad categories of problems, out of 15, are covered by measures aimed at the right direction to mitigate such problems.

Measures such as not charging for registering in the system (www.mercadopublico.cl), the decrease or non-existence of bank guarantees, the total access to all purchases and related data and the fact that financial eligibility is not mandatory for awarded providers of framework agreements, are indicative of very significant actions (and in some cases unique within the OECD) to reduce difficulties that smaller providers face.

Measures implemented in other systems, (especially within the European Union) and their potential effect upon two performance dimensions that are very significant in any government procurement system, namely, savings and participation of MSE providers, are studied in this document.

Although transparency and saving are the main objectives (primary objectives) for government procurement systems, the participation of smaller businesses has also received wide recognition as secondary objective important in the OECD countries (see Annex).

BACKGROUND

One of ChileCompra's permanent motivations has been to include smaller businesses in the public procurement market. Of course, succeeding in integrating small businesses has potential costs, especially in relation to efficiency: managing a large amount of providers can be expensive; prices can even become less competitive due to companies' efficiency problems. On the other hand, it's also worth questioning if taking some popular steps – for example, awarding by lots – would result in more participation of MSE providers.

Consequently, in this work we study the potential "impact" of pro-MSE measures upon these two results (very significant for all procurement systems): saving (efficiency) and the ability measures have to produce more awards for MSE.

Generally speaking, the Chilean public procurement market has been presented as a neutral market, which is correct, but unfortunately the fact that a big portion of ChileCompra's activity is focused on measures that especially benefit smaller providers, has not been emphasized strongly enough.

This study has become an opportunity to show the challenges that a system with more than 10 years of existence must face, and which is being evaluated in compliance with multiple objectives: It is expected that the procurement system builds up savings and gives transparency to government transactions, but it is also expected that it complies with multiple secondary objectives (OECD, 2015), many of which may conflict with primary objectives that define the very continuity of the system (Swedish Competition Authority, 2012).

Figure 1. Amounts involved according to provider size. 2014 and 2015 amounts at 2013 prices

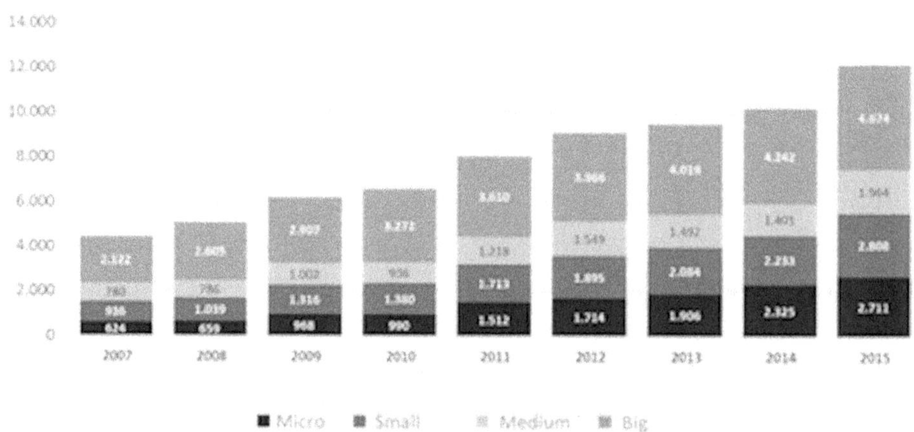

Table 1. Number of providers receiving purchase orders according to their size per year

Size	2007	2008	2009	2010	2011	2012	2013	2014
Big	**2,408** (4.0%) †	**2,403** (3.8%)	**2,354** (3.5%)	**2,394** (3.4%)	**2,318** (3.2%)	**2,217** (3.1%)	**2,130** (2.9%)	**2,056** (2.8%)
Medium	**3,766** (6.3%)	**3,808** (6.1%)	**3,949** (5.8%)	**4,024** (5.7%)	**3,864** (5.3%)	**3,975** (5.5%)	**3,825** (5.3%)	**3,780** (5.1%)
Small	**13,866** (23.3%)	**13,884** (22.1%)	**14,462** (21.3%)	**14,831** (20.9%)	**14,578** (20.1%)	**14,883** (20.5%)	**14,809** (20.3%)	**14,867** (20.1%)
Micro	**39,510** (66.3%)	**42,794** (68.0%)	**47,131** (69.4%)	**49,578** (70.0%)	**51,723** (71.4%)	**51,396** (70.9%)	**52,052** (71.5%)	**53,268** (72.0%)
Total	**59,550** (100%)	**62,889** (100%)	**67,896** (100%)	**70,827** (100%)	**72,483** (100%)	**72,471** (100%)	**72,816** (100%)	**73,971** (100%)

† Percentage between parenthesis

PUBLIC PROCUREMENT CONTEXT

Smaller businesses are the private key players in the public procurement system, not only in terms of quantity, but most importantly, in terms of monetary resources they receive from the system, as shown in the chart below:

This means that in 2015, market participation of smaller businesses reached 45% of the amounts engaged with the system. Before reviewing the instruments used by other countries, it is necessary to review the main indicators that may account for the condition of providers of different sizes.

The following Table 1 shows the number of providers receiving purchase orders according to their size per year.

As can be seen in Table 1, the presence of PYMEs has increased, and to a larger extent so have micro and small businesses.

Of course, the most important measure to evaluate participation per provider size is market participation measured according to the amounts that were negotiated (see Table 2):

Table 2. Market participation over negotiated amounts, according to business size

	MP 2007	MP 2008	MP 2009	MP 2010	MP 2011	MP 2012	MP 2013	MP 2014
MSE	33%	37%	36%	40%	40%	42%	44%	44%
Medium	15%	16%	14%	15%	17%	16%	14%	14%
Big	51%	47%	50%	45%	43%	42%	41%	42%

Table 3. Success rate of bids, according to provider size

Size	2007	2008	2009	2010	2011	2012	2013	2014
Big	536,083 † 179,324 †† (33.5%) †††	470,105 160,824 (34.2%)	528,638 175,736 (33.2%)	482,809 153,378 (31.8%)	452,092 141,425 (31.3%)	413,561 131,157 (31.7%)	342,199 111,261 (32.5%)	268,372 91,875 (34.2%)
Medium	302,610 79,696 (26.3%)	268,640 74,758 (27.8%)	293,434 79,275 (27.0%)	268,197 66,017 (24.6%)	249,237 61,299 (24.6%)	223,829 57,166 (25.5%)	181,862 48,571 (26.7%)	150,896 42,432 (28.1%)
Small	810,344 169,116 (20.9%)	763,559 166,187 (21.8%)	796,378 168,614 (21.2%)	680,514 137,027 (20.1%)	641,423 127,468 (19.9%)	587,644 119,380 (20.3%)	524,828 106,683 (20.3%)	471,787 93,834 (19.9%)
Micro	684,617 138,232 (20.2%)	691,818 151,306 (21.9%)	838,951 172,393 (20.5%)	791,734 155,227 (19.6%)	857,418 158,509 (18.5%)	843,471 156,408 (18.5%)	776,886 142,726 (18.4%)	631,861 13,3742 (21.2%)
General total	**2,333,654 566,368 (24.3%)**	**2,194,122 553,075 (25.2%)**	**2,457,401 596,018 (24.3%)**	**2,223,254 511,649 (23.0%)**	**2,200,170 488,701 (22.2%)**	**2,068,505 464,111 (22.4%)**	**1,825,775 409,241 (22.4%)**	**1,522,916 361,883 (23.8%)**

† Number of bids

†† Number of awarded bids

††† Success percentage = †† / †

As can be seen in Table 2, PYME participation has remained steady since 2012, but smaller businesses participation has increased permanently.

As one would expect, the effort companies must make to win a bidding is different for each size, as shown in the Table 3 below:

The table above shows information about several aspects: in the first place, success rates of the different sizes show significant differences: while big providers are awarded more than 34% of bids submitted, PYME are awarded only around 21% as a whole, with significant differences between micro and medium; it is worth noting

Table 4. Evolution of the number of calls for tender since 2007

Value in UTM	2007	2008	2009	2010	2011	2012	2013	2014
Less than 100	404,843 (90.1%)†	401,955 (88.4%)	399,558 (87.8%)	322,298 (86.6%)	294,497 (82.8%)	266,143 (79.5%)	225,624 (77.0%)	194,895 (73.3%)
Between 100 and 1.000	31,794 (7.1%)	38,940 (8.6%)	42,246 (9.3%)	38,958 (10.5%)	45,163 (12.7%)	50,076 (15.0%)	50,073 (17.1%)	52,144 (19.6%)
More than 1.000	12,782 (2.8%)	13,717 (3.0%)	13,186 (2.9%)	11,002 (3.0%)	16,047 (4.5%)	18,476 (5.5%)	17,309 (5.9%)	18,799 (7.1%)
Total	**449,419 (100%)**	**454,612 (100%)**	**454,990 (100%)**	**372,258 (100%)**	**355,707 (100%)**	**334,695 (100%)**	**293,006 (100%)**	**265,838 (100%)**

† Percentage of column

Table 5. Participation according to provider size (over amounts negotiated), only in Framework Agreement

Size	2007	2008	2009	2010	2011	2012	2013	2014
MSE	27.11%	26.10%	26.03%	28.14%	25.69%	27.74%	30.51%	30.30%
Medium	18.44%	19.01%	19.30%	19.60%	17.83%	18.21%	18.78%	17.28%
Big	54.46%	54.89%	54.66%	52.26%	56.49%	54.06%	50.72%	52.42%

that close to 80% of bids that the public procurement system receives come from PYME providers; finally, it is evident that the number of bids submitted by providers of all sizes has considerably diminished: thus, considering 2007 as a base year, in 2014 the number of bids received by the system diminished to 34%. One of the reasons that explains this situation is shown in the following table displaying the number of calls for tender published per sector from 2007 to 2014.

As shown in the table 4, all kinds of tenders, except for those of higher amounts, have a diminished presence in the system. This has meant an increasing competition among all providers that are available at www.mercadopublico.cl.

Framework agreements represent little more than 20% of the amount negotiated in the public procurement market, consequently the participation of smaller providers is extremely important. Data regarding amounts are shown in the following table 5:

STUDY APPROACH

Since this document studies the measures that could benefit participation of smaller providers in the public procurement market, it is reasonable to determine which difficulties this segment might face when interacting with the public procurement system, and then what instruments exist to address such difficulties.

In order to achieve the aforementioned, we worked on 3 different sources to explore such issues: a survey to smaller providers conducted by ChileCompra's research department called "Opacity in Mercado Publico" (ChileCompra 2014); a study conducted by the European Union called "SMEs' access to public procurement markets and aggregation of demand in the EU" (European Union, 2014), and "The Economic Impact of Late Payments", by William Connell (2014), which distinguishes both aspects. The document European Union Working Papers (European Union, 2014) is a comprehensive synthesis of what can be found in many other documents. The following table 6 summarizing the issues was constructed from the mentioned sources:

Table 6. Main issues MSE faces in public procurement system

Main problems that affect smaller providers	
Very large contracts	Lack of knowledge about procedures
Temporary closing of markets due to the presence of Framework Agreements	Limited skills and experience preparing bids
Unclear requirements	Lack of time to prepare bids
Expensive standards and certification requirements	Lack of dialogue and feed-back with buyers
Limited access to information about new business opportunities	Excessive bureaucracy
Disproportionate levels of technical qualification	Late payments (†)
Disproportionate levels of financial qualification	Lengthy terms of payment (†)
Excessive emphasis on price	

Source: Own elaboration based on UE (2014), Connell (2014) and ChileCompra (2014)

The color of this table indicates the polarity of measures that the procurement system considers about each one. Light green represents the presence of measures mitigating the issue. Dark green indicates the presence of measures that greatly mitigate the issue, and pink indicates the non-existence of measures or such measures that go to the opposite direction of mitigation.

Since the issues are very clear in terms of their meaning, we will include just one brief explanation of them:

1. **Very Large Contracts:** This is a problem because the capacity of small companies to fund big contracts constitute a difficulty, including both financing of working capital and contract guarantees requested by government.
2. **Temporary Closing of Markets Due to the Presence of Framework Agreements:** Framework agreements represent the first purchase option public entities have (except for municipalities), therefore in those items where there are agreements, the possibility that providers, who have not been awarded, can do business with government can be seriously undermined.
3. **Unclear Requirements:** Vagueness of requirements by clients implies the impossibility that smaller businesses that are less experienced in public procurement may submit their best offer to satisfy a buyer's needs.
4. **Expensive Standards and Certification Requirements:** It is very difficult for smaller businesses to have certifications, not only due to the direct and indirect costs they generate, but also because obtaining them takes long periods of time, almost the half-life of a MSE business (for example, CPS, clean production agreements take more than two years).

5. **Insufficient Access to Information Regarding Business Opportunities:** One of the main market failures of public procurement systems is the one related to information asymmetry. If information is not easily accessed and understood, companies could allocate resources to provide it, thus severely undermining the possibility that companies with few workers may obtain useful commercial information to participate in these markets.
6. **Disproportionate Levels of Technical Qualification:** It is reasonable that smaller providers, challenging the market, do not have the standard technical qualifications set by the market, therefore buyers must be careful and only request those qualifications that are strictly mandatory in order to comply with their purchasing objectives and base their purchase requirements on needs rather than solutions in order to allow competition, innovation and renewal of providers.
7. **Disproportionate Levels of Financial Qualifications:** Usually associated to provider's levels of liquidity allowing to guarantee the possibility to operate and respond in case of breach of contract.
8. **Excessive Emphasis on Price:** It is possible that the "excessive" emphasis on price only means that more efficient companies are selected and probably they are not a MSE.
9. **Lack of Knowledge Regarding Procedures:** Smaller businesses have fewer resources (employees, time and money) to understand a system that is highly regulated by procedures, terms and concepts that are only used within the public procurement system. The inability to understand the system may lead to diminish the possibilities of awarding due to reasons different from efficiency or quality of products and services offered by a MSE.
10. **Limited Ability and Experience in Bidding:** Smaller businesses usually have a shorter lifetime than big ones, therefore they have less experience in public procurement.
11. **Lack of Time to Prepare Bids:** Due to reasons already mentioned (lack of time, money and specialization), smaller businesses are likely to need more time to elaborate bids that are suitable to public buyers' needs.
12. **Lack of Dialogue and Feed-Back with Buyers:** This represents a problem in order to have a better definition of requirements and to rectify formal errors in calls for tender processes.
13. **Excessive Bureaucracy:** The existence of procedures that involve knowledge or procedures forcing providers to incur in the so called transaction costs (forced to personally submit their documentation), undermines the possibility that such providers can compete in the public procurement market.

Table 7. Number of problems MSE faces and the responses to those problems given by ChileCompra

		ChileCompra Treatment		
	Identified	**Positive**	**Negative**	**Uncertain**
Problems (number)	15	13	1	1
Problems (%)	100%	87%	7%	7%

14. **Late Payments:** The possibility for smaller businesses to competitively cover the financial cost is weaker (they have less access to credit, and usually the rates they can access are worse than those of bigger businesses).
15. **Lengthy Terms of Payment**: Not only the non-compliance with terms of payment, but also the excessive length of such terms (due to the aforementioned reasons) undermine the possibility for a MSE to bid on competitive products and services or to participate in the business opportunities that Mercado Publico offers. Connell (2014) makes the important distinction between the terms and complying with terms. The fact that companies comply with the terms does not mean that they can finance long payment terms (although it is known to exist).

As can be seen, many of the problems are interrelated.

An aggregated view of them leads to the following global result in Table 7:

That is to say, the ChileCompra system addresses most of the problems exposed, through literature and the very providers, in the right direction, except for two situations.

We are going to analyze each one of them in standardized tables showing the problem; measures taken by ChileCompra, measures taken in other systems or countries, statutory basis of what ChileCompra must do and the polarity of the measure, which represents a positive sign if such measure points (according to expert

Table 8. Problem 1, too big contracts

Problem	ChileCompra Measures	Other measures observed	Obs.	ChileCompra measure polarity
Very large contracts	**Temporary Providers Association**	Division in lots; Partial bids Set aside items	Art. 67bis of Reg.	+

judgement) in the right direction to mitigate the problem. It will show a '?' sign if polarity is questionable and a negative sign if measures taken by ChileCompra point in the opposite direction to mitigate the problem (see Table 8).

As of the amendment to regulations of procurement law on May 12, 2015, company formation is allowed by means of the temporary providers association:

"Article 67bis. If two or more providers join together in order to participate in a procurement process, they shall establish, in the formal engagement document, at least solidarity among parts in relation to all obligations arising from the appointment of a common representative with enough powers.

In the case of acquisitions lower than 1,000 UTM, the representative of the temporary providers association shall, at the time of bidding, enclose the public or private document accounting for the agreement to participate in such a way.

In the case of acquisitions whose amounts are similar or higher than the aforementioned ones and without prejudice to legal provisions and regulations that are applicable, the agreement in which the temporary association is established shall be formalized through public deed as a procurement document with no need for setting up a company.

If the Entity requests such registration in the Providers Registry to sign the contract, each provider member of the temporary association shall be registered. At the moment of submission of bids, members of the association shall determine what background documentation will be submitted to be considered for the relevant evaluation, provided that it does not mean hiding valuable information for the execution of such contract affecting some of its members [...]".

This change is important above all taking into account that the composition of business opportunities of Mercado Publico has been changing, as can be seen in the Figure 2.

Figure 2. Tenders evolution

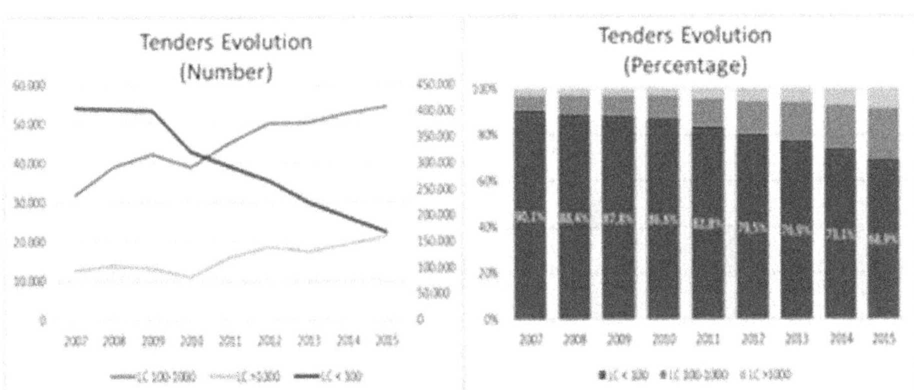

Table 9. Temporary closing of markets due to framework agreements

Problem	ChileCompra Measures	Other measures to be observed	Obs.	ChileCompra measure polarity
Temporary closing of markets due to Framework Agreements	**New calls in FA; Purchases lower than 10 UTM; Framework Agreement as a purchase option**	Restrict the duration of FAs; Restrict renewal of FAs	Art. 8; Art. 16 of Reg. Must be clarified: c) What does it mean not to be in a CM d) Reasons to buy out of CM	+

We can see here that business opportunities of higher amounts have been growing significantly, therefore giving more opportunities for smaller providers to participate is more important today than it was in the past.

Temporary closing of markets due to framework agreements is a problem (see Table 9) that has been addressed through two mechanisms: on the one hand, allowing new calls in the existing framework agreements, on the other hand, by means of a regulatory amendment in 2015, which allows for the purchase of small quantities (less than 10 UTM) to small providers and finally, and this is very important, by means of an exit mechanism that has always existed within the system, namely, said framework agreement mechanism must be understood as a "purchase option", this is, in the full sense of the term, a preferential purchase option, however in the case of an existing bid that gives more value to buyers (lower price and/or higher quality and/or shorter delivery times), the buyer may decide not to use the framework agreement, thus allowing competitive bids that are not contained in the agreements to have an important possibility to award.

Figure 3. Participation in framework agreements

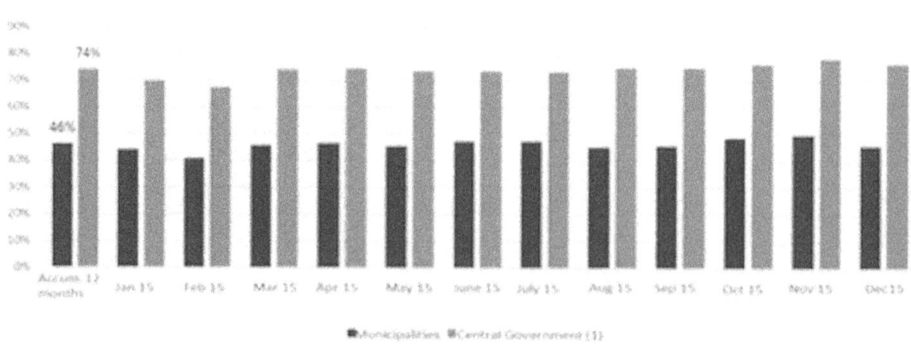

Table 10. Unclear requirements

Problem	ChileCompra Measures	Other measures to be observed	Obs.	ChileCompra measure polarity
Unclear requirements	**Procurement directives; Buyer courses; Buyer guides; RFIs; Observatory**	Restrict the duration of FAs; Restrict renewal of FAs	f) Form bidding bases; Fold publication before tender NA (Columbia)	+

The Figure 3 data can be explained by understanding framework agreements as a purchase option:

The previous results represent the number of purchase orders of all items (ONU) present in framework agreements and are bought through framework agreements in Municipalities (which are not obliged to use framework agreements) and central government (Table 10).

Table 11. Claim categories

Reasons for claims / excluding payments	Amount	%
Badly defined criteria	**3,056**	**14.6%**
Awarding does not stick to evaluation criteria stated in bidding bases	3,002	14.3%
Insufficient and unclear justification to endorse an awarding or to declare it void	2,818	13.4%
Bid without justification or with wrong justification is discarded	2,634	12.6%
Tender has not awarded in the Website (it remains "closed" status)	2,355	11.2%
Bids that do not comply with the bidding bases were received and /or awarded	1,815	8.7%
Questions that arose in the forums have not been answered	1,432	6.8%
Conditions established in the bidding bases are discriminatory	1,313	6.3%
Inopportune deadlines are established at some stages of tender	1,043	5.0%
Unclear product / service requirement	**719**	**3.4%**
Non-compliance of contract /delay in bank guarantee refunding	459	2.2%
Documentation already accredited in ChileProveedores is requested	185	0.9%
Regularization of tender that was awarded outside the Website	98	0.5%
Registration in ChileProveedores to bid in tenders is requested	43	0.2%
	20,972	100.00%

Source: www.mercadopublico.cl

The results shown in the following Table 11 corresponding to claims submitted to the system indicate that this is a problem that, although limited, exists in significant quantity:

Unclear bidding bases, reaching about 4 thousand claims (among 233,000 tenders in 2015), are highlighted in green. It is worth noting that the public procurement observatory reviews all claims and makes suggestions to purchasing entities in order to improve all aspects that may have caused problems to bidders.

The system mitigates unclear requirements by means of procurement boards, which give recommendations to simplify requirements to buyers (directives designed for buyers) and courses emphasizing how to write clear and understandable bidding bases (evaluation criteria, procurement mechanisms), procurement guides and RFIs (consultation to market) that permit contact with companies operating in the industry. This, along with a good knowledge of the market, should help buyers to clearly establish the needs to be covered by procurement (Table 11).

According to the DCCP, this problem is still quite unexplored by ChileCompra, since it is not possible to know in detail what buyers are demanding in their bidding bases. However, it is possible to have certainty about what is demanded in framework agreements (let's keep in mind that they represent 21% of the system amounts and 40% of purchase orders). There is evidence that no certification is requested, except for mandated framework agreements, for example in health, where some sponsor requests some certification that is essential to fulfill its objective (for example, medicine framework agreements).

Other countries CPB investigation shows that this problem can be mitigated by means of a purchase request or strictly functional requirements allowing providers to compete for performance rather than for certifications. Also, the use of MEAT, which means awarding the most economically advantageous bid, avoids this problem (however, it causes only price-based competency, which is also a barrier for a MSE, as will be shown in Table 12).

This problem has been faced by ChileCompra since the beginning of the system. Through the existence of www.mercadopublico.cl, the transactional web site where all purchases are made public regardless of the amount, the smallest providers of

Table 11. Standards and certification requirements

Problem	ChileCompra Measures	Other measures to be observed	Obs.	ChileCompra measure polarity
Expensive standards and certification requirements	-	(UE) Use of MEAT(†); Functional requirements; Cost per life cycle	N/A	?

Table 12. Insufficient access to information

Problem	ChileCompra Measures	Other measures to be observed	Obs.	ChileCompra measure polarity
Insufficient access to information regarding business opportunities	www.mercadopublico.cl_ **T suggested; RSS; E-mails;** ...	TED (UE) http://ted.europa.eu/TED/search/searchResult.do	Law Art. 20 Art. 28Reg Art. 57Reg	+

the system have access to all business opportunities. Additionally, the system has a customized reporting system for providers, which permits the monitoring of items of interest, as well as to receive tender recommendations on the basis of an algorithm, which selects business opportunities, based on similarities and preferences of providers.

On a comparative basis, the information displayed in the European Union system of tenders (TED) was analyzed and is shown in Figure 4:

A simple comparison shows that the Chilean system displays more information than that of the European Union, at least with respect to the following aspects:

- All tenders (and purchases) are shown regardless of the thresholds.
- All bids are shown (TED doesn't) allowing smaller providers to improve their ability to competitively bid in the system.

"Excessive" technical qualifications: It is likely to be strongly related to the provider's years of operation and size, therefore it could present a barrier. This could explain the results (Table 14) in MODEL 2.

Table 13. Disproportionate levels of technical requirements

Problem	ChileCompra Measures	Other measures to be observed	Obs.	ChileCompra measure polarity
Disproportionate levels of technical qualification	Bank guarantee reduction; Elimination of bank guarantees (?)	Regulations on technical qualification request;	Art. 29 of Reg. addresses the issue superficially (-)	+

Figure 4. Sample of European Union's TED web site
Source: http://ted.europa.eu/TED/search/searchResult.do

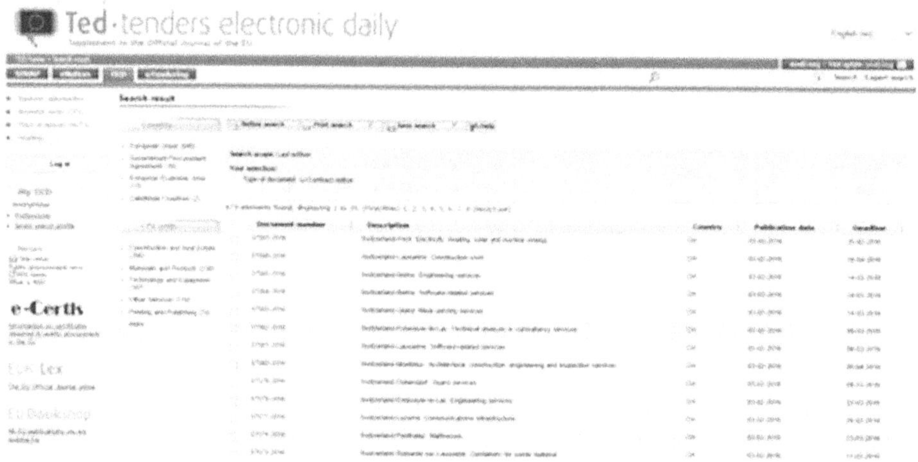

Table 14. Disproportionate levels of financial qualification

Problem	ChileCompra Measures	Other measures to be observed	Obs.	ChileCompra measure polarity
Disproportionate levels of financial qualification	Framework agreements do not request financial qualification; Except for Public Works	Restrictions to financial qualification in items in which it exists	Law, Art. 4: Those who demonstrate their financial situation will be entitled to procure (-)	+

"Excessive" financial qualification requirements: An analysis about current Ratio (i.e. Current asset / current liability), requested by other procurement systems, shows that in this sense Chile takes strong measures that are pro-MSE.

Of course there are problems associated with the situation of non-requirement of minimum levels of liquidity or maximum debt levels. Table 15, based on the Ministry of Finance's data, shows the general ratio asset/liability:

Therefore, if measures applied in other countries were applied here, smaller companies' ability to participate would be visibly undermined.

Regarding evaluation criteria, procurement law points out as follows:

Table 15. Assets and liabilities ratio

		Small		Micro	
Assets/Liabilities ratio		**130,218**	**45.82%**	**123,966**	**43.62%**
Less than 1		16,185	12.43%	19,485	15.72%
Between 1 and 2		95,363	73.23%	77,628	62.62%
Between 2 and 3		9,903	7.60%	11,925	9.62%
Between 3 and 4		3,545	2.72%	5,240	4.23%
Between 4 and 5		1,377	1.06%	3,283	2.65%
More or less than 5		3,845	2.95%	6,405	5.17%

1. Law 19,886, Art. 6: "Call for bidding bases shall establish conditions that allow the most advantageous combination of all benefits of goods or services to be acquired and all their associated current and future related costs. [And they will not be able to deal] only [...] with the price of the bid".
2. Ibidem, Art. 10°: "[…] The successful bidder will be the one who makes the most advantageous proposal, taking into account the conditions established in the bidding bases and evaluation criteria as per regulations".

Procurement regulations (decree 250 of the Ministry of Finance) redound in the same aspects:

- Article 20: "Bidding bases shall establish the conditions to achieve the most advantageous combination of all benefits of goods and services to be acquired and all their current and future related costs. […]"*The bidding entity will not only deal with the possible price of goods and/or services*, but with all the conditions impacting benefits or costs that are expected to be received from such goods and /or services. On determining the conditions, the bidding entity shall tend towards effectiveness, efficiency and quality of goods and services to be procured and savings in its procurements.

Table 16 shows some descriptive statistics regarding price weighting in tenders, according to the amount to be procured:

As shown in the chart above, according to regulations, there are no tenders awarded just by price and in general, criteria different from price are more preponderant (the median is 40%). Additionally, as the bidding amount grows, the importance of the criterion diminishes.

To accomplish this, ChileCompra has worked on the following lines (Table 17):

Table 16. Price weighing in tenders

Price weighing in tenders, 2014					
Bidding amount†	**Media**	**Median**	**Standard Deviation**	**Max**	**Min**
<= $4.5 MM	45.63	40	17.61	99	1
($4.5MM – $45 MM]	40.05	40	18.64	99	1
> $45 MM	39.90	40	21.38	99	1
Total	44.12	40	18.29	99	1

† These are the three thresholds existed until 2014: up to 100 UTM, between 100 UTM and 1000 UTM and higher than 1000 UTM. Since 2015, (1000 UTM – 5000 UTM] and > 5000 UTM are aggregated

Source: own elaboration based on ChileCompra's data base.

Table 17. Knowledge and experience mitigation

Problem	ChileCompra Measures	Other measures to be observed	Obs.	ChileCompra measure polarity
A - Lack of knowledge regarding procedures **B – Limited ability and experience bidding to tenders**	**Free training for providers;** **Help Desk;** **ChC Centers;** **ChileProveedores;**	Training and directives (EU)		+

- **Free Training for Providers:** ChileCompra, through its centers throughout the country and its registry of providers, provides free on-site and virtual (e-learning and online talks) training regarding the use of the platform, public procurement regulations and procurement mechanisms.
- **Help Desk:** ChileCompra has a specialized help desk, which offers three levels of service and high standards of users' satisfaction. In this service channel, Buyers and Providers may solve both difficult situations and basic questions.
- **Regional Centers:** ChileCompra has 16 centers throughout the country, which offer free and expert personalized consultancy on Public Procurement, as well as a mobile center that visits zones that are difficult to access.
- **ChileProveedores:** The registry of providers speeds up paperwork and simplifies the submission of the necessary administrative documents to formalize contracts.
- Advanced training program: This program gives providers tools to make their businesses grow, including subjects such as business models, commercial management, and team work, among others.

- **Mentoring for Women/Female Providers:** The aim of this program is to strengthen leadership and empowerment of women that are government providers.
- **Minimum 5-Days-Period Deadline:** The minimum deadline period was increased between the publication of terms and receipt of bids, resulting in 5 calendar days in the case of tenders covering procurements higher than 100 UTM and lower than 1,000 UTM, in the event that it is about procurement of goods or services of simple and objective specification, and that it demands less effort to prepare bids (Table 18).
- **Observatory:** A monitoring of published processes is performed to make sure all stages have enough time, to identify limited deadlines and to give public bodies a notification of the detected situation where they are asked to consider lengthier deadlines that encourage greater participation of providers.
- **Publication of Procurement Plans:** A module at www.mercadopublico.cl containing Annual Procurement Plans, through which entities publish their procurement intentions. Continuous optimization of such procurement plans so that providers may find real business opportunities, by reviewing procurement processes public entities have scheduled to conduct. The necessity to improve the quality of information published and the use of tools to monitor the Annual Procurement Plan is reinforced with public procurers.
- **Forum for Questions:** During public tender processes at www.mercadopublico.cl, there is an moment for clarifications, where providers make questions during a period of time. The questions are answered by buyers through the information system and are visible for all stakeholders (Table 19).
- **Reverse Forum:** It is the electronic system that arranges clarifications made by entities related to biddings submitted by providers during the evaluation period of bids. This is accomplished through a bid clarification forum which

Table 18. Lack of time mitigation

Problem	ChileCompra Measures	Other measures to be observed	Obs.	ChileCompra measure polarity
Lack of time to prepare bids	**Amendments to regulations on minimum 5-days-period deadline ; Procurement observatory (verifies that all stages have enough time); Publication of procurement plans**	Publication of intentions to buy, before the tender	Time: Art. 25 c. X of Reg. Purchase plan: Art. 57 of Reg.	+

Table 19. Lack of communication mitigation

Problem	ChileCompra Measures	Other measures to be observed	Obs.	ChileCompra measure polarity
Lack of communication and feedback with buyers	**Forum for questions;** ***Foro inverso;*** **Evaluation of providers;** **Networking;** **ChileCompra fair**	Tender Q&A (specific); Dialogue with buyer in requirements and specifications (EU); Debriefing (qualitative, post awarding)	Time: Art. 25 c. X of Reg. Purchase plan: Art. 57 of Reg.	+

guarantees a transparent process by making all interactions between entities and bidders public.

- **Provider Evaluation:** A star rating tool is provided at www.mercadopublico.cl. This tool evaluates the quality of service with a scoring system from 1 to 5 stars. Its use is being promoted in free training courses. Additionally, it is possible that in the ChileProveedores registry, the buyer may write in the provider data sheet recommendations or claims. Also, during 2016, a provider contractual behavior tool will be provided, which will inform buyers about compliance failures of providers.
- **Networking:** It's a space created by ChileCompra through which simultaneous meetings between providers and buyers are coordinated.
- **Fairs:** Aimed at spreading Mercado Publico's business opportunities where several training workshops for providers and buyers are provided.
- **Online Tenders, Electronic Bidding, and Simple Sworn Declaration:** The electronic platform www.mercadopublico.cl allows providers, both throughout the country and abroad, to participate in calls for tender processes by publishing their bids online. Also, it urges public procurers not to request more information than what is available in the Providers Registry and in case they need it, ChileCompra suggests requesting simple sworn declarations (Table 20).
- **ChileProveedores Registry:** The ChileProveedores registry facilitates commercial transaction between the state and its providers, validating online the necessary requirements to do business with the state. Additionally, it has a digital repository of documents, which validates, digitalizes, classifies and stores hard and electronic documentation of the company requested in tenders. It validates, for instance, financial, tax, legal and commercial information, among others.

Table 20. Excessive bureaucracy

Problem	ChileCompra Measures	Other measures to be observed	Obs.	ChileCompra measure polarity
Excessive bureaucracy	**Electronic bids and tenders; Simple statements; Delivery of awarded documents only; ChileProveedores**	Not to request documents that were submitted in the past by the bidder; Documents request is made directly with the relevant authority	Art. 28 of Reg. Art. 30 of Reg.	+

- **ChileProveedores Registry:** This on-line registry contains agreements of information transferring and daily instant updating of abilities and inabilities of providers. Such agreements were subscribed with source institutions such as Labor Bureau, Treasury of the Republic, Internal Revenue Service, Superintendency of Insolvency and *Entrepreneurship*, among others.

In order to respond to this issue, ChileCompra created the Timely Payment Program (Table 21), which addresses the issue by means of providing timely information, training and consulting to buyers (because there are management problems that cause delays), management of claims for payment. ChileCompra acts as an intermediary to look for a solution and strategic alliances with public entities involved in the issue.

In 2015, a model aimed at management of claims for payment submitted to www.mercadopublico.cl. This model has executives who check and administer responses to such incidents on a daily basis. In this case, claims are referred by ChileCompra to relevant public bodies, including municipalities. Some achievements in this matter in the year 2015 are:

Table 21. Late payment

Problem	ChileCompra Measures	Other measures to be observed	Obs.	ChileCompra measure polarity
Late payments	**Chile pays; Claims for payment service;**	Interest payment; Sanctions for late payment; Advances; Interim payments; Direct payments to subcontractors; *CPB* pays	Art. 79bis of Reg.	+

- During 2015, a total of 15,742 claims for payment were submitted against public bodies, corresponding to a 0.5% of purchase orders sent through the system, reaching 2 million.
- 52% of all claims submitted to the web site are against the health sector, 33% against municipalities, 10% against central government and 5% against the Chilean military.
- Of all claims managed, 44% end in a successful management with regularized documents or a known date for payment
- A total of 1,443 MSE providers benefited from payment management.

A solution implemented in South Korea, which probably has the most reputed public procurement system in the world, refers to CPB, which is in charge of paying providers once services have electronically informed their agreement with products and services received. After paying, CPB gets back the amount payed from public services, so that providers are not subject to possible late payments.

Finally, it is important to take a look at the experience in the United States and Europe. In both cases, the right to demand interest payments when there are delays has been established by law. According to the people who elaborated this study, this is the only problem in which regulations point in a direction that is opposite to the mitigation of the problem described. Article 79bis of the procurement law regulations points out the following:

"Notwithstanding the above, [payment within 30 days], it will be possible to establish a deadline different from the one established in the bidding bases in case of public or private tenders, or in contracts in case of direct dealings, situations that shall be supported by sound reasons".

Although the described rule solves the problem of knowledge, it definitely does not solve the problem of access; that is to say, the financial cost of the contract will be of public knowledge, but it doesn't mean the provider will be able to finance it. On the other hand, it calls attention to the fact that a rule as a regulation of procurement law may depart from the rule related to invoice payment that indicates a maximum term (without exceptions) of 30 days. Consequently, the recommendation is to modify the referred article.

RESULTS

The aim of this section is to respond to the request made by the Finance Ministry in relation to the impact of implementing new measures benefiting a MSE. As mentioned earlier, impact has been interpreted as the following two aspects formulated in the form of questions:

1. Would awarding more MSEs impact savings in a negative way?
2. Would allowing batches and partial awarding increase the market share of MSEs?

Certainly, results depend strongly on the way things are done today (It must be kept in mind that the current system is not first-price sealed-bid kind) and how definitions are adopted (savings).

Figure 5 shows the conditional probability that a MSE business wins a bidding depending on tender amount. The axis Y shows two values, 0 and 1, being 1 the probability that a MSE awards and 0 the probability that it does not award:

Figure 6 shows the conditional probability that saving occurs depending on the importance (weighing) assigned to tender price. Axis Y shows two values, 0 and 1,

Figure 5. Conditional probability for MIPE awarding

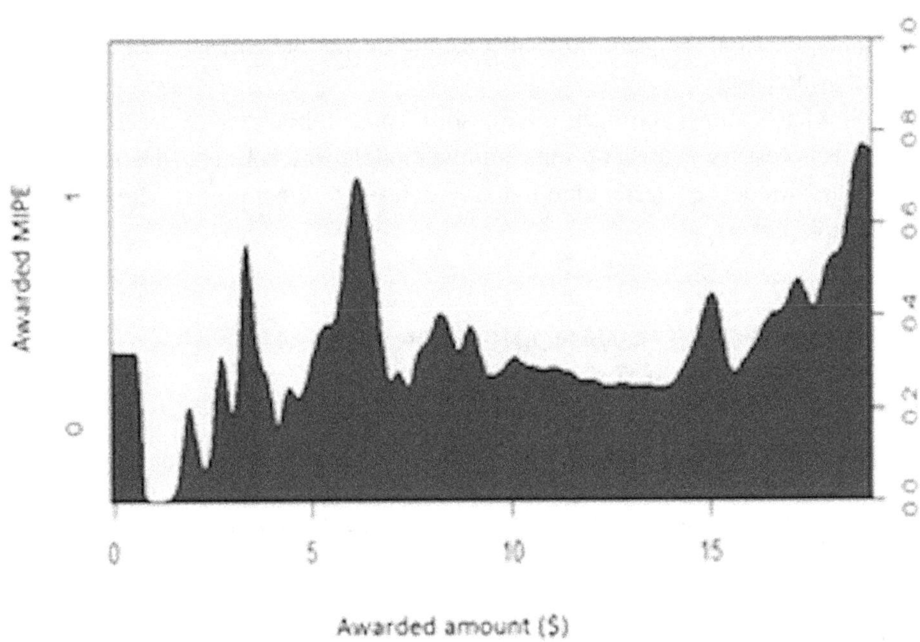

Figure 6. Conditional probability for saving

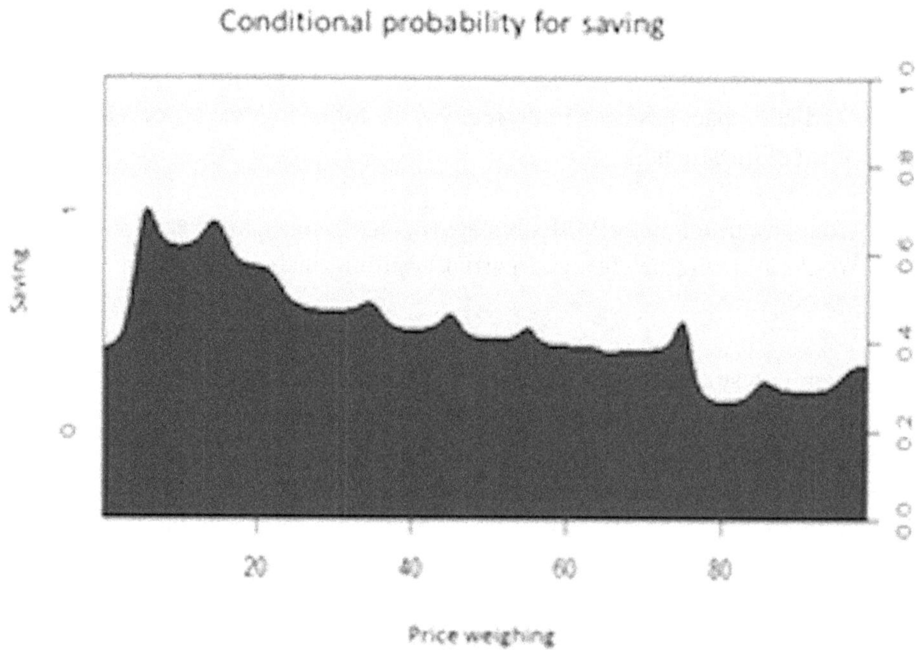

being 1 the probability that saving occurs and 0 the probability that saving does not occur:

As can be seen, the probability that saving occurs increases as price weighing of tender increases.

Both charts above approach the questions posed, however in order to answer them it is necessary to draw up some simple model that can be tested using the system's data. Models correspond to logistic regressions where results are controlled by multiple factors.

MODEL 1: WOULD AWARDING MORE MSES NEGATIVELY IMPACT SAVINGS?

To answer this question the following model was specified:

$$\text{Savings} = \Upsilon_0 + \Upsilon_1 \text{ Precio} + \Upsilon_2 \text{ MSE} + \Upsilon_3 \text{ofertas} + \Upsilon_4 \text{ tipoON} + \Upsilon_5 \text{ Region} + \Upsilon_6 \text{ Rubro} + e \quad (1)$$

The variables included in the model are:

Dependent Variable

Savings: 0 if saving did not occur, 1 if saving occurred (Table 22)

Independent Variable

Percentage: Price weighing in tender varies in a range of [1, 99]
MSE: 1 is it is MSE, 0 if it is not.
CantOfertas: quantity of bids submitted in tender.
TipoON: the type of business opportunity (or tender), TipoONL1, TipoONLE, TipoONLP to reflect amounts lower that 100 UTM, between 100 and 1,000 UTM and higher than 1,000 UTM respectively
Region: 1 is it is the Metropolitan Region, 0 if the procurement is made in other regions.
Rubro: we distinguish between goods and services. The reference category is service.

The following result is obtained using data from 2014:

As usual, it must be kept in mind that references for categorical variables are not shown.

Table 22. Dependent variable: Savings

	Dependent variable: Savings (0,1)				
	Estimate	**Std. Error**	**z value**	**Pr(>|z|)**	
(Intercept)	-2.5052179	0.0378446	-66,197	< 2e-16	***
Porcentaje	0.0148336	0.0005147	28,822	< 2e-16	***
MSE					
MSE	0.0806238	0.0228887	3,522	0.000428	***
CantOfertas	0.5276533	0.005284	99,859	< 2e-16	***
TipoON					
LE	-0.2814715	0.0245629	-11,459	< 2e-16	***
LP	-0.1401546	0.0545362	-2.57	0.010172	*
Region					
Metropolitana	0.1418062	0.0210063	6,751	1.47E-11	***
Rubro					
Productos	0.205967	0.0193341	10,653	< 2e-16	***
Signif. codes: 0 '***' 0.001 '**' 0.01 '*' 0.05 '.' 0.1 ' ' 1					

Odds Ratio (OR) de intercepto = $e^{-2.5052179}$ = 0.0816578

Therefore, given that OR (p) = p/(1-p), the probability is that a savings close to 9% occurs in the base case.

- **Percentage:** As might be expected, a positive relationship exists between price weighing in tender and savings. Therefore, $e^{0.0148336}$= 1.014944164.
- **MSE:** its OR indicates the variation in the probability of occurrence of savings when awarding a MSE concerning the benchmark category (0= medium or big provider). Therefore, $e^{0,0806238}$ = 1,083963033.
- **CantOfertas:** number of bids submitted. $e^{0.0148336}$= 1.014944164.
- **TipoON:** LE's OR is $e^{-0.2814715}$= 0.754672424, while LP's OR is $e^{-0.1401546}$ = 0.869223843.
- **Region**: its OR is $e^{0.0148336}$= 1.152353301
- **Rubro**: $e^{0.2059670}$= 1.228712656

CONCLUSION: Results show that MSEs increase the odds of having savings (controlling by the main characteristics of procurement processes).

MODEL 2: 1. Would Allowing Partial and Lot Awards Increase the Market Share of MSEs?

To answer this question, the following model was specified:

$$\text{AdjudicaMSE} = \Upsilon_0 + \Upsilon_1 \text{ Porcentaje} + \Upsilon_2 \text{ tipoON} + \Upsilon_3 \text{ Region} + \Upsilon_4 \text{ Rubro} + e \quad (2)$$

Dependent Variable

MSE: 0 when a MSE does not award, 1 when a MSE awards (Table 23)

Independent Variables

Explanatory and controlled variables are a subset of variables used in the previous model.

Results obtained are shown in the following Table 23:

In the first place it can be observed that all explanatory variables show a negative sign.

- **Percentage**: This model shows that as price weighing increases 1 percentage point, probability to award a MSE diminishes: OR= $e^{-0,002404}$= 0,99759889

Table 23. Dependent variable: MSE

	Dependent variable: MSE (0.1)				
	Estimate	**Std. Error**	**z value**	**Pr(>|z|)**	
(Intercept)	2.327639	0.0315788	73,709	< 2e-16	***
Percentage	-0.002404	0.0005223	-4,603	4.17E-06	***
TipoON					
LE	-0.1715077	0.0265349	-6,463	1.02E-10	***
LP	-0.8067473	0.0554403	-14,552	< 2e-16	***
Region					
Metropolitan	-0.295085	0.0204849	-14,405	< 2e-16	***
Rubro					
Products	-1.2267044	0.0225451	-54,411	< 2e-16	***
Signif. codes: 0 '***' 0.001 '**' 0.01 '*' 0.05 '.' 0.1 ' ' 1					

- **TipoON:** This is the most interesting variable. It shows that the probability to award a MSE diminishes with tenders of higher amount. Following OR with respect to the benchmark category of this variable that refers to tenders lower than 100.

TipoONLE OR= $e^{-0.1715077}$= 0.842393782

TipoONLP OR= $e^{-0.8067473}$= 0.446307412

- **Region**: MSE providers have less probability to award in Santiago than in other regions with
- OR = $e^{-0.295085}$ = 0.744468305
- **Rubro**: Perhaps unexpected, the probability to award a MSE is lower when tender is about goods (service tender is the benchmark category) with an OR = $e^{-1.2267044}$= 0.293257446.

  CONCLUSION: The results show that the probability to increase MSE awarding would increase if procurement awarded volume are kept low.

CONCLUSION OF THIS SECTION

Taking measures increasing the probability to award MSE providers such as allowing lot bids in higher procurement and partial bids (bids for a subset of products in a tender) would not affect the probability that saving occurs. Conclusions are summarized in the following Table 24:

Data Used

Data used in this section correspond to transactions in 2014: Awarded tenders and bids submitted in 2014. The number of observations is 68,547 (equivalent to the number of tenders), which correspond to tenders for a sole line of product, goods and services in all regions of the country. Also, they refer to public tenders only (L1, LE y LP).

CONCLUSION

We have shown in detail that ChileCompra addresses, with specific instruments, most of the problems faced by a MSE in the Mercado Publico. Also, we have emphasized the fact that the MSE benefiting more in this market should not significantly affect the savings achieved by the system, and as long as contracts are smaller, we can expect more participation of smaller businesses in such contracts. Finally, for each

Table 24. Summary of effects

<table>
<tr><th colspan="2">Saving (savings probability)
(MODEL 1)</th><th colspan="2">MSE (MSE awarding probability)
(MODEL 2)</th></tr>
<tr><th>Variable</th><th>Impact</th><th>Variable</th><th>Impact</th></tr>
<tr><td>Percentage</td><td>+</td><td>Percentage</td><td>-</td></tr>
<tr><td>MSE</td><td>MSE increases probability of savings</td><td>TipoON</td><td>The higher the amount, the lesser probability of MSE</td></tr>
<tr><td>CantOfertas</td><td>+</td><td>Region</td><td>Metropolitan Region diminishes the probability of MSE</td></tr>
<tr><td>TipoON</td><td>The higher the amount, the lesser probability of saving</td><td rowspan="3">Rubro</td><td rowspan="3">Product diminishes probability of MSE</td></tr>
<tr><td>Region</td><td>Metropolitan Region increases the probability of savings</td></tr>
<tr><td>Rubro</td><td>Product increases probability of saving</td></tr>
</table>

problem, a set of solutions to be explored has been shown, among which there are six that are relevant and currently not used by ChileCompra:

1. Set asides (purchases reserved for a group of stakeholders)
2. Partial bids
3. Lot awarding
4. Payment of interests due to late payment (EU, USA)
5. Centralized payment (KONEPS)
6. Rules limiting the technical qualification requirement

The following is a detailed explanation of each one of them:

Set Asides (Purchases Reserved for a Group of Stakeholders)

Purchases to which only smaller providers have access. As we mentioned earlier, an example of this kind of practice can be seen in the Columbian Efficient Procurement Law (Decree 1510 dated July 17, 2013. Title IV, Chapter II, Articles 152 to 155).

"Article 152. Calls restricted to Mipyme. Government entities must restrict the call for Contracting Process for the modality of public tender, abbreviated selection and merit-based competition to national Mipyme that has a minimum of (1) year of existence:

1. The value of the Contracting Process is lower than one hundred and twenty five thousand United States dollars (US $125,000) liquidated at an exchange ratio determined, to this effect, every two years by the Ministry of Commerce, Industry and Tourism; and
2. Government Entity has received requests from at least three (3) national Mipyme to restrict the call to national Mipyme. Government Entity shall receive such requests, at least, one (1) day before the Opening of the Contracting Process.

Article 153. Territorial restrictions. Government Entities can make calls restricted to national Mipyme domiciled in departments or municipalities where the contract is going to be executed. The Mipyme shall prove its domicile through business registry or certificate of existence and legal representation of the company."

Partial Bids

With this procedure, smaller providers can submit bids for a lower quantity than required by the public entity (in terms of number of units or time), so that they can compete with smaller providers who otherwise would not be able to bid nor award in the process. This measure, in effect and form, is similar to lot awarding, which is explained below:

Lot Awarding

It refers to purchases in which the total amount (number of units, time or another aspect) is divided into smaller quantities in order to allow more participation of smaller businesses or businesses operating only in certain locations. According to several specialists' opinion (Dimitri, Piga, & Spagnolo, 2006), the decision of dividing into lots must consider the following aspects:

- Possible complementarity of the different parts of the contract: Dividing a contract can be a bad idea, from an economical point of view, if complementarities of certain business are lost by doing so (due to production processes or others).
- Objectives of the division: The number of lots must respond to authority objectives. For example, there can be lot procurement in which one lot bids as usual, and the other is reserved for new potential providers entering the market.
- Cost structure of providers: If unitary cost of goods (not grouped) has an important component of variable cost, then grouping is a good idea (may lower the costs); otherwise, lot procurement can be equally efficient.
- Number of competitors: If there is a good number of competitors, the economic "evidence" suggests that competition can be stronger if purchases are grouped.
- Understanding properly the relation there must be between the number of lots and the number of providers (for example, limiting each bidder to be potentially awarded only one lot, which would weaken the competition) (Dimitri, Piga, & Spagnolo (2006, p. 175).

Payment of Interest Due to Late Payment (EU, USA)

Since 2001 in the European Union, interests and other costs that arose from payments that were not made within 30 days must be paid (for further details, please see annex with directives of the European Union). In the United States it works in a similar way.

The European Union has been especially aware of the necessity of assessing the impact of this measure, but at the date of the elaboration of this study data did not exist. Instead, there is a study elaborated by the same commission (Connell, 2014), which studies the financial cost of late payments in procurement in TED, such as exiting the market, cash flow problems, necessity to incur loans, and in general, financial costs businesses face. It is worth mentioning that, to our knowledge, there are no studies on cost-benefit regarding this measure, where late payment could be associated with an increase in the price of goods and services purchased by government, and that could consequently rationally recommend the application of this measure in our country. Nevertheless, it seems reasonable to suppose that applying such a measure would allow for lower prices in the procurement system and also transactions made by government with providers would be perceived as more legitimate. This problem appears as number three in the hierarchy of importance, at least in the segment of smaller providers.

Centralized Payment (KONEPS)

In the case of South Korea, CPB called KONEPS is in charge of making payments to providers. This ensures a timely payment (informally we have been told that in 2013 the average payment waiting time was less than 1 day). Afterwards, KONEPS is in charge of getting back, from each public entity, the amounts it has paid to providers.

This measure requires integration of the procurement system (a full good and service reception system and invoice notification) with financial system (accounting system). A cost-benefit study of this measure has not been elaborated, at least publicly. However, it is reasonable to think that this measure would cause the procurement system to be perceived as more legitimate, and in those more competitive markets, government would pay less for goods and services acquired.

Rules Restricting Technical Qualification Requirement

The recommendation is to encourage, to the extent possible, tenders with descriptions that allow competition among different solutions that are not thoughtlessly supported by technical qualifications, which sometimes are unnecessary, or that follow obsolete standards. In this matter, it is essential to understand more deeply how to support innovation (products providing innovative solutions to the needs of entities).

The advantages of investing time to understand how to stimulate innovative responses are many, because the public sector is a significant player, in almost all markets it participates in, due to its size.

Other Considerations

It must be kept in mind that in selecting some of the alternatives from 1 to 3, evaluation costs of buyers will increase because they will receive more offers, will have managed contracts with a higher number of providers and will coordinate the needs of public entities, with incomplete capacity of multiple providers to satisfy those needs. The aforementioned can lead to rejection from buyers, unless they are provided with the technical means to somehow mitigate such costs and administrative burden. In this sense, implementation of these kinds of tools also will impact ChileCompra.

The fact that ChileCompra does not follow a Demsetz model is an incentive for MSEs to reach larger market shares (derives from MODEL 2). The probability that savings occurs when awarding a MSE is marginally higher compared with larger providers (derived from MODEL 2). The probability that MSE awards diminishes as amounts increase. More MSEs could be awarded through lot system or allowing partial bids (derived from MODEL 2).

Finally, it is important to remember that the results of models presented depend strongly on the behavior of the current system, and those changes in the rules (awarding lower price) should translate into different results. Similarly, changes in conventions or definitions of saving will change such results.

REFERENCES

Carpineti, L., Piga, G., & Zanza, M. (2006). *The Variety of Procurement Practice: Evidence from Public Procurement. In Handbook of Procurement.* Cambridge University Press.

ChileCompra. (2014). *Opacidad en el Mercado Público.* Author.

Connell, W. (2014). *The Economic Impact of Late Payments.* European Union Working Papers.

Dimitri, N., Piga, G., & Spagnolo, G. (2006). *Handbook of Procurement.* New York: Cambridge University Press. doi:10.1017/CBO9780511492556

Escobar, D. (2009). Eliminating Barriers for MSE's in the Public Procurement Marketplace of Chile.*Proceedings of the 3rd International Public Procurement Conference.*

European Union. (2014). *SMEs' access to public procurement markets and aggregation of demand in the EU.* EU.

FNE. (2011). *Compras Públicas y Libre Competencia.* Santiago: FNE.

OECD. (2015). *Government at a Glance 2015.* OECD.

Swedish Competition Authority. (2012). *The Cost of Different Goals of Public Procurement.* Västerås: Edita Västra Aros AB.

Vogel, L. (2009). *Macroeconomic effects of cost savings in public procurement.* European Commission, Economic Papers.

World Bank. (2011). *Framework Agreements.* Author.

KEY TERMS AND DEFINITIONS

CPB: Centralized Purchasing Body is an organism equivalent to ChileCompra, that is to say, it is the governing body in charge of government procurement and in most countries is in charge of carrying out framework agreements, providing a system for the government procurement market and establishing some degree of regulation. Further information is available at (OECD, 2015).

Call for Tender: Competitive procurement process, which has a list of requirements. In the case of Chile, the call for tenders are of the kind first-price sealed-bid, this means they are not only defined by price, but also by non-monetary attributes M ≥ 1 (for example, quality, delivery conditions, sustainability, etc.), which is known as "scoring auctions" or MEAT.

First-Price Sealed-Bid (Demsetz): Tender (or auction) in which the lowest bid price (highest bid price) offered. For further references and variations of this kind of procedure see (Carpineti, Piga, & Zanza, 2006).

Lot Purchasing: This is a procedure that consists of dividing goods or services to be bought into fractions of different qualities. The objective of this procedure is to allow a larger amount of total bids, thus increasing the probability that MSE providers may compete and win biddings. Other uses have to do with preserving regional providers who cannot compete on a national basis. Further information about this kind of procedure is available at (Dimitri, Piga, & Spagnolo, 2006).

MEAT: Most Economically Advantageous Tender. This criterion allows the public body to take into account criteria reflecting qualitative, technical and sustainable aspects of the bid, and price at the moment of the award decision. Further details are available at (European Union, 2014).

Mercado Público: Is the electronic web site or market place where suppliers and buyers perform activities related to procurement (sending purchase orders, advertising calls for tenders, etc.) and also is the site where providers make their bids for tender processes, receive purchase orders from their awarded bids, etc. Further information is available at www.mercadopublico.cl.

MSE: Micro and small businesses. In Chile (2015), it refers to companies that sell less than UTM 250,000 (monthly tributary measure. 1000 UTM equals USD 67913) a year. In the European Union, it refers to companies with less than 50 workers. It is a more complex situation in the United States because there are 3 variables that can determine the size of the company: sales, number of workers and industry in which it operates.

Partial Bids: The idea of this procedure is to allow providers to bid smaller quantities than those requested by the public body (for example, in terms of the number of units or time) so that they can compete with smaller providers, which otherwise would not be able to bid nor award in the process.

Framework Agreement: In Chile, framework agreements are products and services catalogues posted in a web site as a virtual store. Under a certain threshold (1000 UTM[1]), products of this store can be bought without competitive processes on the part of public agencies. Providers are selected by means of a public tender designed by ChileCompra which is also in charge of both catalogues and providers administration. All rules and commercial conditions (price, delivery schedules and others) will stay in force throughout the duration of the agreement, usually several years. Further information about this kind of agreement is available at (World Bank, 2011).

Procurement Directives: Procurement directives are general recommendations elaborated by the Government Procurement Directorate, hereafter DCCP, according to its advisory role as per article 30, letter a) of Law N° 19.886. They are non-binding guidelines for public bodies and providers, but adding them as good practices facilitates a better management of procurement processes within the current legal framework. Further information is available at ChileCompra's web site: http://goo.gl/HmrRAO.

Savings: in the case of Chile, it involves the difference between the awarded amount and the average price received in the process (therefore it can be negative or positive). The benchmark price from which we will calculate the "savings" corresponds to the average price of tender bids. In each tender *i*, saving (in currency units) is calculated as: $Saving_i = q_i * \left(\overline{p}_i - pa_i\right)$ Where q_i : Quantity awarded in tender i. $\overline{p}_i$: Average price of bids in tender i. pa_i: Awarded Price in tender i. For example: If 10 couches were awarded at USD 350 each, and the average price of bids was USD 400, saving is: $Saving = 10 * \left(400 - 350\right)$ = USD 500

Set Asides: Procurement reserved for smaller providers. An example of how this operates in Columbia where it is likely that previous to publication (the moment that bidding bases are made known before being published), national businesses or PYME (SMB, small and medium-size businesses) formally issue a communication to the public body informing that they are in condition to supply what is requested. In the event that the authority receives three notifications of this kind, the process will be closed (or set aside) for this kind of provider.

Temporary Association of Providers: Association that is composed of natural or legal entities to submit a bid in case of call for tenders, or to entering a contract in case of direct interaction. These associations are regulated under the amendment to Regulations of Public Procurement Law. See Art. 67bis of the Regulation.

Chapter 9 Electronic Government Procurement in Latin America and the Caribbean

Leslie Harper
Inter-American Development Bank, USA

Daniel Sanchez
Inter-American Development Bank, USA

ABSTRACT

The chapter explores the topic of electronic government procurement (e-GP) in Latin America and the Caribbean (LAC), the factors that affected the development of such systems, how they evolved differently across the region and the challenges going forward. The information included in this chapter will provide insight on how e-GP implementation has been a key element in public procurement reform in LAC as well as important lessons from the region.

INTRODUCTION

Since the mid-1990s when e-GP systems first began to emerge in Latin America and the Caribbean (LAC), the region has made considerable progress both in terms of degree of interaction/transaction of the systems and in having advanced modules. While the approach has differed greatly amongst countries and sub-regions,

DOI: 10.4018/978-1-5225-2203-4.ch009

the overall tendency has been a notable shift towards more widespread use and adoption of such systems. This chapter will explore how such factors such as the establishment of public procurement entities, new business models and political buy-in influenced the adoption of e-GP. It will also cover the key differences that characterize the development of e-GP in the Caribbean and discuss some of the pending issues that e-GP systems still face in the region, such as the challenges of shifting from a control to an efficiency perspective in public procurement and its effect on e-GP and continued impact of legacy systems. Finally, the chapter will conclude with areas for future research.

BACKGROUND

History of e-GP in Latin America and the Caribbean

Latin America and the Caribbean (LAC) is a region characterized by three main waves of e-GP implementation. The first wave focused on the development of incipient procurement informational portals that began to appear in the late 1990s to early 2000s, an era when countries in LAC didn't have the political or budgetary support that is commonly found today for procurement modernization and implementation of sophisticated e-GP systems. Additionally, there was limited institutional capacity, organizational structure and human resources with the expertise to support such an undertaking. This environment influenced heavily the future of e-GP implementations and countries that pioneered development had to rely on and leverage other initiatives that had the support and resources necessary, in the case of LAC, the e-government and anti-corruption initiatives (Concha, 2011).

At the time, newly created e-government agencies were occupied by disseminating and publishing government information online and focused on creating standards and tools to create, manage and populate websites and informational portals for the central government. E-government agencies were eager to further their impact by converting analog services to digital and create platforms that went beyond the simple provision of vertical information online (Concha, 2011) Helping in the development of e-GP was the fact that it is one of the few government functions that has both back office and front office transactions, so it was a natural fit as the partnership would help both up and coming areas of government to gain notoriety and highlight their importance and potential.

Furthermore, high-profile corruption scandals of the late 90s generated an outcry among the population and government officials were blamed for not having proper controls in place. This created the political environment conducive to implement measures to increase transparency and ensure greater accountability in public

Figure 1.
Source: INGP Survey (2013)

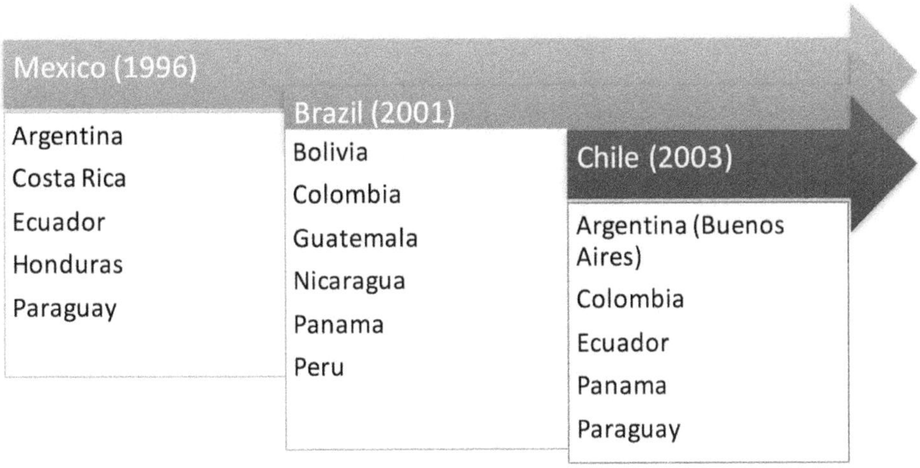

expenditure. As budgetary and financial management functions were more politically sensitive, entailed more complex interventions and required longer periods for overhaul, e-GP became the tool of choice to fulfill the demands and highlight progress in gaining more transparency, control and accountability in the use of public resources (Volosin, 2010).

The first wave was typified by early adopters that began the process of digitalization with information portals and in some cases interactive features including countries such as Brazil, Chile and Mexico (Volosin, 2010). These pioneers not only started the wave of e-GP implementations in the region, but influenced and assisted developments in a number of countries (see Figure 1).

INTERACTIVITY AND THE SEARCH FOR EFFICIENCY

The second wave of e-GP implementation took place between the mid to late 2000s. It consisted of the development of systems with early interactive and transactional functionalities.

Specialized procurement agencies and units were created in most countries of the region and with them a new focus occurred. The new entities had to worry not only about control, but also providing services to other government agencies as they now gave back-office support to the central government and front-office services to private sector suppliers. As the focus shifted towards having more efficient services, e-GP became the tool chosen to streamline procedures for posting bids to procure

Figure 2. e-GP Timeline
Source: Authors' analysis with information from e-GP Map (2011)

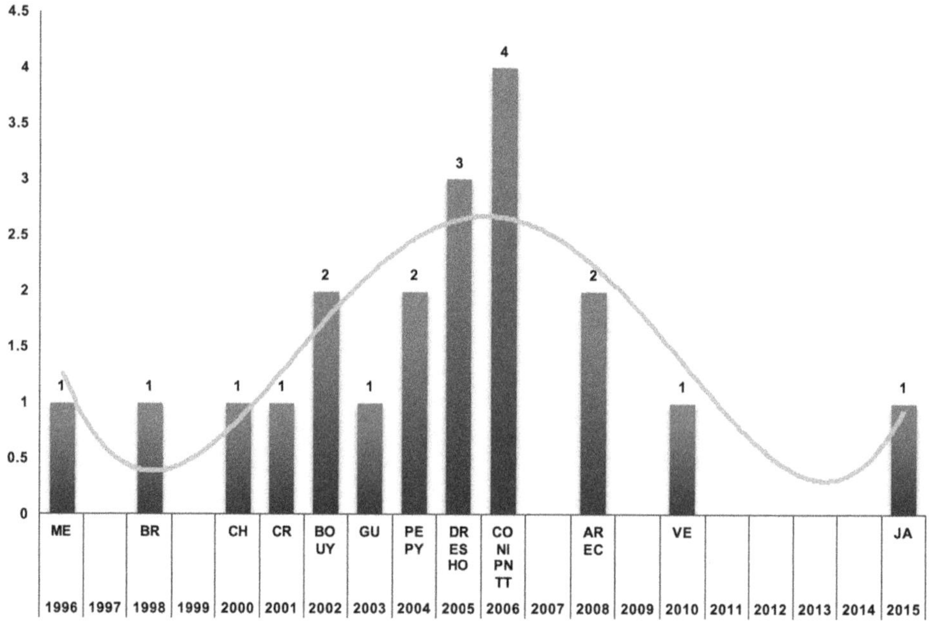

goods and services and to simplify and avoid duplication of paperwork and requirements for private sector firms.

With the exception of the Caribbean, during this period most LAC countries developed e-GP systems with varying degrees of interactivity, and in many cases such as Chile, Mexico, Brazil, Paraguay, Ecuador and Panama one can see the first iterations of transactional platforms (e-GP Map, 2011).

TRANSACTIONAL PLATFORMS

The third wave of modernization is characterized by large scale implementations beyond the capacity of in-house IT departments, whereby governments are undertaking adoption of off-the-shelf solutions or customized developments with a mix of in-house and external resources.

There is a wide array in terms of the functionalities of e-GP systems in LAC. While it is difficult to neatly categorize phases for something as complex and multifaceted as e-GP, there are three main stages commonly used: information, interaction and transaction (World Bank, 2004).

Figure 3. Stages of e-GP Implementation
Source: Authors own analysis with information from (OECD, 2016) and e-GP Map (2011)

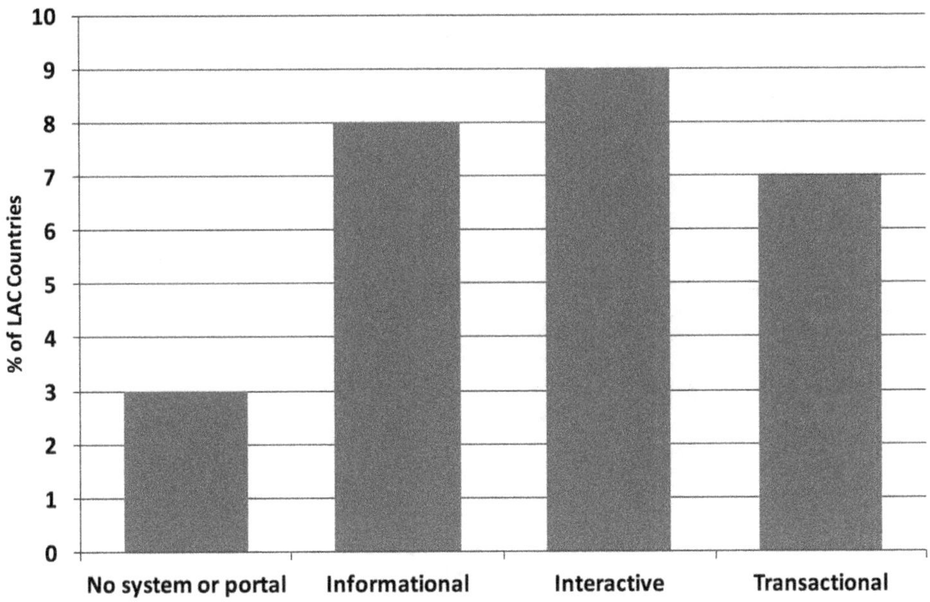

Informational stage includes countries with portals that enable the publication of tender opportunities. The establishment of an information portal is an important first step that enables procurement notices to reach a wider audience, replacing or in addition to the traditional publication of such notices in the local newspaper or gazette. In this grouping you will find most of the Caribbean countries such as Guyana and in Central America, countries such as Guatemala and Honduras. Countries tended to start with publishing notices on the Ministry of Finance website and then gradually moving towards a dedicated information portal for public procurement (World Bank, 2004).

The interaction stage involves the capacity to download bidding documents and register as a supplier. Countries with these types of functionalities include Costa Rica, El Salvador and Nicaragua, the Dominican Republic and Uruguay. Colombia is also in this category, although that will change shortly with the second phase of their e-GP system (SECOP II) expected to be operational in 2017 (OECD, 2016).

Finally, there is the transactional stage, which includes the capacity to carryout online bidding and awarding. (World Bank, 2004). This includes countries such as Brazil, Chile, Ecuador, Jamaica, Mexico, Panama and Paraguay. Few countries as yet have electronic functions related to the contract management aspects of the procurement cycle (OECD, 2016).

Figure 4. e-GP Functionalities in LAC
Source: OECD (2016)

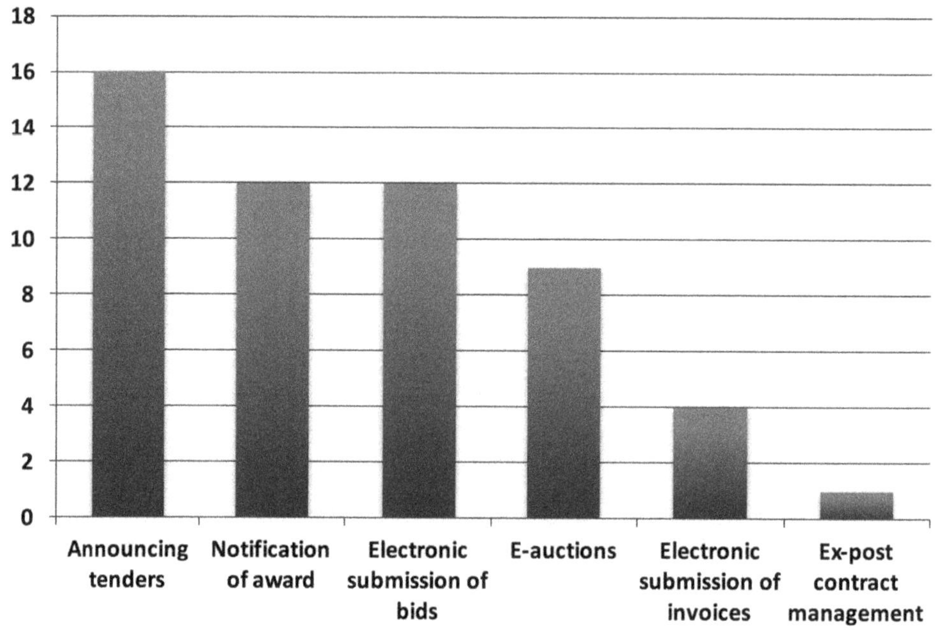

Current Status of e-GP in the Region

By the 2010s almost every country in the region has at least an information portal and many have launched e-tendering and supplier registry modules.

As can be seen from a 2015 OECD-LAC survey of 22 countries in the region, the most common functionalities are announcing tenders (86%), e-auctions (41%), with the smallest category being ex-post contract management (14%) (OECD, 2016).

THE CARIBBEAN

E-GP in the Caribbean has taken a different path than in Latin America. Given the characteristics of expenditure management in the region, these countries started to implement e-GP later, around the late-2000s, which turned out to be beneficial. At this point in time there were enough commercially available tools and expertise to start the development of more advanced platforms and go from basic informational portals straight to transactional platforms developed by external firms and based in COTS solutions. In this manner, the Caribbean region is leapfrogging the traditional roadmap for e-GP development.

Limitations inherent to small nations made it prohibitively expensive to have large IT departments, which meant that the adoption of off the shelf solutions was the most practical strategy. International firms capable of deploying human and technological resources have been preferred over the in-house development teams favored among their Latin American neighbors. This has resulted in faster development times and fewer government resources used as firms naturally try to be efficient with overhead costs and include cumbersome activities such as training and change management as part of a comprehensive project.

Finally, the particularities of the region have made it possible to take steps towards a regional approach to e-GP. The small size of the individual procurement markets has prompted the countries to start to explore the use of regional platforms for procurement, such as in the OECS with pharmaceuticals and the CARICOM information platform.

The Caribbean countries were the last in the region to implement procurement portals and many continue to rely substantially on their local newspaper or gazette or posting on the general website of the Ministry of Finance. Some have procurement portals under development, but for the most part there is an absence of centralized e-GP systems. In many ways, the slower progress makes sense as the incentives to develop e-GP, such as the savings and efficiency gains commonly associated with e-GP implementation were not as significant as they were in Latin America. One of the arguments for e-GP is increased competition as it is easier for more suppliers to participate in the public procurement process. However, this incentive is not as great as the region has a more limited number of suppliers due to the small size and populations of the countries.

This setup mixed with the surpluses from the tourism and commodities industries characteristic of countries in this region, created little to no incentive to overhaul public expenditure systems, even fewer incentives to develop centralized e-GP solutions. However, the 2008 financial crisis had a negative impact on the Caribbean, which put fiscal pressure on the countries to make better use of limited resources and focus on improving efficiency and effectiveness of their public expenditure (IMF, 2013). At 15-20% of GDP, public procurement is a common target for reform as a means to generate savings. This situation had a positive effect on the development of a new array of systems to streamline and modernize expenditure functions, including public procurement.

Two countries that stand out in the region for e-GP are Jamaica and Barbados. Jamaica launched a new e-GP system in 2015, which includes functions ranging from the publication of opportunities, transactional platform, electronic submission of bids, e-tendering, notification of awards, supplier registry and framework agreements. Barbados also has an advanced e-procurement system, having purchased a COTS which will be integrated into the government's public financial management system. However, the current legislation does not enable electronic transactions and the e-procurement system while developed has not been activated pending the approval of the new procurement legislation. This is expected to occur in late 2016 (Williams, 2016).

In the case of Trinidad & Tobago, while there is no central procurement platform, starting in 2006 the country built two separate electronic systems as part of a public sector reform program. These systems include an e-Auction platform used in limited instances by state owned enterprises for receiving and tendering quotations on goods and some services (e.g., water, paper goods, etc.); and TT Connect Tender Notices Online dedicated tenders website, which provided a searchable listing of tender notices. The former was developed by the Telecommunications Services of Trinidad & Tobago Limited (TSTT), with customization of an off-the-shelf solution for the Government of Trinidad & Tobago and the latter by iGovTT, a state-owned enterprise, under the Ministry of Science and Technology (Theodate, 2015).

Regional Platform

Another characteristic of the Caribbean region is the geographic, demographic and economic incentives for a regional approach to public procurement. Aggregating demand through a common platform would be beneficial given the small size of the countries.

A good example is the single electronic platform for the procurement of pharmaceuticals that the OECS member states share and use. The OECS countries1 are small and it was expensive for each country to procure its own pharmaceuticals both in terms of the staff with sufficient technical expertise to develop bids as well as ability to negotiate a lower price given the limited quantities that were needed for each country.

In 1986, the Pharmaceutical Procurement Service (PPS) was created as an agency of the OECS to pool procurement for the Ministries of Health of the nine member states. This proved quite successful, as regional PPS prices were on average 44% lower than prices negotiated by individual governments or found in national markets.

In 2013, the OECS launched the Electronic Government for Regional Integration Project (eGRIP), which involved a variety of e-government solutions, among them the first regional pharmaceutical e-procurement system that built on the success of the PPS. This e-procurement system includes modules for centralized registration, e-tendering, basic contract management, system and security administration and online help (Crane, 2016).

Currently, CARICOM is working on a Regional Integration Electronic Public Procurement System, which will serve as a procurement information portal for the Caribbean. The process in practice has been slow though and the challenge going forward will be overcoming issues such as the differences in legislation, national politics and pushback from the private sector (Shillingford, 2014).

As seen above, the Caribbean countries have an opportunity to not only catch up but achieve high levels of functionality in their first implementations as there are no legacy systems to phase out and dismantle as there are in Latin America. In addition, there are cutting-edge IT tools and software solutions that were not available during the first wave of e-GP systems. At the same time, there is an opportunity to increase efficiency and savings by taking advantage of aggregated demand through pooled procurement. It is likely that there will be a wave of e-GP implementations in the Caribbean within the next five years, including advanced efforts towards regional platforms.

MAIN FOCUS

The evolution of e-GP systems in LAC has been very successful in many cases (Brazil, Chile, Mexico, Panama) achieving levels of efficiency and functionality similar to the ones found in high income economies and OECD countries (OECD, 2014).

A particular mix of strategic partnerships, demand for transparency and policy decisions has created a favorable environment in the LAC region to develop e-GP systems accompanied by the institutional and legal frameworks necessary. However, the strategies and policy decisions made can become a liability in the next phase of developing these systems.

Regulatory Framework

Over the past few years, LAC countries have undertaken the task to further existing e-GP systems to a transactional stage. However, this time the task is much more complex than publishing and exchanging procurement information through portals which was governed by existing information disclosure regulations.

New laws and regulations were necessary to enable and govern modern commercial practices and especially electronic transactions for the benefit of public procurement. It is here where the LAC region enters a period of drafting new legislation and regulations.

Besides enabling electronic transactions, the new regulatory frameworks strengthened the public procurement entities and gave them the resources and flexibility necessary to implement new business models that generate savings and aggregate demand, such as reverse auctions and framework agreements. This had a positive effect on e-GP implementation, as in many cases IT departments had to develop the capacity to manage new systems that had transactional modules, e-reverse auction functionalities and virtual stores attached to framework agreements.

However, many countries delayed their modernization and reform programs as they were waiting on the passage of a new procurement law. This was unfortunate as changing legislation is a time consuming process and many countries, such as Chile, have demonstrated it is possible to undertake significant modernization with just a decree (Volosin, 2010). For example, lack of a dedicated procurement law that provided for electronic transactions was a key factor that delayed modernization in the Caribbean where countries had dispersed financial acts that did not provide a modern vision of public procurement. The move over the last ten years to update legislation and provide the necessary clauses for e-GP has taken time but once in place will be an important step in the right direction[2] (Shillingford, 2015).

Institutions

Another important factor in the rise of e-GP in LAC has been the establishment of procurement agencies. In contrast to other regions of the world, in LAC these agencies do not purchase on behalf of decentralized procurement offices but rather are responsible for policy and monitoring and have played a major role in pushing reform and modernization in public procurement. By 2016, almost all the countries have entities with such mandate, 64% units under a ministry and 34% as organic government agencies with some degree of budgetary and/or administrative autonomy. These entities have been in charge of setting policies, spearheading efforts to update legislation and designing national training and certification programs. One area where their role has been particularly critical is the implementation, management and expanding adoption of e-GP systems.

Procurement entities have established their importance in their initial years of functioning. However, as many other public agencies; they now have to compete for budgetary resources, relevance, and political support. Therefore, they have the challenge of having to demonstrate value to the public administration and be able to not only improve transparency and controls, but have real quantifiable effects on efficiency, savings and lately in the implementation of public policies aimed to promote strategic economic sectors. One of the most effective tools to achieve this objective has been providing e-GP platforms to procure goods and services and most importantly platforms to implement and manage new business models such as framework agreements and reverse auctions.

Procurement entities with more institutional independence will continue to have a key role in expanding the adoption of e-GP systems to keep on increasing efficiency and generating savings for line ministries and central government agencies. In LAC there seems to be a relationship between independence in this agencies and

Figure 5. Procurement agencies
Source: OECD (2016)

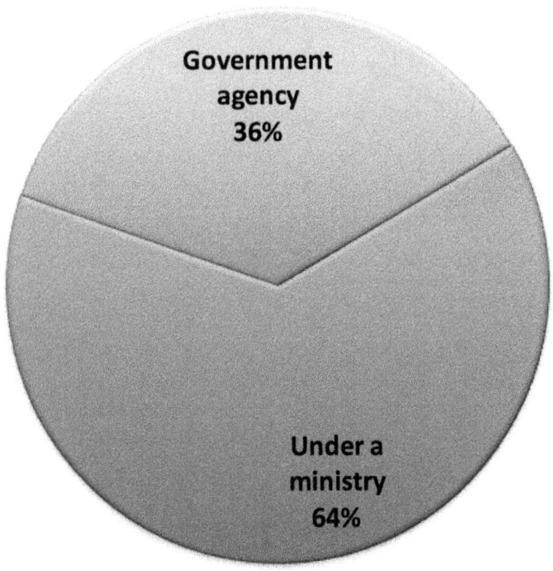

Figure 6. Role of procurement agencies
Source: OECD (2016)

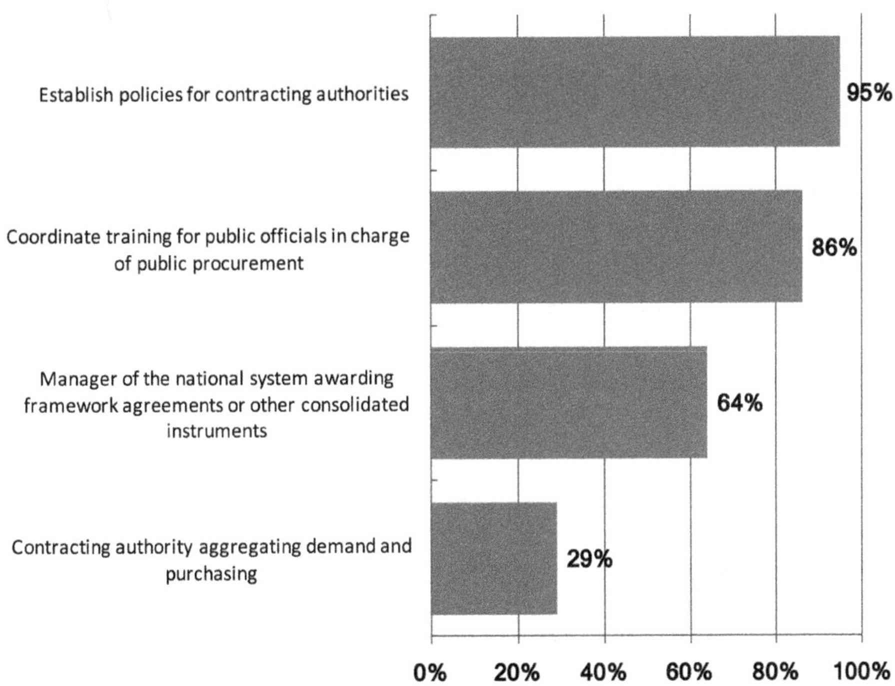

Figure 7. Institutional independence and level of functionality
Source: Authors' analysis with information from OECD (2016)

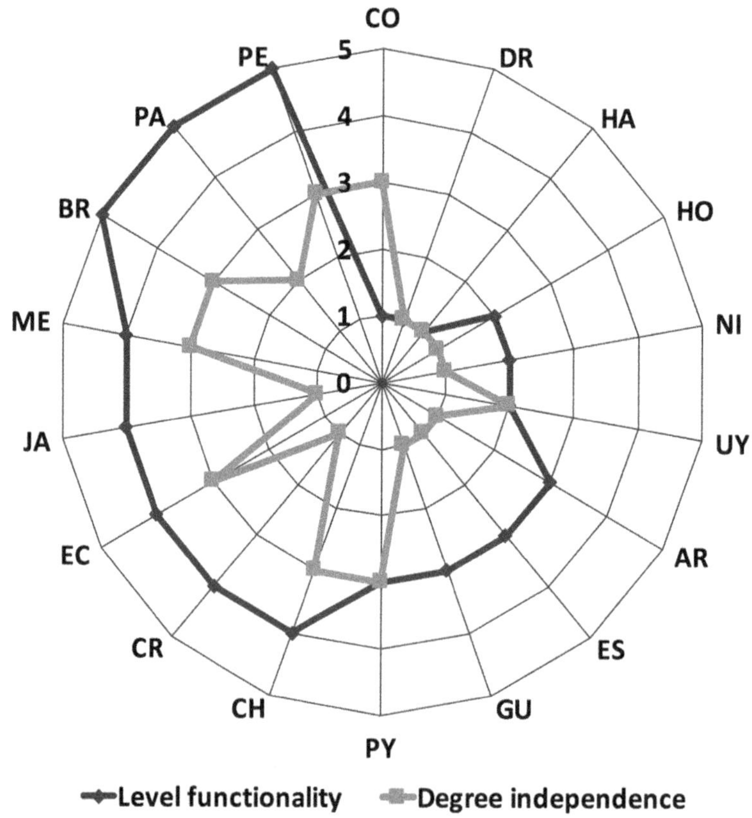

e-GP development and, there is also ample data and experiences from around the world that demonstrate that e-GP can significantly lower transaction costs and entry barriers for suppliers (ADB, 2013). Thus, the strengthening of these entities should be a critical aspect in future e-GP developments.

Development Strategies in LAC: Build Over Buy

In LAC the development strategy selected to implement e-GP systems ended up being its most important catalyzers. Given characteristics of the region, pragmatism was necessary when setting up resources to undertake this project, which had a long term effect on how e-GP systems evolved in this part of the world. The strategic decisions made resulted in modernization projects that led to LAC being one of the regions in the world where e-GP adoption has expanded the fastest in the public sector, albeit with some trade-offs in scope and functionality at the initial stages of development.

In the early 2000s, there were virtually no commercial off-the-shelf solutions (COTS) to facilitate the procurement of goods and services in the public sector. Big software firms concentrated their efforts in developing ERM solutions more suited to the supply chain management needs of the manufacturing and industrial sectors. At the time any attempt to adopt COTS platforms to support public procurement operations would have required significant political support across the central government, high level technical capacity and substantial financial investments on the government side. Most countries didn't have these resources and had to partner with (also incipient) e-government agencies for technological expertise, also they had to leverage political support and resources associated to increasing transparency and strengthening controls to address backlash from high profile corruption scandals.

In order to maximize resources, most countries in LAC chose as their development strategy to build public procurement systems in-house on an ongoing basis, with easy deployment and a long term focus for improvement.

This was a good fit as the systems had to reflect the demand of public procurement as a control function. In-house solutions had the benefit of being faster to implement (from a technological standpoint) and cheaper to build (in the short term). One aspect that facilitated their quick implementation was that reengineering processes that are necessary to adapt COTS solutions were an optional step when it came to in-house developments; in many cases this step was postponed or ignored all together.

The new systems were effective from a control perspective, quickly addressing demand for transparency and controls, however some compromise had to be achieved as much inefficiency in the procurement cycle was carried over to the electronic platforms and the underlying issues inhibiting efficiency and value for money were not necessarily addressed in the early stages of implementation.

On the other side, this strategy also had a positive effect that many project teams later become IT departments that not only strengthened the procurement agencies as a bureaucratic body, but also gave them a seat at the table of e-government discussions. Even now in 2016, 77% of e-GP systems in LAC can be traced to an in-house development, the percentage goes to over 90% if the Caribbean is not included in the count.

For countries that adopted e-GP later, the strategy has tended towards the selection of in-house developments using COTS tools and licenses rather than purely coding and programming systems in house from scratch. This tendency is a result of a couple of factors. It reflects the better options in the market for the public sector that appeared in the mid to late 2000s as well as the growing realization that large IT departments are expensive and difficult to staff. This was particularly the case in smaller countries that adopted e-GP at a later stage that simply did not have

Figure 8. Types of e-GP solutions
Source: Authors own analysis

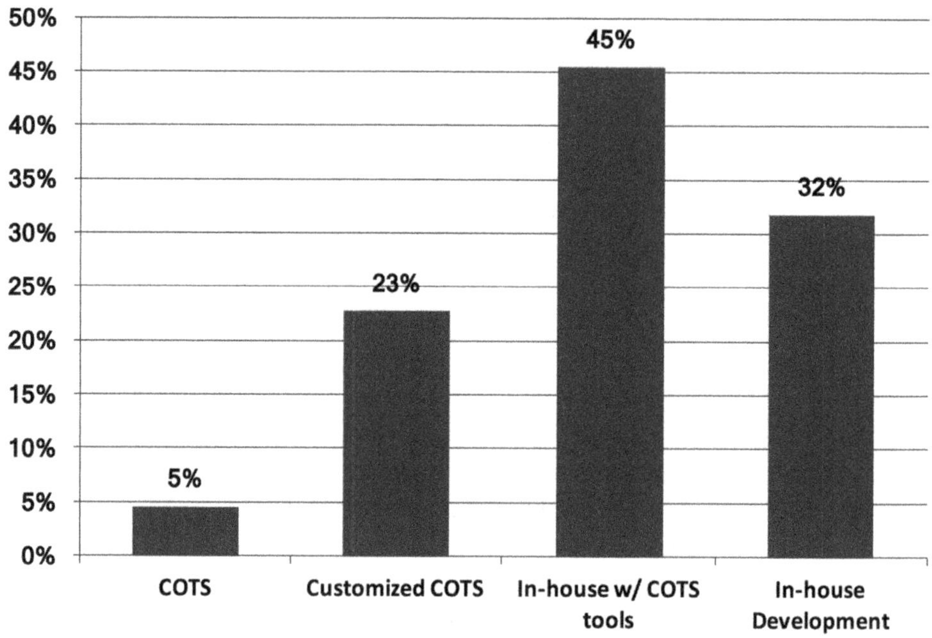

either the budget for such IT departments or availability of people in country with sufficient advanced IT skills to staff the departments, particularly at public sector salaries. This is often seen in the Caribbean and to a lesser degree in Central America.

A benefit to off-the-shelf solutions is that as they are usually designed with an optimal public procurement system in mind, countries that adapt their processes to the new system and therefore are more likely to have a more efficient system. However, this takes time to plan and political will to make the changes needed to adapt to the new system. This has become easier for countries that adopted e-GP later as they did not have legacy systems that were difficult to replace as there were already people in place with an interest in maintaining the current system and status quo. Off-the-shelf solutions are of course not a panacea and have their own issues in the beginning they can be cheaper and faster (the technological part) to install, but have higher costs later on in terms of maintenance and upgrade costs.

It is worth mentioning that another strategic decision that worked for LAC countries was to develop their platforms only for goods and services as they tend to be lower in value and higher in volume than works. In many cases, works are not channeled through the national public procurement system, but rather the Ministry of Works does its own procurement. This is significant as works usually involves a higher percentage of the public budget, given the large infrastructure projects, which can run into the millions of dollars. In Chile for example, works comprises 50% of public expenditures (CPAR, 2008). This means that an important part of the public procurement market does not benefit from the gains in efficiency and competition that can be provided by a modernization of the main e-GP system (Pimenta, 2015). This is starting to change and countries like Chile are looking into ways to further link the two systems. Another area that is often not channeled through the main e-GP system is procurement on the part of State-Owned Enterprises (SOEs). This is of concern as in many cases, public resources are spent outside the budget process without any way of tracking those expenditures.

Tools for Suppliers

Public procurement is not just a back office function and the new technologies have been useful to improve interaction with the private sector especially when lowering their transaction costs. Thus, governments in LAC have increasingly been investing and deploying tools such as supplier registries and Business Intelligence (BI) modules as part of e-GP implementations. As private sector companies had been using these tools for quite a while for business to business transactions, eventually governments caught on to this trend and recognized the benefits of using the new functionalities of electronic procurement to facilitate access and promote competition.

- **Supplier Registries:** Supplier registries as a concept have existed for quite some time in analog form. However, functionalities provided by electronic platforms have made them more effective and easier to use. E-supplier registries within e-GP systems provide the means for private sector companies to register once online, enabling them to be recognized as a provider to the public sector. This is important as it reduces transaction costs and burdensome processes and paperwork that before were needed for each individual procurement process. They are particularly effective when the registry cuts across different government platforms, for example with the tax systems, commerce registry or specialized bodies such as for the provision of industry-specific licenses so that businesses do not have to register multiple times (ADB, 2013).

There is a wide array of degrees of digitalization and automation in supplier registries, in most LAC countries even with the expansion of this tool in its digital form, there are still supplier registration processes that must be done manually, on paper, or that duplicate an electronic procedure. However, in spite of these shortcomings, in LAC supplier registries are particularly important to lower transaction costs for small and medium sized enterprises (SMEs). Chile for example has an advanced platform ChileProveedores, which has reduced transaction costs by 50% since it was established, particularly key as in Chile 54% of the suppliers to the state are SMEs (ChileProveedores, N.D.)

- **Business Intelligence:** Data from the public sector have traditionally been difficult to obtain and understand in LAC. When processes were fully paper based, information on what the government was buying was buried in files across ministries. The rise of e-GP systems improved this situation. However, the problem remains that the data being generated frequently was not easy to access or analyze.

BI addressed those issues by providing analytic tools that let users know who is buying, what they are buying and where they are buying it, thereby providing useful information on supplier assets and capabilities and their market. These types of tools are beneficial for civil society to monitor information related to the government in the area of procurement, procuring units are better able to develop market studies and analyze demand and prices and procurement officers can know the market and plan better. On the other side, it helps suppliers as they will have better information about where the upcoming opportunities will be. This is of particular use for small and medium sized enterprises as they do not have the same market analysis and development capabilities as larger companies (Guinez, 2013).

Starting in the 2010s, the LAC region began to develop BI modules in their e-GP system. To this regard, a pioneer in the region is Chile. Chile has a platform called Analiza that provides information on the public market that takes the data and presents it in a way that is easy to understand and actionable. It includes a list of all transactions, a tool for analyzing and comparing transactions (for example, by framework agreement or purchase order), trends and complaints ranking by purchasing entity. What each entity is buying, by what categories and by how much. Mexico is another country that has implemented BI. Its Information and Market Intelligence Module for Public Procurement (CompraNet-IM), was created in 2012 with five sections: 1) annual public procurement programs, 2) contracting procedures, 3) contracts, 4) providers and suppliers and 5) performance indicators for contracting procedures (Guinez, 2013).

The rise of electronic platforms has enabled governments in LAC to build tools which are revolutionizing how the governments are interacting with the market, to the benefit of the public sector in terms of greater transparency and efficiency, the private sector in terms of knowing the public sector market and targeting their business development accordingly and citizens in terms of better services as a result of the former as well as greater confidence in government.

New Business Models and Aggregation of Demand

Tools to aggregate demand such as framework agreements and reverse auctions are being implemented across the region with increasing frequency as governments realize their potential for savings, both in terms of reduced transaction costs and in terms of lower prices through increased competition. As countries have increasingly seen the value of such tools (especially given the quantity of such transactions), and the benefits that digitalization can bring to the process, there has been a push to adopt e-GP in LAC.

E-GP brings three main benefits to the bidding process for these types of transactions. The first is that it generates an enormous amount of real time data that can help the central procurement unit make planning and budgeting decisions as well as inventory management. This information about purchasing behavior can also help governments adjust and target their procurement policies to facilitate the increased participation of certain groups such as SMEs, local industry and women-owned businesses.

The second is that online platforms which make all the transactions transparent and removes the operator which can reduce opportunities for corruption. Finally it involves increased competition as it is easier for more suppliers to participate in the bidding process – both from other regions of the country and internationally (in the case where it is allowed) as the supplier does not have to be present. This is particularly beneficial for small and medium sized enterprises, which might not have the resources to travel or take time to participate in a live bid (ADB, 2013).

- **Framework Agreements:** Framework agreements are umbrella agreements whereby the price and quantity of the provision of a certain good or service is determined for a set period, particularly useful in cases where the buyer knows that a particular good or service will be needed but not the quantity and when. They are beneficial to the buyer and the supplier in that the tender only happens once rather than multiple times which is costly in terms of time and transaction costs. They are also useful in terms of leveraging purchasing power and generating economies of scale and sharing costs among different agencies and departments of the state (ADB, 2013)

Framework agreements are not new, however electronic platforms make them easier to implement and more effective. Specifically e-GP can help strengthen the decision-making process, planning, management involved in framework agreements through the data that is produced (ADB, 2013) These types of agreements are becoming common throughout Latin America. Some countries that use them, include, Chile, Colombia, Costa Rica, Jamaica, Mexico, Panama, Paraguay, and

Peru. In the case of Colombia for example, framework agreements have been allowed by law since 2007, but did not take off until the creation of the procurement agency Colombia Compra Efficiente the upgrades to the e-GP platform were made. (OECD, 2016). The "Tienda Virtual del Estado Colombiano" – the virtual store system for the framework agreements will be available in the new version of their e-GP system SECOP II. It is expected that the average time to carry out a procurement process will decrease in Colombia from 6 months to ten days with the use of framework agreements.

Panama is another country that has made progress in this area, with framework agreements for 38 different types of goods and services. An example that is frequently cited with regard to Panama are framework agreements for airline tickets. Starting in 2011, 98 public entities have been using the virtual airline ticket store which allows the entire process to be carried out online, including approval by the Ministry of the Presidency and payment with a credit card, which means a quicker approval for payment resulting in a lower ticket price. This framework agreement has generated monetary savings of $25-50 dollars per ticket and savings in transaction costs (INGP, 2013)

- **Reverse Auctions**: Another tool to aggregate demand that is of increasing use in Latin America and the Caribbean are reverse auctions. These tools are also facilitated by e-GP, whereby electronic means can safeguard neutrality and fairness. In this case, the buyer sets the base price and suppliers compete to provide the good at the lowest price. When this is carried out electronically, it is completely impersonal as the electronic system automatically selects the winner (Pinto, 2009).

It is not a panacea though as it does not prevent collusion, and is vulnerable to manipulation. It usually only works well in relatively large markets where there are sufficient number of providers to generate competition, otherwise they will not be effective in generating additional savings. For example, reverse auctions are successful in an enormous country like Brazil, but might not be recommendable in a very small country, where to the contrary the price might be higher as there are so few suppliers to particliple in the procurement process. In other words, reverse auctions can help the contracting agency take advantage and harness the existing potential for competition, but they cannot generate competition that does not exist (Volosin, 2013).

Countries that have reverse auctions include Brazil, Chile, Colombia, Costa Rica, Ecuador, Jamaica, Mexico, Panama, Peru and Uruguay. Brazil is the leader in the region in this area, which makes sense given its large size and number of potential providers. Brazil established its procurement portal, ComprasNet in 1998, and it became fully transactional in 2000, including the capacity for reverse auctions. Over 70% of all procurement transactions are through reverse auctions and by all accounts they have been very successful in Brazil (INGP, 2013). By 2008, 30% of the federal government was using the site, which allows for all levels of government and at the federal level. The time it takes for a procurement procedure was reduced from 60 to 14 days on average. (Pinto, 2009). The original investment was US $7 million, with savings of 1.5 million in the first two years (Volosin, 2010). Peru has been using reverse auctions since 2006, which are mandatory in the procurement of simple goods and services.

As the focus of public procurement in LAC takes a more strategic approach rather than just one of control and as there is a greater pressure to do more with less, tools that can support those objectives have become more critical. Governments have adopted tools such as framework agreements and reverse auctions as they generate actionable data, greater competition and a better targeting of procurement processes.

Challenges Ahead

While the LAC region has made considerable progress in the development of e-GP, there are still pending challenges that need to be resolved in order for governments to keep on modernizing these systems and make the most of the tools.

- **Control-Efficiency- Public Policies:** As has been mentioned throughout this chapter, there is the age-old problem in public procurement, which is how to balance the need for control and corruption prevention, as public resources are involved, with the need for efficiency and to do public procurement strategically. (Sanchez, 2013). This balancing act has played out and is reflected in the development and implementation of e-GP. Closely linked to that problem is the fact that public procurement is a dry topic that is hard for the average person and politician to understand.

To overcome this, government officials often build political support and momentum for reform and modernization efforts through corruption scandals. And indeed, anti-corruption efforts have created a favorable political environment to embed greater transparency in procurement operations, being e-GP the preferred tool to achieve this goal. However, the ultimate expected impact of a modern procurement system is not to guarantee due process, although that is important also, but to maximize value for money and achieve a more efficient and targeted use of public resources. As seen in previous sections of this chapter, internal control functions and oversight of procurement operations have been major driving forces to modernize public procurement and especially to adopt e-GP systems.

Nevertheless, this focus on control comes at the expense of efficiency and a cost as it adds more procedures to the procurement cycle and thus increases administrative costs. In addition, it didn't create incentives to overhaul and streamline operational procedures to add efficiency and reduce costs of the procurement cycle. In other words, as e-GP systems were implemented, controls tended to be increased, some inefficiencies remained as they were converted from analog to digital and in many cases efforts were duplicated as paper procedures were difficult to phase out.

In spite of the wide adoption of e-GP systems in the region, it could be argued that there is still considerable potential to be tapped in this tool to gain efficiency and value for money. Over the past ten years, the region has increased its transparency and accountability thanks to the new technology in place. However, there is a real opportunity to make corrections and carryout a thorough exercise to streamline procedures and requirements to maximize value for money and thus the quality of public goods and services provided to the citizens of LAC.

- **Focus of the Reform:** Another challenge that the region that needs to be addressed is the tendency to focus on e-GP as an end rather than a means to greater modernization of procurement as an expression of a country's public policy and development strategy. Considerable human and financial resources have been invested to adopt new technologies in procurement operations and they have been approached as if this were the reform itself.

e-GP systems should be considered a tool among many in an overall reform and not be designed as a stand-alone initiative to solve a particular function, as though purchasing a word processing software or mobile app. Their development must be accompanied by the proper business process analysis (correcting any inefficiencies), regulatory and legal framework (enabling e-transactions), change management strategies, sequencing with the government's overall e-government program, etc. One often hears about successful e-GP systems like ChileCompra, which has been adopted with great results, but its success also responds to a wide set of reforms enabling the modernization of the public administration as a whole and in line with a strong history of public management in Chile.

As much as the LAC region has made important advances in transparency and oversight, there is still work to be done in phasing out unnecessary and redundant paper procedures, as well as carrying out comprehensive assessments, and overhauls to streamline the procurement cycle.

Political, economic and technical context is important, which is why no matter how admired systems like ChileCompra are, simply copying and replicating its functionalities is unlikely to produce the same results and impact as it did in Chile.

Holistic procurement reforms in line, properly sequenced with e-government and public financial reforms and in accordance with country context are needed.

- **Legacy Systems:** LAC countries have invested considerable political, financial and human resources in the development of e-GP systems. As discussed earlier in this chapter, virtually all LAC countries have some form of e-GP, and out of those, almost half of them have functionalities to electronically submit bids, and as many as half of the countries in the region are in some stage of design or implementation of transactional systems. Additionally, many countries have included advanced modules such as those for business intelligence and supplier registries, as well as platforms to support framework agreements and reverse auctions.

However, information technology moves at an incredibly fast pace and many of the standards, tools and platforms that these e-GP systems rely on are quickly becoming out of date. Maintenance, operating and upgrade costs will only increase as support and technical expertise will become increasingly hard to find, especially in low income countries of the region. In spite of this, it is often difficult to move away from legacy systems, especially if they were successful; and expenses and efforts tend to be misplaced in building additional functionalities on top of the existing platforms, instead of leaning towards commercial off the shelf solutions where maintenance and development is taken care of by the supplier.

- **IT Departments and Legacy Systems:** A by-product of the tremendous effort undertaken by the region to implement e-GP systems has been the emergence of IT departments/units specialized in e-GP, either housed within public procurement entities or as part of bigger IT departments within ministries of finance. This has created bureaucracies with their corresponding incentives to justify their need for human and budgetary resources, as well as their continued existence. These departments or units are usually fully specialized and invested in the maintenance and operation of existing legacy systems.

Procurement reforms in LAC have often been carried out in isolation, which has created e-GP systems and corresponding bureaucracies that participate in wider electronic government efforts but not necessarily integrated with them. Procurement entities have little to no incentive to cede maintenance and operation of e-GP systems to government agencies better equipped to carry those functions. In many cases, e-GP has not been integrated or developed at the same pace as other expenditure systems.

All that was mentioned above illustrates a situation where there are limited incentives to adopt modern procurement technologies based on commercial off the shelf solutions that are developed and maintained by an external supplier, and there are also no incentives to adopt modern institutional arrangements where an e-government agency provides IT services for all government functions. Virtually eliminating the need of oversized IT departments embedded within the different levels and agencies of the public administration.

Modern Procurement Technologies

The need for streamlined supply chain management and sourcing in the private sector has prompted the development of new technological tools and platforms that could have a great effect in the public sector. Now there is a wide array of procurement platforms and solutions that leverage the technological advancements of the last decade, as opposed to the years when e-GP systems were starting to be developed and few off-the-shelf solutions were available. However, these new platforms could go against many institutional and operational models currently in place along with established legacy systems implemented between the late 1990s and the 2000s. As challenging as it will be, ready-to-deploy solutions seem to be increasingly well-suited to replace platforms currently in place that took a lot of effort and political capital to develop.

In many ways the procurement function is going through a new technological revolution. Heavy emphasis on demand forecasting in the private sector and large amounts of data generated by systems in the public sector has prompted software firms to develop new platforms/systems that can provide functionalities for complex analytics.

The significant investments made on IT infrastructure and software during the 2000s cannot be replicated; however, internet penetration in LAC continues to be high among developing economies. Furthermore, modern IT infrastructure puts suppliers in a privileged position as they need fewer and minimum computer resources to access complex e-GP systems. These factors will likely lead towards cloud-based platforms where infrastructure and software capabilities are contracted as a service permeating the public administration soon rather than later.

These new technologies seem to have the potential to impact procurement operations and results heavily; however, in the process of adopting them legacy systems will have to be phased-out and IT departments will have to face a major restructuring to fit the new needs of the public administration.

FUTURE RESEARCH DIRECTIONS

There are still big gaps in research in this topic for Latin America. While there are many areas that should be considered for future research, some key ones include the role of institutions and e-GP, specifically policy and monitoring units and how they have affected the development of such systems and what are the lessons from those experiences. So many attempts at e-GP around the world have failed and an underlying issue in many of the cases is likely the lack of a strong entity that can have an overall vision for the system that goes way beyond just the purchase of software. This is particularly the case in Latin America where these entities have spearheaded reform and modernization efforts.

There also needs to be more research on the returns of investments in e-GP. While some of the benefits are difficult to quantify such as improved governance, others are easier such as savings. Those numbers are critical for the Heads of Procurement to have to gain political support for deepening the reforms. Along those lines, actionable data is also of growing importance in the region, and how these systems are generating data and the use and impact of BI systems is an area that warrants further study.

Finally, an in-depth look at e-GP and its link to the overall public financial management system, particularly IFMIS could be explored further given the impact of public procurement on the execution of the budget.

CONCLUSION

E-GP over the last twenty years has advanced as governments have realized that it is much more than an administrative function, but rather has strategic value in terms of being a tool for public policy and contributing to overall improved public administration. (Sanchez, 2013). This is reflected in the widespread adoption of e-GP since the late nineties until present day. Countries are still investing in modernizing systems as they continue to seek the gains in transparency, efficiency and savings that these tools provide.

However, there are still pending issues that need to be addressed. The traditional focus on control has not for the most part been overcome. This is reflected in the continued trend of in-house solutions for e-GP systems that allow small and constant modifications to the flow of information and processes. For e-GP systems to fulfill their full potential, their development should have an optimal balance between efficiency, control and public policy.

Additionally, the legacy systems produced under in house development will make it difficult to make a switch towards having systems that keep up to date with modern trends in technology, which are changing at an ever faster rate. Countries will also face the need to adopt modern IT software standards and platforms if they are going to take advantage of new trends such as cloud computing.

In conclusion, the region has made great strides in terms of the approval of legislation, creation and strengthening of procurement agencies, building in-house capacity, developing tools for suppliers and helping line ministries implement new business models. Given its circumstances, LAC has progressed significantly in terms of creating a conducive environment for future e-GP implementations, by laying out a good foundation. However there is still work to be done in order to adopt new technologies for revamped e-GP systems while maintaining a focus on efficiency and savings.

REFERENCES

Asian Development Bank. (2013). Mandaluyong City, Philippines: Asian Development Bank.

Chile Proveedores. (n.d.). Retrieved July 10, 2016, from http://www.chileproveedores.cl/chprovdnn/serviciosybeneficios.aspx

Concha, G. & Porrua, M., & Pimenta, C. (2011). E-*Government procurement observatory, maturity model and early measurements.* Academic Press.

Crane, R., & Marius, M. (2016). *Regional approaches to e-government initiatives in the Caribbean.* ECLAC.

Guinez, C. (2013). *Business Intelligence para las Compras Públicas.* Washington, DC: Inter-American Development Bank.

Hunja, R. (2010). *Forging New Frontiers in Public Procurement.* Retrieved from: http://blogs.worldbank.org/governance/forging-new-frontiers-in-public-procurement

Inter-American Development Bank. (2011). *Electronic Government Procurement Map.* Washington, DC: Campero, Harper, Concha, Vizcaíno, Sánchez.

Inter-American Development Bank and the Government of Chile. (n.d.). Chile: evaluación del sistema nacional de compras y contrataciones Públicas (CPAR), op. cit., p. 33.

Inter-American Network on Government Procurement (INGP). (2013). *Conference proceedings.* Retrieved July 10, 2016, from http://www.RICG.org

International Monetary Fund. (2013). *Caribbean small states: challenges of high debt and low growth.* Retrieved July 10, 2016 from: https://www.imf.org/external/np/pp/eng/2013/022013b.pdf

Lapido, O. A. S., & Sopher. (2009). Accountability in Public Expenditures in Latin America and the Caribbean – Revitalizing Reforms in Financial Management and Procurement. Washington DC: The World Bank.

Organization for Economic Cooperation and Development. (2014). *Government at a Glance: Latin America and the Caribbean 2014: Towards Innovative Public Financial Management.* Paris: OECD Publishing.

Organization for Economic Cooperation and Development and Inter-American Development Bank. (2016). *Towards Efficient Public Procurement in Colombia.* Paris: OECD Publishing.

Organization for Economic Cooperation and Development and Inter-American Development Bank. (2016). *Government at a Glance: Latin America and the Caribbean 2017.* Paris: OECD Publishing.

Organization of American States. (2005). *Inter-American Forum on Government Procurement: Chile, Mexico and Costa Rica Case Studies.* Washington, DC: OAS.

Pimenta, C., & Pessoa, M. (2015). *Public Financial Management in Latin America: The Key to Efficiency and Transparency.* Washington, DC: Inter-American Development Bank. doi:10.18235/0000083

Pinto, S. (2009). *Subastas inversas electrónicas y su aplicación en las compras gubernamentales: La experiencia de Latinoamérica.* Washington, DC: Inter-American Development Bank.

Sanchez, A. (2013). The Role of Public Procurement. In R. Allen, R. Hemming, & B. Potter (Eds.), *The International Handbook of Public Financial Management* (pp. 312–335). London, UK: Palgrave. doi:10.1057/9781137315304_15

Segal, G., & Taylor, M. (2001). *Electronic Procurement How Technology is Changing Government Purchasing.* Retrieved from: http://reason.org/news/show/electronic-procurement

Shillingford-McKlimon, S., & Gayle-Sinclair, S. (2014). *CARICOM: Small market–big money. Amalgamating the Procurement Market to Transform Small Size into an Economic Advantage.* Academic Press.

Theodate, M. (2015). *Desk Review of Caribbean Country Procurement.* Washington, DC: Inter-American Development Bank.

Veiga Malta, J., Schapper, P., Calo-Gonzalez, O., & Berroa, D. (2011). *Old Rules New Realities: Are Existing Public Procurement Systems Addressing Current and Future Needs?* Washington, DC: The World Bank- LAC.

Volosin, N. (2010). *Promoviendo compras públicas electrónicas para el desarrollo: Análisis comparativo de Brasil, Chile y México y recomendaciones para una agenda de incidencia e implementación en la Argentina*. Buenos Aires: Fundación Poder Ciudadano.

Williams, R., & Marius, M. (2016). *Regional approaches to e-government initiatives in the Caribbean*. Santiago: Economic Commission for Latin America and the Caribbean.

World Bank, Inter-American Development Bank, & Asian Development Bank. (2004). *Electronic Government Procurement Roadmap*. Available at http://siteresources.worldbank.org/INFORMATIONANDCOMMUNICATIONANDTECHNOLOGIES/Resources/e-GPRoadMap.pdf

ENDNOTES

1. The OECS is a nine member grouping comprising Antigua and Barbuda, Commonwealth of Dominica, Grenada, Montserrat, St Kitts and Nevis, St. Lucia and St Vincent and the Grenadines.
2. In other regions, this has been done with a decree but in the Caribbean there has been resistance to taking that route.

Chapter 10
Public Procurement Framework in India: An Overview

Prabir Panda
Independent Researcher, India

G. P. Sahu
MN National Institute of Technology Allahabad, India

ABSTRACT

Studies highlight that public procurement in any country acts as a barometer of public confidence in fairness and transparency of public institutions. A number of cases related to corruption in public procurement in the country have been highlighted by media on regular basis. These incidents raise questions regarding robustness of the procurement framework in vogue in the country. Though no special legislative framework dealing with public procurement exists in the country, the administrative guidelines on the subject are quite exhaustive. Procurement is not a state subject; hence law can be made by the Centre for entire country. However, no separate law governing public procurement has been enacted in India. However, public procurement in India is not bereft of its share of issues. Multiplicity of instructions, absence of procurement law and singular emphasis on upfront value of acquisition without considering life cycle cost mars public procurement in India. Further, social and environmental sustainability has also not received the attention it deserves. Studies highlight that migration of public procurement to Internet could provide us savings of up to 25% by streamlining 30% of Indian Union Budget spent on provisioning of goods / services. However, any such endeavor has 70% chances of failure. With only 13% e-procurement research focusing on public sector make matter worse. In

DOI: 10.4018/978-1-5225-2203-4.ch010

the above backdrop, the chapter would cover: Importance of public procurement, Difference between public and corporate procurement, Overview of procurement framework of the country - covering constitutional/ legislative/ administrative provisions, generic public procurement process, various types of procurements – limited tender, open tender, single tender, issues in public procurement of the country and e-procurement initiatives by Government of India and status thereof.

INTRODUCTION

In India, by February, finance ministry in Central/ State Government prepare an annual budget for the upcoming financial year (01 April to 31 March next year). This budget brings out anticipated income and planned expenditure for the financial year. The budget is presented in Parliament/ state legislature in the month of Feb/ Mar. Once the budget is passed, Ministry of Finance, Government of India (GoI) allots funds to Ministries/ Departments of the Central Government for meeting their budgeted expenditure. This function is undertaken by the state finance ministry in case of state governments. Available estimates indicate that about 30% of Indian budget (OECD, 2010) or 3.4 - 5.7% of the GDP (DIT, 2011) is spent on procurement of goods / provisioning of services. These huge sums of public funds need to be spent in consonance with laid down rules and regulations which are meant to ensure that public procurement is uniform, transparent, efficient and cost effective.

In succeeding paragraphs, this chapter delves upon the framework used for affecting public procurement in India. The framework in the context of this chapter deemed to cover both processes and powers for affecting public procurement. This chapter is divided in four major sections. In second section, constitutional, legislative and administrative provisions governing public procurement in India are covered. While third section covers general overview of public procurement process in India, section four covers various issues affecting it. In the last section, authors cover generic recommendations for improving transparency and efficiency of public procurement in India. The structure followed for third section is shown in Figure 1.

BACKGROUND

Governments across the world are increasingly embracing ICT for the benefits of their citizenry which entails improvement in delivery of public service, augmenting public access to information and encouragement of e-participation in civic affairs (Kaliannan, Awang and Raman, 2009). However, Moon (2004) underlined that there is general negative perception among the masses about public procurements.

Public Procurement Framework in India

Figure 1. Public procurement framework in India

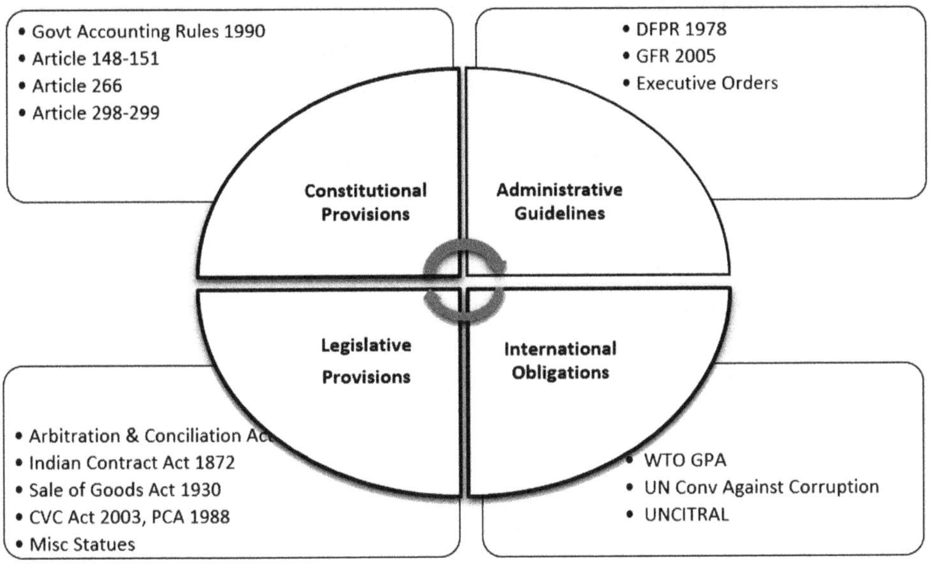

This is in stark contrast to corporate procurement which is considered to efficient and effective. Therefore, before proceeding further, it would be appropriate to enunciate differences in considerations and the approaches between public and corporate procurement. Firstly, in corporate sector the procurement decisions are driven more by strategic considerations like opportunities through long term arrangements, apportioning supply risks, effective cost of procurement etc., than in the public sector. While public procurements meticulously follow "Lowest bid wins", "separation between the vendor and user is needed to avert subsequent accusations of favoritism", "fixed pricing and contract term" etc., corporate procurements are only concerned about profits (MacManus, 2002). The public procurement is also constrained by government rules which are guided by considerations of equity, transparency, competition or sectoral reservations (like Small Scale Industries etc.). In the above, backdrop, succeeding paragraphs cover constitutional, legislative and administrative provisions governing public procurement in India.

PUBLIC PROCUREMENT FRAMEWORK: CONSTITUTIONAL PROVISIONS

India is a 'Union of States' and is governed in terms of the Constitution of India. Indian constitution came into force on 26 January 1950. The constitution provides for a parliamentary form of government with two Houses known as the Council of States (Rajya Sabha) and the House of the People (Lok Sabha). President of India, is constitutional but ceremonial head of the Executive of the Union as Indian Constitution requires President to exercise his/ her powers in accordance with aid and advice of Council of Ministers which is headed by Prime Minister [Article 74(1) of Constitution]. Consequently, actual executive authority lies with Council of Ministers. The Prime Minister must enjoy majority in the lower house of Indian Parliament called Lok Sabha. The constitution provides for similar provisions for states. In case of states, Governor (appointed by President of India) is constitutional head of state executive and functions on aid and advice of Council of Ministers which is headed by Chief Minister. Further, Indian Constitution provides for division of legislative powers between Central Government and State Government through clearly laid down Union List, State List and Concurrent List.

While the Indian Constitution is quite exhaustive and covers all essential aspects related to smooth functioning of the union with clear demarcation of power and roles among executive, legislature and judiciary. However, it is silent on public procurement issues except for following provisions incidental thereto:

1. **Article 148:** Deals with appointment of Comptroller and Auditor-General of India (C&AG) by President of India. The C&AG is responsible for audit of books of accounts of Central and state governments and render report to President/ Governor.
2. **Article 149:** Lays down duties and powers of C&AG.
3. **Article 150:** Empowers President of India to issue directions regarding the form in which accounts of the Union and of the States is to be kept.
4. **Article 151:** Requires President of India and Governors of States to place C&AG audit reports before Parliament and state legislatures respectively.
5. **Article 266:** Contains stipulations regarding consolidated funds and public accounts of India and that of State government. The article requires expenditure to be appropriated only in accordance with the provisions of the constitution.
6. **Article 298:** Authority to contract for goods and services.
7. **Article 299:** Legally binding contracts are to be executed for and on behalf of the President of India/ Governor of state in writing by officers specifically authorised to do so. However, constitutional head of the Executive i.e. the President/ Governor is not personally liable in respect of any executed contract.
8. Fundamental rights of the suppliers as a common citizen e.g. of being treated equally (while soliciting tenders).

In consonance with the powers conferred under Article 150, President of India (on the advice of C&AG) issued Government Accounting Rules, 1990 (Revised

Edition) which came in effect from 01 Apr 1990. For the guidance of Government Departments, C&AG drafted general principles of Government accounting are also included in the Rules.

PUBLIC PROCUREMENT FRAMEWORK: STATUES

Union List, State List, or the Concurrent List of Indian Constitution does not contain any reference to 'Procurement' as a subject. Therefore, in accordance with Article 248 of the Constitution, Union Parliament is empowered to make any laws on the subject for the entire country. Even if procurement deemed to be covered by "Acquisition and Requisition of property" and "Contracts" (42 and 7 of concurrent list), both centre and state governments can legislate. However, no law governing public procurement has been passed by Indian parliament, few states like Tamil Nadu Nadu and Karnataka have implemented public procurement laws.

In aftermath of public outcry against corruption in public expenditure, GoI instituted a committee under Mr. Vinod Dhall, Ex-Chief CCI for suggesting public procurement reforms. The committee submitted its report in Jun 2011. Based on the committee recommendations, 'Public Procurement Bill, 2012' was introduced in Lok Sabha on 14 May 2012. On 28 May 12, the bill was referred to a parliamentary standing committee. The bill expired with dissolution of previous Lok Sabha. Recently, GoI revived the bill. Inputs on the bill were sought from public by 20 Apr 15. The bill is being handled by Public Procurement Division (PPD) under Min of Finance. The bill is yet to be passed. PPD had sought public view on the draft Public Procurement Bill, 2012 by 20 Apr 2015 vide OM F.No. 2/1/2012-PPD dated 06 Apr 2015. The authors of this chapter had forwarded comments and suggestions on the bill to Ministry of Finance, Government of India. Some of these suggestions/recommendations are covered in later part of this chapter.

In the absence of a constitutional or legislative framework specially dealing with public procurements, the officers dealing with public procurements are guided by various ancillary statues such as Indian Contract Act 1872, Sale of Goods Act 1930, Prevention of Corruption Act 1988, Arbitration and Conciliation Act 1996, Information Technology Act 2000, Competitions Act 2002, Central Vigilance Commission Act 2003, Right to Information Act, 2005 etc. These ancillary statutes shape various aspects of public procurement. Further, as per constitutional scheme in India, expenditure from public exchequer is subject to statutory audit by C&AG (Article 148 to 151, Comptroller and Auditor General's [Duties, Powers and Conditions of Service] Act 1971), therefore, accounting standards prescribed C&AG and Government Accounting Rules 1990 are followed in the country.

PUBLIC PROCUREMENT FRAMEWORK: ADMINISTRATIVE GUIDELINES

Notwithstanding above, detailed rules and instructions on public procurement are contained in various executive orders/ guidelines like General Financial Rules issued by Government of India. As per Article 266 of Indian constitution, powers for incurring expenditure out of consolidated funds/ contingency funds are vested in Central/ State Government in conjunction with respective legislatures. In order to achieve efficiency in administrative functioning, it is imperative that sanctioned expenditure is incurred at lowest level of executive consistent with the objective of the expenditure. Accordingly, GoI issued 'Delegation of Financial Power Rules, 1978' which prescribes the manner and extent of delegation of financial powers to lower Competent Financial Authorities (CFA) for decentralized procurement. Similarly, Financial Regulations Vol I & II, provide general principles of financial management.

CFAs in India are required to follow 'General Financial Rules, 2005' issued by Ministry of Finance, GoI while incurring expenditure from public funds. In order to cater for subtle differences in the nature of procurements, Rule 135 of GFR 2005 empowers GoI Ministries and Departments to issue departmental manuals on procurement. In pursuance of the rule, major ministries and departments have issued detailed purchase procedures for their internal use such as Ministry of Defense (MoD) (Defense Procurement Procedure, 2013, and Defense Procurement Manual, 2009), Director General Supplies and Disposal (DGS&D Manual), etc. The modes for procurement of goods and services utilizing public funds are laid down in Chapter 6 of GFR 2005 which permits expenditure up to Rs. 15,000 (on each occasion) without inviting tender (Rule 145), from Rs. 15,001 up to Rs. 1,00,000 by a purchase committee (Rule 146) and expenditure beyond Rs. 1 lakh only by obtaining bids (Rule 149). Invariably two bids system (separate Technical bid and Commercial bid) is followed (Rule 152). However, the rule of competitive bidding is not applicable to purchases made directly under rate contract (Rule 147). The GFR chapter also lays down guiding principles for single tender enquiry (Rule 154) and Sectoral Purchase Preference Policy (Rule 144). In order to avert perceived conflict with Indian Contract Act, OM No. 29(1)/2014-PPD dated 28 Jan 2014 (issued by Ministry of Finance, Govt of India) mandates government departments to incorporate a clause in RFPs with stipulation that bids with 'NIL consideration' would be summarily rejected.

Since the GFR was last revised in 2005, it has largely been out of sync with development in ICT area. Consequently, in order to leverage technology for cost effective and expeditious procurement, Procurement Policy Division of Ministry of Finance, Govt of India, inserted a sub-rule under Rule 141 of GFR vide OM No.

F.26/4/2016-PPD dated 03 May 2016, which inter-alia requires DGS&D to host a Government e-Marketplace (GeM) portal. The GeM (akin to e-marketplace portals like Flipkart, Amazon etc.,) permits government department to affect procurements of items available on GeM upto Rs. 50,000/- without following paper procedure related to procurement. The procedure for procurement and payment on GeM was stipulated vide OM No. F.26/4/2016-PPD dated 26 May 2016. Further, inter-governmental procurement of goods and services have been streamlined by GoI by amending Rule 126 of GFR 2005 vide OM No. F.29/1/2015-PPD dated 13 Apr 2016.

Apart from FR and GFR provisions, various sectoral manuals are also issued by Ministry of Finance, Govt of India for guiding public procurement process. Three such important manuals are related to Policies and Procedures for Purchase of Goods, Works and Consultancy. These manuals were issued in 2006 and were largely out of sync. Consequently, the manuals were revised under the aegis of PPD, Min of Finance, GoI. Views of selective stakeholders (including author of this chapter) on the alpha draft of the revised Manuals were sought by 15 Jun 2016 through email vide OM F.No. 17/6/2014-PPD dated 24 May 2016. Based on the inputs so received from civil/ official domain experts/ stakeholders, the manuals were revised. Attendant beta draft of the revised manuals have now been placed in public domain vide OM No. F.17/6/2014-PPD dated 22 Aug 2016. Comments on the manuals could be given by general public till The revised manuals aims to incorporate many novel concepts in public procurement like Life Cycle costing, e-payment gateway, GeM etc.,

The pictorial depiction of type and mode of public procurement envisaged under Indian system is covered in Figure 2.

Figure 2. Types and modes of tendering

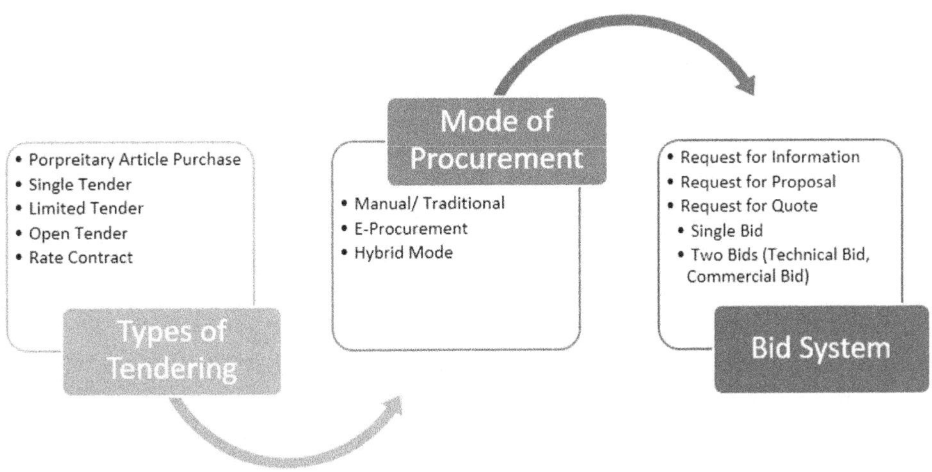

Above procurement guidelines are also followed by the state governments/ UTs. While most States / UTs regulate public procurement through Government Orders, many state governments like the state of Tamil and Karnataka have enacted statues governing public procurement. The cardinal principles of public procurement are spelt out in Office Memorandum No. 8 (3)-E.II (A) 0-02 issued by GoI which envisages:

1. Maximizing economy, efficiency and effectiveness in public procurement through expeditious procurement of goods/ provisioning of services at the most economical price.
2. Treat all prospective suppliers / bidders fairly and equitably without any bias.
3. Affect procurements at most economical price by fostering competition among prospective suppliers for supply of goods/ services.
4. Strive for transparency in procurement.

While Information Technology Act 2000 provides legal framework for e-commerce by the government agencies, e-procurement adoption has been somewhat slow in India. Consequently, a number of government orders were issued for expediting the migration process. For example, OM No.8 (5)/EII (A)/2006 dated 10 January 2007 stipulated that:

1. In respect of procurement through DGS&D rate contracts, Ministries should commence placing orders through of DGS&D website as soon as possible but not later than 01 April 2007.
2. In case of other procurements, the Ministries may make their own arrangements for switching over to mandatory e-procurement beyond identified threshold limits w.e.f 01 April 2007 with certain compliance norms.

Another government order on expenditure management (OM No. 7(3) E-Coord/2006 dated 22 July 2006) mandates migration to e-procurement and e-payments in order to improve efficiency in procurement process and thereby reduce overall procurement cost. Central Vigilance Commission of India has also directed implementation of e-Payment & e-Receipt (CVC office order No. 98/ORD/1 dated 20 October 2004) and issued guidelines for e-procurement systems security (CVC circular No. 009/VGL/002 dated 17 September 2009).

Even after launch of National e-Government Program (NeGP) in 2006 [with E-Government Procurement (E-GP) as integrated Mission Mode Project (MMP)], adoption of e-procurement has been slow in India. Various Government Orders (GO) on e-procurement (cited above) remained unimplemented (DIT, 2011). Consequently, post review of E-GP MMP progress on 29 June 2010, NeGP Apex

Committee (chaired by the Cabinet Secretary), felt the need of regulatory intervention by Ministry of Finance, GoI for mandatory adoption of e-procurement system for government procurements. Consequently, GoI (vide OM No. 10/3/2012-PPC dated 30 Mar 2012), made it mandatory for central government agencies to publish Tender Enquiries [with Estimated Contract Value (ECV) above Rs. 10 Lakh] on Central Public Procurement Portal. In addition, E-GP MMP implementation strategy was refined for a three pronged approach. Central government agencies/ State Governments were given the choice to implement E-GP through one of the following routes (DIT, 2011):

1. **Use the e-Procurement Solution Developed by NIC (GePNIC)** which provides generic but customizable functionalities related to the government tendering / procurement requirements.
2. **Use DGS&D e-Procurement Portal** for procurement of common user items through Rate Contracts.
3. **Use Any Third Party e-Procurement Solution** preferably on a Private Public Partnership (PPP) model as has been done by Chhattisgarh and Andhra Pradesh subject to certification by STQC regarding security and transparency.

GENERIC PUBLIC PROCUREMENT IN INDIA

Rule 150 of the GFR 2005, CVC CTE Manual 2002 (Para 6.1 and 6.2) and CVC Guideline No. 005/VGL/4 dated 01 September 2006 (http://cvc.nic.in), stipulate that for ECV of Rs. 1 lakh and above, wide publicity of the tender is to be given. Further, as per policies in vogue, government agencies send classified advertisements regarding public procurements [Request for Quotation (RFQ), Request for Information (RFI) or Request for Proposal (RFP)] to the Directorate of Audio-Visual Publicity (DAVP), Ministry of Information and Broadcasting (I&B) (in case of central government) or publicity/ public relations department (in case of state governments) who in turn release it for publication in national/ local dailies.

Apart from delay and expenditure incurred in publication of the advertisement, the manual process of invitation of bids, bid evaluation and finalization of contract induces significant time lag from initiation of procurement process to its fruition. A typical public procurement process flow chart is depicted in Figure 3. The process may vary slightly depending upon departmental rules in vogue. The process depicted in the figure may be abridged at the discretion of CFA on case-to-case basis on operational necessity. For example, discretion has been given to respective department/ ministry to affect procurement up to Rs. 25 lakh through limited tender enquiry without following advertised procurement route.

Figure 3. Generic public procurement in India

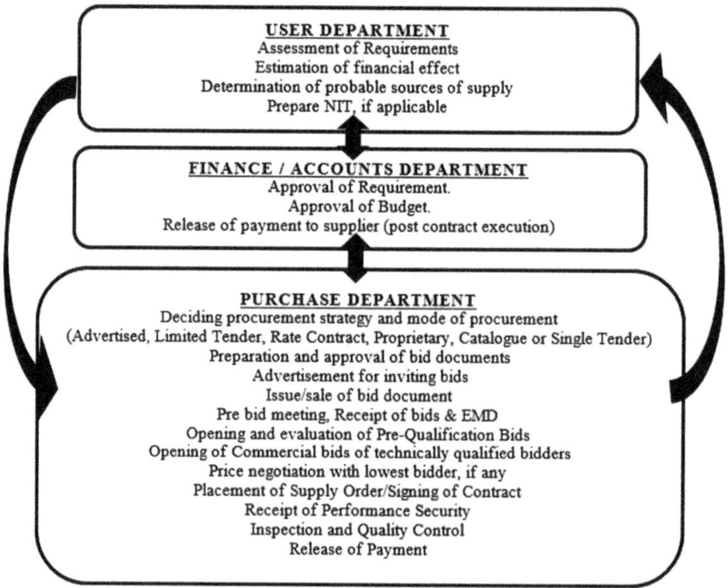

Source: Panda and Sahu (2011)

Typically, user department oversees technical evaluations of product/ service, inspection, quality control and execution of contract. Tendering and subsequent stages of procurement and payment related activities are coordinated by the purchase department with user and accounts departments. There is a continuous interaction and consultation between the user, finance and procurement departments from initiation of demand for purchase to release of payment to the vendor.

COMMONALITY IN PROCUREMENT PROCESS IN INDIA

Even in the absence of legal framework; the public procurement procedure followed across India is somewhat similar. As per Panda and Sahu (2015), the similarity emanates from:

1. General adherence to rules and instructions issued by Ministry of Finance, GoI by all state governments and union territories. Some of the cardinal books in this regard are DFPR and GFR.
2. Applicability of various central statues (in terms of Article 251, 253-254 of Indian Constitution) such as Indian Contract Act 1872, Sale of Goods Act 1930, Comptroller and Auditor General's (Duties, Powers and Conditions

of Service) Act 1971, Government Accounting Rules 1990, Competition Act, 2002 [amended vide Competition (Amendment) Act, 2007], Arbitration and Conciliation Act, 1996 [amended vide Arbitration and Conciliation (Amendment) Act, 2015], Micro, Small and Medium Enterprises Development (MSME Development) Act, 2006, Information Technology Act, 2000 (governing e-commerce), etc., to state governments.

3. In case of projects funded projects, the procurement guidelines issued by funding agency like World Bank, IMF, ADB etc. are to be followed.
4. All e-procurement solutions must adhere to the basal requirements specified by DIT and to be audited by STQC (directed by CVC vide circulars dated 23 Jun 2010 and 12 Jan 2012), therefore all e-GP systems in the country are somewhat similar.

GOI PROCUREMENT PORTALS

In order to harness potential of information technology for efficient and transparent procurement, following centralized portal are being operated under the aegis of Government of India:

1. **Rate Contract Based e-Procurement Platform:** DGS&D was established in 1951 for rendering procurement services to Central and State Governments by finalizing Rate Contracts for common user items and contracts against their ad-hoc demands. The contract is utilized by various ministries and their associated departments for affecting procurement. The DGS&D platform permits management of procurement requisitions, placement of supply orders and subsequent receipt and inspection. The payment to the Rate Contract (RC) holder for supplies is made directly by the concerned ministries/ department. In the event of payment being made by DGS&D's on their behalf, the book adjustment is subsequently carried out with the concerned ministry. URL of the portal is http://www.dgsnd.gov.in/.
2. **Central Public Procurement Portal (CPPP):** The website has been created and is being operated by National Information Corporation which is under Ministry of Commerce, GoI. The portal has two modules i.e. E-Publish and E-Procure which provide different levels of functionalities. The portal is a single point access public procurements being undertaken by various central government organizations. The URL of the portal is http://eprocure.gov.in/. The portal also hosts the tenders published by states/ UTs (E-GP MMP).

3. **Government e-Marketplace (GeM):** Based on recommendations of Group of Secretaries made to Hon'ble Prime Minister, Government directed DGS&D to create a one stop Government e-Marketplace (GeM) to facilitate on line procurement of common use Goods & Services required by various Government Departments / Organizations / PSUs. GeM aims to enhance transparency, efficiency and speed in public procurement by providing for e-bidding and reverse e-auction as well as demand aggregation. The URL of the portal is https://gem.gov.in/.
4. **e-Auctioning:** Using Internet technology to dispose of unserviceable/ discarded or surplus public goods which are no longer needed by various government departments is called e-auctioning. It is carried out through M/s MSTC, a Govt. of India enterprise. The entire process from the listing of goods for auction, reserve price to the actual auctioning can be carried out by various departments through MSTC web site http://www.mstcindia.co.in/. Vendors registered with M/s MSTC can participate in the online auction process.

CHALLENGES IN PUBLIC PROCUREMENT IN INDIA

The public procurement in India has many issues of concern. First and foremost of these issues is existence of multiple procurement guidelines and procedures. The stipulations contained in various rules, guidelines and directions are not always in harmony with each other and therefore lead to varied interpretation of procurement provisions. In addition, a large number of institutions like Ministry of Finance, CVC, CAG, BEE, Bureau of Indian Standards (BIS) etc., control various aspects of public procurement. Obscurity in their regulatory roles results in overlapping functions and jurisdictions (Panda and Sahu, 2013). Even the 'Public Procurement Bill, 2012' under consideration by GoI has many lacunas like:

1. The bill is only applicable to central government and its entities and that too for procurements above Rs. 0.50 Cr.
2. The bill does not cover procurements related to disaster management or with security/ strategic connotations. In addition, central government may exempt any procurement or procuring entity from any of the provisions of the Bill in public interest. The procedure for exemption is likely to be spelt out in procurement rules (to be notified and amended by GoI later once the act is passed). Hence, exemption would be in the purview of the executive and would not require legislative approval.

3. The bill does not conform to international obligations of the country under various agreements and conventions like World Trade Organization Government Procurement Agreement, UN Convention against Corruption etc.
4. Bill is sketchy and silent on key issues such as centralized registration of vendors, sustainability issues etc.

In addition, analysis of the ancillary statues and administrative guidelines (governing public procurement) indicates that emerging issues such as balancing Social, Environmental and Economic considerations take a back seat in procurement decisions due primacy of cost effectiveness. The specific issues highlighted by Panda and Sahu (2013) in this regard are related to:-

- **Economic Considerations:** Maximizing economy is central theme of public procurement policies in India. Deciding L1 (winning bidder) solely on the basis of only price defies the sustainability imperatives in procurement. Lifetime costs associated with an acquisition such as operating costs related to energy consumption, maintenance and final environmentally safe disposal are often ignored in bid formulation and evaluation. Lately, lifetime costing has incorporated in few big ticket defense procurements.
- **Social Sustainability:** Social sustainability does not find explicit mention in public procurement policies in India. However, it is a pervasive factor guiding public policies. Social sustainability takes many forms like waiver from earnest money deposit, preferences in price, reservation of items for low-tech labor intensive small scale industries. These policies strive to enable these smaller entities to compete with big corporations for government contracts. Consequently, this policy of providing exclusive market access negates efficiency generated by competition.
- **Environmental Footprint/ Sustainability:** Environmental/ carbon footprint related considerations do not form part of procurement decisions. The objective of Energy Conservation Act 2001 was to foster country's transition to a more energy efficient and sustainable future. However, till date only Rule 160 of GFR and recent guidelines (OM No. 26/6/12-PPD dated 21 Jan 13) on procurement of energy efficient electrical appliances (Air conditioners, Refrigerators, Fan and Water Heaters) are the cornerstone of this noble objective. State governments are not bound to follow the guidelines the issued by central government in this regard.

In addition to the above, absence of centralized repository of procurement related data (last purchase price, procuring and supplying agency etc.,) is the biggest impediment in generating MIS report for managerial decision making for public purchases.

Similarly, in the absence of centralized registration of vendors, department-wise registration not only leads to wastage of time but also acts as an entry barrier for newer entrants. Resultantly, public procurement market in India is fragmented and is mired in departmental silos.

WORLD PERSPECTIVE ON PUBLIC PROCUREMENT

Procurement is an important function of governments' world over. Consequently, various international bodies like United Nations Commission for International Trade Law (UNCITRAL Model Law), WTO (Government Procurement Agreement), World Bank, OECD etc., have framed guidelines and agreements. These guidelines/ frameworks strive to promote integrity and transparency in public procurements. The multi-lateral agreements on public procurement are based on WTO GPA and United Nations Convention against Corruption. WTO GPA is broadly consistent with and reinforces the values and objectives of other important international instruments (Panda and Sahu, 2013). In fact a many countries have borrowed the principles contained in GPA and UNCITRAL Model Law for drafting their national procurement laws like Uganda, Paraguay etc. In addition, multi-lateral agencies have been working on frameworks for evaluating public procurement system of countries. One such framework in respect of developing countries has been devised by the OECD together with the World Bank. EU on the other hand has evolved its own framework for assessing public procurement system of member countries. The aim of these frameworks is to stipulate an integrated set of tools and good practices to improve procurement systems and the outcomes they produce as well as to assist in the periodical assessments of the domestic legislation. While many important aspects of best practices contained therein are already part of administrative guidelines issued by GoI, there is a need of providing it legislative backing as recommended by 2nd Administrative Reforms Commission of India (DARPG, 2010b).

REVIEW OF E-PROCUREMENT IN INDIA

Consequent to persistent thrust on migration to e-procurement by GoI, as on date, almost all state governments and union territories have implemented e-GP. Most of these implementations have been through GePNIC except few states who have followed PPP route for implementation of e-procurement solution. Andhra Pradesh and Chhattisgarh are among the state who were among the first few states to implement e-GP through PPP route. There are only limited number of e-GP Application Service Providers in India. Notable among them are C1 India (http://www.c1india.

com/), Nextenders (India) Pvt. Ltd. (http://nextenders.com), nCode Solutions (https://www.ncodesolutions.com/) and Antares Systems Ltd. (http://www.antar-essystems.com). Irrespective of e-GP implementation route, actual utilization of implemented e-GP solutions in the country has been dismal save few states like Andhra Pradesh, Chhattisgarh, Gujrat etc,. In their study, Panda and Sahu (2015) found a positive correlation between e-GP implementation and e-readiness level as brought out in e-Readiness Assessment Report 2008 (DIT and NCAER, 2010). E-readiness found not only contributing to e-procurement implementation but also to subsequent utilization. Interested readers could refer to Panda and Sahu (2015) for details regarding mode of implementation, utilization of implemented solutions and issues connected thereto.

A number of studies have tried to evolve Critical Success Factors related to e-GP. These studies have underlined Top Management Support, E-Procurement Implementation Strategy, Business Case and Project Management, Business Process Re-engineering, Change Management, Training and Education, Adoption by Stakeholders, Technology Standards, System Integration, Security and Authentication, and Performance Measurement as factors contributing to e-GP system success (Panda and Sahu, 2013). Further studies on level of evolution of e-GP solutions in India, underline that E-GP systems in country are at Stage 2 of project evolution in terms of 4 stage evolution model suggested by Lyne and Lee (2001). However, efforts are on for upstream and downstream integration of other procurement functions such as requisition management etc., in E-GP system.

WAY FORWARD

In order to achieve a single public procurement market in India which fosters competition, efficiency and transparency, the following recommendations are made. These recommendations build upon the findings of various studies conducted in India on success of e-GP system in Andhra Pradesh and Chhattisgarh notably that was carried out by Panda and Sahu (2011). It is felt that majority of the issues could best be addressed by enactment of a central procurement law covering all aspects of public procurement.

1. Political leadership needs to take more interest in case of E-GP systems where system usage is low. E-GP projects should be expedited by committing necessary resources and by constituting core committees within each ministry/department.
2. In India, revenue procurements have been decentralized and carried out by designated CFAs spread across the government hierarchy. Therefore, demand

aggregation in classical sense is neither feasible nor desirable. Availability of centralized procurement data would enable rate contract finalizing agencies and CFAs to gauze accurate consumption data and procurement price which could then be exploited for cost effective procurement.

3. Centralized registration of vendors at National Level is necessary. This would preclude entry barriers for the vendors and requirement of re-registering with each procuring agency. Payment Gateways may be integrated with E-GP systems.
4. GFR 2005 provisions may be suitably incorporated in Public Procurement Bill or the rules to be made thereunder. Procurement processes may be simplified to enable easier mapping in the e-procurement platform. Non value adding processes may be discontinued. Environmental sustainability must be made part of procurement decisions. Bid challenge related issues may be formally assigned to CVC.
5. Central repository for Public Procurement data at a National Data Centre may be considered. MIS data derived from this repository which may be used for making better procurement decisions. With availability of accurate consumption data, rate contracts may be concluded at cheaper rates.
6. Capacity building may be augmented through creation of 'National Institute of Public Procurement'. Institute may undertake research in collaboration with industry and recommend measures for optimization of public spending. Government may make course on public procurement mandatory for Procurement Officers/ CFAs.

CONCLUSION

This chapter brings out framework governing public procurements in India. The existing framework (though predominantly administrative in nature), is quite exhaustive and incorporates best practices in this regard. Further, Government of India has taken steps which have potential of radically reforming public procurement process in India. The approach encompasses standardizing procurement process (i.e. rules, regulations and guidelines), migration to E-GP and vigilant monitoring mechanism (i.e. CVC). These mechanisms, though good, must aim to harness the entire spectrum of potentialities provided by Information Technology today. The solution therefore lies in removal of barriers to creation of single public procurement market. It would make public procurement in India truly efficient, transparent and effective.

REFERENCES

Anderson, R.D. (2007). Renewing the WTO Agreement on Government Procurement: Progress to date and Ongoing Negotiations. *Public Procurement Law Review, 16.*

Arbitration and Conciliation Act 1996. (n.d.). Retrieved from http://lawmin.nic.in/la/Arbitration.pdf

C&AG [Duties, Powers and Conditions of Service] Act 1971. (n.d.). Retrieved from http://www.cag.gov.in/content/dpc-act

Central Vigilance Commission Act 2003. (n.d.). Retrieved from http://cvc.nic.in/cvcact.pdf

Chief Technical Examiner (CTE) Manual. (2002). Retrieved from http://cvc.nic.in/

Clausen, B., Kraay, A., & Nyiri, Z. (2009). *Corruption and Confidence in Public Institutions Evidence from a Global Survey.* Policy Research Working Paper 5157. Retrieved from http://econ.worldbank.org

Competitions Act 2002. (n.d.). Retrieved from http://www.cci.gov.in/competition-act

Constitution of India. (n.d.). Retrieved from https://india.gov.in/my-government/constitution-india

CVC 005/VGL/4 dated 01 September 2006. (n.d.). Retrieved from http://cvc.nic.in/

CVC circular No. 009/VGL/002 dated 17 September 2009. (n.d.). Retrieved from http://cvc.nic.in/

CVC circulars dated 23 Jun 2010 and 12 Jan 2012. (n.d.). Retrieved from http://cvc.nic.in/

CVC office order No. 98/ORD/1 dated 20 October 2004. (n.d.). Retrieved from http://cvc.nic.in/

Defence Procurement Manual. (2009). Retrieved from http://www.dgqadefence.gov.in/documents/ DPM2009.pdf

Defence Procurement Procedure. (2013). Retrieved from http://mod.nic.in/writereaddata/DPP2013.pdf

Delegation of Financial Power Rules. (1978). Retrieved from http://finmin.nic.in/

DGS&D Manual. (n.d.). Available at http://cga.nic.in/writereaddata/DGS&DManual.pdf

DIT. (2011). *Saraansh: A compendium of Mission Mode Projects under NeGP*. Retrieved from http://www.mit.gov.in

Government Accounting Rules. (1990). Retrieved from http://www.cga.nic.in/writereaddata/b3.pdf

Indian Contract Act 1872. (n.d.). Retrieved from http://comtax.up.nic.in/Miscellaneous%20Act/the-indian-contract-act-1872.pdf

Information Technology Act 2000. (n.d.). Retrieved from http://www.dot.gov.in/act-rules/information-technology-act-2000

Kaliannan, M., Awang, H., & Raman, M. (2009). Electronic Procurement: A Case Study of Malaysias e-Perolehan (e-procurement) Initiative. *International Journal of Electronic Governance*, *2*(2-3), 103–117. doi:10.1504/IJEG.2009.029124

MacManus, S. A. (2002). Understanding the incremental nature of e-procurement implementation at the state and local levels. *Journal of Public Procurement*, *2*(1), 5–28.

Manual on Policies and Procedures for Purchase of Goods. (n.d.). Retrieved from http://finmin.nic.in/

Moon, M. J. (2004). *State E-Procurement Management in the Information Age: Practices, Prospects and Challenges*. Texas A&M University.

Neupane, A., Soar, J., & Vaidya, K. (2012). The potential of e-procurement technology for reducing corruption. *International Journal of Information Technology and Management*, *11*(4), 273–287. doi:10.1504/IJITM.2012.049997

OECD. (2010). *Report on Collusion and Corruption in Public Procurement in India*. Retrieved from http://www.oecd.org/dataoecd/19/20/44530808.pdf

Office Memorandum No. 7(3) E-Coord /2006 dated 22 July 2006. (n.d.). Retrieved from http://finmin.nic.in/

Office Memorandum No. 8 (5)/EII (A)/2006 dated 10 January 2007. (n.d.). Retrieved from http://finmin.nic.in/

Office Memorandum No. 10/3/2012-PPC dated 30 Mar 2012. (n.d.). Retrieved from http://finmin.nic.in/

Office Memorandum No. 2/1/2012-PPD dated 06 Apr 2015. (n.d.). Retrieved from http://finmin.nic.in/

Office Memorandum No. 29(1)/2014-PPD dated 28 Jan 2014. (n.d.). Retrieved from http://finmin.nic.in/

Office Memorandum No. 17/6/2014-PPD dated 24 May 2016. (n.d.). Retrieved from http://finmin.nic.in/

Office Memorandum No. F.17/6/2014-PPD dated 22 Aug 2016. (n.d.). Retrieved from http://finmin.nic.in/

Office Memorandum No. 8 (3)-E.II (A) 0-02. (n.d.). Retrieved from http://finmin.nic.in/

Panda, P., & Sahu, G. P. (2011). E-Procurement Implementation: Comparative Study of Governments off Andhra Pradesh and Chhattisgarh. *IUP Journal of Supply Chain Management*, *8*(2), 34–67.

Panda, P., & Sahu, G. P. (2013). *Fulfilling Public Procurement Expectations in India: Need of Legislative Intervention.* ICEGOV '13, Seoul, South Korea. doi:10.1145/2591888.2591905

Panda, P., & Sahu, G. P. (2015). E-Government Procurement Implementation in India: A cross sectional study. Int. J. *Business Information Systems*, *18*(1), 1–25. doi:10.1504/IJBIS.2015.066124

Panda, P., Sahu, G. P., & Gupta, P. K. (2010). Combating Corruption in Public Procurements through E-Procurement: Challenges and Opportunities. In Governance Issues and Corruption (pp. 173-196). Haryana, India: Intellectual Foundation.

Panda, P., Sahu, G. P., & Gupta, P. K. (2011). E-Government Procurement Implementation: Necessity of National Procurement Law. In N. Bhatt & A. Aggarwal (Eds.), *E-Governance: Policies and Practices* (pp. 170–183). New Delhi, India: Excel India Publishers. doi:10.2139/ssrn.1898759

Prevention of Corruption Act 1988. (n.d.). Retrieved from http://www.persmin.gov.in/DOPT/EmployeesCorner/ Acts_Rules/PCAct/pcact.pdf

Public Procurement Bill. (2012). Retrieved from http://finmin.nic.in/the_ministry/dept_expenditure/ ppcell/58_2012_LS_EN.pdf

Right to Information Act 2005. (n.d.). Retrieved from http://www.rti.gov.in/rtiact.asp

Sale of Goods Act 1930. (n.d.). Retrieved from http://finmin.nic.in/

Transparency International. (2012). *Global Corruption Report 2012*. Retrieved from http://www.transparency.org/

UNPAN. (2012). *United Nations' e-Gov Rankings2012*. Retrieved from http://unpan3.un.org/egovkb/datacenter/countryview.aspx

WEF. (2010). *Global Competitiveness Report 2010*. Retrieved from http://www3.weforum.org/docs/WEF_GlobalCompetitivenessReport_2010-11.pdf

KEY TERMS AND DEFINITIONS

Competent Financial Authorities: Government officers/ committees who are empowered through specific government orders to incur expenditure from public funds to the extent to which financial powers have been delegated.

E-Procurement: This chapter uses the definition of e-procurement articulated by Panda and Sahu (2015) i.e. "Evolutionary migration of all manual procurement related functions (being undertaken by an organization) to ICT platform(s) for documented objectives after undertaking procurement process re-engineering necessary for their e-adoption."

Public Procurement: All procurements of goods or provisioning of services wherein the procurement is affected by a government agency (Central/ State Govt or their subordinate/ attached offices) and payment is made from the public funds.

Chapter 12
Benefits of E-Procurement Systems Implementation:
Experience of an Australian Municipal Council

Nergiz Ilhan
Monash University, Australia

Md Mahbubur Rahim
Monash University, Australia

ABSTRACT

E-procurement systems are widely discussed in the eBusiness literature in which it is claimed that businesses generally experience three types of benefits (e.g. operational, tactical, and strategic) from implementing these systems. However, limited studies have so far been reported in the e-government literature on the benefits e-procurement systems have provided for the Australian municipality context. This chapter thus reviews the existing literature and reports e-procurement benefits experience of a large Australian municipal council. The findings indicate that the council's experience is limited to the attainment of operational and tactical benefits, and no evidence has been found about gaining any strategic benefits. In addition, several factors are identified that influenced those benefits. The lessons learned from the experience of the council are discussed and contributions made to the e-procurement literature for the public government context are highlighted.

DOI: 10.4018/978-1-5225-2203-4.ch012

INTRODUCTION

In recent years, many business organisations worldwide have streamlined and automated their manual procurement process using software solutions that are known as e-procurement systems (Ilhan & Rahim, 2013). These systems are generally package solutions that use web-based technologies to render support for the procurement process (Smart 2010). Examples of popular e-procurement solutions include SAP EBP, Straightbuy, and Oracle iProcurement, among others. These systems are generally initiated by the buying organisations, operate from their own IT infrastructure, automate procurement process, and send procurement related documents to suppliers over the Internet. When successfully implemented, e-procurement systems can offer three types of benefits (e.g. operational, tactical, and strategic) to organisations (Puschmann & Alt, 2005; Croom & Brandon-Jones, 2007; Caniato et al.; 2011).

Being attracted by the reported success of e-procurement systems in the private sector, government agencies too have begun implementing these systems to help them reduce their operational costs, exercise greater control over purchasing, and improve image by involving greater information exchange with suppliers for timely receipt of the items they seek to purchase. In the e-government literature, some studies have reported adoption phenomenon of e-procurement systems in the government organisations. Examples of include the works of Moe (2004), Henriksen and Mahnke (2005), Moon (2005), Doherty et al. (2013), Adebayo, and Evans (2015), and Ronald and Omwenga (2015). Relatively limited information is however available on how e-procurement systems are actually used in the Australian local government context (Rahim and Bantwal 2012; Rahim and Kurnia, 2014). As such, it is not clearly known on how municipal councils in Australia are experiencing three types of benefits (mentioned in the literature) from implementing e-procurement systems, and how the attainment of those benefits are being shaped by the context of the municipal councils. Evaluating the perceptions of the Australian municipal council managers who are involved with the e-procurement systems is important. This is because interesting insights and lessons can be learned on how council context can affect the attainment of e-procurement systems benefits, for context is known to influence how implementation of IT systems are negotiated and in what ways outcomes of implementing IT systems emerge (Staehr, et al, 2012; Bernroider and Schmöllerl (2013). Hence, the research question addressed in this chapter is: how are various benefits experienced by the Australian municipal councils? Addressing this question is useful because future growth in e-procurement systems market can be slower than expected when councils report unsatisfactory beneficial outcomes.

RELATED LITERATURE

Key Themes Related to e-Procurement Benefits

From a review of the e-procurement literature, four key themes have been identified related to the benefits organisations can experience from the successful implementation of e-procurement systems. Each theme is briefly discussed below.

Description of Benefits

This theme is about an identification and description of e-procurement systems benefits. Popular benefits include cost savings (Parida et al., 2005), greater accuracy (Reddick, 2004), time savings (Osmonbekov et al, 2002), control improvement by reducing maverick buying practices (Puschmann and Alt, 2005), and image building (Kaliannan, 2009), among others. The digitization of documents pertaining to the manual procurement process means that there is very little involvement of physical papers. In addition, digitized procurement documents can be dispatched quickly bypassing purchasing of mail stamps (Reddick, 2004). Together, these electronic activities are expected to contribute towards cost savings. This assertion is confirmed by Parida et al (2005) who report that those organisations that use e-procurement systems have reported savings of up to 42%, especially in larger firms where purchase orders can cost between $70 to $300 to process. In a recent work, Lewis-Faupel et al (2014), report the presence of more than 3% cost savings associated with e-procurement in the public works conducted in India.

Automation for creating purchase related documents in turn help bring a reduction in the number of errors. Thus, an improvement in data accuracy and procurement order quality occurs (Reddick, 2004). According to Rahim et al (2008), a requisition form often has to wait at several locations before it is picked up and sent to the next relevant department for processing. Waiting times may be experienced where someone has to pick up the requisition from the buyer, where someone has to verify it at an approval station and where the supplier has to manually shift through potentially hundreds of such orders originating from various locations (Kalakota and Robinson, 1999). Hence, considerable timesavings are expected when an e-procurement system sends the requisition directly to all the concerned parties. This view is also supported by Osmonbekov et al (2002) and.

A lack of control in the procurement of goods and services may lead to such problems as maverick purchasing practices (Garrido et al, 2006), difficulty in maintaining audit trails and reduced visibility of overall spending (Attaran, 2001). The traditional procurement process does not adequately address these issues. By automating the procurement process, e-Procurement systems can improve control of purchasing practices. For example, use of punch out systems which allow purchasing from the e-catalogues of approved suppliers only can greatly reduce maverick buying (Puschmann and Alt, 2005). E-procurement systems further address the difficulty in maintaining audit trails by electronically linking purchase orders, invoices and receipts (Croom, 2001; Angeles, 2006).

Several studies have indicated that organisations in the public sector make use of e-Procurement systems in an effort to create a positive image of their organisations (Leipold et al, 2004; Kaliannan, 2009). Building a positive image is important because it helps an organization to provide: a) a fair opportunity for all stakeholder participation, b) develop a means of establishing accountability, and c) act as a catalyst for spearheading IT innovations. In another study, Croom and Brandon-Jones (2007) report that the image of government agencis can be enhance as e-procurement systems help in enforcing contact compliance. Likewise, Carlo (2012) acknowledge the capability of using e-procurement in the government sector by improving transparency in procurement process.

Ranking of e-Procurement Benefits

Little similarity is noted in the ranking of e-procurement benefits suggested by various scholars. For example, Davila et al. (2003) identify the top three benefits as a reduction in purchasing transaction costs, purchasing order fulfilment time, purchasing cycle time, whereas Leipold (2004) observe such benefits as transparency, reduction in process complexity (via enhanced simplification), and compliance as the top three most important benefits.

Taxonomy of Benefits

This theme focuses on classifying e-procurement systems benefits into several categories. Categories of benefits however vary from two to four. For example, Croom (2000), De Buer (2002) and Mukhopadhay and Kekre (2002) divide benefits into three categories: operational, tactical, and strategic. In contrast, Kalakota and Robinson (2001) identify two categories of e-procurement benefits: efficiency and effectiveness. However, Piotrowitz and Irani (2010) classify e-procurement benefits in four categories: financial, growth and learning, customer and business process.

Antecedents of Benefits

This theme is concerned with identifying factors that affect realization of e-procurement benefits. Studies by Hsu and Chen (2004), Rahim and Bantwal (2012),

Rotchu (2013), and Karthik and Kumar (2013) represent this theme. A number of factors like management support (Arabind 2003), compatibility (Dorig et al, 2005), integration (Karthik, & Kumar, 2013; Fernandes & Vieira (2015), and presence of e-catalogues (Costa et al., 2013) have been identified as important factors that influence e-procurement benefits.

Arabind (2003) argue that management support is essential to ensure the realization of benefits from using e-procurement systems. Management support is useful to sponsor investments in such aspects as training, resistance change, e-catalogue, integration, and changes in procurement process. Dorig et al (2005) describe compatibility as the suitability of the e-Procurement system to the work-styles of the users. Croom and Johnston (2003) suggest that compatibility between employees' work-habits and e-Procurement systems enable employees to take control of their own purchasing decision while simultaneously automating procurement security procedures. This provides the employee with a feeling of empowerment and encourages responsible purchasing habits. Increased employee empowerment in turn leads to greater ownership of the purchasing process and therefore achieves accountability and transparency.

Integration is defined as the extent to which data and applications through different communications networks can be shared and accessed for organizational use (Wyse & Higgins, 1993). As e-procurement is inter-organizational in nature (Hsu and Chen, 2004), two types of integration (e.g. internal and external) can influence how a reduction in manual data entry can affect gaining benefits (Rahim, Ilhan and Chen, 2011). Internal integration is concerned with establishing electronic interface between an e-procurement system and other internal systems (e.g. financial systems) for seamless data exchange. External integration involve making an interface with the suppliers' front-end systems to facilitate electronic exchange of documents. An e-procurement system has even the ability to support e-catalogues (Vaidya, et al., 2006). Use of e-catalogues promotes organizational policy to guide employees for buying from approved suppliers only. Hence, maverick buying practice can be largely minimized.

Literature Gaps

In summary, it is acknowledged that although benefits of e-procurement systems have been discussed in the literature, it is still unclear how the Australian municipality councils realize benefits from e-procurement systems implementation and how the council context influences those benefits. The case study reported in this chapter seeks to address this concern.

RESEARCH APPROACH

A case study approach was chosen in order to identify how a municipal council in Australia experiences benefits from implementing an e-procurement system and in what way the context of the council can affect the realization of those benefits. Selection of case study is considered appropriate because it provides rich insights into the contextual situation of the council and is thus in line with the recommendations provided by Yin (2003). As the details are not adequately known on how a council in Australia experiences benefits from an e-procurement systems implementation, we thus consider our research to be in the formative stage. A single municipal council was thus chosen as a case organization because we wanted to explore the rich e-procurement benefits experience of that council that has been using an e-procurement system for a considerable period.

The unit of analysis is an individual council because a council (unlike a manufacturing company) is most likely to have one single e-procurement system implementation in support of its procurement process. Data from the council was gathered from multiple sources, including semi-structured interviews, e-mail communications, e-procurement related documents maintained by the council, and information posted on the council website. A total of four senior managers who have an intimate involvement with the e-procurement systems initiative at the council were interviewed. They include: e-procurement project director, e-procurement coordinator, procurement administrator, and IT manager. An interview protocol was developed which included questions on the background of interviewees, reasons for e-procurement implementation, benefits of e-procurement, and council contextual situation influencing those benefits. We have used a coding scheme (Neuman 2003) to extract themes from the interview transcripts and data sources (e.g. emails, interview transcripts), and then matched them against three types of e-procurement benefits (i.e. operational, tactical, and strategic) mentioned in the literature. Data analysis was thus done using the pattern matching logic described by Yin (2003). In general, established methodological guidelines provided by Yin (2003) and Sarker and Lee (2000) were applied to generate reliable and valid findings.

CASE ORGANISATION

A large Australian municipal council with over 400 staff and A$130 million operating budget was selected. The council serves about 200,000 residents and provides them with traditional and online e-services alike. The e-services support web based online processes and transactions over the Internet. These services are developed, maintained, and supported by the IT department of the council. The council's key hardware platforms involve Authority, Expedit, and some major software applications including Civica, Fujitsu, and an ERP system. After careful consideration the council decided to adopt Straightbuy system with the intention to automate the purchasing process in order to reduce cycle times, eliminate manual and paper based processes, reduce rouge purchasing and better information management. The council utilized the Straightbuy system for improving purchase information management, auditing and as well as efficiently handling document flows. Straightbuy is Australian owned comprehensive web based procurement and supply chain management package that supports quoting, requisitioning, approvals, ordering and reporting. Straightbuy allows the council to map its procurement policy into the workflow business rules and then electronically routes internal requisitions prepared by council staff (with email notifications) to the council managers for their approval.

The council's financial systems were well integrated with Straightbuy system and purchasing process was automated more on the council's side and semi-automated on the suppliers's side. The council found that adequate but had plans on getting suppliers integrated into the Straighbuy system in the future. The council sought to use the Straightbuy system to reduce internal procurement related costs and to improve control and these objectives were among their initial anticipated operational and tactical benefits. Currently, 400 users (council employees) and 1200 suppliers are registered in the Straightbuy system. This e-procurement system is well integrated with the other major software systems (e.g.Civica, Fujitsu, ERP system) used by the council. On a typical working day, about 50 purchasing transactions are carried out using the Staightbuy system. As most suppliers of the council lack e-commerce capabilities, purchase orders generated by the e-procurement system are sent to the suppliers as either e-mail or internet fax.

CASE STUDY FINDINGS

Drawing on case study data, we have identified that the council experiences several operational and tactical benefits. However, the council has reported no evidence about the realisation of strategic benefits. These benefits are summarised in Table 1 and are briefly discussed below.

Operational Benefits

The council has reported experiencing three instances of operational benefits: paper cost savings, transaction cost savings, and a faster processing of purchase orders (timesavings). The council has saved postal stamps by sending purchase orders in the form of e-mail/internet fax generated by the Straightbuy e-procurement system.

Table 1. A summary of e-procurement systems benefits experienced by the council

Benefit Types	Examples of Benefits	Observed	Remarks
Operational	Paper cost savings	Y	The council has experienced operational benefit
	Reduced transaction costs	Y	
	Time savings	Y	
Tactical	Reduced maverick buying	Y	The council has experienced tactical benefit
	Better understanding the purchasing needs	Y	
	Improved decision making ability	Y	
Strategic	Improved relationship with suppliers	N	The council has not reported experiencing any strategic benefits
	Enhanced council image	N	

Note: Y means Yes, N means No

Savings in transaction costs have further emerged as a result of cutting the cost of manual errors made during the ordering process. Those errors were avoided by establishing an electronic link between the Straightbuy e-procurement system and relevant data extracted from the back-end systems. Drawing on the council's top management support, the council has made payment to the vendors of its mainframe based ERP system and the Straightbuy e-procurement system for developing an electronic interface that links these two systems to avoid data re-entry. This sentiment is echoed by the e-procurement project director as follows:

Integration was done to automate the whole thing. The purchase order information was keyed in only once.

Savings in purchase order transaction costs have been clearly worked out by the council managers in dollar terms. The e-procurement project director has made the following bold claims concerning a substantial reduction in purchase order transaction costs:

The cost of purchasing went down from AS$56 to AS$17, and that was further reduced to AS$7. We saved on errors and the new Straightbuy system enabled our purchasing staff to determine the best price as well.

The council has also reported time savings due to more accurate ordering through an electronic link between internal systems and Straightbuy system.

Tactical Benefits

The Straightbuy e-procurement system has further contributed to the attainment of three tactical benefits: reduced maverick buying, better understanding the purchasing needs, and improved decision making ability. By receiving support from the top management of the council, many of the purchasing rules were centralized and even automated by the Straightbuy system. Appropriate approval and authorization protocols were incorporated into the system, which in turn helped the council in streamlining its procurement processes. This has enabled the procurement manager to better trace purchase orders placed by the council staff. Moreover, the use of e-catalogues further encouraged a reduction in maverick buying practices. According to the IT manager:

They definitely do, because of the two aspects of the centralization of the purchasing system if you like and the system has its own set of rules like purchase approval and that gives us a high degree of control.

Furthermore, procurement policies were amended at the council with the consent given by the council's top management. Employees were then instructed to select the products from approved suppliers whose information were made available within the Straightbuy e-procurement system. This sentiment is reflected by the procurement administrator as follows:

Yes, I think it achieved better control. We are ensuring that our employees are using preferred suppliers rather than adding another supplier into the system.

With the Straightbuy e-procurement system in place, the council management is now able to generate reports that are more sophisticated and trace purchasing preferences and trends of various departmental units, which in turn help the council managers to better understand their procurement needs. This view is reflected by the procurement administrator as follows:

Reports are now available that monitor purchasing made by various departments. We can now see who ordered what. It helps us clearly understand the needs of our staff.

The council acknowledges that the introduction of Straightbuy e-procurement system has enabled its employees to make more informed procurement choice related decisions by referring to product price and approved supplier related information collected from e-catalogues. Decisions concerning the range of suppliers from who the council purchases products and services can be better understood. According to the e-procurement coordinator:

The Straightbuy e-procurement system makes it easier in the sense that we can now find our suppliers a lot simpler, we have more consistency where our suppliers are coming from.

Strategic Benefits

The management of the council believes that their suppliers considered the council as one of the key account customers. The council is also seen to stand as a representative of the government. As such, the council is in a much more powerful position. Hence, the suppliers are keen to maintain a good working relationship and comply with the council's directives. Therefore, the council management does not believe that the Straightbuy e-procurement system has strengthened existing relationship with the suppliers by sending them purchase orders in terms of emails generated by the Straightbuy system rather than dispatching them through postal services. Hence, the introduction of the Straightbuy system has not been perceived to enhance council image. This view is echoed by the e-procurement coordinator as follows:

Our suppliers see us as a big customer. Therefore, they usually do not fuss, instead they put in the effort of trying to keep the relationship good.

The council has exhibited no intentions whatsoever to share greater information (e.g. annual procurement budget of council) with its suppliers. This is due to the lack of management approval to facilitate confidential information exchange with suppliers. The council only shares fundamental information about the product and services it orders through the e-procurement system. According to the e-procurement coordinator:

Not much, our suppliers only get product information from us. Other than that, there is a lack of communication between the council and the suppliers.

In terms of resources, the council does not share computing, any other technical or man-power with its suppliers because the Straightbuy e-procurement system pretty much runs on the council's own IT infrastructure. Suppliers just receive purchase orders in terms of e-mails and internet faxes generated by the Straightbuy system. The e-procurement coordinator made the following remarks:

No resources are shared between the council and suppliers, we are just buying off our suppliers.

Concerning knowledge sharing with its suppliers, the council has not recognized any benefits. This sentiment is expressed by the procurement administrator as follows:

With our suppliers we are not sharing knowledge at all because no one is driving e-procurement systems, it is the lack of knowledge from our part on how best to derive any strategic benefits from sharing procurement related information with our suppliers.

Thus, in summary due to the lack of external integration (electronic linkage between the Straightbuy system and suppliers' IT systems involved with customer order taking process) and reluctance of council management for sharing additional knowledge (e.g. yearly procurement plan of the council, annual procurement budget of the council) and resources (e.g. supplier training in Straightbuy) with suppliers, no improvement in supplier relationship has taken place. As a result, supplier caring image of the council has not been established. This sentiment is expressed by the procurement administrator officer as follows:

I do not think e-procurement system has any role in facilitating relationship with our suppliers. There is not any serious dialog happening in between our Straightbuy system and suppliers' IT system.

DISCUSSION

It appears that some of the operational and tactical benefits reported in the scholarly literature have been indeed experienced by the participating case council. Hence, our research offers support to the observations of such scholars as Neef (2001), Panayiotou et al (2004), Wen and Wei (2007), Rahim (2008) and Ronchi et al.(2010) with regard to the attainment of benefits from the implementation of e-procurement systems.

In contrast, no evidence was found from the case council in support of gaining strategic benefits. The reason for not achieving strategic benefits can be explained by the views of the top management of the council. Managers at the council acknowledged that the top management of their council does not view e-procurement with strategic significance. The top management has deliberately chosen Straightbuy e-procurement system that required little involvement on the part of the suppliers as they were considered outsiders. This particular finding is found to be in line with Corini (2000) and Min and Galle (2003) who argue that management commitment and support is needed to seek strategic use of e-procurement systems. This is possible when senior management does not consider suppliers as outsiders (Pan, 2005).

The view of the top management of the council for implementing their Straightbuy e-procurement system is fundamentally found to be internal focused. The management sought to use the system to reduce internal procurement related costs and improve internal control. This observation is in agreement with the views of Croom and Jones (2007). In a case study of e-procurement systems adoption in a UK based public sector organization, they found that although e-procurement solution was recognized to have a potential for enhancing business relationship with suppliers (strategic purpose) but the solution was not considered to be a pre-requisite for building close relationships with suppliers and was intended to improve internal efficiency and productivity only. Therefore, without further empirical investigation it is difficult for us to ascertain whether this observation applies to all municipal councils in Australia.

CONCLUSION

Even though adoption phenomenon of e-procurement systems in the broader public sector is receiving a growing attention in the scholarly literature, relatively less has been reported about the outcomes of implementing such systems in the local government context. We have thus addressed this concern by describing the e-procurement benefits experience of a large municipal council in Australia. We have found evidence for the attainment of some operational and tactical benefits. However, no evidence has been found about any strategic benefits experienced by that council. Additionally, several factors have been identified that are reported to affect those benefits. For example, management motivation, internal integration and procurement process streamlining positively affected operational benefits. In contrast, lack of management motivation and absence of external integration influenced the council for not experiencing strategic benefits.

Hence, the lesson learned from our case study is that the implementation of e-procurement systems by municipal councils does not automatically lead to all three types of benefits cited in the literature. Our findings thus make a modest contribution towards better understanding the benefits from e-procurement systems implementation in the local government context, and in directing future empirical research in this area. We however acknowledge that although our research findings shed some insightful lights into the outcomes of e-procurement systems implementation in one large Australian municipal council, those findings however cannot be generalized across the entire sector. Additional case studies are thus needed in the Australian local government sector to improve the validity of our research findings. Further research is also needed to examine the influence of a broader range of potential local government context related factors that would constrain how certain e-procurement system benefits can emerge within municipality context.

REFERENCES

Adebayo, V. O., & Evans, R. D. (2015). Adoption of e-procurement systems in developing countries: A Nigerian public sector perspective. In *2015 2nd International Conference on Knowledge-Based Engineering and Innovation* (pp. 20-25). IEEE. doi:10.1109/KBEI.2015.7436015

Ageshin, E. (2001). E-Procurement at Work: A Case Study. *Production and Inventory Management Journal*, 48-53.

Andersen, K. V., Juul, N. C., Korzen-Bohr, S., & Pedersen, J. K. (2003). Fractional Institutional Endeavors and Eprocurement in Local Government. *Proceedings of the 16th Bled eCommerce Conference: eTransformation*, 961-973.

Bensaou, M. (1999, Summer). Portfolios of Buyer-Supplier Relationships. *Sloan Management Review*, 35–44.

Bernroider, E. W., & Schmöllerl, P. (2013). A technological, organisational, and environmental analysis of decision making methodologies and satisfaction in the context of IT induced business transformations. *European Journal of Operational Research*, *224*(1), 141–153. doi:10.1016/j.ejor.2012.07.025

Caniato, F., Longoni, A., & Moretto, A. (2012). Effective eProcurement implementation process. *Production Planning and Control*, *23*(12), 935–949. doi:10.1080/09537287.2011.586652

Carlo Bertot, J., Jaeger, P. T., & Grimes, J. M. (2012). Promoting transparency and accountability through ICTs, social media, and collaborative e-government. Transforming Government: People. *Process and Policy*, *6*(1), 78–91.

Carr, A.S., & Smeltzer, L.R. (2002). The Relationship between Information Technology Use and Buyer-Supplier Relationships: An Explanatory Analysis of the Buying Firm's Perspective. *IEEE Transactions on Engineering Management*, *49*(3), 293-304.

Corini, J. (2000, March). Integrating E-Procurement and Strategic Sourcing. *Supply Chain Management Review*, 3-7.

Costa, A. A., Arantes, A., & Tavares, L. V. (2013). Evidence of the impacts of public e-procurement: The Portuguese experience. *Journal of Purchasing and Supply Management*, *19*(4), 238–246. doi:10.1016/j.pursup.2013.07.004

Croom, S., & Brandon-Jones, A. (2007). Impact of e-procurement: Experiences from implementation in the UK public sector. *Journal of Purchasing and Supply Management, 13*(4), 294–303. doi:10.1016/j.pursup.2007.09.015

Dale, C. (2003). The Competitive Networks of Tourism E-Mediaries:New Strategies, New Advantages. *Journal of Vacation Marketing, 9*(2), 109-118.

Davila, A., Gupta, M., & Palmer, R. (2003). Moving Procurement Systems to the Internet: The Adoption and Use of E-Procurement Technology Models. *European Management Journal, 21*(1), 11-23.

Day, S.G., & Hubbard, J.K. (2003). Customer Relationships Go Digital. *Business Strategy Review, 14*(1), 17-26.

Doherty, N. F., McConnell, D. J., & Ellis-Chadwick, F. (2013). Institutional responses to electronic procurement in the public sector. *International Journal of Public Sector Management, 26*(6), 495–515. doi:10.1108/IJPSM-04-2012-0048

Fernandes, T., & Vieira, V. (2015). Public e-procurement impacts in small-and medium-enterprises. *International Journal of Procurement Management, 8*(5), 587–607. doi:10.1504/IJPM.2015.070904

Garrido, M. J., Gutierrez, A. M., & San Jose, R. (2006). The impact of e-procurement on the structure of the buying centre. *International Journal of Electronic Business, 4*(6), 463–482. doi:10.1504/IJEB.2006.011696

Garrido-Samaniego, M.J., Gutierrez-Arranz, A.M., & Jose-Cabezudo, R.S. (2010). Assesing the Impact of E-Procurement on the Structure of the Buying Centre. *International Journal of Information Management, 30*(2), 135-143.

Hardy, C., & Williams, S. (2005). Public E-Procurement in Action: Policies, Practices and Technologies. *IFIB International Feredation for Information Processing 2005.*

Henriksen, H. Z., & Mahnke, V. (2005). E-procurement adoption in the Danish public sector: The influence of economic and political rationality. *Scandinavian Journal of Information Systems, 17*(2), 2.

Hsu, J. S. C., & Chen, E. T. (2015). Managers' Perceived Benefits of Using Electronic Procurement in Taiwan. *Communications of the IIMA*, *4*(2), 3.

Ilhan, N. (2011). *Understanding E-Procurement Systems Implementation Processes and Benefits in the Victorian Local Government Sector: A Business Relationship Perspective* (MS Thesis). Caulfield School of IT, Monash University.

Jarach, D. (2002). The Digitalisation of Market Relationships in the Airline Business: The Impact and Prospects of E-Business. *Journal of Air Transport Management*, *8*(8), 115–120. doi:10.1016/S0969-6997(01)00039-4

Johnson, M., & Whang, S. (2002). E-Business and Supply Chain Management: An Overview and Framework. *Production and Operations management, 11*(4), 413-423.

Kalakota, R., & Robinson, M. (1999). e-Business. In Roadmap for Success. Addison Wesley.

Kaliannan, M., Raman, M., & Dorasamy, M. (2009, September). E-procurement adoption in the malaysian public sector: organizational perspectives. In Enterprise Distributed Object Computing Conference Workshops, 2009. EDOCW 2009. 13th (pp. 189-194). IEEE. doi:10.1109/EDOCW.2009.5331999

Karthik, V., & Kumar, S. (2013). Investigating 'degree of adoptioneffects on e-procurement benefits. *International Journal of Procurement Management*, *6*(2), 211–234. doi:10.1504/IJPM.2013.052470

Kim, J.I., & Shunk, D.L. (2004). Matching Indirect Procurement Process with Different B2b E-Procurement Systems. *Computers in Industry*, (53), 153-164.

Leek, S., Turnbull, P.W., & Naude, P. (2003). How Is Information Technology Affecting Business Relationships? Results from a UK Survey. *Industrial Marketing Management*, (32), 119-126.

Lewis-Faupel, S., Neggers, Y., Olken, B. A., & Pande, R. (2014). *Can electronic procurement improve infrastructure provision? evidence from public works in India and Indonesia (No. w20344)*. National Bureau of Economic Research.

Min, H., & Galle, W.P. (2003). E-Purchasing: Profiles of Adopters and Nonadopters. *Industrial Marketing Management, 32*(3), 227-233.

Moe, C. E. (2004). Public e-Procurement–Determinants of Attitudes Towards Adoption. In Electronic Government (pp. 278-282). Springer Berlin Heidelberg. doi:10.1007/978-3-540-30078-6_46

Moon, M. J. (2005). E-procurement management in state governments: Diffusion of e-procurement practices and its determinants. *Journal of Public Procurement*, *5*(1), 54.

Morgan, R.M., & Hunt, S.D. (1994). The Commitment-Trust Theory of Relationship Marketing. *Journal of Marketing, 58*(3), 20-38.

Naseebullah, H.M.F.B., & Dominic, P.D.D. (2010). *The Role of Factors in Business-to-Business E-Procurement Implementation.* 2010 International Information Technology (ITSim) Symposium, Kuala Lumpur, Malaysia.

Neef, D. (2001). *E-Procurement: From Strategy to Implementation*. Prentice Hall Inc.

Neuman, W. L. (2003). *Social Research Methods: Qualitative and Quantitative Approaches*. Allyn & Bacon.

Osmonbekov, T., Bello, D. C., & Gilliland, D. I. (2002). Adoption of electronic commerce tools in business procurement: Enhanced buying center structure andprocesses. *Journal of Business and Industrial Marketing*, *17*(2/3), 151–166. doi:10.1108/08858620210419781

Pan, G. S. (2005). Information systems project abandonment: A stakeholder analysis. *International Journal of Information Management*, *25*(2), 173–184. doi:10.1016/j.ijinfomgt.2004.12.003

Panayiotou, N. A., Gayialis, S. P., & Tatsipopulos, I. P. (2004). An E-Procurement System for Governmental Purchasing. *International Journal of Production Economics*, *90*(1), 79–102. doi:10.1016/S0925-5273(03)00103-8

Parida, U., & Parida, V. (2005). *E-procurement: An Indian and Swedish perspective*. Academic Press.

Puschmann, T., & Alt, R. (2005). Successful Use of E-Procurement in Supply Chains. *International Journal of Supply Chain Management, 10*(2), 122-133.

Rahim, M., Ilhan, N., & Chen, X. (2011). Factors affecting benefits of e-procurement systems: Experience of an Australian City Council. In *11th International Conference on Electronic Business* (pp. 265-272). PA Living.

Rahim, M., & Kurnia, S. (2014). *Understanding E-Procurement System Benefits Using Organisational Adoption Motivation Lens: A Case Study*. PACIS.

Rahim, M. M. (2008). *Identifying Factors Affecting Acceptance of E-Procurement Systems: An Initial Qualitative Study at an Australian City Council.* The 10th International Business Information Management Association (IBIMA) Conference, Kuala Lumpur, Malaysia.

Rahim, M.M., & As-Saber, S.N. (2011). E-Procurement Adoption Process: An Arduous Journey for an Australian City Council. *International Journal of Electronic Finance, 5*(2), 150–168.

Rahim, M. M., & Bantwal, A. P. (2012). Perceived Benefits from a Local Government Public Procurement Initiative: A Diffusion of Innovation Perspective. In Inter-Organizational Information Systems and Business Management: Theories for Researchers. IGI Global. doi:10.4018/978-1-60960-768-5.ch016

Reddick, C. G. (2004). The growth of e-procurement in American state governments: A model and empirical evidence. *Journal of Public Procurement*, *4*(2), 151.

Rogers, E. M. (1995). Diffusion of Innovations (4th ed.). New York: The Free Press.

Ronald, N. K., & Omwenga, J. Q. (2015). Factors Contributing to Adoption of E-Procurement in County Governments: A Case Study of County Government of Bo`met. *International Journal of Academic Research in Business and Social Sciences*, *5*(10), 233–239.

Ronchi, S., Brun, A., Golini, R., & Fan, X. (2010). What Is the Value of an It E-Procurement System? *Journal of Purchasing and Supply Management*, (16), 131-140.

Sarker, S., & Lee, A. S. (2000). *Using a Positivist Case Research Methodology to Test Three Competing Theories-in-Use of Business Process Redesign*. International Conference on Information Systems (ICIS), Brisbane, Australia.

Schoenherr, T., & Tummala, V. M. R. (2007). Electronic Procurement: A Structured Literature Review and Directions for Future Research. *International Journal of Procurement Management, 1*(1/2), 8-37.

Sin, L.Y.M., Tse, A.C.B., Yau, O.H.M., Chow, R.P.M., Lee, J.S.Y., & Lau, L.B.Y. (2005). Relationship Marketing Orientation. *Scale Development and Cross Cultural Validation Journal of Business Research*, (58), 185-194.

Smart, A.F. (2010). E-Procurement and Its Impact on Supply Management-Evidence from Industrial Case Studies. *International Journal of Logistics: Research and Applications, 13*(6), 423-440.

Staehr, L., Shanks, G., & Seddon, P. B. (2012). An explanatory framework for achieving business benefits from ERP systems. *Journal of the Association for Information Systems*, *13*(6), 424.

Tanner, C., Wolfle, R., Schubert, P., & Quade, M. (2008). Current Trends and Challenges in Electronic Procurement: An Empirical Study. *Electronic Markets, 18*(1), 6-18.

Tatsis, V., Mena, C., Wassenhove, L., & Whicker, L. (2006). E-Procurement in the Greek Food and Drink Industry: Drivers and Impediments. *Journal of Purchasing and Supply Management*, *12*(15), 63–74. doi:10.1016/j.pursup.2006.04.003

Trkman, P., & McCormack, K. (2010). Estimating the Benefits and Risks of Implementing E-Procurement. *IEEE Transactions on Engineering Management, 57*(2), 338-348.

Vaidya, K., Sajeev, A. S. M., & Callender, G. (2006). Critical factors that influence e-procurement implementation success in the public sector. *Journal of Public Procurement, 6*(1/2), 70.

Yang, K., & Rho, S. Y. (2007). E-government for better performance: Promises, realities, and challenges. *International Journal of Public Administration, 30*(11), 1197–1217. doi:10.1080/01900690701225556

Yin, R. K. (2003). *Applications of Case Study Research.* Sage Publications Inc.

Chapter 13
Electronification of the Public Procurement System:
A Comparative Analysis of the Experience of the Russian Federation and Ukraine

Sergey Tsygankov
Southern Federal University, Russia

Ekaterina Gasanova
Southern Federal University, Russia

ABSTRACT

This chapter analyzes the reform of public procurement systems in Russia and Ukraine in the context of electronization, as well as a comparative analysis of the effectiveness of such reforms. The goal is to determine the prospects of expanding the scope of e-procurement based on the analysis of the implementation of the reform of public procurement systems effects in Russia and Ukraine. Public procurement is a fundamental component of social and economic policy of any state, by means of this mechanism the government has the ability to create and influence the industry for future changes in production structures, increase efficiency and more rapid transition to an innovative new type of economy. Procurers are dependent on funds that provide their functioning and providing services to the population. Provision of works, goods and services to such customers is carried out by means of public

DOI: 10.4018/978-1-5225-2203-4.ch013

procurement market, which, enhances the efficiency and transparency of spending money through a contractual relationship satisfying the needs of the state. The share of public procurement (including procurement of state-owned companies) is more over 25% of Russia's GDP, while in Ukraine - more than 7%. That's why it is possible to make a comparative analysis of public procurement reform in Russia and the Ukraine, whose legal approach is quite close (Tsygankov & Syropyatov, 2014).

INTRODUCTION

The state regulation of economic relations and processes is the most evident in the organization of the public procurement system. The indicator of the maturity of this sector is directly related to the efficiency of the system of public expenditure. The analysis of public requirements should be based on the macroeconomic interpretation of a requirement as a basic category of the modern economic theory reflecting inner motives (incentives) that encourage the efficient use of scarce resources for the production of essential goods ensuring the satisfaction of needs.

As a part of the system of economic needs as a whole, the state requirements are closely connected with processes of the extended social reproduction and with market mechanisms. The modern market economy, its condition and development potential have a decisive impact on the public needs, forming these needs and determining priorities in addressing them.

The volume and structure of public needs, which are determined by the relevant public authorities, dictate a set of objectives which should be met in the process of public and municipal procurement.

The challenge to meet the public requirements creates the need to finance them, i.e. to present them in the form of a state order. Thus, the public (government) needs quantified in the public spending generate a set of actions at different levels of the economic management, which include financing and procurement processes of those material goods, services and works that are necessary for the functioning of the state. The developing public procurement system should provide the fullest satisfaction of increasingly complex needs of the state. Ensuring a high level of satisfaction of social requirements dictates the need to increase the flexibility, elasticity of structural changes in the public procurement system following the changes in the public requirements. Indicators of the scale of public procurement are the volume and structure of the public procurement market. Determination of the categorial content of the public procurement market requires evidence that their distribution system is characterized by all indicators (attributes) of the market. However, with respect to the category of "market" the scientific literature offers diverse interpretations that are differentiated not only depending on the approach to the identification of its nature, but also depending on the context of use of this category. In particular, the market is defined as (Boyer, 1997, p. 62):

- A place where the seller and the buyer meet (historically the first definition of the market);
- A particular territory where purchase and sale take place (a wider geographic interpretation of the market concentrated in cities or countries);
- An aggregate of demand and supply of goods or services, which reflects the sectorial affiliation of the market;
- A self-regulating mechanism of the interaction of supply and demand that determines the market price of goods and services (characterizes the interaction of economic agents);
- An economic mechanism of competition between independent economic agents.

The analysis of historical forms of the market exchange makes it possible to distinguish five criterial (attributive) features that isolate the market of the historically prior "pre-market" forms:

1. Regularity of exchange operations;
2. Mainly monetary nature;
3. Mutual benefit for the parties involved;
4. Voluntary exchange;
5. Presence of competitiveness or competition (Radaev, 2010, p.23).

The public procurement market is an effective mechanism for the distribution of budget funds in the market economy, ensuring the interaction between the state and business for the satisfaction of social needs on the basis of the principle of substantive rationality, which is associated with the orientation on final goals and cannot be reduced to a simple calculation, but it is related to the choice of these goals.

Participants of the public procurement market are the state represented by competent authorities of all levels of government for the implementation of the budget expenditure, on the one hand, and bidders (one of which will be the supplier of goods or contractor, provider of services), on the other hand. However, the state only personifies the society as a consumer of goods, to the production or delivery of which the government spending (except for the maintenance of the state apparatus) are directed.

The revealed specific character of the public procurement market structure suggests that the budget orders market is a quasi-market. The category of "quasi-market" can be defined as an "aggregate of stable institutional forms of interaction (transactions) between economic agents organized by the state, in which manufacturers compete for the right to provide services to consumers, whose spending is financed by the state" (Korytsev, 2009, p .6).

In the area of public procurement, this means that "applicants to enter into government contracts are competing by offering better deal terms to government agencies" (Korytsev, 2006, p. 112). Quasi-markets represent a mechanism of interaction, in which market incentives are combined with government resources. In this context, the economic mechanism is usually less effective than the real market; therefore, it became widespread only in those areas where the desire to preserve the power prevailed over the benefits of the economic efficiency (for example, in the field of public procurement). The efficiency of functioning of the public procurement market means that the very competitive bidding procedures should be implemented at the lowest possible cost. In international practice, the major direction of solving the problem of the trading cost reduction is unification and electronification of all public procurement procedures. The need to fully meet the public requirements forms the requirement to finance such activities and generates a set of actions at different levels of the economic management, which include the processes of financing those material goods, works and services that are useful for the functioning of the state.

ELECTRONIFICATION OF THE PUBLIC PROCUREMENT SYSTEM IN RUSSIA

Extensive electronification of the public procurement system in Russia started in 2011. Electronic auctions became obligatory for customers of all levels: federal, constituent entity of the Russian Federation and municipal. Electronic auctions are held on the 5 electronic platforms selected by the Government of the Russian Federation in 2010. The main objective of the development of e-commerce based on modern forms of the information exchange is to reduce costs arising from decision-making and their registration according to the legal practice of economic entities. This transition, which has become technically possible due to the development of information technology, is an unprecedented event in the public procurement market, a historic step in the direction of global IT development that led to many positive changes in the public procurement system, such as:

1. Document management in the electronic form significantly reduced the transaction costs of customers and suppliers, previously they were compelled to share all the documents related to the public auction and conclusion of a contract only in the paper form.

Table 1. Aggregate coefficient of average efficiency for electronic auctions

	2011	2012	2013	2014
Coefficient of average efficiency	0.13	0.16	0.09	0.11

2. Increased awareness and business access to public procurement due to the fact that all procurement notices are placed on a single portal on the Internet.
3. The application for participation in the electronic auction is subdivided into 2 parts:

The first part - information on goods, works and services that are the subject of the contract; The second part - information on the procurement party, including on his compliance with the requirements of the law to persons supplying goods, performing works and rendering services that are the subject of the contract (license, permit to work, etc.). The customer receives the information about the procurement party which has filed an application to participate in the auction only after the auction procedures and not prior to them; this completely eliminates the pressure on the supplier by an unscrupulous customer.

In order to assess the effectiveness of application of common rules and standards in the public procurement system, we find the indicator of the electronic auction performance in the procurement system in 2011-2014[1]. Firstly, we calculate the amount of prices of concluded contracts (PC) and the amount of initial maximum prices of contracts (IMPC) over this period. The efficiency is measured in the economic theory as a quotient of the difference in utility and costs incurred, which, in turn, can be expressed as a ratio of utility to costs minus one. In the public procurement system, the initial maximum prices of contracts evaluate the utility of contracts, and the price of the concluded contract evaluates the costs of the state.

Thus, the coefficient of average efficiency of the procurement method can be measured according to the following formula:

Average coefficient of efficiency = $\sum$ (The initial maximum contract price-contract price) / $\sum$ (contract price)

Based on the data in Table 1, according to the above formula we calculate the aggregate coefficient of average efficiency for electronic auctions in 2011-2014:

The aggregate coefficient of average efficiency for public electronic auctions in 2011 is 0.13, and considering that the proportion of the initial (maximum) prices of procurement contracts placed with an electronic auction in the Russian Federation over the period was 27%[2], we calculate:

$$\text{Efficiency}_{e\text{-}auc} = \text{CAE (general) x } 27\% = 3.51\%$$

Therefore, the procedures of the selection of suppliers of goods (works, services) using an auction procedure improve the efficiency of the public procurement system by an average of 3.51% in 2011. We calculate the similar indicator for 2012-2014.

The aggregate coefficient of average efficiency for electronic auctions in 2012 is 0.16, and considering that the proportion of the initial (maximum) prices of procurement contracts placed with an electronic auction in the Russian Federation over the period was 41.1%[3], we calculate:

$$\text{Efficiency}_{e\text{-}auc} = \text{CAE (general) x } 41.1\% = 6.6\%$$

Thus, it is possible to make a conclusion that the introduction of electronic auctions increases the efficiency of the public procurement system in 2012 by an average of 6.6%.

The aggregate coefficient of average efficiency for electronic auctions in 2013 is 0.15, and considering that the proportion of the initial (maximum) prices of procurement contracts placed with an electronic auction in the Russian Federation over the period was 57%[4], we calculate:

$$\text{Efficiency}_{e\text{-}auc} = \text{CAE (general) x } 57\% = 5.13\%$$

Thus, it is possible to make a conclusion that the introduction of electronic auctions increases the efficiency of the public procurement system in 2013 by an average of 5.13%.

The aggregate coefficient of average efficiency for public electronic auctions in 2014 is 0.4, and considering that the proportion of the initial (maximum) prices of procurement contracts placed with an electronic auction in the Russian Federation over the period was 51.8%[5], we calculate:

$$\text{Efficiency}_{e\text{-}auc} = \text{CAE (general) x } 51.8\% = 20.7\%$$

Thus, it is possible to make a conclusion the introduction of electronic auctions increases the efficiency of the public procurement system in 2014 by an average of 20.7%.

The analysis of the empirical evidence leads to the conclusion that the introduction of electronic auctions helps to reduce the transaction costs, to minimize the corruption of sales transactions.

High efficiency of the electronic auction in 2014 can be attributed to the entry into force of a new law on public procurement on 1 January 2014. From 1 January 2014 the market of state and municipal procurement operates within the framework of the contract system[6]. The contract system in procurement of goods, works and services for state and municipal needs is an aggregate of participants of the contract system in the field of procurement (federal executive authority for regulation of the contract system in the field of procurement, executive authorities of constituent entities of the Russian Federation for regulation of the contract system in the field of procurement, and other federal executive authorities, state authorities of constituent entities of the Russian Federation, local government authorities authorized to perform statutory regulation and control in the field of procurement, State Atomic Energy Corporation "Rosatom", customers, procurement parties, including those recognized as providers (contractors, principals), authorized bodies, authorized institutions, specialized agencies, electronic platforms operators) and actions performed by them, including with the use of a unified information system in the field of procurement, in accordance with the legislation of the Russian Federation and other normative legal acts on the contract system in the field of procurement that are aimed at meeting the state and municipal requirements. The law on the contract system applies to procurement of federal, regional and municipal levels and refers to the range of customers, which includes government bodies of the federal and regional levels, municipal authorities, state and municipal institutions as well as public institutions. The law covers a range of issues related to procurement, namely:

- Procurement planning;
- Selection of suppliers (contractors, principals);
- Conclusion of contracts;
- Peculiarities of contract performance;
- Procurement monitoring;
- Audit in procurement;
- Control over compliance with the legislation of the Russian Federation and other normative legal acts on the contract system in the area of public and municipal procurement.

Thus, the contract system significantly expanded its influence as compared with the Federal Law No. 94-FZ of July 21, 2005 "On placing orders for goods, works and services for state and municipal needs"[7]: it covers the entire procurement cycle from its planning and reasoning to the stage of the contract performance in order to increase the efficiency of the public procurement system. More over electronifcation of system of public procurements is extending now: the government of the Russian Federation plans to hold electronically not only auctions, but also tenders and other methods of procurement to reduce the corruption and to increase the transparency in this sphere.

ELECTRONIFICATION OF THE PUBLIC PROCUREMENT SYSTEM IN UKRAINE

Ukraine also has interesting experience in procurement. In April 2014, a new version of the Law of Ukraine "On public procurement"[8] came into effect. The working group on development of amendments included experts from the World Bank, the European Union, specialists of the Ministry of Economic Development and Trade, and other departments as well as representatives of leading civil society organizations in the fight against corruption in public procurement. In accordance with the task of the working group, the new version of the Law is designed to meet the key requirements of the World Bank and the EU, it also contains a number of anti-corruption rules and regulations aimed at improving the transparency of the public procurement system, which has been requested by the public of Ukraine for a long time. In addition, the adoption of the new version of the Law was a prerequisite for quick loans from international organizations.

At the same time, in Ukraine there is a process of transition to public procurement exclusively based on electronic procedures for the determination of suppliers on the basis of "ProZorro" e-procurement system. At the end of 2015, the system involved more than 2,200 state-owned companies which arranged about 37 thousand tenders. The total value of registered tenders amounted to about 7 billion UAH. At the end of last year, savings made 12% of tender amounts or more than 500 million UAH. Due to electronification of the procurement system, the indicator of the number of participants in electronic auctions is 2.72, whereas before it was an average of 2. Competition forces the providers to offer more competitive prices resulting in savings of up to 12-18%.

"Prozorro" system has already received the prize of the World Procurement Awadrs-2016 in the category of Public Sector Award. In February, the Law "On public procurement"[9] was adopted that ensured the implementation of the e-procurement system in 2016 in two stages: from April 1 - for the central government authorities, from August 1 - for other customers. The main elements of the public procurement system reform in Ukraine are the following:

Table 2. The statistical analysis of the public procurement system of the Russian Federation in 2011-2014[10]

Year	Indicator*	Total for bidding and other procurement method, Thoussand rubles	Including							
			By types of bidding, thoussand rubles					Other methods of order placement (without bidding), thousand Rubles		
			Tenders		Auctions				Procurement from a single supplier, executor, contractor	
			Opened	Closed	Opened	Opened in the electronic form	Closed	By request for quotations	Without bidding	Small volume procurement
2011	IMPC	8 778 536 338	927 375 419	133 544 497	114918302	2 632 681 938	284673988	214 589 970	3 794 763 217	383021024
	Procurement coefficient		0,105	0,0152		0.3	0.032	0.024	0.43	0.044
	Price of contract	8 309 758 423	834 820 229	132411566	108236772	2 339 964 096	251108405	183 930 287	3 794 763 217	383 021 024
	Savings	0.053	0.01	0.008	-	0.11	0.12	0.14	0	0
2012	IMPC	9137414797	1341304800	301491339	-	3751944322	391260667	211389193	2720410787	419613689
	Procurement coefficient		0.147	0.033		0.411	0.043	0.023	0.298	0.046
	Price of contract	8339935471	1211027387	285924300	-	3232257063	293442156	177260089	2720410787	419613689
	Savings	0.087	0.097	0.052	-	0.139	0.250	0.161	0.087	0.097
2013	IMPC	9 023 266 717	1149611302	351293617	-	3658578840	526561651	200039901	2681327331	455854075
	Procurement coefficient		0.13	0.039		0.4	0.058	0.022	0.3	0.05
	Price of contract	8211557215	972061551	333266460	-	3129691830	471867856	167488112	2681327331	455854075
	Savings	0.09	0.15	0.05	-	0.14	0.1	0.16	0	0
2014	IMPC	8 218 324 630	1280794103	197719712	-	3303850462	202900251	84312294	2 632 243 976	260425612
	Procurement coefficient		0.15	0.024		0.4	0.024	0.01	0.32	0.031
	Price of contract	7 376 811 087	1179927260	174120241	-	2 655 541 660	184 793 171	68273376	2632243976	260425612
	Savings	0.11	0.91	0.12	-	0.2	0.09	0.19	0	0

* **IMPC, thous. rub.:** Total initial price of contracts (lots) put at auction and amount of contracts (agreements) for other methods of placing orders for state and municipal needs;
Procurement Coefficient: Share of a corresponding method of placing orders in the total amount (RUR) of procurement for state and municipal needs;
Price of Contract, RUR: Total value of contracts and agreements for state needs;
Savings, %: Savings for a corresponding method of placing orders for state and municipal needs, the ratio of the difference between "IMPC" and "Price of contract" to "IMPC"

- Eliminating and preventing corruption
- Non-discrimination and objective evaluation of bids
- Simplicity and ease of procedures application
- Transition to electronic document management
- Full reporting and analysis of all public procurement

Moreover, an important element in the success of the Ukrainian reform is an increase of the level of business confidence in competitive bidding. Over many years of the rent-seeking behaviour of officials and restriction of access for independent parties, small and medium businesses lost faith in the fact that it could be profitable to sell their products or services to the state.

CONCLUSION

Thus, we see that despite the successful steps in the electronification of the public procurement system in Ukraine, in Russia this process has started at least 5 years earlier and has already given some positive results in terms of the transparency of the procurement process and budget savings. That is why for the Ukrainian authorities it makes sense to use positive elements of the reform in Russia, as "the legal mentality of these two countries is quite close" (Tsygankov & Syropyatov, 2014).

REFERENCES

Boyer, R. (1997). *The Variety and Unequal Performance of really Existing Markets: Farewell to Doctor Pangloss? Contemporary Capitalism: The Embeddedness of Institutions*. Cambridge, UK: Cambridge University Press.

Korytsev, M. (2009). *Institutional structure and mechanisms of functioning of quasi-markets in the public sector* (p. 6). Rostov-on-Don.

Korytsev, M. (2006). Quasi-market of public procurement: Options for organization and efficiency loss. *Terra Economicus*, *4*(2), 112.

Radaev, V. (2010). What is the market: Economic and sociological approach. *Economia e Sociologia (Evora, Portugal)*, *7*(5), 23.

Tsygankov, S., & Syropyatov, V. (2014). *Comparative analysis of public procurement systems in Ukraine and the Russian Federation. In Modern problems of regional development: Collection of scientific articles* (p. 120). Academic Publishing House of the Agricultural University Plovdiv.

ENDNOTES

1 Data for the calculation are given in Table 2

2 Data for the calculation are given in Table 2

3 Data for the calculation are given in Table 2

4 Data for the calculation are given in Table 2

5 Data for the calculation are given in Table 2

6 Federal Law No. 44-FZ of April 5, 2013 "On the contract system in procurement of goods, works and services for state and municipal needs" // "Consultant Plus" Legal Reference System

7 Federal Law No. 94-FZ of July 21, 2005 "On placing orders for goods, works and services for state and municipal needs" // "Consultant Plus" Legal Reference System

8 The Law of Ukraine No. 1197-VII of April 10, 2014 "On public procurement" // http://zakon4.rada.gov.ua

9 UNIAN news agency - Poroshenko has signed the law on electronic public procurement // Available at: http://economics.unian.net/finance/1267858-poroshenko-podpisal-zakon-o-goszakupkah-v-elektronnom-rejime.html

10 Calculated by the authors in the course of research on observational data on the form No. 1 bids // Official website of the Russian Federal Service of State Statistics // www.gks.ru Results of bidding and other methods of placing orders for goods, works and services only for state needs

Compilation of References

A Guide to the Project Management Body of Knowledge. (2013). Newton Square, PA: Program Management Institute.

Aberdeen Group. (2007). *The Spend Analysis Benchmark Report*. Aberdeen Group. Retrieved from https://www.unspsc.org/Portals/3/Documents/Aberdeen_Spend_Analysis_Report.pdf

Aberdeen Group. (2008). *The e-Procurement benchmark report*. Aberdeen Group. Retrieved from http://onget.net/documents/Aberdeen_eproc_sept2008.pdf

Abu–Shanab, E. A., Harb, Y. A., & Al–Zoubi, S. Y. (2013). E–government as an anti–corruption tool: Citizens perceptions. *International Journal of Electronic Governance*, *6*(3), 232–248. doi:10.1504/IJEG.2013.058410

Abu-Shanab, E. A. (2013). *The Relationship between Transparency and E-Government: An Empirical Support*. Paper presented at the Electronic Government and Electronic Participation, Joint Proceedings of Ongoing Research of IFIP EGOV and IFIP ePart 2013EGOV/ePart Ongoing Research, Koblenz, Germany.

Acquisition Systems. (n.d.). Retrieved from: https://www.acquisition.gov/?q=Acquisition_Systems

Adamu, H., Shatimah, A., & Aliyu, M. (2016). Role of Information and Communication Technology as a Means of Tackling Corruption in Nigeria. *International Journal of Innovative Research and Creative Technology*, *1*(5), 478–480.

Adebayo, V. O., & Evans, R. D. (2015). Adoption of e-procurement systems in developing countries: A Nigerian public sector perspective. In *2015 2nd International Conference on Knowledge-Based Engineering and Innovation* (pp. 20-25). IEEE. doi:10.1109/KBEI.2015.7436015

Ae Chun, S., Luna-Reyes, L. F., Sandoval-Almazán, R., Carlo Bertot, J., Jaeger, P. T., & Grimes, J. M. (2012). Promoting transparency and accountability through ICTs, social media, and collaborative e-government. *Transforming Government: People,Process and Policy*, *6*(1), 78–91.

Ageshin, E. (2001). E-Procurement at Work: A Case Study. *Production and Inventory Management Journal*, 48-53.

Agrahari, A. (2007). Analyzing e-procurement adoption efforts: Case study of an Indian steel manufacturer. In A. Pani & A. Agrahari (Eds.), *E-procurement in emerging economies: Theory and cases* (pp. 197–231). Hershey, PA: Idea Group Publishing. doi:10.4018/978-1-59904-153-7.ch008

Agranoff, R. (2003). *Leveraging Networks: A Guide for Public Managers Working Across Organizations*. Bloomington, IN: Indiana University, School of Public and Environmental Affairs.

Agranoff, R. (2004). Another look at bargaining and negotiating in intergovernmental management. Journal of Public Administration: Research and Theory, 14(4), 495–512. doi:10.1093/jopart/muh033 doi:10.1093/jopart/muh033

Ahn, M. J., & Bretschneider, S. (2011). Politics of E-Government: E-Government and the Political Control of Bureaucracy. *Public Administration Review*, *71*(3), 414–424. doi:10.1111/j.1540-6210.2011.02225.x

Aibinu, A. A., & Al-Lawati, A. M. (2010). Using PLS-SEM technique to model construction organizations' willingness to participate in e-bidding. *Automation in Construction*, *19*(6), 714–724. doi:10.1016/j.autcon.2010.02.016

Aladwani, A. M. (2016). Corruption as a source of e-Government projects failure in developing countries: A theoretical exposition. *International Journal of Information Management*, *36*(1), 105–112. doi:10.1016/j.ijinfomgt.2015.10.005

Albano, G. L., Russo, F. A., Castaldi, G., & Zampino, R. (2015). Evaluating small businesses' performance in public e-procurement: Evidence from the Italian government's e-marketplace. *Journal of Small Business Management*, *53*(Suppl. 1), 229–250. doi:10.1111/jsbm.12190

Al-Hakim, L., Abdullah, N. A., & Ng, E. (2012). The effect of inter-organization trust and dependency on e-procurement adoption: A case of Malaysian manufacturers. *Journal of Electronic Commerce in Organizations*, *10*(2), 40–60. doi:10.4018/jeco.2012040103

Almeida, J., & Fautino, P. (2009). Implementing national measures on public procurement under the EC Directives: the portuguese experience.*International Public Procurement Conference*.

Alsac, U. (2013). The Developments of E-procurement in Turkey. In L. V. Tavares (Ed.), *E-Public Procurement in Europe: Public Management, Technologies and Processes of Change* (pp. 48–55). Lisbon: OPET Publishing.

Ambali, A. R. (2010). Determinants of e-government satisfaction: The case study of e-procurement. In H. Rahman (Ed.), *Handbook of research on e-government readiness for information and service exchange: Utilizing progressive information communication technologies* (pp. 465–479). Hershey, PA: IGI Global. doi:10.4018/978-1-60566-671-6.ch023

Andersen, K. V., Juul, N. C., Korzen-Bohr, S., & Pedersen, J. K. (2003). Fractional Institutional Endeavors and Eprocurement in Local Government. *Proceedings of the 16th Bled eCommerce Conference: eTransformation*, 961-973.

Anderson, J. E. (2015). Public Policymaking. Stamford, CT: Cengage Learning.

Anderson, R.D. (2007). Renewing the WTO Agreement on Government Procurement: Progress to date and Ongoing Negotiations. *Public Procurement Law Review, 16.*

Andrade, P., Alturas, B., & Oliveira, T. (2012). Electronic procurement: The supplier perspective. In J. Varajão, M. Cruz-Cunha, & A. Trigo (Eds.), *Organizational integration of enterprise systems and resources: Advancements and applications* (pp. 213–232). Hershey, PA: IGI Global. doi:10.4018/978-1-4666-1764-3.ch012

Angelov, S., & Grefen, P. (2008). An e-contracting reference architecture. *Journal of Systems and Software, 81*(11), 1816–1844. doi:10.1016/j.jss.2008.02.023

APEC. (1999). *Non-Binding Principles on Government Procurement: Report by the Chair of the Government Procurement Experts Group.* Retrieved from http://mddb.apec.org/documents/2006/GPEG/GPEG2/06_gpeg2_005.pdf

Arantes, A., Aguiar Costa, A., & Valadares, L. (2013). The Evaluation Of Mandatory E-Public Procurement In Portugal: Perceptions And Results Of The National Survey (2010-2012).*1st European Conference on e-Public Procurement* (pp. 63-74). Barcelona, Spain: ebook.

Arbitration and Conciliation Act 1996. (n.d.). Retrieved from http://lawmin.nic.in/la/Arbitration.pdf

Arnold, U., & Schnabel, M. (2008). Economic effects of electronic reverse auctions: A procurement process perspective. In D. Parente (Ed.), *Best practices for online procurement auctions* (pp. 57–76). Hershey, PA: IGI Global. doi:10.4018/978-1-59904-636-5.ch005

Arpit, B. (2012). E-Government and Social Media as Openness and Anti-Corruption Strategy. *Research Journal of Management Sciences, 1*(1), 48–52.

Arrowsmith, S., Linarelli, J., & Wallace, D. (2000). *Regulating Public Procurement: National and International Perspectives.* Kluwer Law International.

Arrowsmith, S. (2002). The EC Procurement Directives, national procurement policies and better governance: The case for a new approach. *European Law Review, 27*(1), 3–24.

Arrowsmith, S. (2005). *The Law of Public and Utilities Procurement.* Sweet & Maxwell.

Arrowsmith, S. (2009). EC Regime on Public Procurement. In Thai, K. V. (Ed.), International Handbook of Public Procurement (pp. 251-289). CRC Press, Taylor and Francis Group.

Asgarkhani, M. (2005). Digital government and its effectiveness in public management reform: A local government perspective. *Public Management Review, 7*(3), 465–487. doi:10.1080/14719030500181227

Asian Development Bank. (2013). *E-Government Procurement Handbook.* Retrieved April 27, 2016, from http://www.adb.org/sites/default/files/institutional-document/34064/files/e-government-procurement-handbook.pdf

Asian Development Bank. (2013). Mandaluyong City, Philippines: Asian Development Bank.

Assar, S., & Boughzala, L. (2008). Empirical evaluation of e-procurement platforms in France. *International Journal of Value Chan Management*, 30-42.

Australian Government. (2001). Department of Finance, Financial Management and Accountability Act 1997 No. 154 of 1997 as amended.

Australian Government. (2008). Department of Finance, Commonwealth Procurement Guidelines. Financial Management Guidance No.1.

Azmi, K. S. A., & Rahman, A. A. L. A. (2015). E-Procurement: A Tool to Mitigate Public Procurement Fraud in Malaysia? *The Electronic Journal of E-Government, 13*(2), 150-160.

Bakos, J. Y. (1997). Reducing buyer search costs: Implications for electronic marketplaces. *Management Science, 43*(12), 1676–1692. doi:10.1287/mnsc.43.12.1676

Bayazit, O. (2014). Investigating adoption of e-procurement systems: An empirical study. *International Journal of Information Systems and Supply Chain Management, 7*(2), 47–66. doi:10.4018/ijisscm.2014040103

Bayram, S., & Vayvay, Ö. (2013). E-procurement system and adoption for SMEs. In *Supply chain management: Concepts, methodologies, tools, and applications* (pp. 950–966). Hershey, PA: IGI Global. doi:10.4018/978-1-4666-2625-6.ch055

Bensaou, M. (1999, Summer). Portfolios of Buyer-Supplier Relationships. *Sloan Management Review*, 35–44.

Bernroider, E. W., & Schmöllerl, P. (2013). A technological, organisational, and environmental analysis of decision making methodologies and satisfaction in the context of IT induced business transformations. *European Journal of Operational Research, 224*(1), 141–153. doi:10.1016/j.ejor.2012.07.025

Bertot, J. C., Jaeger, P. T., & Grimes, J. M. (2010). Using ICTs to create a culture of transparency: E-government and social media as openness and anti-corruption tools for societies. *Government Information Quarterly, 27*(3), 264–271. doi:10.1016/j.giq.2010.03.001

Betts, M., Black, P., Christensen, S. A., Dawson, E., Du, R., Duncan, W., & Nieto, G. et al. (2010). Towards secure and legal e-tendering. *Journal of Information Technology in Construction, 11*, 89–102.

Betts, M., Black, P., Christensen, S., Dawson, E., Du, R., Duncan, W., . . . Gonzalez, J. (2006). Towards secure and legal e-tendering. ITcon, 89-102.

Beynon-Davies, P. (2005). Constructing electronic government: The case of the UK inland revenue. *International Journal of Information Management, 25*(1), 3–20. doi:10.1016/j.ijinfomgt.2004.08.002

Bhatnagar, S. C., & Singh, N. (2010). Assessing the Impact of E-government: A Study of Projects in India. *Information Technologies & International Development, 6*(2), 109–127.

Bhuiyan, S. H. (2011). Modernizing Bangladesh public administration through e-governance: Benefits and challenges. *Government Information Quarterly*, *28*(1), 54–65. doi:10.1016/j.giq.2010.04.006

Bikshapathi, K., RamaRaju, P., & Bhatnagar, S. (2006). *E-Procurement in Government of Andhra Pradesh, India.* Retrieved from siteresources.worldbank.org/INTEGOVERNMENT/Resources/APeProcurement.doc

Bircan, T., & Çeviker-Gürakar, E. (2015). Business networks and public procurement in Turkey. In V. Benson & S. Morgan (Eds.), *Implications of social media use in personal and professional settings* (pp. 249–267). Hershey, PA: IGI Global. doi:10.4018/978-1-4666-7401-1.ch013

Block, C., & Neumann, D. (2008). A decision support system for choosing market mechanisms in e-procurement. *Negotiation, Auctions, and Market Engineering*, *2*, 44–57. doi:10.1007/978-3-540-77554-6_3

Bobar, V., Mandic, K., & Suknovic, M. (2015). Bidder selection in public procurement using a fuzzy decision support system. *International Journal of Decision Support System Technology*, *7*(1), 31–49. doi:10.4018/ijdsst.2015010103

Boer, L., Harink, J., & Heijboer, G. (2001). *A model for assessing the impact of electronic procurement forms.* In *10th International Annual IPSERA Conference*, Jönköping, Sweden.

Bolton, P. (2006). Government procurement as a policy tool in South Africa. *Journal of Public Procurement*, *6*(3), 193–217.

Bovis, C. (2006). *EC Public Procurement: Case Law and Regulation.* Oxford, UK: Oxford university Press.

Boyer, R. (1997). *The Variety and Unequal Performance of really Existing Markets: Farewell to Doctor Pangloss? Contemporary Capitalism: The Embeddedness of Institutions.* Cambridge, UK: Cambridge University Press.

Brammer, S., & Walker, H. (2011). Sustainable procurement in the public sector: An international comparative study. *International Journal of Operations & Production Management*, *31*(4), 452–476. doi:10.1108/01443571111119551

Brantley, W. (2015, December). Agile Project Management for Improved Contract Development and Execution. In *Government Contract Management Symposium.* Symposium conducted at the meeting of National Contract Management Association, Washington, D.C.

Bromberg, D., Saldivar, K., & Fudge, M. (2012). E-procurement: Understanding implementation. In A. Manoharan & M. Holzer (Eds.), *E-governance and civic engagement: Factors and determinants of e-democracy* (pp. 72–92). Hershey, PA: IGI Global. doi:10.4018/978-1-61350-083-5.ch004

Brookings. (2009). *Effective and Transparent Governance of Public Expenditures in Latin America and the Caribbean - Revitalizing Reforms in Financial Management and Procurement.* Washington, DC: Brookings Institution - Transparency and Accountability Project.

Bruno, G., Esposito, E., Mastroianni, M., & Vellutino, D. (2005). Analysis of public e-procurement web site accessibility. *Journal of Public Procurement, 5*(3), 344.

C&AG [Duties, Powers and Conditions of Service] Act 1971. (n.d.). Retrieved from http://www.cag.gov.in/content/dpc-act

Cabras, I. (2010). Use of E-procurement in Local Authorities Purchasing and Its Effects on Local Economies: Evidence from Cumbria, UK. European Planning Studies, 18(7), 1133–1151. doi:10.1080/09654311003744209 doi:10.1080/09654311003744209

Caldwell, N., & Howard, M. (2011). *Procuring complex performance: Studies of innovation in product-service management.* New York, NY: Routledge.

Caloghirou, Y., Protogerou, A., & Panagiotopoulos, P. (2016). Public procurement for innovation: A novel eGovernment services scheme in Greek local authorities. *Technological Forecasting and Social Change, 103*, 1–10. doi:10.1016/j.techfore.2015.10.016

Campbell, D. (2012). Public managers in integrated services collaboratives: What works is workarounds. Public Administration Review, 72(5), 721–730. doi:10.1111/j.1540-6210.2012.02545.x doi:10.1111/j.1540-6210.2012.02545.x

Caniato, F., Longoni, A., & Moretto, A. (2012). Effective eProcurement implementation process. *Production Planning and Control, 23*(12), 935–949. doi:10.1080/09537287.2011.586652

Carpineti, L., Piga, G., & Zanza, M. (2006). *The Variety of Procurement Practice: Evidence from Public Procurement. In Handbook of Procurement.* Cambridge University Press.

Carr, A.S., & Smeltzer, L.R. (2002). The Relationship between Information Technology Use and Buyer-Supplier Relationships: An Explanatory Analysis of the Buying Firm's Perspective. *IEEE Transactions on Engineering Management, 49*(3), 293-304.

Carter, C. R., Kaufmann, L., Beall, S., Carter, P. L., Hendrick, T. E., & Petersen, K. J. (2004). Reverse auctionsgrounded theory from the buyer and supplier perspective. *Transportation Research Part E, Logistics and Transportation Review, 40*(3), 229–254. doi:10.1016/j.tre.2003.08.004

CEN - CENELEC. (2016, June). *Work Programme 2016 - European standardization and related activities.* Retrieved from CEN-CENELEC Management Centre: http://www.cencenelec.eu/news/publications/publications/cen-cenelec-wp2016_en.pdf

Central Vigilance Commission Act 2003. (n.d.). Retrieved from http://cvc.nic.in/cvcact.pdf

Chandramowli, S., Transue, M., & Felder, F. A. (2011). Analysis of barriers to development in landfill communities using interpretive structural modeling. *Habitat International, 35*(2), 246–253. doi:10.1016/j.habitatint.2010.09.005

Chang, H. S., & Kristiansen, P. (2006). Selling Australia as "clean and green". *The Australian Journal of Agricultural and Resource Economics, 50*(1), 103–113. doi:10.1111/j.1467-8489.2006.00330.x

Chief Technical Examiner (CTE) Manual. (2002). Retrieved from http://cvc.nic.in/

Chile Proveedores. (n.d.). Retrieved July 10, 2016, from http://www.chileproveedores.cl/chprovdnn/serviciosybeneficios.aspx

ChileCompra. (2014). *Opacidad en el Mercado Público.* Author.

Christos, G., Ziouvelou, X., Yovanof, G., & Ramfos, A. (2011). An open source e-procurement application framework for B2B and G2B. In M. Cruz-Cunha & J. Varajão (Eds.), *Innovations in SMEs and conducting e-business: Technologies, trends and solutions* (pp. 76–97). Hershey, PA: IGI Global. doi:10.4018/978-1-60960-765-4.ch005

Clausen, B., Kraay, A., & Nyiri, Z. (2009). *Corruption and Confidence in Public Institutions Evidence from a Global Survey.* Policy Research Working Paper 5157. Retrieved from http://econ.worldbank.org

Cline, K. D. (2000). Defining the implementation problem: Organizational management versus cooperation. Journal of Public Administration: Research and Theory, 10(3), 551–571. doi:10.1093/oxfordjournals.jpart.a024281 doi:10.1093/oxfordjournals.jpart.a024281

Collaborate. (n.d.). In *Merriam-Webster Dictionary.* Retrieved September 04, 2016, from http://www.merriam-webster.com/dictionary/collaborate

Comite, U. (2012). Innovative processes and managerial effectiveness of e-procurement in healthcare. In A. Manoharan & M. Holzer (Eds.), *Active citizen participation in e-government: A global perspective* (pp. 206–229). Hershey, PA: IGI Global. doi:10.4018/978-1-4666-0116-1.ch011

Communicate. (n.d.). In *Merriam-Webster Dictionary.* Retrieved September 04, 2016, from http://www.merriam-webster.com/dictionary/communicate

Competitions Act 2002. (n.d.). Retrieved from http://www.cci.gov.in/competition-act

Concha, G. & Porrua, M., & Pimenta, C. (2011). E-*Government procurement observatory, maturity model and early measurements.* Academic Press.

Conference on Digital Transformation. (2016, February 16). *Declaration on the digital transformation.* Retrieved from Digital Transformation 2016: http://www.digitaltransformation2016.eu/docs/declaration.pdf

Connell, W. (2014). *The Economic Impact of Late Payments.* European Union Working Papers.

Constitution of India. (n.d.). Retrieved from https://india.gov.in/my-government/constitution-india

Contracting, A. (n.d.). *Defense Acquisition University (DAU) Acquisition Community Connection.* Retrieved from: https://acc.dau.mil/CommunityBrowser.aspx?id=24962

Corini, J. (2000, March). Integrating E-Procurement and Strategic Sourcing. *Supply Chain Management Review*, 3-7.

Costa, A. A., Arantes, A., & Tavares, L. V. (2013). Evidence of the impacts of public e-procurement: The Portuguese experience. *Journal of Purchasing and Supply Management*, *19*(4), 238–246. doi:10.1016/j.pursup.2013.07.004

Costa, A. A., & Tavares, L. V. (2014). Social e-business as support for construction e-procurement: E-procurement network dynamics. *Automation in Construction*, *43*, 180–186. doi:10.1016/j.autcon.2014.03.019

Crane, R., & Marius, M. (2016). *Regional approaches to e-government initiatives in the Caribbean*. ECLAC.

Croom, S. R., & Brandon-Jones, A. (2005). Key issues in e-procurement: Procurement implementation and operation in the public sector. *Journal of Public Procurement*, *5*(3), 367–387.

Croom, S., & Brandon-Jones, A. (2007). Impact of e-procurement: Experiences from implementation in the UK public sector. *Journal of Purchasing and Supply Management*, *13*(4), 294–303. doi:10.1016/j.pursup.2007.09.015

CVC 005/VGL/4 dated 01 September 2006. (n.d.). Retrieved from http://cvc.nic.in/

CVC circular No. 009/VGL/002 dated 17 September 2009. (n.d.). Retrieved from http://cvc.nic.in/

CVC circulars dated 23 Jun 2010 and 12 Jan 2012. (n.d.). Retrieved from http://cvc.nic.in/

CVC office order No. 98/ORD/1 dated 20 October 2004. (n.d.). Retrieved from http://cvc.nic.in/

Dale, C. (2003). The Competitive Networks of Tourism E-Mediaries:New Strategies, New Advantages. *Journal of Vacation Marketing*, *9*(2), 109-118.

Davila, A., Gupta, M., & Palmer, R. (2003). Moving procurement systems to the Internet: The adoption and use of e-procurement technology models. *European Management Journal*, *21*(1), 11–23. doi:10.1016/S0263-2373(02)00155-X

Davila, A., Gupta, M., & Palmer, R. (2003). Moving Procurement Systems to the Internet: The Adoption and Use of E-Procurement Technology Models. *European Management Journal*, *21*(1), 11-23.

Dawson, G. F., & Probert, E. J. (2007). A sustainable product needing a sustainable procurement commitment: The case of green waste in Wales. *Sustainable Development*, *15*(2), 69–82. doi:10.1002/sd.307

Day, S.G., & Hubbard, J.K. (2003). Customer Relationships Go Digital. *Business Strategy Review*, *14*(1), 17-26.

De Boer, L., Harink, J., & Heijboer, G. (2002). A conceptual model for assessing the impact of electronic procurement. *European Journal of Purchasing & Supply Management*, *8*(1), 25–33. doi:10.1016/S0969-7012(01)00015-6

Deasy, M., White, G. R. T., Parfitt, S., & Ringwald, K. (2014). Asymmetric procurement in the public sector. *Strategic Change*, *23*(1/2), 21–29. doi:10.1002/jsc.1957

Defence Procurement Manual. (2009). Retrieved from http://www.dgqadefence.gov.in/documents/DPM2009.pdf

Defence Procurement Procedure. (2013). Retrieved from http://mod.nic.in/writereaddata/DPP2013.pdf

Delegation of Financial Power Rules. (1978). Retrieved from http://finmin.nic.in/

Demirbas, T., Eroglu, E., & Çetinkaya, Ö. (2013). The benefits and barriers of electronic public procurement system: A case study on public hospitals in Turkey. In P. Ordóñez de Pablos, J. Lovelle, J. Gayo, & R. Tennyson (Eds.), *E-procurement management for successful electronic government systems* (pp. 131–146). Hershey, PA: IGI Global. doi:10.4018/978-1-4666-2119-0.ch008

Devaraj, S., Vaidyanathan, G., & Mishra, A. N. (2012). Effect of purchase volume flexibility and purchase mix flexibility on e-procurement performance: An analysis of two perspectives. *Journal of Operations Management, 30*(7/8), 509–520. doi:10.1016/j.jom.2012.08.001

DGS&D Manual. (n.d.). Available at http://cga.nic.in/writereaddata/DGS&DManual.pdf

Dillard, M., Jr. (2014, November). Applying Agile Methodology to Acquisition and Contracting Support. In *Government Contract Management Symposium*. Symposium conducted at the meeting of National Contract Management Association, Washington, DC.

Dimitri, N., Piga, G., & Spagnolo, G. (2006). *Handbook of Procurement*. New York: Cambridge University Press. doi:10.1017/CBO9780511492556

DIT. (2011). *Saraansh: A compendium of Mission Mode Projects under NeGP*. Retrieved from http://www.mit.gov.in

Doherty, N. F., McConnell, D. J., & Ellis-Chadwick, F. (2013). Institutional responses to electronic procurement in the public sector. *International Journal of Public Sector Management, 26*(6), 495–515. doi:10.1108/IJPSM-04-2012-0048

Dorasamy, N. (2013). Conditions determining the success of public e-procurement. In N. Pomazalová (Ed.), *Public sector transformation processes and Internet public procurement: Decision support systems* (pp. 185–209). Hershey, PA: IGI Global. doi:10.4018/978-1-4666-2665-2.ch009

DRE. (2007, February 19). *Diário da República, 1ª série*. Retrieved from Diário da Repúblic Eletrónico - DRE: https://dre.pt/application/file/517923

DRE. (2008a). *Diário da República, 1ª série*. Obtido de Diário da República Eletrónico - DRE: https://dre.pt/application/file/248099

DRE. (2008b). *Diário da República, 1ª série*. Obtido de Diário da República Eletrónico - DRE: https://dre.pt/application/file/239497

DRE. (2008c). *Diário da República, 1ª série*. Obtido de Diário da República Eletrónico - DRE: https://dre.pt/application/file/575266

DRE. (2009, July 30). *Diário da República, 2ª série.* Retrieved from Diário da República Eletrónico - DRE: https://dre.pt/application/file/757133

DRE. (2015). *Diário da República, 1ª série.* Obtido de Diário da República Eletrónico - DRE: https://dre.pt/application/file/70017225

Dwivedi, Y. K., Weerakkody, V., & Janssen, M. (2012). Moving towards maturity: Challenges to successful e-government implementation and diffusion. *ACM SIGMIS Database*, *42*(4), 11–22. doi:10.1145/2096140.2096142

Eadie, R., Perera, S., & Heaney, G. (2013). Electronic procurement in the construction industry. In N. Pomazalová (Ed.), *Public sector transformation processes and Internet public procurement: Decision support systems* (pp. 118–161). Hershey, PA: IGI Global. doi:10.4018/978-1-4666-2665-2.ch007

Eakin, D. (2003). Measuring e-procurement benefits. Summit: Canada's Magazine on Public Sector Purchasing.

EBRD. (2011). *Public Procurement Assessment Review of laws and practice in the EBRD region.* EBRD.

EBRD. (2013). *Turning best practice into policy: public procurement reform agenda.* EBRD.

Edler, J., & Georghiou, L. (2007). Public procurement and innovation: Resurrecting the demand side. *Research Policy*, *36*(7), 949–963. doi:10.1016/j.respol.2007.03.003

Edler, J., & Yeow, J. (2016). Connecting demand and supply: The role of intermediation in public procurement of innovation. *Research Policy*, *45*(2), 414–426. doi:10.1016/j.respol.2015.10.010

Edquist, C., & Zabala-Iturriagagoitia, J. M. (2012). Public procurement for innovation as mission-oriented innovation policy. *Research Policy*, *41*(10), 1757–1769. doi:10.1016/j.respol.2012.04.022

Elbahnasawy, N. G. (2014). E-government, internet adoption, and corruption: An empirical investigation. *World Development*, *57*, 114–126. doi:10.1016/j.worlddev.2013.12.005

Engelbrekt, K. (2011). EU enlargement and the emboldening of institutional integrity in Central and Eastern Europe: The "tough test" of public procurement. *European Law Journal*, *17*(2), 230–251. doi:10.1111/j.1468-0386.2010.00546.x

Escobar, D. (2009). Eliminating Barriers for MSE's in the Public Procurement Marketplace of Chile.*Proceedings of the 3rd International Public Procurement Conference.*

Essig, M., & Arnold, U. (2001). Electronic procurement in supply chain management: An information economics based analysis of electronic markets. *Journal of Supply Chain Management*, *37*(4), 43–49. doi:10.1111/j.1745-493X.2001.tb00112.x

EU. (2010). *EC Green Paper on expanding the use of e-Procurement in the EU.* European Commission. Retrieved from http://ec.europa.eu/internal_market/consultations/docs/2010/e-procurement/green-paper_en.pdf

European Bank for Reconstruction and Development-EBRD. (2015). *Guide to Electronic Procurement Reform*. Retrieved April 25, 2016 from http://www.ebrd.com/what-we-do/sectors/legal-reform/public-procurement.html

European Commission. (2010). *Green Paper on Expanding the Use of e-Procurement in the EU Brussels*. European Commission.

European Commission. (2009). Smarter, faster, better eGovernment, 8th Benchmark Measurement. Brussels, Belgium: European Commission.

European Union. (2014). *SMEs' access to public procurement markets and aggregation of demand in the EU*. EU.

Federal Acquisition Regulation. 15.2 C.F.R. § 15.201. (2016). Retrieved from: https://www.acquisition.gov/?q=browsefar

Federal Acquisition Regulation. 2.1 C.F.R. § 2.101 (b)(2) (2016). Retrieved from: https://www.acquisition.gov/?q=browsefar

Federal Acquisition Regulation. 6.3 C.F.R. § 6.300. (2016). Retrieved from: https://www.acquisition.gov/?q=browsefar

Federal Acquisition Regulation. 7.1 C.F.R. § 7.104 [a]. (2016). Retrieved from: https://www.acquisition.gov/?q=browsefar

Federal Acquisition Regulations (FAR), The U.S. Small Business Administration, SBA. gov. (n.d.). Retrieved from: https://www.sba.gov/content/federal-acquisition-regulations-far

Federici, T. (2009). Introducing e-procurement in a local healthcare agency. In A. Scupola (Ed.), *Cases on managing e-services* (pp. 218–237). Hershey, PA: IGI Global. doi:10.4018/978-1-60566-064-6.ch015

Fernandes, T., & Vieira, V. (2015). Public e-procurement impacts in small-and medium-enterprises. *International Journal of Procurement Management*, *8*(5), 587–607. doi:10.1504/IJPM.2015.070904

Fet, A., Michelsen, O., & de Boer, L. (2011). Green public procurement in practice: The case of Norway. *Society and Economy*, *33*(1), 183–198. doi:10.1556/SocEc.33.2011.1.13

Filho, J. R., & Mota, F. P. (2012). Public e-procurement implementation: Insights from the structuration theory. In K. Vaidya (Ed.), *Inter-organizational information systems and business management: Theories for researchers* (pp. 222–233). Hershey, PA: IGI Global. doi:10.4018/978-1-60960-768-5.ch014

Fink, D. (2006). Value decomposition of e-commerce performance. *Benchmarking: An International Journal*, *13*(1/2), 81–92. doi:10.1108/14635770610644592

FNE. (2011). *Compras Públicas y Libre Competencia*. Santiago: FNE.

Frederickson, H. (1999). The repositioning of American public administration. *PS Political Science & Politics*, *32*(4), 701–711. doi:10.1017/S1049096500056547

Fuks, K., Kawa, A., & Wieczerzycki, W. (2009). *Improved e-sourcing strategy with multi-agent swarms*. Paper presented at the Computational Intelligence for Modelling Control and Automation International Conference, Vienna, Austria.

Furuholt, B., & Wahid, F. (2008). *E-government Challenges and the Role of Political Leadership in Indonesia: the Case of Sragen*. Paper presented at the Hawaii International Conference on System Sciences. doi:10.1109/HICSS.2008.134

Gardenal, F. (2010). Public E-procurement-Define, Measure and Optimize Organizational Benefits. *Proceedings of the* 4th *International Public Procurement Conference*. Retrieved April 24, 2016, from http://www.ippa.org/IPPC4/Proceedings/05e-Procurement/Paper5-1.pdf

Garrido, M. J., Gutierrez, A. M., & San Jose, R. (2006). The impact of e-procurement on the structure of the buying centre. *International Journal of Electronic Business*, *4*(6), 463–482. doi:10.1504/IJEB.2006.011696

Garrido-Samaniego, M.J., Gutierrez-Arranz, A.M., & Jose-Cabezudo, R.S. (2010). Assesing the Impact of E-Procurement on the Structure of the Buying Centre. *International Journal of Information Management, 30*(2), 135-143.

Gelderman, K., Ghijsen, P., & Schoonen, J. (2010). Explaining non-compliance with European Union procurement directives: A multidisciplinary perspective. *JCMS: Journal of Common Market Studies*, *48*(2), 243–264.

Genis-Gruber, A., & Tas, B. K. (2013). Does national culture affect e-procurement implementations?: Analysis of differences through a unified model. In M. Khosrow-Pour (Ed.), *E-commerce for organizational development and competitive advantage* (pp. 171–190). Hershey, PA: IGI Global. doi:10.4018/978-1-4666-3622-4.ch009

Georghiou, L., Edler, J., Uyarra, E., & Yeow, J. (2013). Policy instruments for public procurement of innovation: Choice, design and assessment. *Technological Forecasting and Social Change*, *86*, 1–12. doi:10.1016/j.techfore.2013.09.018

Gichoya, D. (2005). Factors affecting the successful implementation of ICT projects in government. *The Electronic Journal of E-Government, 3*(4), 175-184.

Gil-García, J. R., & Pardo, T. A. (2005). E-government success factors: Mapping practical tools to theoretical foundations. *Government Information Quarterly*, *22*(2), 187–216. doi:10.1016/j.giq.2005.02.001

Golden, W., Hughes, M., & Scott, M. (2003). Implementing E-Government in Ireland: A Roadmap for Success. *Journal of Electronic Commerce in Organizations*, *1*(4), 17–33. doi:10.4018/jeco.2003100102

Goldsmith, S., & Eggers, W. (2004). *Governing by network*. Washington, DC: Brookings Institution Press.

Golob, T. F. (2003). Structural equation modeling for travel behavior research. *Transportation Research Part B: Methodological*, *37*(1), 1–25. doi:10.1016/S0191-2615(01)00046-7

Goodrich, S. (2015, February). 6 simple fixed for the federal procurement process. Federal Times. Retrieved from: http://www.federaltimes.com/story/government/acquisition/blog/2015/02/20/procurement-fix-legislation-rule/23754523/

Gorvett, R., & Liu, N. (2006). *Interpretive structural modeling of interactive risks*. Paper presented at the 2006 Enterprise Risk Management Symposium, Chicago, IL.

Government Accounting Rules. (1990). Retrieved from http://www.cga.nic.in/writereaddata/b3.pdf

Grönlund, Å. (2010). Using ICT to combat corruption - tools, methods and results. In C. Strand (Ed.), *Increasing transparency and fighting corruption through ICT-empowering people and communities* (pp. 7–27). SPIDER - The Swedish Program for ICT in Developing Regions.

Guinez, C. (2013). *Business Intelligence para las Compras Públicas*. Washington, DC: Inter-American Development Bank.

Gunasekaran, A., McGaughey, R. E., Ngai, E. W. T., & Rai, B. K. (2009). E-procurement adoption in the Southcoast SMEs. *International Journal of Production Economics*, *122*(1), 161–175. doi:10.1016/j.ijpe.2009.05.013

Gunasekaran, A., & Ngai, E. W. T. (2008). Adoption of e-procurement in Hong Kong: An empirical research. *International Journal of Production Economics*, *113*(1), 159–175. doi:10.1016/j.ijpe.2007.04.012

Günther, E., & Scheibe, L. (2006). The hurdle analysis. A self-evaluation tool for municipalities to identify, analyse and overcome hurdles to green procurement. *Corporate Social Responsibility and Environmental Management*, *13*(2), 61–77. doi:10.1002/csr.92

Hall, M., & Purchase, D. (2006). Building or bodging? Attitudes to sustainability in UK public sector housing construction development. *Sustainable Development*, *14*(3), 205–218. doi:10.1002/sd.265

Hardy, C., & Williams, S. (2005). Public E-Procurement in Action: Policies, Practices and Technologies. *IFIB International Feredation for Information Processing 2005*.

Harink, J. H. A. (2003). *Internet technology to purchase* (PhD Thesis). University of Twente, Netherland.

Hashim, R., & Mazuki, M. A. (2013). Electronic procurement (e-procurement) implementation in municipalities: Lessons learned. In P. Ordóñez de Pablos, J. Lovelle, J. Gayo, & R. Tennyson (Eds.), *E-procurement management for successful electronic government systems* (pp. 220–238). Hershey, PA: IGI Global. doi:10.4018/978-1-4666-2119-0.ch014

Hashim, R. (2012). Issues in electronic procurement project implementation in local government. In J. Wang (Ed.), *Project management techniques and innovations in information technology* (pp. 285–296). Hershey, PA: IGI Global. doi:10.4018/978-1-4666-0930-3.ch017

Hassan, H., Tretiakov, A., Whiddett, D., & Adon, I. (2014). Extent of e-procurement use in SMEs: A descriptive study. *Procedia: Social and Behavioral Sciences*, *164*, 264–270. doi:10.1016/j.sbspro.2014.11.076

Hawking, P., Stein, A., Wyld, D. C., & Foster, S. (2004). E-procurement: Is the ugly duckling actually a swan down under? *Asia Pacific Journal of Marketing and Logistics*, *16*(1), 3–26. doi:10.1108/13555850410765140

Hekkert, M., Suurs, R. A. A., Negro, S. O., Kuhlmann, S., & Smits, R. (2007). Functions of innovation systems: A new approach for analysing technological change. *Technological Forecasting and Social Change*, *74*(4), 413–432. doi:10.1016/j.techfore.2006.03.002

Henriksen, H. Z., & Mahnke, V. (2005). E-procurement adoption in the Danish public sector: The influence of economic and political rationality. *Scandinavian Journal of Information Systems*, *17*(2), 2.

Ho, L. W. P., Dickinson, N. M., & Chan, G. Y. S. (2010). Green procurement in the Asian public sector and the Hong Kong private sector. *Natural Resources Forum*, *34*(1), 24–38. doi:10.1111/j.1477-8947.2010.01274.x

Ho, C. F., Wu, W. H., & Tai, Y. M. (2004). *An e-procurement impact model based on supply chain orientation: An empirical investigation*. Paper presented at the 4th Workshop on Knowledge Economy and Electronic Commerce, Kaohsiung, Taiwan.

Hsu, J. S. C., & Chen, E. T. (2015). Managers' Perceived Benefits of Using Electronic Procurement in Taiwan. *Communications of the IIMA*, *4*(2), 3.

Huang, D. C., Tran, Q. D., Nguyen, T. Q., & Nazir, S. (2016). Initial adoption vs. institutionalization of e-procurement in construction firms: The role of government in developing countries. In *Web design and development: Concepts, methodologies, tools, and applications* (pp. 1417–1437). Hershey, PA: IGI Global. doi:10.4018/978-1-4666-8619-9.ch064

Hunja, R. (2010). *Forging New Frontiers in Public Procurement*. Retrieved from: http://blogs.worldbank.org/governance/forging-new-frontiers-in-public-procurement

IAC. (2011). *Ibero-American social electronic identification framework*. Approved by the XIII Ibero American Conference of Ministers of the Federal Administration and Reform of the State, Asunción, Paraguay.

Ilhan, N. (2011). *Understanding E-Procurement Systems Implementation Processes and Benefits in the Victorian Local Government Sector: A Business Relationship Perspective* (MS Thesis). Caulfield School of IT, Monash University.

Imamoglu, M. Y., & Rehan, M. (2011). Evaluation of Turkish public e-procurement systems: An analysis of critical success factors. In D. Piaggesi, K. Sund, & W. Castelnovo (Eds.), *Global strategy and practice of e-governance: Examples from around the world* (pp. 144–156). Hershey, PA: IGI Global. doi:10.4018/978-1-60960-489-9.ch009

IMPIC, I.P. (2011). *Contratação Pública em Portugal – Relatório Síntese 2010*. Lisboa: IMPIC, IP.

IMPIC. IP. (2016a). *Condições Tecnicas de Interligação.* Obtido de Portal BASE: http://www.base.gov.pt/mediaRep/inci/files/base_docs/Req_Interligacao_PE_BASE_20160407.pdf

IMPIC. IP. (2016b, June 18). *Plataformas certificadas.* Retrieved from Portal BASE: http://www.base.gov.pt/Base/pt/PlataformasEletronicas/PlataformaEletronicasLicenciadas

Imran, A., & Gregor, S. (2010). Uncovering the Hidden issues in e-Government adoption in a least Developed Country: The Case of Bangladesh. *Journal of Global Information Management, 18*(2), 30–56. doi:10.4018/jgim.2010040102

Indian Contract Act 1872. (n.d.). Retrieved from http://comtax.up.nic.in/Miscellaneous%20Act/the-indian-contract-act-1872.pdf

Information Technology Act 2000. (n.d.). Retrieved from http://www.dot.gov.in/act-rules/information-technology-act-2000

Inter-American Development Bank and the Government of Chile. (n.d.). Chile: evaluación del sistema nacional de compras y contrataciones Públicas (CPAR), op. cit., p. 33.

Inter-American Development Bank. (2011). *Electronic Government Procurement Map.* Washington, DC: Campero, Harper, Concha, Vizcaíno, Sánchez.

Inter-American Network on Government Procurement (INGP). (2013). *Conference proceedings.* Retrieved July 10, 2016, from http://www.RICG.org

International Monetary Fund. (2013). *Caribbean small states: challenges of high debt and low growth.* Retrieved July 10, 2016 from: https://www.imf.org/external/np/pp/eng/2013/022013b.pdf

ISACA. (2011). *Risk Perception and Trust in Cloud.* Retrieved from http://www.isaca.org/Journal/archives/2010/Volume-4/Pages/Risk-Perception-and-Trust-in-Cloud.aspx

Ishak, M. W., & Said, J. (2015). Assessing the role of anti-corruption initiatives in reducing lobbyist involvement in e-procurement: A case study of Mardi. *Procedia Economics and Finance, 31*, 485–494. doi:10.1016/S2212-5671(15)01182-X

Jarach, D. (2002). The Digitalisation of Market Relationships in the Airline Business: The Impact and Prospects of E-Business. *Journal of Air Transport Management, 8*(8), 115–120. doi:10.1016/S0969-6997(01)00039-4

Johnson, M., & Whang, S. (2002). E-Business and Supply Chain Management: An Overview and Framework. *Production and Operations management, 11*(4), 413-423.

Jones, D. S. (2002). Procurement Practices in the Singapore Civil Service: Balancing Control and Delegation. *Journal of Public Procurement, 2*(1), 29–53.

Joongi, K. (2006). *National Integrity Systems:Transparency International Country Study Report: Republic of Korea.* Transparency International Secretariat Alt Moabit 96, 10559. Retrieved from http://www.transparency.org

Kalakota, R., & Robinson, M. (1999). e-Business. In Roadmap for Success. Addison Wesley.

Kaliannan, M., Awang, H., & Raman, M. (2009). Electronic Procurement: A Case Study of Malaysias e-Perolehan (e-procurement) Initiative. *International Journal of Electronic Governance*, *2*(2-3), 103–117. doi:10.1504/IJEG.2009.029124

Kaliannan, M., Raman, M., & Dorasamy, M. (2009, September). E-procurement adoption in the malaysian public sector: organizational perspectives. In Enterprise Distributed Object Computing Conference Workshops, 2009. EDOCW 2009. 13th (pp. 189-194). IEEE. doi:10.1109/EDOCW.2009.5331999

Kamarulzaman, N. H., & Eglese, R. W. (2015). Managing purchasing with different e-procurement solutions. In E. Sabri (Ed.), *Optimization of supply chain management in contemporary organizations* (pp. 246–279). Hershey, PA: IGI Global.

Karagoz, H. (2014). Procurement Procedures at Unions of Public Hospitals. *Journal of Health Efficiency*, *2*, 26–31.

Karthik, V., & Kumar, S. (2013). Investigating 'degree of adoptioneffects on e-procurement benefits. *International Journal of Procurement Management*, *6*(2), 211–234. doi:10.1504/IJPM.2013.052470

Karv, J. (2015). *E-Government and its ability to reduce corruption-The case of Estonia* (Master Thesis). Lund University, Lund, Sweden.

Kasemsap, K. (2015a). The role of cloud computing adoption in global business. In V. Chang, R. Walters, & G. Wills (Eds.), *Delivery and adoption of cloud computing services in contemporary organizations* (pp. 26–55). Hershey, PA: IGI Global. doi:10.4018/978-1-4666-8210-8.ch002

Kasemsap, K. (2015b). The role of cloud computing in global supply chain. In N. Rao (Ed.), *Enterprise management strategies in the era of cloud computing* (pp. 192–219). Hershey, PA: IGI Global. doi:10.4018/978-1-4666-8339-6.ch009

Kasemsap, K. (2016a). The roles of business process modeling and business process reengineering in e-government. In J. Martins & A. Molnar (Eds.), *Handbook of research on innovations in information retrieval, analysis, and management* (pp. 401–430). Hershey, PA: IGI Global. doi:10.4018/978-1-4666-8833-9.ch015

Kasemsap, K. (2016b). The role of strategic outsourcing in global business. In G. Alor-Hernández, C. Sánchez-Ramírez, & J. García-Alcaraz (Eds.), *Handbook of research on managerial strategies for achieving optimal performance in industrial processes* (pp. 325–357). Hershey, PA: IGI Global. doi:10.4018/978-1-5225-0130-5.ch016

Kashta, R. (2012), E-procurement System in Albania, Impact and Lessons Learned. *Proceedings of the 5th International Public Procurement Conference.* Retrieved April 25, 2016, from http://www.ippa.org/IPPC5/Proceedings/Part2/PAPER2-5.pdf

Kassim, E. S., & Hussin, H. (2013). A success model for the Malaysian government e-procurement system: The buyer perspective. *International Journal of Electronic Government Research*, *9*(1), 1–18. doi:10.4018/jegr.2013010101

Kaufmann, D., Kraay, A., & Mastruzzi, M. (2006). *Measuring Corruption: Myths and Realities*. Washington, DC: The World Bank.

Kazakhstan. (2011). *Kazakhstan Centre for E-Commerce website*. Retrieved from https://ecc.kz

Ke, W., & Wei, K. K. (2004). Successful e-government in Singapore. *Communications of the ACM*, *47*(6), 95–99. doi:10.1145/990680.990687

Khorana, S., Ferguson-Boucher, K., & Kerr, W. A. (2015). Governance issues in the EU's e-procurement framework. *JCMS: Journal of Common Market Studies*, *53*(2), 292–310.

Kifle, H., & Low Kim Cheng, P. (2009). E-government Implementation and Leadership: The Brunei Case Study. *Electronic. Journal of E-Government*, *7*(3), 271–282.

Kim, C.-K. (2014). Anti-corruption initiatives and e-government: A cross-national study. *Public Organization Review*, *14*(3), 385–396. doi:10.1007/s11115-013-0223-1

Kim, S., Kim, H. J., & Lee, H. (2009). An institutional analysis of an e-government system for anti-corruption: The case of OPEN. *Government Information Quarterly*, *26*(1), 42–50. doi:10.1016/j.giq.2008.09.002

Kim, J.I., & Shunk, D.L. (2004). Matching Indirect Procurement Process with Different B2b E-Procurement Systems. *Computers in Industry*, (53), 153-164.

Klerkx, L., & Leeuwis, C. (2009). Establishment and embedding of innovation brokers at different innovation system levels: Insights from the Dutch agricultural sector. *Technological Forecasting and Social Change*, *76*(6), 849–860. doi:10.1016/j.techfore.2008.10.001

Knudsen, D. (2003). Aligning corporate strategy, procurement strategy and e-procurement tools. *International Journal of Physical Distribution & Logistics Management*, *33*(8), 720–734. doi:10.1108/09600030310502894

Kohli, J. (2012). Red Flags in E-procurement/E-tendering for Public Procurement and Some Remedial Measures. *Proceedings of the 5th International Public Procurement Conference*. Retrieved April 24, 2016, from http://www.ippa.org/IPPC5/Proceedings/Part2/PAPER2-6.pdf

Konradt, U., Lückel, L., & Ellwart, T. (2012). The role of usability in business-to-business e-commerce systems: Predictors and its impact on user's strain and commercial transactions. *Advances in Human-Computer Interaction*, *2012*, 1–11. doi:10.1155/2012/948693

Korytsev, M. (2006). Quasi-market of public procurement: Options for organization and efficiency loss. *Terra Economicus*, *4*(2), 112.

Korytsev, M. (2009). *Institutional structure and mechanisms of functioning of quasi-markets in the public sector* (p. 6). Rostov-on-Don.

Kotwani, A. (2013). Transparency and accountability in public procurement of essential medicines in developing countries. In *Supply chain management: Concepts, methodologies, tools, and applications* (pp. 1437–1452). Hershey, PA: IGI Global. doi:10.4018/978-1-4666-2625-6.ch085

Krishnan, S., Teo, T. S., & Lim, V. K. (2013). Examining the relationships among e-government maturity, corruption, economic prosperity and environmental degradation: A cross-country analysis. *Information & Management, 50*(8), 638–649. doi:10.1016/j.im.2013.07.003

Krüger, K. (2009). Ban-on-negotiations in tender procedures: Undermining the best value for money. In International Handbook of Public Procurement (pp. 631-658). CRC Press, Taylor and Francis Group.

Krysiak, M. K., Tucker, C., Spitzer, D., & Holland, K. (2008). E-procurement: State government learns from the private sector. In A. Anttiroiko (Ed.), *Electronic government: Concepts, methodologies, tools, and applications* (pp. 1566–1583). Hershey, PA: IGI Global. doi:10.4018/978-1-59904-947-2.ch118

Lapido, O. A. S., & Sopher. (2009). Accountability in Public Expenditures in Latin America and the Caribbean – Revitalizing Reforms in Financial Management and Procurement. Washington DC: The World Bank.

Lee, J. Y. (2007). The government e-procurement system in Korea. In A. Anttiroiko & M. Malkia (Eds.), *Encyclopedia of digital government* (pp. 896–900). Hershey, PA: IGI Global. doi:10.4018/978-1-59140-789-8.ch134

Lee, C., & Huang, T.-y. (2014). *E-government Use and Citizen Empowerment: Examining the effects of online information on political efficacy*. Academic Press.

Lee, W., & Quaddus, M. (2006). *Buyer–supplier relationship in the adoption of e-purchasing in the small and medium printing industries in Singapore: An empirical test using structural equation modelling*. Paper presented at the 10th Pacific Asia Conference on Information Systems (PACIS 2006), Kuala Lumpur, Malaysia.

Leek, S., Turnbull, P.W., & Naude, P. (2003). How Is Information Technology Affecting Business Relationships? Results from a UK Survey. *Industrial Marketing Management*, (32), 119-126.

Leipold, K., Klemow, J., Holloway, F., & Vaidya, K. (2004). The World Bank e-procurement for the selection of consultants: Challenges and lessons learned. *Journal of Public Procurement, 4*, 319–339.

Leistner, C. N. (2013). Measuring the impact of tools on the leanness of e-procurement processes. In D. Graham, I. Manikas, & D. Folinas (Eds.), *E-logistics and e-supply chain management: Applications for evolving business* (pp. 44–88). Hershey, PA: IGI Global. doi:10.4018/978-1-4666-3914-0.ch004

Lewis-Faupel, S., Neggers, Y., Olken, B. A., & Pande, R. (2014). *Can electronic procurement improve infrastructure provision? evidence from public works in India and Indonesia (No. w20344)*. National Bureau of Economic Research.

Lin, A., & Chen, S. (2013). Structuring information systems-in-use: Studying the replication of an e-procurement system through a practice lens. *Journal of Global Information Management, 21*(1), 1–18. doi:10.4018/jgim.2013010101

Linders, D., & Wilson, S. C. (2011). What is open government?: one year after the directive. *Proceedings of the 12th Annual International Digital Government Research Conference: Digital Government Innovation in Challenging Times*. doi:10.1145/2037556.2037599

Luk, S. C. Y. (2009). The impact of leadership and stakeholders on the success/failure of e-government service: Using the case study of e-stamping service in Hong Kong. *Government Information Quarterly*, *26*(4), 594–604. doi:10.1016/j.giq.2009.02.009

Lupu, D., & Lazăr, C. G. (2015). Influence of e-government on the Level of Corruption in some EU and Non-EU States. *Procedia Economics and Finance*, *20*, 365–371. doi:10.1016/S2212-5671(15)00085-4

Luthra, S., Kumar, V., Kumar, S., & Haleem, A. (2011). Barriers to implement green supply chain management in automobile industry using interpretive structural modeling technique: An Indian perspective. *Journal of Industrial Engineering and Management*, *4*(2), 231–257. doi:10.3926/jiem.2011.v4n2.p231-257

Macintosh, A. (2004). Characterizing e-participation in policy-making.*Proceedings of the 37th Annual Hawaii International Conference on.*

MacManus, S. A. (2002). Understanding the incremental nature of e-procurement implementation at the state and local levels. *Journal of Public Procurement*, *2*(1), 5–28.

Madeja, N., & Schoder, D. (2003). *The adoption of e-procurement and its impact on corporate success in electronic business*. Paper presented at the 3rd International Conference on Electronic Business (ICEB 2003), Singapore.

Mahmood, S. A. I. (2010). Public procurement and corruption in Bangladesh confronting the challenges and opportunities. *Journal of Public Administration and Policy Research*, *2*(6), 103-111.

Manthou, V., Bialas, C., & Stefanou, C. J. (2016). Benefits and barriers of e-sourcing and e-purchasing in the healthcare sector: A case study. In P. Papajorgji, F. Pinet, A. Guimarães, & J. Papathanasiou (Eds.), *Automated enterprise systems for maximizing business performance* (pp. 71–87). Hershey, PA: IGI Global. doi:10.4018/978-1-4666-8841-4.ch005

Manual on Policies and Procedures for Purchase of Goods. (n.d.). Retrieved from http://finmin.nic.in/

Marín, J. L., Rodríguez, M., Marín, Á., Calmeau, R., Alvarez, J. M., & Labra, J. E. (2013). Euroalert.net: Aggregating public procurement data to deliver commercial services to SMEs. In P. Ordóñez de Pablos, J. Lovelle, J. Gayo, & R. Tennyson (Eds.), *E-procurement management for successful electronic government systems* (pp. 114–130). Hershey, PA: IGI Global. doi:10.4018/978-1-4666-2119-0.ch007

Martín, S. B., & Peñalvo, F. J. (2013). Electronic government systems for e-procurement procedure in the EU. In P. Ordóñez de Pablos, J. Lovelle, J. Gayo, & R. Tennyson (Eds.), *E-procurement management for successful electronic government Systems* (pp. 29–51). Hershey, PA: IGI Global. doi:10.4018/978-1-4666-2119-0.ch003

Masson, B. (2014). *Digital disruption ushering in a new era of public services in Europe: a call to action*. Obtido de The Lisbon Council: http://www.lisboncouncil.net/publication/publication/117-delivering-public-service-for-the-future.html

McLinden, G., & Durrani, A. Z. (2013). Corruption in Customs. *World Customs Journal*, *7*(2), 3–10.

Meehan, J., & Bryde, D. (2011). Sustainable procurement practice. *Business Strategy and the Environment*, *20*(2), 94–106. doi:10.1002/bse.678

Meek, J., Schildt, K., & Witt, M. (2006). *Local government administration in a metropolitan context*. University of LaVerne.

Min, H., & Galle, W.P. (2003). E-Purchasing: Profiles of Adopters and Nonadopters. *Industrial Marketing Management, 32*(3), 227-233.

Mistry, J. J., & Jalal, A. (2012). An empirical analysis of the relationship between e-government and corruption. *The International Journal of Digital Accounting Research, 12*(18), 145-176.

MIT Center for Digital Business and Capgemini Consulting. (2013). *Digital transformation: A roadap for billion dollar organisations*. Retrieved from http://digitalcommunity.mit.edu/docs/DOC-1084

Mital, M., Pani, A., & Ramesh, R. (2014). Determinants of choice of semantic web based software as a service: An integrative framework in the context of e-procurement and ERP. *Computers in Industry*, *65*(5), 821–827. doi:10.1016/j.compind.2014.03.002

Moe, C. E. (2004). Public e-Procurement–Determinants of Attitudes Towards Adoption. In Electronic Government (pp. 278-282). Springer Berlin Heidelberg. doi:10.1007/978-3-540-30078-6_46

Mohammad, H., Almarabeh, T., & Ali, A. A. (2009). E-government in Jordan. *European Journal of Scientific Research*, *35*(2), 188–197.

Moon, M. J. (2004). *State E-Procurement Management in the Information Age: Practices, Prospects and Challenges*. Texas A&M University.

Moon, M. J. (2005). E-procurement management in state governments: Diffusion of e-procurement practices and its determinants. *Journal of Public Procurement*, *5*(1), 54.

Morgan, R.M., & Hunt, S.D. (1994). The Commitment-Trust Theory of Relationship Marketing. *Journal of Marketing, 58*(3), 20-38.

Morris, A., Stahl, A., & Herbert, R. (2000). *E-procurement: Streamlining processes to maximize effectiveness*. Houston, TX: Luminant Worldwide Corporation.

Multilateral Development Banks. (2004). *Electronic Government Procurement Roadmap*. Retrieved April 24, 2016, from http://idbdocs.iadb.org/wsdocs/getdocument.aspx?docnum=645469

Nagle, T., Finnegan, P., & Hayes, J. (2009). From tough negotiation to complex integration: Implications of adversarial and collaborative relationships on electronic procurement systems. *Information Resources Management Journal*, *22*(4), 64–84. doi:10.4018/irmj.2009061904

Naseebullah, H.M.F.B., & Dominic, P.D.D. (2010). *The Role of Factors in Business-to-Business E-Procurement Implementation.* 2010 International Information Technology (ITSim) Symposium, Kuala Lumpur, Malaysia.

Nath, R., & Angeles, R. (2005). Relationships between supply characteristics and buyer-supplier coupling in e-procurement: An empirical analysis. *International Journal of E-Business Research*, *1*(2), 40–55. doi:10.4018/jebr.2005040103

National Contract Management Association (NCMA) World Congress 2016 Breakout Sessions. (2016, July). Retrieved from: http://www.ncmahq.org/wc16/speakers/sessions

Neef, D. (2001). *E-Procurement: From Strategy to Implementation.* Prentice Hall Inc.

Neuman, W. L. (2003). *Social Research Methods: Qualitative and Quantitative Approaches.* Allyn & Bacon.

Neupane, A., Soar, J., Vaidya, K., & Yong, J. (2014). Willingness to adopt e-procurement to reduce corruption: Results of the PLS Path modeling. *Transforming Government: People,Process and Policy*, *8*(4), 500–520.

Neupane, A., Soar, J., & Vaidya, K. (2012). Evaluating the anti-corruption capabilities of public e-procurement in a developing country. *The Electronic Journal on Information System in Developing Countries*, *55*(2), 1–17.

Neupane, A., Soar, J., & Vaidya, K. (2012). The potential of e-procurement technology for reducing corruption. *International Journal of Information Technology and Management*, *11*(4), 273–287. doi:10.1504/IJITM.2012.049997

Neupane, A., Soar, J., & Vaidya, K. (2014). Anti-Corruption Capabilities of Public E-Procurement Technologies: Principal-Agent Theory. In K. J. Bwalya (Ed.), *Technology Development and Platform Enhancements for Successfull Global E-government Design.* IGI Global. doi:10.4018/978-1-4666-4900-2.ch010

Neupane, A., Soar, J., & Vaidya, K. (2015). Anti-corruption capabilities of public e-procurement technologies: Principal-agent theory. In *Business law and ethics: Concepts, methodologies, tools, and applications* (pp. 355–373). Hershey, PA: IGI Global.

Neupane, A. (2014). *The potential of public e-procurement technology to reduce corruption in public procurement* (PhD Thesis). University of Southern Queensland, Toowoomba, Australia.

Neupane, A., Soar, J., Vaidya, K., & Aryal, S. (2014). The potential for ICT tools to promote public participation in fighting corruption. In C. M. Akrivopoulou & N. Garipidis (Eds.), Human Rights and the Impact of ICT in the Public Sphere. Hershey, PA: Information Science Reference, IGI Global. doi:10.4018/978-1-4666-6248-3.ch010

Neupane, A., Soar, J., Vaidya, K., & Yong, J. (2012). Role of public e-procurement technology to reduce corruption in government procurement. *Proceedings of the 5th International Public Procurement Conference (IPPC5).*

New Zealand. (2006). *Mandatory Rules for Procurement by Government Department.* Retrieved from http://www.procurement.govt.nz/procurement/pdf-library/agencies/Mandatory%20Rules%20for%20Procurement%20by%20Departments.pdf/view

Niewadomska, E., & Weiner, S. (2013). Measuring Success in Public Procurement Reform. *Law in Transition Online*, *2*, 6–21.

Nissinen, A., Parikka-Alholaa, K., & Ritab, H. (2009). Environmental criteria in the public purchases above the EU threshold values by three Nordic countries: 2003 and 2005. *Ecological Economics*, *68*(6), 1838–1849. doi:10.1016/j.ecolecon.2008.12.005

Novosák, J., Hájek, O., & Machu, J. (2013). Public procurement in the Czech Republic: Focused on regional development and e-procurement. In N. Pomazalová (Ed.), *Public sector transformation processes and Internet public procurement: Decision support systems* (pp. 210–226). Hershey, PA: IGI Global. doi:10.4018/978-1-4666-2665-2.ch010

O'Connell, M. (2012, June). Services Acquisition Reform Act (2003). Federal News Radio. Retrieved from: http://federalnewsradio.com/acquisition/2012/06/services-acquisition-reform-act-2003/

OECD. (2011). *Demand-side innovation policies.* Paris, France: Organization for Economic Cooperation and Development.

OECD. (2015). *Government at a Glance 2015.* OECD.

OECD. (2002). *Government Procurement: A synthesis report.* Retrieved from https://www.oecd.org/gov/budgeting/43506020.pdf

OECD. (2006). *Methodology for Assessment of National Procurement Systems.* Retrieved from http://www.oecd.org/dataoecd/1/36/37130136.pdf

OECD. (2008). *Fighting Cartels in Public Procurement.* Retrieved from http://www.oecd.org/dataoecd/45/63/41505296.pdf

OECD. (2010). *Report on Collusion and Corruption in Public Procurement in India.* Retrieved from http://www.oecd.org/dataoecd/19/20/44530808.pdf

OECD. (2013). *Public Governance Reviews Public Procurement Review of the State's Employee's Social Security and Social Services Institute in Mexico.* Retrieved from https://books.google.com/books?isbn=9264197303

OECD. (2015, February 18). *OECD Recommendation of the Council on Public Procurement.* Retrieved from Decisions, Recommendations and other Instruments of the Organisation for Economic Co-Operation and Development: http://acts.oecd.org/Instruments/ShowInstrumentView.aspx?InstrumentID=320&InstrumentPID=348&Lang=en

OECD/DAC. (2003). *Mainstreaming the Procurement Function into the Public Expenditure Policy and Effectiveness Dialogue (OECD/DAC).* World Bank Roundtable, Paris, France. Available at www.oecd.org

Office Memorandum No. 10/3/2012-PPC dated 30 Mar 2012. (n.d.). Retrieved from http://finmin.nic.in/

Office Memorandum No. 17/6/2014-PPD dated 24 May 2016. (n.d.). Retrieved from http://finmin.nic.in/

Office Memorandum No. 2/1/2012-PPD dated 06 Apr 2015. (n.d.). Retrieved from http://finmin.nic.in/

Office Memorandum No. 29(1)/2014-PPD dated 28 Jan 2014. (n.d.). Retrieved from http://finmin.nic.in/

Office Memorandum No. 7(3) E-Coord /2006 dated 22 July 2006. (n.d.). Retrieved from http://finmin.nic.in/

Office Memorandum No. 8 (3)-E.II (A) 0-02. (n.d.). Retrieved from http://finmin.nic.in/

Office Memorandum No. 8 (5)/EII (A)/2006 dated 10 January 2007. (n.d.). Retrieved from http://finmin.nic.in/

Office Memorandum No. F.17/6/2014-PPD dated 22 Aug 2016. (n.d.). Retrieved from http://finmin.nic.in/

Office of Federal Procurement Policy. (2011, February 2). "Myth-Busting": Addressing Misconceptions to Improve Communication with Industry during the Acquisition Process. Memorandum for Chief Acquisition Officers; Senior Procurement Executives; Chief Information Officers. Washington, DC: Daniel I. Gordon, Administrator for Federal Procurement Policy, Author.

OGC. (2005). *e-Procurement in Action.* Office of Government Commerce. Retrieved from http://www.umic.pt/images/stories/publicacoes/embedded_object[1].pdf

Ojha, A., Palvia, S., & Gupta, M. (2008). A model for impact of e-government on corruption: Exploring theoretical foundations. In J. Bhattacharya (Ed.), *Critical thinking in e-governance* (pp. 160–170). New Delhi: Gift Publishing.

Oliveira, A. F., & Joia, L. A. (2013). E-procurement associated with MRO: The case of Caixa Econômica Federal. In P. Ordóñez de Pablos, J. Lovelle, J. Gayo, & R. Tennyson (Eds.), *E-procurement management for successful electronic government systems* (pp. 52–72). Hershey, PA: IGI Global. doi:10.4018/978-1-4666-2119-0.ch004

Olken, B. A., & Pande, R. (2011). Corruption in developing countries. *Annual Review of Economics. Annual Reviews, 4*(1), 479–509.

OMahoney, J., Heusinkveld, S., & Wright, C. (2013). Commodifying the commodifiers: The impact of procurement on management knowledge. *Journal of Management Studies*, *50*(2), 204–235. doi:10.1111/joms.12008

Organization for Economic Cooperation and Development and Inter-American Development Bank. (2016). *Towards Efficient Public Procurement in Colombia*. Paris: OECD Publishing.

Organization for Economic Cooperation and Development and Inter-American Development Bank. (2016). *Government at a Glance: Latin America and the Caribbean 2017*. Paris: OECD Publishing.

Organization for Economic Cooperation and Development. (2014). *Government at a Glance: Latin America and the Caribbean 2014: Towards Innovative Public Financial Management*. Paris: OECD Publishing.

Organization of American States. (2005). *Inter-American Forum on Government Procurement: Chile, Mexico and Costa Rica Case Studies*. Washington, DC: OAS.

Osmonbekov, T., Bello, D. C., & Gilliland, D. I. (2002). Adoption of electronic commerce tools in business procurement: Enhanced buying center structure andprocesses. *Journal of Business and Industrial Marketing*, *17*(2/3), 151–166. doi:10.1108/08858620210419781

Otsuki, K. (2011). Sustainable partnerships for a green economy: A case study of public procurement for home-grown school feeding. *Natural Resources Forum*, *35*(3), 213–222. doi:10.1111/j.1477-8947.2011.01392.x

Palmujoki, A., Parikka-Alhola, K., & Ekroos, A. (2010). Green public procurement: Analysis on the use of environmental criteria in contracts. *Review of European Community & International Environmental Law*, *19*(2), 250–262. doi:10.1111/j.1467-9388.2010.00681.x

Pan, G. S. (2005). Information systems project abandonment: A stakeholder analysis. *International Journal of Information Management*, *25*(2), 173–184. doi:10.1016/j.ijinfomgt.2004.12.003

Panayiotou, N. A., Gayialis, S. P., & Tatsiopoulos, I. P. (2004). An e-procurement system for governmental purchasing. *International Journal of Production Economics*, *90*(1), 79–102. doi:10.1016/S0925-5273(03)00103-8

Panda, P., Sahu, G. P., & Gupta, P. K. (2011). E-Government Procurement Implementation: Necessity of National Procurement Law. In N. Bhatt & A. Aggarwal (Eds.), *E-Governance: Policies and Practices* (pp. 170–183). New Delhi, India: Excel India Publishers. doi:10.2139/ssrn.1898759

Panda, P., & Sahu, G. P. (2011). E-Procurement Implementation: Comparative Study of Governments off Andhra Pradesh and Chhattisgarh. *IUP Journal of Supply Chain Management*, *8*(2), 34–67.

Panda, P., & Sahu, G. P. (2015). E-Government Procurement Implementation in India: A cross sectional study. Int. J. *Business Information Systems*, *18*(1), 1–25. doi:10.1504/IJBIS.2015.066124

Panda, P., & Sahu, G. P. (2013). *Fulfilling Public Procurement Expectations in India: Need of Legislative Intervention*. ICEGOV '13, Seoul, South Korea. doi:10.1145/2591888.2591905

Panda, P., Sahu, G. P., & Gupta, P. K. (2010). Combating Corruption in Public Procurements through E-Procurement: Challenges and Opportunities. In Governance Issues and Corruption (pp. 173-196). Haryana, India: Intellectual Foundation.

Pani, A. K. (2007). Perspectives from IOIS, EDI, and channel management: Research issues in e-procurement. In A. Pani & A. Agrahari (Eds.), *E-procurement in emerging economies: Theory and cases* (pp. 1–20). Hershey, PA: Idea Group Publishing. doi:10.4018/978-1-59904-153-7.ch001

Parida, U., & Parida, V. (2005). *E-procurement: An Indian and Swedish perspective*. Academic Press.

Patra, M. R. (2007). A service-oriented agent-based model for electronic procurement. In A. Pani & A. Agrahari (Eds.), *E-procurement in emerging economies: Theory and cases* (pp. 233–264). Hershey, PA: Idea Group Publishing. doi:10.4018/978-1-59904-153-7.ch009

Peck, F., & Cabras, I. (2011). The impact of local authority procurement on local economies: The case of Cumbria, North West England. *Public Policy and Administration*, *26*(3), 307–331. doi:10.1177/0952076709356859

Phang, C. W., & Kankanhalli, A. (2008). A framework of ICT exploitation for e-participation initiatives. *Communications of the ACM*, *51*(12), 128–132. doi:10.1145/1409360.1409385

Pimenta, C., & Pessoa, M. (2015). *Public Financial Management in Latin America: The Key to Efficiency and Transparency*. Washington, DC: Inter-American Development Bank. doi:10.18235/0000083

Pinto, S. (2009). *Subastas inversas electrónicas y su aplicación en las compras gubernamentales: La experiencia de Latinoamérica*. Washington, DC: Inter-American Development Bank.

PMC, R. C. (2014). *Analysis of the State Procurement System of Georgia*. USAID Georgia.

Podlogar, M. (2007). E-procurement success factors: Challenges and opportunities for a small developing country. In A. Pani & A. Agrahari (Eds.), *E-procurement in emerging economies: Theory and cases* (pp. 42–75). Hershey, PA: Idea Group Publishing. doi:10.4018/978-1-59904-153-7.ch003

Polemi, D., & Papastergiou, S. (2006). *A secure e-ordering web service*. Academic Press.

Pomazalová, N., & Rejman, S. (2013). The rationale behind implementation of new electronic tools for electronic public procurement. In N. Pomazalová (Ed.), *Public sector transformation processes and Internet public procurement: Decision support systems* (pp. 85–117). Hershey, PA: IGI Global. doi:10.4018/978-1-4666-2665-2.ch006

Preuss, L., & Walker, H. (2011). Psychological barriers in the road to sustainable development: Evidence from public sector procurement. *Public Administration*, *89*(2), 493–521. doi:10.1111/j.1467-9299.2010.01893.x

Preuss, L. (2007). Buying into our future: Sustainability initiatives in local government procurement. *Business Strategy and the Environment, 16*(5), 354–365. doi:10.1002/bse.578

Prevention of Corruption Act 1988. (n.d.). Retrieved from http://www.persmin.gov.in/DOPT/EmployeesCorner/ Acts_Rules/PCAct/pcact.pdf

Previtali, P. (2012). European public e-procurement: The Italian experience. In A. Manoharan & M. Holzer (Eds.), *Active citizen participation in e-government: A global perspective* (pp. 230–249). Hershey, PA: IGI Global. doi:10.4018/978-1-4666-0116-1.ch012

PricewaterhouseCoopers. (2013). *E-procurement Golden Book of Good Practice*. Retrieved April 27, 2016, from http://ec.europa.eu/archives/dgs/internal_market/studies/docs/e-procurement-golden-book-of-good-practice_en.pdf

Public Procurement Bill. (2012). Retrieved from http://finmin.nic.in/the_ministry/dept_expenditure/ ppcell/58_2012_LS_EN.pdf

Puschmann, T., & Alt, R. (2005). Successful use of e-procurement in supply chains. *Supply Chain Management: An International Journal, 10*(2), 122–133. doi:10.1108/13598540510589197

Puschmann, T., & Alt, R. (2005). Successful Use of E-Procurement in Supply Chains. *International Journal of Supply Chain Management, 10*(2), 122-133.

Quander, A. Y., & Woppert, J. N. (2010, September). Analysis of Alpha Contracting from Three Perspectives: Government Contracting, the Government Program Office, and Industry. Retrieved from Defense Acquisition University (DAU) Acquisition Community Connection: https://acc.dau.mil/CommunityBrowser.aspx?id=417098

Rabaey, M. (2013). A complex adaptive system thinking approach of government e-procurement in a cloud computing environment. In P. Ordóñez de Pablos, J. Lovelle, J. Gayo, & R. Tennyson (Eds.), *E-procurement management for successful electronic government systems* (pp. 193–219). Hershey, PA: IGI Global. doi:10.4018/978-1-4666-2119-0.ch013

Racca, G., & Albano, G. L. (2013). Collaborative Public Procurement and Supply Chain. In D. Martinez-Alfonso (Ed.), *The SAGE Handbook of Strategic Supply Management* (pp. 179–213). London: SAGE Publications Ltd. doi:10.4135/9781446269886.n8

Radaev, V. (2010). What is the market: Economic and sociological approach. *Economia e Sociologia (Evora, Portugal), 7*(5), 23.

Rahim, M. M., & Bantwal, A. P. (2012). Perceived benefits from a local government public procurement initiative: A diffusion of innovation perspective. In K. Vaidya (Ed.), *Inter-organizational information systems and business management: Theories for researchers* (pp. 251–271). Hershey, PA: IGI Global. doi:10.4018/978-1-60960-768-5.ch016

Rahim, M., & Kurnia, S. (2014). *Understanding E-Procurement System Benefits Using Organisational Adoption Motivation Lens: A Case Study*. PACIS.

Rahim, M. M. (2008). *Identifying Factors Affecting Acceptance of E-Procurement Systems: An Initial Qualitative Study at an Australian City Council*. The 10th International Business Information Management Association (IBIMA) Conference, Kuala Lumpur, Malaysia.

Rahim, M., Ilhan, N., & Chen, X. (2011). Factors affecting benefits of e-procurement systems: Experience of an Australian City Council. In *11th International Conference on Electronic Business* (pp. 265-272). PA Living.

Rahim, M.M., & As-Saber, S.N. (2011). E-Procurement Adoption Process: An Arduous Journey for an Australian City Council. *International Journal of Electronic Finance, 5*(2), 150–168.

Rahman, H., & Ramos, I. (2013). Technology Development and Platform Enhancements for Successful Global E-Government Design. In K. J. Bwalys (Ed.), Stages of E-Government Maturity Models: Emergence of E-Governance at the Grass Roots (p. 228). Academic Press.

Reddick, C. G. (2004). The growth of e-procurement in American state governments: A model and empirical evidence. *Journal of Public Procurement*, *4*(2), 151.

Reddick, C. G. (2007). Government e-procurement through the Internet. In A. Anttiroiko & M. Malkia (Eds.), *Encyclopedia of digital government* (pp. 901–905). Hershey, PA: IGI Global. doi:10.4018/978-1-59140-789-8.ch135

Reddy, K., & Rampersad, R. (2013). Black economic empowerment, ICT, and preferential public procurement in South Africa. In N. Pomazalová (Ed.), *Public sector transformation processes and Internet public procurement: Decision support systems* (pp. 254–275). Hershey, PA: IGI Global. doi:10.4018/978-1-4666-2665-2.ch012

Rehan, M. (2013). An analysis of public e-procurement system: An overview of Turkish system. *International Journal of Technology Diffusion*, *4*(4), 66–81. doi:10.4018/ijtd.2013100104

Rehme, J., Kindstrom, D., & Brege, S. (2005). Know your why's how's: Towards a contingency model for industrial e-procurement. In N. Shin (Ed.), *Strategies for generating e-business returns on investment* (pp. 125–142). Hershey, PA: Idea Group Publishing. doi:10.4018/978-1-59140-417-0.ch006

Report of the Acquisition Advisory Panel to the Office of Federal Procurement Policy and the United States Congress. (2007, January). Retrieved from: http://www.ndia.org/Advocacy/AcquisitionReformInitiative/Documents/4-24102_GSA.pdf

Resca, A., & Federici, T. (2013). Implementing e-procurement in public healthcare: The knowledge management issue. In *Supply chain management: Concepts, methodologies, tools, and applications* (pp. 984–1001). Hershey, PA: IGI Global. doi:10.4018/978-1-4666-2625-6.ch057

Reunis, M. R. B., Santema, S. C., & Harink, J. H. A. (2006). Increasing e-ordering adoption: A case study. *Journal of Purchasing and Supply Management*, *12*(6), 322–331. doi:10.1016/j.pursup.2007.01.006

Right to Information Act 2005. (n.d.). Retrieved from http://www.rti.gov.in/rtiact.asp

Robinson, P., Wale, D., & Dickson, G. (2010). *Events management*. Cambridge, MA: CABI Publishing. doi:10.1079/9781845936822.0000

Rogers, E. M. (1995). Diffusion of Innovations (4th ed.). New York: The Free Press.

Rolfstam, M. (2013). *Public procurement and innovation: The role of institutions*. Cheltenham, UK: Edward Elgar Publishing. doi:10.4337/9780857930521

Roman, A. V. (2013). The "mental revolution" of the public procurement specialist: Achieving transformative impacts within the context of e-procurement. In N. Pomazalová (Ed.), *Public sector transformation processes and Internet public procurement: Decision support systems* (pp. 1–16). Hershey, PA: IGI Global. doi:10.4018/978-1-4666-2665-2.ch001

Ronald, N. K., & Omwenga, J. Q. (2015). Factors Contributing to Adoption of E-Procurement in County Governments: A Case Study of County Government of Bo`met. *International Journal of Academic Research in Business and Social Sciences*, *5*(10), 233–239.

Ronchi, S., Brun, A., Golini, R., & Fan, X. (2010). What Is the Value of an It E-Procurement System? *Journal of Purchasing and Supply Management*, (16), 131-140.

Sale of Goods Act 1930. (n.d.). Retrieved from http://finmin.nic.in/

Salin, A. S. A. P., & Abidin, Z. Z. (2011). *Information and communication technologies and local governance trend: A case study of a smart city in Malaysia*. Paper presented at the 2010 International Conference on Business and Economics Research, Kuala Lumpur, Malaysia.

Sanchez, A. (2013). The Role of Public Procurement. In R. Allen, R. Hemming, & B. Potter (Eds.), *The International Handbook of Public Financial Management* (pp. 312–335). London, UK: Palgrave. doi:10.1057/9781137315304_15

Sarantis, D., Charalabidis, Y., & Askounis, D. (2010). A goal-driven management approach based on knowledge exploitation for e-government programs. International Journal of Electronic Government Research, 6(3), 14–30. doi:10.4018/jegr.2010070102

Sarker, S., & Lee, A. S. (2000). *Using a Positivist Case Research Methodology to Test Three Competing Theories-in-Use of Business Process Redesign*. International Conference on Information Systems (ICIS), Brisbane, Australia.

Saxena, K. (2005). Towards excellence in e-governance. *International Journal of Public Sector Management*, *18*(6), 498–513. doi:10.1108/09513550510616733

Schapper, P. R., Veiga Malta, J., & Gilbert, D. (2009). An Analytical Framework for the Management and Reform of Public Procurement. In International Handbook of Public Procurement (pp. 87-103). CRC Press, Taylor and Francis Group.

Schoenherr, T., & Tummala, V. M. R. (2007). Electronic Procurement: A Structured Literature Review and Directions for Future Research. *International Journal of Procurement Management*, *1*(1/2), 8-37.

Segal, G., & Taylor, M. (2001). *Electronic Procurement How Technology is Changing Government Purchasing*. Retrieved from: http://reason.org/news/show/electronic-procurement

Shakya, R. K. (2012). *Procurement governance framework: Success to e-government procurement (E-GP) system implementation*. Retrieved from http://woppaa.org/wp-content/uploads/2012/09/PAPER-II.16-PROCUREMENT-GOVERNANCE-FRAMEWORK.pdf

Shakya, R. K. (2015). e-Procurement for good governance in public procurement. Saarbrucken, Germany: Scholars' Press.

Shakya, R. K. (2015). *Good governance in public procurement: An evaluation of the role of e-procurement system* (3714138, Capella University). ProQuest Dissertations and Theses, 225.

Shakya, R. K. (2016). E-Procurement: Paradigm Shift From the Traditional Public Procurement. In *Procurement and Contract Management for the Curious: Why Study Procurement and Contract Management?* (pp. 1544–1880). Curious Academic Publishing. Retrieved Nov 11, 2016 from http://amzn.to/1T3kl4T

Sheng, M. L. (2008). Global integrated supply chain implementation: The challenges of e-procurement. In F. Tan (Ed.), *Global information technologies: Concepts, methodologies, tools, and applications* (pp. 3243–3249). Hershey, PA: IGI Global. doi:10.4018/978-1-59904-939-7.ch229

Shillingford-McKlimon, S., & Gayle-Sinclair, S. (2014). *CARICOM: Small market–big money. Amalgamating the Procurement Market to Transform Small Size into an Economic Advantage*. Academic Press.

Shrivastava, U., & Bhattacherjee, A. (2015). ICT as a corruption deterrent: a research note. *Proceedings of the Seventh International Conference on Information and Communication Technologies and Development*. doi:10.1145/2737856.2737864

Sin, L.Y.M., Tse, A.C.B., Yau, O.H.M., Chow, R.P.M., Lee, J.S.Y., & Lau, L.B.Y. (2005). Relationship Marketing Orientation. *Scale Development and Cross Cultural Validation Journal of Business Research*, (58), 185-194.

Singh, M. D., & Kant, R. (2008). Knowledge management barriers: An interpretive structural modeling approach. *International Journal of Management Science and Engineering Management*, *3*(2), 141–150.

Smart, A.F. (2010). E-Procurement and Its Impact on Supply Management-Evidence from Industrial Case Studies. *International Journal of Logistics: Research and Applications, 13*(6), 423-440.

Somasundaram, R. (2007). Challenges in implementation of e-procurement in the Indian government. In A. Pani & A. Agrahari (Eds.), *E-procurement in emerging economies: Theory and cases* (pp. 76–100). Hershey, PA: Idea Group Publishing. doi:10.4018/978-1-59904-153-7.ch004

SPA. (2011). *Annual Report*. Tbilisi: State Procurement Agency.

Staehr, L., Shanks, G., & Seddon, P. B. (2012). An explanatory framework for achieving business benefits from ERP systems. *Journal of the Association for Information Systems, 13*(6), 424.

Steinfeld, J. M., & Thai, K. V. (2013). Technology advancement and e-procurement in the US. In N. Pomazalová (Ed.), *Public sector transformation processes and Internet public procurement: Decision support systems* (pp. 68–84). Hershey, PA: IGI Global. doi:10.4018/978-1-4666-2665-2.ch005

Swanson, M., Weissman, A., Davis, G., Socolof, M., & Davis, K. (2005). Developing priorities for greener state government purchasing: A California case study. *Journal of Cleaner Production, 13*(7), 669–677. doi:10.1016/j.jclepro.2003.12.011

Swedish Competition Authority. (2012). *The Cost of Different Goals of Public Procurement.* Västerås: Edita Västra Aros AB.

Syquia, J. L. C. (2007). *Reforming Public Procurement in Emerging Market Countries. A USAID's sponsored view on procurement reform.* USAID. Retrieved April 27, 2016, from http://kdid.org/sites/kdid/files/resource/files/Reforming%20Public%20Procurement%20in%20Emerging%20Market%20Countries.pdf

Talib, F., Rahman, Z., & Qureshi, M. N. (2011). An interpretive structural modelling approach for modelling the practices of total quality management in service sector. *International Journal of Modelling in Operations Management, 1*(3), 223–250. doi:10.1504/IJMOM.2011.039528

Tanner, C., Wolfle, R., Schubert, P., & Quade, M. (2008). Current Trends and Challenges in Electronic Procurement: An Empirical Study. *Electronic Markets, 18*(1), 6-18.

Tarantini, M., Loprieno, A. D., & Porta, P. L. (2011). A life cycle approach to green public procurement of building materials and elements: A case study on windows. *Energy, 36*(5), 2473–2482. doi:10.1016/j.energy.2011.01.039

Tatsis, V., Mena, C., Wassenhove, L., & Whicker, L. (2006). E-Procurement in the Greek Food and Drink Industry: Drivers and Impediments. *Journal of Purchasing and Supply Management, 12*(15), 63–74. doi:10.1016/j.pursup.2006.04.003

Tavares, L. (2009). *A gestão das aquisições públicas: guia de aplicação do Código dos Contratos Públicos.* Observatório de Prospectiva da Engenharia e da Tecnologia.

Tavares, L. (2010). *White paper: Public e-Tendering in the European Union: Trust in eVolution.* EVA - European Vortal Academy.

Teich, J., Wallenius, H., & Wallenius, J. (1999). Multiple-issue auction and market algorithms for the world wide web. *Decision Support Systems, 26*(1), 49–66. doi:10.1016/S0167-9236(99)00016-0

Teo, T. S. H., Lin, S., & Lai, K. (2009). Adopters and non-adopters of e-procurement in Singapore: An empirical study. *Omega: International Journal of Management Science, 37*(5), 972–987. doi:10.1016/j.omega.2008.11.001

Testa, F., Annunziata, E., Iraldo, F., & Frey, M. (2016). Drawbacks and opportunities of green public procurement: An effective tool for sustainable production. *Journal of Cleaner Production, 112*, 1893–1900. doi:10.1016/j.jclepro.2014.09.092

Testa, F., Iraldo, F., Frey, M., & Daddi, T. (2012). What factors influence the uptake of GPP (green public procurement) practices? New evidence from an Italian survey. *Ecological Economics, 82*, 88–96. doi:10.1016/j.ecolecon.2012.07.011

Testa, F., Iraldo, F., & Frey, M. (2011). The effect of environmental regulation on firms' competitive performance: The case of the building & construction sector in some EU regions. *Journal of Environmental Management, 92*(9), 2136–2144. doi:10.1016/j.jenvman.2011.03.039 PMID:21524840

Theodate, M. (2015). *Desk Review of Caribbean Country Procurement.* Washington, DC: Inter-American Development Bank.

Thomson, J., & Jackson, T. (2007). Sustainable procurement in practice: Lessons from local government. *Journal of Environmental Planning and Management, 50*(3), 421–444. doi:10.1080/09640560701261695

TI. (2012). *Transparency International: Georgia 51st in 2012 Corruption Perceptions Index.* TI.

TI. (2013, June 14). Retrieved from http://www.transparency.ge/en/node/3117

Timmermans, B., & Zabala-Iturriagagoitia, J. M. (2013). Coordinated unbundling: A way to stimulate entrepreneurship through public procurement for innovation. *Science & Public Policy, 40*(5), 674–685. doi:10.1093/scipol/sct023

Toktaş-Palut, P., Baylav, E., Teoman, S., & Altunbey, M. (2014). The impact of barriers and benefits of e-procurement on its adoption decision: An empirical analysis. *International Journal of Production Economics, 158*, 77–90. doi:10.1016/j.ijpe.2014.07.017

Transparency International. (2012). *Global Corruption Report 2012.* Retrieved from http://www.transparency.org/

Trkman, P., & McCormack, K. (2010). Estimating the Benefits and Risks of Implementing E-Procurement. *IEEE Transactions on Engineering Management, 57*(2), 338-348.

Truong, D. (2016). The relationship between B2B e-procurement solutions and the purchasing portfolio: An empirical study. *International Journal of Knowledge-Based Organizations, 6*(2), 55–69. doi:10.4018/IJKBO.2016040104

Tsygankov, S., & Syropyatov, V. (2014). *Comparative analysis of public procurement systems in Ukraine and the Russian Federation. In Modern problems of regional development: Collection of scientific articles* (p. 120). Academic Publishing House of the Agricultural University Plovdiv.

Turkish Prime Ministry. (2016). *The Constitution of Turkey. Ankara, Turkey.* Turkish Prime Ministry. Retrieved April 27, 2016, from http://www.mevzuat.gov.tr/MevzuatMetin/1.5.2709.doc

Turkish Public Procurement Authority. (2006). *Annual Performance Report for the Year 2006*. Ankara, Turkey: Turkish Public Procurement Authority.

Turkish Public Procurement Authority. (2012a). *Public Procurement Law*. Ankara, Turkey: Turkish Public Procurement Authority. Retrieved April 27, 2016, from http://www2.ihale.gov.tr/english/4734_English.pdf

Turkish Public Procurement Authority. (2012b). *EKAP Survey for User Satisfaction*. Ankara, Turkey: Turkish Public Procurement Authority. Retrieved April 27, 2016, from http://www2.ihale.gov.tr/duyurular2012/20120404_EKAP_Kullanim_Anketi.pdf

Turkish Public Procurement Authority. (2016a). *2015 Report for Public Procurement Statistics*. Ankara, Turkey: Turkish Public Procurement Authority. Retrieved April 27, 2016, from http://dosyalar.kik.gov.tr/genel/Raporlar/2015_yil_sonu_kamu_alimlari_raporu_v2.pdf

Turkish Public Procurement Authority. (2016b). *Annual Performance Report for the Year 2015*. Ankara, Turkey: Turkish Public Procurement Authority. Retrieved April 27, 2016, from http://www2.ihale.gov.tr/duyurular2012/2015_Faaliyet_Raporu.pdf

United Nations. (2011). *Expert Group Meeting Report: E-Procurement: Towards Transparency and Efficiency in Public Service Delivery*. New York, NY: United Nations.

UNPAN. (2012). *United Nations' e-Gov Rankings2012*. Retrieved from http://unpan3.un.org/egovkb/datacenter/countryview.aspx

Uthayasankar, S. (2014). *Exploring the application of web 2.0 technologies in the context of e-government* (PhD thesis). Brunel University.

Vaidya, K., Campbell, J., Soar, J., & Gardner, S. (2012). Assimilation of inter-organizational information systems: Insight from change resistance theory in public electronic procurement. In K. Vaidya (Ed.), *Inter-organizational information systems and business management: Theories for researchers* (pp. 18–32). Hershey, PA: IGI Global. doi:10.4018/978-1-60960-768-5.ch002

Vaidya, K., Sajeev, A., & Gao, J. (2005). E-procurement assimilation: an assessment of e-business capabilities and supplier readiness in the Australian public sector.*Proceedings of the 7th international conference on Electronic commerce*. doi:10.1145/1089551.1089630

Vaidya, K. (2007). *Electronic Procurement in the Australian Public Sector: The Organizational Assimilation Process and Its Impact on Public Procurement Performance*. University of New England.

Vaidya, K. (2007). Organizational assimilation of e-procurement: An institutional perspective and the research model. In A. Pani & A. Agrahari (Eds.), *E-procurement in emerging economies: Theory and cases* (pp. 21–40). Hershey, PA: Idea Group Publishing. doi:10.4018/978-1-59904-153-7.ch002

Vaidya, K., Sajeev, A. S. M., & Callender, G. (2006). Critical factors that influence e-procurement implementation success in the public sector. *Journal of Public Procurement, 6*(1/2), 70.

Vaidya, K., Sajeev, A. S., & Callender, G. (2006). Critical factors that influence e-procurement. Journal of Public Procurement, 6.

Vaidyanathan, G., Devaraj, S., & D'Arcy, J. (2012). Does security impact e-procurement performance? Testing a model of direct and moderated effects. *Decision Sciences*, *43*(3), 437–458. doi:10.1111/j.1540-5915.2012.00354.x

Vaidyanathan, G., & Devaraj, S. (2008). The role of quality in e-procurement performance: An empirical analysis. *Journal of Operations Management*, *26*(3), 407–425. doi:10.1016/j.jom.2007.08.004

van Duinkerken, W., Batenburg, R., & Versendaal, J. (2008). The added value of e-procurement for buyer-supplier interaction. In N. Kock (Ed.), *Encyclopedia of e-collaboration* (pp. 14–20). Hershey, PA: IGI Global. doi:10.4018/978-1-59904-000-4.ch003

van Lente, H., Hekkert, M., Smits, R., & van Waveren, B. (2003). Roles of systemic intermediaries in transition processes. *International Journal of Innovation Management*, *7*(3), 1–33. doi:10.1142/S1363919603000817

Veiga Malta, J., Schapper, P., Calo-Gonzalez, O., & Berroa, D. (2011). *Old Rules New Realities: Are Existing Public Procurement Systems Addressing Current and Future Needs?* Washington, DC: The World Bank- LAC.

Vincent-Jones, P. (2006). *The new public contracting: Regulation, responsiveness, relationality*. Oxford, UK: Oxford University Press. doi:10.1093/acprof:oso/9780199291274.001.0001

Vogel, L. (2009). *Macroeconomic effects of cost savings in public procurement*. European Commission, Economic Papers.

Volosin, N. (2010). *Promoviendo compras públicas electrónicas para el desarrollo: Análisis comparativo de Brasil, Chile y México y recomendaciones para una agenda de incidencia e implementación en la Argentina*. Buenos Aires: Fundación Poder Ciudadano.

Walker, H., & Brammer, S. (2009). Sustainable procurement in the United Kingdom public sector. *Supply Chain Management: An International Journal*, *14*(2), 128–137. doi:10.1108/13598540910941993

Wang, E. T. G., & Seidmann, A. (1995). Electronic data interchange: Competitive externalities and strategic implementation policies. *Management Science*, *41*(3), 401–418. doi:10.1287/mnsc.41.3.401

WB. (2008). World Bank.

Weerakkody, V., Irani, Z., Lee, H., Osman, I., & Hindi, N. (2015). E-government implementation: A birds eye view of issues relating to costs, opportunities, benefits and risks. *Information Systems Frontiers*, *17*(4), 889–915. doi:10.1007/s10796-013-9472-3

WEF. (2010). *Global Competitiveness Report 2010*. Retrieved from http://www3.weforum.org/docs/WEF_GlobalCompetitivenessReport_2010-11.pdf

Westerman, G., Bonnet, D., & Mcaffe, A. (2014). *Leading digital.* Boston: Harvard Business Review Press.

World Bank England and Wales. Northern Ireland. (2006). *The Public Contracts Regulations, No 5*. Retrieved from http://www.oecd.org/unitedkingdom/39647169.pdf

World Bank. (2001). *Colombia: Country Procurement Assessment Report.* Washington, DC: The World Bank.

World Bank. (2004). *Chile: Country Procurement Assessment Report.* Washington, DC: The World Bank.

World Bank, Inter-American Development Bank, & Asian Development Bank. (2004). *Electronic Government Procurement Roadmap*. Available at http://siteresources.worldbank.org/INFORMATIONANDCOMMUNICATIONANDTECHNOLOGIES/Resources/e-GPRoadMap.pdf

World Bank. (2011). *Framework Agreements.* Author.

Wu, F., Zsidisin, G. A., & Ross, A. D. (2007). Antecedents and outcomes of e-procurement adoption: An integrative model. *IEEE Transactions on Engineering Management*, *54*(3), 576–587. doi:10.1109/TEM.2007.900786

Xinli, H. (2015). Effectiveness of information technology in reducing corruption in China: A validation of the DeLone and McLean information systems success model. *The Electronic Library*, *33*(1), 52–64. doi:10.1108/EL-11-2012-0148

Yamamoto, G. T., & Karaman, F. (2007). Barriers to e-procurement adoption: The Turkish case. In A. Pani & A. Agrahari (Eds.), *E-procurement in emerging economies: Theory and cases* (pp. 101–125). Hershey, PA: Idea Group Publishing. doi:10.4018/978-1-59904-153-7.ch005

Yang, K., & Rho, S. Y. (2007). E-government for better performance: Promises, realities, and challenges. *International Journal of Public Administration*, *30*(11), 1197–1217. doi:10.1080/01900690701225556

Yang, J., & Zhang, R. Y. (2009). *The research and analysis of e-procurement for iron and steel enterprises.* Paper presented at the International Conference on Information Management, Innovation Management and Industrial Engineering, Xian, China.

Yin, R. K. (2003). *Applications of Case Study Research.* Sage Publications Inc.

Yu, S., Mishra, A. N., Gopal, A., Slaughter, S., & Mukhopadhyay, T. (2015). E-procurement infusion and operational process impacts in MRO procurement: Complementary or substitutive effects? *Production and Operations Management*, *24*(7), 1054–1070. doi:10.1111/poms.12362

Zhu, Q., Geng, Y., & Sarkis, J. (2013). Motivating green public procurement in China: An individual level perspective. *Journal of Environmental Management*, *126*, 85–95. doi:10.1016/j.jenvman.2013.04.009 PMID:23666074

About the Contributors

Rajesh Kumar Shakya is currently working with the World Bank as an e-Procurement Specialist. He is an International expert on e-Government Procurement (e-GP), Framework Agreements, Green Public Procurement, and public procurement strategies. He has got international experience working for more than 35 countries from Asia, Africa, Caribbean, Central Asia, and Europe. He has worked with the World Bank, USAID, Asian Development Bank, Eastern African Community, Inter-American Development Bank, Caribbean Development Bank, and other government and development agencies. Dr. Shakya is the Ph.D. with Distinction in Public Administration from the Capella University, USA. His book entitled "e-Procurement for good governance in public procurement" was published in 2015, and another book on "Green Public Procurement Strategies for Environmental Sustainability" is under publication in 2017. He has presented and published several papers on e-Government Procurement, Framework agreements, green procurement, ICT and e-Governance.

* * *

Umit Alsac is an Independent Public Procurement Consultant. Before this job, he served as one of the project managers of Turkey's public e-procurement project at the Public Procurement Authority of the Republic of Turkey. Between May 2009-May 2015, he actively involved with development, design and testing of apllications in EKAP, Turkey's centralized public e-procurement system. His research interests include e-procurement, framework agreements, settlement of disputes in public procurement and public health sector procurement.

Sunil Aryal is a lecturer at School of Engineering and IT, Faculty of Science and Technology, Federation University Australia. In terms of research, he is interested in the application of ICT to solve real-world problems in different domains. His research interest includes data mining, machine learning, artificial intelligence, IT for socio-economic development. Before coming to academia, he worked in IT industry as a software developer and data analyst for a number of years.

Ana Chania has more than six years' experience in public procurement and more than five years' experience of middle management in business sector in Georgia. She heads analytical department at State Procurement Agency (SPA) of Georgia. At the same time, she provides trainings at SPA's Training Center and has already trained more than 1000 public officials. Mrs. Chania has a strong background in Public Procurement and is one of the leading executive officers in State Procurement agency. Mrs Chania represents the SPA while sharing Georgian experience of public procurement reform with foreign delegations and visitors. She is in charge of producing SPA analytical documents and publications (Annual reports, e-Procurement User manuals, Q&A regarding e-procurement process, market analyses, and other research documents. Mrs. Chania holds Master Degree in Business Administration.

João de Almeida is a lawyer by training and holds post graduate degrees in European Union Law, Public Procurement Law and Business Administration. He became a Public Procurement Consultant in 2012 shortly after completing a five-years term as a Member of the Executive Board of the Portuguese National Agency for Public Procurement (ANCP), a central purchasing body (CPB) created in 2007. In addition to actively participate in the management of this CPB, he played a key role in the legislative and organizational changes undertaken between 2007 and 2012 within the framework of the Portuguese public procurement system reform, which included the launch of a mandatory fully fledged e-procurement system that is widely recognized as a best practice case. The World Bank, the European Commission, the European Bank for Reconstruction and Development, the Council of Europe and the Islamic Development Bank are among the institutions he has been supporting through his consultancy in the field of public procurement over the last five years. His current research, conducted with the purpose of delivering better and innovative solutions to his clients and projects, focus mainly on topics relating to central purchasing, framework agreements, public procurement performance measurement, e-procurement and, more recently, on barriers to international trade raised by national public procurement regulations and practices.

Kakha Demetrashvili has more than 20 years of experience in international public aid and development programs as a senior management team member, team leader, project manager and a consultant to a wide variety of donor, governmental and non-governmental organisations. His experience is worldwide but since 1995 mainly in Central- and Eastern Europe in general, and the South Caucasus area in particular. He has a strong background in Public Management, ICTD, and eGovernance in the context of democratic development and good governance. Since 1997 being as a project manager, team leader and a leading expert/consultant/analyst of

UNDP, EU/EC, USAID, CoE, WB, Dr. Demetrashvili was involved in a variety of specialized democratic governance programs including public administration reform, civil service reform, parliamentary strengthening, public finance management reform, government oversight, supreme audit reform, civil registry reform, decentralization and local governance reform, regional development, reform of electoral administration, E-Governance, ICT4D, strengthening of civil society institutions, human rights and national minorities issues, as well as institutional-building and capacity development projects. In January, 2013 Dr. Demetrashvili has been appointed as a deputy head of a leading Georgian EGOV and IT agency – Financial-Analytical Service at the Ministry of Finance, supervising development of an ePFMS - Electronic Public Finance Management System. Since June, 2014 Dr. Demetrashvili has employed as a Deputy Chairman of the State Procurement Agency of Georgia. Dr. Demetrashvili is engaged as a full Professor at the Georgian Technical University leading bachelors' and masters' courses in computer integrating manufacturing and mechatronics.

Gasanova Ekaterina is an instructor of Pilot procurement center SFU and working as a senior Expert Advisor of the Fund "Promotion - XXI Century", the state procurement system since 2010.

Leslie Harper has over 18 years of experience as an international development professional working on Latin America and the Caribbean, with a focus on public sector reform and management. She has coordinated the topic of public procurement modernization for the Institutions for Development Department since 2008, including portfolio and knowledge management. She built up the topic in the Department from practically non-existent to a coherent, comprehensive and well-funded program that includes programs in 24 of the 26 IDB member countries. She leads an $80 million-dollar portfolio of public procurement and public financial management, including two policy based loan series in Suriname, 4 investment loans and 11 technical assistance programs. She has participated as a team member providing technical advice in the area of public procurement for investments loans in Colombia, Dominican Republic, Jamaica and Trinidad. She also leads a major initiative supporting public procurement modernization in the Caribbean with funding from the IDB's Regional Public Good program to support the development of a regional procurement market place. To support that goal, she created the Caribbean Public Procurement Network, which brings together professionals working on the reform and modernization of the topic. She is the team leader of DataGov, a high-profile initiative that provides 800 public management indicators to users around the world, including the development of public procurement performance indicators. At its peak it was the IDB's most visited database, it is currently undergoing an overhaul. Prior to joining the IDB, she worked in Chile for two years on a local government strengthening project as a Peace Corps Volunteer in a rural municipality.

Nergiz Ilhan is currently a PhD student at RMIT University. She has completed her MS by research at Monash University. She has over 6 years of teaching experience (as a tutor) at Monash University. She has so far published three research papers in the area of e-procurement.

Kijpokin Kasemsap received his BEng degree in Mechanical Engineering from King Mongkut's University of Technology, Thonburi, his MBA degree from Ramkhamhaeng University, and his DBA degree in Human Resource Management from Suan Sunandha Rajabhat University. Dr. Kasemsap is a Special Lecturer in the Faculty of Management Sciences, Suan Sunandha Rajabhat University, based in Bangkok, Thailand. Dr. Kasemsap is a Member of the International Association of Engineers (IAENG), the International Association of Engineers and Scientists (IAEST), the International Economics Development and Research Center (IEDRC), the International Association of Computer Science and Information Technology (IACSIT), the International Foundation for Research and Development (IFRD), and the International Innovative Scientific and Research Organization (IISRO). Dr. Kasemsap also serves on the International Advisory Committee (IAC) for the International Association of Academicians and Researchers (INAAR). Dr. Kasemsap is the sole author of over 250 peer-reviewed international publications and book chapters on business, education, and information technology.

Arjun Neupane completed his PhD in Information System and Master of Information Technology (MIT) at the School of Management and Enterprise, Faculty of Business, Education, Law and Arts of the University of Southern Queensland, Australia. He did Bachelor of Computer Application from Pokhara University Nepal. Currently, he is working on developing an Anti-corruption artefact, based on the Design Science Research (DSR). His research interests are applied information System, electronic government and procurement, ICT for Development, and Anti-corruption research. He has published in prestigious international journals, conference paper and book chapter. He has extensive teaching and research on anti-corruption.

Prabir Panda received his M.S. in Software Systems from Birla Institute of Technology and Science, India and M.Phil. in Computer Science from Vinayaka Mission University, Salem, India. He received Ph.D. in Management from Motilal Nehru National Institute of Technology Allahabad, India. He is currently working in the area of e-procurement and has more than 12 years experience in Supply Chain Management. His research has appeared in a number of reputed journals, edited books and the conference proceedings of many national and international conferences.

Md Mahbubur Rahim is currently a Senior Lecturer at the Faculty of Information Technology, MONASH University, Australia. He has research interests in such areas as E-business, E-government, Social media impact, IT enabled sustainability practices, and IT strategies. Rahim has widely published in over 80 refereed journals, conference proceedings and edited books. His total number of google scholar citations stands at 933 with an h-index of 15. He is also the recipient of the BEST PAPER AWARD at ACIS2011 and e-CASE2008 conferences. Rahim has successfully supervised research projects of 3 PhD students and 2 Masters students in the areas of E-commerce, ERP systems, IT government, IT security, and E-procurement. He has received a number of research grants including a prestigious ARC Discovery grant. Currently, Rahim serves on the editorial board for the Journal of Administration & Governance.

Isabel Rosa is currently working as a policy officer in the Innovative and e-Procurement unit, DG GROW, European Commission. She is a PhD candidate in Governance of Digital Transformation. Shear earlier worked as the Director of Licensing Directorate in IMPIC (Portuguese e-procurement regulator); Coordinator of the National Public Contracts Portal development; Deputy General Secretary of the Ministry of Public Works, Transports and Communications; Chair of the ICT Commission in the Ministry of Public Works, Transports and Communications.

G. P. Sahu, Associate Professor, has more than 14 years of experience in teaching. He has received his PhD in management from Indian Institute of Technology Delhi. His research interests are in the areas of MIS and E-governance. He has published around 56 research papers in international journals and conferences. He has coordinated several international conferences. He has also edited 5 books in the area of E-governance. Dr. Sahu has acted as a reviewer for several international journals, and is also a Guest Editor with the International Journal of Electronic Governance. He has been Co-Convener, E-district for the CSI-Nihilent E-Governance National Awards, India.

Daniel Sánchez has more than 12 years of experience in international development in the sectors of public financial management and modernization of the state. He is currently working on various programs aimed at promoting the modernization of public expenditure management, including procurement and public financial management systems in Latin America and the Caribbean. He has participated in various international forums in the USA. And Europe representing the IDB. Mr. Sánchez holds an MBA in Finance from the joint program of the Universidad Católica Boliviana and the Harvard Institute for International Development. He also holds an MA in Public Sector Communication from American University and has conducted public financial management studies at the Kennedy School of Government at Harvard University.

Paul Roland Schapper is an international specialist in public e-procurement and procurement systems and practice. He has a career spanning 35 years with 18 years in procurement, including as Supply Commissioner, Director-General for the Department of Industry and Technology, Chief Executive Officer for the Department of Contract and Management Services, CEO for the Office of Public Sector Management, and Professorial Fellow for Governance in Western Australia. Dr Schapper has developed strategic e-procurement frameworks or engaged in e-procurement capacity development, e-procurement legislation reform and procurement practice for more than 30 countries. He has been a peer reviewer for the World Bank and was a founding member on the editorial board of the Journal of Digital Evidence. Dr Schapper has also lectured at the International Development Law Institute (Rome).

Jacqueline Shiner founded OSA Proposals in 2007 to focus on pricing for large and small-business customers. Shortly after starting OSA proposals, she was recruited to serve as the Business Manager at Tetra Tech ARD in Burlington, Vermont. At Tetra Tech, she was involved in all aspects of proposal development, pricing strategy, contract negotiations and mentoring small business partners. She also supported other operating units on complex and critical proposals. In 2015, she left Tetra Tech and relaunched OSA Proposals. She currently supports two-dozen clients including Fortune 500 businesses, emerging growth companies and non-profits. Prior to founding OSA Proposals, Jacque was senior pricing specialist at General Dynamics Armament and Technical Products. She held similar positions at SAIC and Pearson Government Solutions. She has worked extensively with U.S. defense, intelligence and USAID entities for the past 16 years. She started her career in Information Technology, working as an IT Specialist for the Republican National Committee and, later, in the financial industry before moving into government contracting. Jacque Shiner earned her B.S. in Finance from George Mason University in Virginia and is currently pursuing her Master's in Public Administration at Norwich University in Northfield, Vermont. She resides in Stowe, Vermont and served on the Planning Commission between 2007 and 2013.

Jeffrey Soar holds the Chair in Human-Centred Technology at the University of Southern Queensland where he researches technology innovation for human benefit. He came into research from a career at the highest levels of ICT management within large public and private organisations. He was CIO in several government departments in Australia and New Zealand including Director of Information and Technology for NZ Police where he managed the largest-ever ICT project impacting across emergency services. In academia he established two demonstration smart homes with the latest in innovations for independent living, entertainment, security and energy. His research has been supported by 7 Australian Research Council grants as well as over 30 grants from national and international technology and service organisations. His current research projects are in Technology for Economic Development, E-Learning and M-Learning, E-Government, E-Health, Decision Support, Mobile, Cloud, Algorithms, Adoption and Benefits Realisation, Human Computer Interaction and User Experience.

Sergey Tsygankov is an instructor of Pilot procurement center SFU and the Head of the state order placement Fund "Promotion - XXI Century", the state procurement system since 2010.

Kishor Vaidya is Adjunct Senior Lecturer at the University of Southern Queensland, and Honorary Professional Associate at the Faculty of Information Sciences and Engineering of the University of Canberra. Dr Vaidya has a Master's degree in Information Systems from Central Queensland University and a PhD from the University of New England. He is the author of the book Electronic Procurement: Impact on Procurement Performance. He has published over 30 peer reviewed articles in various journals, book chapters, and international conference proceedings. His current research interests include adoption and assimilation of inter-organisational information systems, organizational theories, and theory-based evaluation of e-Business/e-Government initiatives. More recently, he has developed his research interests in issues relating to ICT for developing countries, including using ICT to combat corruption in public procurement."

Robert Wright has over 25-years of experience in increasingly more responsible positions to envision, develop, and implement innovative programs/policies/grant acquisition strategies impacting public and private sectors, to organize people and events, and to communicate positive ideas and images intended to improve organizational productivity and support innovative decision-making. Dr. Wright has held senior management positions in the areas of public safety, emergency management, workforce development and health care policy. These positions included Senior Policy Analyst, MassHealth, Commonwealth of Massachusetts, Senior Program Manager, Executive Office of Public Safety, Commonwealth of Massachusetts, and Program Coordinator, Southern New Hampshire Services. Dr. Wright received his BA from the University of Chicago, an MPA from Suffolk University, Boston, MA, and a Doctorate in Public Administration from the University of LaVerne, LaVerne, CA. His research has focused upon the implementation of major federal programs. Dr. Wright is an Editorial Review Board Member, Journal of Emergency Management. He has also published articles pertaining to program evaluation and emergency management. These publications include "Key Performance Measure Considerations in Implementation & Policy Design: Assessing the Workforce Investment Act Program" International Journal of Knowledge, Culture and Change Management, Volume 9, Issue 7, pp.89-110 and "The Department of Homeland Security and the Entrepreneurial Management and Public Policy Model: A Work in Progress (book chapter)," Wendy Haynes & Robert J. Wright, in Entrepreneurial Management and Public Policy, Van R. Johnston, Editor. New York: Nova Science Publishers, Inc., 2008. Dr. Wright currently teaches at Capella University, Minneapolis, MN as a Lead Core Faculty, in the Doctoral Program of Public Administration, School of Public Servic Leadership. He has been recognized for excellence in teaching as a recipient of the Harold Able Award 2014 as well as thee President's Award for Teaching Excellence, 2012. Dr. Wright also holds a teaching position as a Senior Adjunct Faculty in the Graduate School of Continuing Education, Norwich University, Northfield, VT. Areas of expertise concern Workforce Development, Program Evaluation, Public Sector Leadership, Public Sector Collaboration, and Emergency Management. Total Years Teaching: 8 years graduate level in the area of Public Administration (MPA/DPA degrees).

Index

F

G

I

L

M

P

Q

R

S

T

U

V

www.ingramcontent.com/pod-product-compliance
Lightning Source LLC
LaVergne TN
LVHW062113200926
848484LV00007B/1662
* 9 7 8 1 5 2 2 5 2 2 0 3 4 *